POETIC THEOLOGY

POETIC THEOLOGY

God and the Poetics of Everyday Life

William A. Dyrness

WILLIAM B. EERDMANS PUBLISHING COMPANY
GRAND RAPIDS, MICHIGAN / CAMBRIDGE, U.K.

© 2011 William A. Dyrness
All rights reserved

Published 2011 by
Wm. B. Eerdmans Publishing Co.
2140 Oak Industrial Drive N.E., Grand Rapids, Michigan 49505 /
P.O. Box 163, Cambridge CB3 9PU U.K.
www.eerdmans.com

Library of Congress Cataloging-in-Publication Data

Dyrness, William A.
Poetic theology: God and the poetics of everyday life / William A. Dyrness.
    p.   cm.
Includes bibliographical references (p.   ) and index.
ISBN 978-0-8028-6578-6 (pbk.: alk. paper)
1. Aesthetics — Religious aspects — Christianity.
2. Theology — Methodology.
3. Religion and poetry.   I. Title.

BR115.A8D97   2011
261.5'7 — dc22

2010040494

Unless otherwise noted, the Scripture quotations in this publication are from the New Revised Standard Version of the Bible, copyright © 1989 by the Division of Christian Education of the National Council of Churches of Christ in the U.S.A., and used by permission.

To Ted Dyrness (1933-2010),
who saw the poetry in the trees
he studied and loved

Contents

PREFACE ix

The Method of Poetic Theology

1. Prelude to Aesthetic Theology: Theological Reflections on Love, Desire, and the Affections — 3
2. The Historical Model: *Theologia Poetica* — 37
3. Poetic Stewardship of Life — 71

Building Blocks for a Poetic Theology: How Did We Get Here?

4. Re-reading the Nineteenth-Century Romantic Heritage — 99
5. Twentieth-Century Aesthetics: In Search of a Theological Voice — 125
6. Dante, Bunyan, and the Search for a Protestant Aesthetics — 153
7. Calvin, the Locked Church, and the Recovery of Contemplation — 187

The Trajectory of Poetic Theology: Where Can We Go?

8. The Aesthetics of Church — 217
9. Aesthetics and Social Transformation — 253

CONTENTS

Conclusion

10. Living and Reflecting Poetically: Systematic Implications   283

    BIBLIOGRAPHY   313

    INDEX   327

Preface

This book seeks to connect poetry and theology. It probably ought to have been written in poetry. But if it were, the poets would not read it because it was theology, and the theologians would not read it because it was poetry. And so it is written in the pigeon-toed prose of theology — a dog barking at the moon. Theology has always been handicapped, of course, when it tries to speak of God. Especially recently, it has had to borrow language from science, philosophy, and even from economics to try to shape some recognizable image of God. Needless to say, this has left many feeling like something was missing. For its part, poetry has recently had its own problems with God, frequently retreating to the confines of individual consciousness or to metaphors without reference. So readers of poetry have occasionally felt a lack of . . . something.

So here we are, left with a theology without poetry, and a poetry without God. This dilemma has given rise to the following reflections. For I believe these disciplines, though they are currently estranged, were born together and need to be reconciled. This work of apologetic and cultural theology will attempt to forge pathways between them. I will seek to show that theology invariably deals in images of love and desire, which attract and connect the human soul to God, the source of light and life. But I will also argue that human longing for a good (even beautiful) life inclines people inevitably to shape poetic practices that become objects of their devotion — things for which they live and die. Further, I will argue that contemporary people, busy shaping devotional objects and practices for themselves, seek by means of these to find a way to flourish beyond what is given in life. This devotion and construction, I will argue, has religious, even theological significance.

It expresses something essential about the divine image, and its processes and products should be honored even if the devotion itself must eventually be re-oriented.

It is clear already that I am using the poetic in a broader sense than simply poems or paintings, and this calls for some initial explanation. For some time now I have been reflecting on God's interest and involvement in the work of art and artists. Most recently I have taken to asking people how these artistic objects actually function in their experience, especially in their practices of devotion.[1] What I have discovered is that works of art — painting, poetry, or architecture — do not function independently of the context in which they are experienced. And for most people most of the time, this context reflects the complex arrangements of modern life. The poetry that matters to most people, then, is what we might call the poetics of everyday life. So in this book I have broadened my focus to include many kinds of symbolic objects and practices — those projects that embody the desires and dreams around which people orient their lives. For some these center on specifically religious practices, but for many others these include commitments to various aesthetic, recreational, and even political causes that engender their own special devotional practices.

It turns out that this broader understanding of the poetic has ancient authorization. Aristotle defined poetry as a "making," which he said is "to imitate and represent various objects through the medium of color and form, or again by the voice." Further, this imitation is produced by "rhythm, language, or 'harmony.'"[2] It is true that Aristotle largely had in mind what we call today the fine arts, and I will pay special attention to these. But I believe the practices of the fine arts are particular and refined instances of a more general human inclination to make beautiful things — the desire, as we say, to make something of one's life.

The projects that are the focus of this broader discussion have two characteristics. First, they respond to fundamental human desires. They are objects and practices that go well beyond simple functional purposes, though they often fulfill these as well. They express deeper

---

1. This research on Christian populations, published in *Senses of the Soul: Art and the Visual in Christian Worship* (Eugene, Ore.: Cascade Books, 2008), is currently being expanded to include Jewish, Muslim, and Buddhist devotion. See also William Dyrness, *Visual Faith: Theology, Art, and Worship in Dialogue* (Grand Rapids: Baker Book House, 2001).

2. Aristotle, *Poetics*, trans. S. H. Butcher (Mineola, N.Y.: Dover, 1997), p. 1.

longings and reach for purposes that satisfy the affections. These symbolic constructions express Augustine's fundamental insight that people are defined not simply by what they know but by what (and who) they love. Second, these targets of desire coalesce into various objects and practices whose figure and texture evoke praise, even wonder — or at least are intended to do so. So with Aristotle we will focus on the rhythm, language, and harmony of these practices and explore their shared characteristics. As Philip Sidney put this in his sixteenth-century defense of poetry, the poet "ever sets virtue so out in her best colors ... that one must be enamored of her."[3]

But, in defending poetic practice, Sidney also points out that Scripture itself is filled with poetry that figures forth to teach and delight.[4] David's Psalms are divine poems that "give a face to God," enabling readers to "see" God coming in majesty, or riding on the waves of the sea.[5] Moreover, these images go beyond teaching to "entice" one to enter into the way of virtue.[6] Besides the Psalms, the Bible engages readers' imaginations in the parables of Jesus and in the elaborate visions of the Apostles and the Prophets. The great events of Scripture are invariably clothed in color and light, from the growing light of creation through the cloud of fire in the wilderness, to the tongues of fire at Pentecost, suggesting that these intend not just to teach but to spark delight or fear. These biblical precedents, especially in what is known as the wisdom tradition, suggest that poetic theology was part of God's intention all along.

Readers will be aware of how much remains to be done to adequately develop a poetic theology — though they will not feel it as keenly as the author. The language is lacking, the habits of thought and practice missing or poorly developed — I am still a dog barking. But the moon toward which I gesture in these pages is really there. One day, someone may stand on it; I do not do so in this book.

Five of the chapters here include materials previously published, and I would like to express my appreciation to these publishers for allowing me to reprint some of this material. As I reviewed my recent work, I became aware that the central focus was something that I am

---

3. Philip Sidney, "A Defense of Poetry," *Miscellaneous Prose of Philip Sidney*, ed. K. Duncan-Jones and Jan van Dorsten (Oxford: Clarendon Press, 1973 [1595]), p. 90.

4. Sidney, "A Defense of Poetry," p. 79.

5. Sidney, "A Defense of Poetry," p. 77.

6. Sidney, "A Defense of Poetry," p. 92.

trying to define as poetic theology. Chapters One, Two, and Three were written specifically for this book and develop the methodology of such theology in some detail. Chapters Four and Five develop historical material and sources for poetic theology that I surveyed more briefly for the article titled "The Arts" in the *Oxford Handbook of Systematic Theology*.[7] Chapter Six on Protestant aesthetics, which expands on an article published in the *International Journal of Systematic Theology*, seeks to describe what is unique about a Protestant and Reformed approach to poetic theology. This material was also presented as the biennial Aesthetics Lectureship at Wheaton College in March 2004, and I am grateful to Professor Joel Sheesley for the invitation and his hospitality on that occasion. Chapter Seven uses material from a 2006 article in the *Image* journal pointing out ways in which Reformation spirituality constricted the full appreciation of poetic theology.[8] Chapters Eight and Nine show how this idea works its way into the worship of the church and into the practices of everyday life, especially those concerned with social transformation. Chapter Eight, titled "The Aesthetics of Church," uses material published in *The Community of the Word*.[9] Chapter Nine on aesthetics and transformation was presented in an earlier form as a lecture at the University of the Philippines in Manila in July 2002; I want to thank the leadership of the Institute for Study in Asian Church and Culture, especially their director and founder, Dr. Melba Padilla Maggay, for this invitation and their warm hospitality. All of this material has been extensively revised and expanded to shape it into what I hope is a coherent argument, though repetitions and digressions certainly remain. Chapter Ten, which attempts to summarize my argument and suggest ways it might apply to the study of theology, includes material given in various lectures but is largely rewritten for this book.

---

7. *Oxford Handbook of Systematic Theology*, ed. John Webster, Kathryn Tanner, and Iain Torrance (Oxford: Oxford University Press, 2007), pp. 561-79. This material is used by permission of Oxford University Press.

8. See "Dante, Bunyan, and the Case for a Protestant Aesthetics," *International Journal of Systematic Theology* 10 (Summer 2008): 285-302; and "Contemplation for Protestants: Where the Reformation Went Wrong," *Image*, no. 49 (Spring 2006): 71-79. This was given first as a lecture at the Image Conference at the University of Houston in Houston, Texas in November 2005.

9. See "Spaces for an Evangelical Ecclesiology," in *The Community of the Word*, ed. Mark Husbands and Daniel J. Treier (Downers Grove, Ill.: InterVarsity Press, 2005), pp. 251-72. Volume copyright © 2005 by Mark Husbands and Daniel J. Treier. Used by permission of InterVarsity Press, P.O. Box 1400, Downers Grove, IL 60515.

Preface

Many colleagues, students, and friends contributed to the conversation evident in this book, and I would like to acknowledge some of them here. Some of the material was given at the Woods Lectureship at Dubuque Theological Seminary on April 17-18, 2006, and at the WIC Lectureship at Covenant College on February 12-14, 2009, and I want to express my gratitude for the hospitality of these institutions and the colleagues there. The welcome and quiet provided by the Huntington Library in San Marino, California, continues to provide a wonderful setting where most of these pages were written, and I am grateful to many colleagues there. I am especially grateful for colleagues and friends who read and commented on portions of the manuscript: Mark Burrows, Robert K. Johnston, and Katherine Lee. And I want to thank all of the students in the "Theology of Beauty Seminar" in the fall of 2008; they read chapters whether they wanted to or not. For many related conversations on many issues explored here, I want to thank John Witvliet, Clayton Schmit, Todd Johnson, John Thomson, David Morgan, Leah Buturain Schneider, Michael Bruner, Richard Peace, and Patricia Benner. These all deserve a better book, and several of them will certainly write it (or have done so). Thanks also to Jon Pott, who encouraged me to move ahead with this project; to Richard Hicks, who checked references and developed the bibliography, and who did everything a good editor needs to do; and especially to my editor at Eerdmans, Mary Hietbrink, who was a wise reader and did much to make this a better book.

Pasadena, California
Feast of the Ascension
May 2009

The Method of Poetic Theology

CHAPTER 1

Prelude to Aesthetic Theology: Theological Reflections on Love, Desire, and the Affections

Introduction

Consider the following representative sample of contemporary twenty-first century, middle-class Americans:

- Adam has just celebrated his thirtieth birthday and works in financial services in downtown Los Angeles. He is an avid USC football fan and organizes his fall around the schedule of the Trojans. Every year he will make at least one trip to an away game, and he holds season tickets to all home games. During the fall his week is spent scouring newspapers and sports blogs for clues about the strengths and weaknesses of this week's opponent, and the readiness (and injury report) of his team. Saturday morning he rises early, dons his red-and-yellow sweatshirt, and goes to a buddy's house to carpool with friends to the Coliseum. He looks forward to the feeling of being part of eighty thousand people on their feet cheering a great play — he finds this experience to be deeply moving.
- Lisa and her husband live in Salt Lake City. They love to ski and can't wait for ski season to arrive. Lisa has arranged her part-time work schedule in the local hospital so that she and a friend can make the short drive to the nearest slope at least twice a week. The couple's fall and winter program always includes trips to ski resorts with their friends. Even in the off-season Lisa watches the sales so that she can keep up with the latest ski equipment. Her favorite experience is to feel the cold mountain air as she drifts down the slopes. It is there that she feels most alive.

- Brad loves to fish and has found several lakes near his Los Angeles home that he can visit — he is sure to fish in one or another at least once a week. He services heating and air-conditioning systems and is quick to tell his customers about the five-pound bass he caught last week. He checks online fishing sites regularly to see what people are catching and keeps his fishing gear (and the beer!) in the trunk of his car so he can make a quick trip with his friends. When he is fishing, the quiet of the lake and the birds flying overhead give him a sense of peace.
- Sophia works as a graphic designer, but would love to paint full-time — part of her study is equipped as a studio where she spends long hours painting. Her weekly schedule will usually include a gallery opening, or a museum visit with her friends. Her home is full of original prints, and the coffee table is crowded with art books. Recently she was appointed to the cultural affairs council of her local community. She loves to spend time in front of her favorite work, sketching, or simply meditating — it is there that she feels most fulfilled.

These people are unremarkable in many ways, but they have this in common: All of them would say that they are relatively happy, and all of them would also claim that religion plays no role in either their happiness or their daily lives. As a result, the lives of people like this would commonly be described as secular. But in what follows I want to dispute, or at least challenge, this characterization.[1] While they may have given up the formal institution of religion, none have given up the satisfactions that religion has traditionally supplied: all of them have found activities that they enjoy and that give them a sense of fulfillment. Furthermore, their regular practices have given a kind of ritual structure to their lives that gives them strength and offers them meaning.

Devotion, Ritual, and Community

Many, perhaps most, contemporary people with college degrees and middle-class jobs live their lives these days without paying much atten-

---

1. For a nonreligious interpretation of these phenomena, see Phil Zuckerman, *Society without God: What the Least Religious Nations Can Tell Us about Contentment* (New York: New York University Press, 2008).

tion to religion. Even if they would claim to believe in God (as some 90 percent of them do!) and attend church or synagogue at various times, they will live most of their lives as functional atheists; God does not play much of a role in their daily lives. But I want to argue that this fact does not give a complete picture of what might be called their religious lives. For it is clear from even the brief examples above that many of them have committed themselves to causes and values around which they orient their lives. These causes, and the practices they inspire, are clearly the object of their affections as much as of their reason and will. As a result, one can fairly say that they are devoted to these things, and that they pursue them with specific practices that anthropologists would call rituals. These shared rituals, moreover, provide social contexts in which these people find their meaning and forge their identities. It is while pursuing these practices, they tell us, that they feel most alive.

To be sure, sports, fishing, and the arts are not religious in any traditional sense, but, for many of our contemporaries, they have *taken the place of* religious practices. And like religious practices, they have become things for which they live — and perhaps for which they might even die! Indeed, the argument I want to develop will go further and argue that the significance they derive from these activities has not only a human meaning but a possible theological reference as well. That is, the drive that moves them to pursue the goods associated with their passions is a movement of the soul that, if nurtured more deeply and oriented rightly, would lead them to God.

If something like this is true, it follows that a major work of theology today, at least of the apologetic sort, might be to explore these drives as though they were theologically significant. Accordingly, pursuing conversations about God today might not in the first instance be about the truth of Christianity, but about the presence and work of God in the contemporary situation and, especially, in the passions that move people to act, build, and create. It would proceed on the assumption that God is already deeply involved in their lives, and is already in conversation with them. The presence or absence of God would thus be reconsidered in the light of these passionate commitments. I would like to propose that people are not so much misled by the devotional urges they find in themselves, or by the legitimate activities that express these drives, but by failing to understand their direction and their limitations, by failing to see that life lived *only* for these things is finally not fulfilling. But the argument I want to make is that life lived with a more holistic understanding of these good things is more satisfying, even as it gives a deeper and richer meaning to these practices.

But is such a religious reading of culture really possible? I recognize that there are many barriers to mounting an argument of this kind — some of which I will deal with in due course. But I think it is important to begin with practices and creative activities of the sort I described simply because for many people today these activities define and give meaning to their lives. So an argument of this kind is important for strategic reasons, something I will explore in the third chapter. But the religious reading of these projects suggests that there are theological reasons as well — something I want to develop in this chapter and the next. I will seek to develop my argument in two ways. First, I will try to show that, for people like Adam and Sophia, aesthetic experience, broadly conceived, and the rituals and created objects that express this, are fundamental to the shaping and expressing of their human identity. That is to say, they are not optional extras, but fundamental to the growth and flourishing of persons. But this part of the argument goes further: aesthetic and symbolic projects are also spiritual sites where the affections, the goods of the world, and religious longings meet and interact. Second, then, I will argue that symbolic practices of this kind can also be "theological" in the broad sense of the word. That is, they are places where, because of God's continuing presence in creation and God's redemptive work in Christ and by the Spirit, God is also active, nurturing, calling, and drawing persons — and indeed, all creation — toward the perfection God intends for them.

Where Is a Theology of Desire to Be Found?

Before turning to my argument, I need to recognize a handicap that I work with. I claim to be doing a kind of apologetic theology — that is, I will be reflecting on the presence and purposes of God in relation to cultural patterns and trends. Theology as it is ordinarily studied does not appear well-equipped to carry out this sort of investigation. Some theologians have wrestled in various ways with art and aesthetics, and we will consider their contributions in due course; others are highly suspicious of this sort of approach, and we will consider some of these as well. But in general one could describe a particular modern way of doing theology that has emerged in the last few centuries. This method emphasizes the rational formulation, expression, and understanding of God's purposes as these are contained in Scripture. Only after we have reached a firm understanding of Christian truth, according to this dominant view, are we encouraged to apply it to our lives in the world. The truth comes first; practices and attendant feelings follow. This is the proper order of things.

A good illustration of this modern way of thinking about theology, and an indication of how far we have come, is contained in a story that I learned as a young evangelical Christian. In an illustration of the Christian life from the popular writer Watchman Nee, living as a Christian was pictured in the form of three figures — named Fact, Faith, and Feeling — walking along the top of a wall.[2] According to this picture, for me to live out the Christian life rightly, it was essential that I get the order of these three figures right. Fact — the truths about Christ and his death for my salvation — had to go first; then Faith could follow, "keeping her eyes on Fact"; Feeling, last of all, would follow along, and all would be well. But if Faith would take her eyes off Fact, and turn around to see how Feeling was getting on, she would surely fall off the wall, and Feeling would tumble after her.

There are a bundle of theological (even psychological) assumptions hidden in this innocent little illustration. There is the supposition that all that we know about Christ is unambiguous "fact"; that faith has to do (primarily) with knowledge of these assured facts; and finally, and most significantly for our purposes, that emotions are unreliable and, in the end, dispensable factors in the Christian life. For many Christians, at least in the evangelical tradition, this picture of things has seemed unarguably true. It is a picture, which, as Wittgenstein says, holds us captive. (A parallel case might be made for classical liberal theology, which has simply replaced these facts and faith with different specified commitments and practices, and similarly overlooked the emotions, though I will not pursue that possibility here.) There is more than a little irony in this. The evangelical tradition has been among the most opposed to the use of images and metaphors in doing theology; Watchman Nee, the source of this illustration, is especially opposed to

---

2. Watchman Nee, *The Normal Christian Life* (Ft. Washington, Pa.: Christian Literature Crusade, 1963 [1957]), pp. 55-56.

these things.³ Yet in this case, in spite of this resistance, images emerge, and, unbidden, do their work.

So in part, I want to undo, or at least challenge, the work that this image has done. And I want to do this by focusing directly on the role of aesthetics, ritual, and images in our religious life — inside and outside of church. Whatever room we make or do not make for these dimensions of our lives, it is fair to say that all of us, as people immersed in families and communities, live on stories and pictures — whether it is the rush of a roaring football stadium or the quiet whoosh of the ski slope. The problem is that too often when it comes to theology we make little allowance for this arena — dealing as it does with emotions and desires. This was felt to be an interesting subject for our spare time, for diversion, but it was not given any substantial importance in the exploration of the Christian faith. Aesthetics has to do with more than feelings, as I will argue, but it certainly includes centrally our emotional life, our feeling for what happens, as Antonio Damasio puts it. Damasio makes use of recent brain studies and his own extensive clinical experience to argue that our basic sense of self — what he calls our core consciousness — is based on images or mental patterns, and that particular images involve fundamentally our emotions.⁴ "Consciousness begins," he believes, "as the feeling of what happens when we see or hear or touch."⁵ Genuine creativity needs additional skills, experience, and training, but it is always rooted in the possibilities and the feelings that consciousness offers.⁶ And this consciousness invariably includes representations that the body offers and our feeling response to them. The relevance of this to my argument is clear: The aesthetic desires and the habits and objects that embody these are fundamental to our human identity.

Clearly the little picture I was given was not only misleading — it may have had things backward: the role played by feelings is prior to and influential on the pictures we finally make of the world (i.e., on our knowing); moreover, faith itself cannot be understood apart from a

---

3. See, for example, his book titled *Love Not the World* (Wheaton, Ill.: Tyndale House, 1978 [1968]).

4. See Antonio R. Damasio, *The Feeling of What Happens: Body and Emotion in the Making of Consciousness* (San Diego, New York: Harcourt/Harvest Book, Inc., 1999), pp. 10, 125.

5. Damasio, *The Feeling of What Happens*, p. 26.

6. Damasio, *The Feeling of What Happens*, p. 315.

healthy awareness of the role of feeling. Thankfully, more and more emphasis is being given to this aspect of Christian devotion and theological reflection. Within the church, ancient devotional practices are experiencing widespread revival, especially among younger Christians, and these have always given full weight to our being embodied creatures indwelling special places and times. Indeed, all the practices of corporate worship — prayer, song, preaching, and so on — involve actions which necessarily have emotional and aesthetic dimensions to them. Outside the church, the media-saturated environment in which we all live inevitably raises issues of style and emotion. These concerns lie behind the discussions in this book. And they are developed as a means to opening conversations with Adam, Lisa, Brad, Sophia, and others like them.

In defense of our theological teachers, one might argue that during the last couple of centuries there were valid reasons for avoiding a focus on affections in theology. Given the excess to which this focus led, major theological figures purposefully avoided these emphases. The appeal to passions of peoples and races ("blood and soil") led Karl Barth to emphasize clarity and understanding, and to reflect on theology as *scientia*. In a very different context, the anti-intellectualist, feeling-saturated piety of his fundamentalist background led Carl Henry to emphasize Christianity as a rational system. In both cases, the theologians' aversion to emotion and their emphasis on real knowledge were understandable. Both of these also sought to escape the humanistic confines of classical liberalism, and their move to focus on the objectivity of God and God's Word is also sound — even praiseworthy.

Both of these theologians represent what is broadly called the Reformed tradition, which represents the perspective of this book as well. This tradition is well-known for being cautious about the role of feeling and affections. But however justified such suspicion may have been in the past, it is clearly problematic today. For it is increasingly clear that in contemporary culture, for many people, the search for truth has been overtaken by the search for what is pleasing — that during the last half-century, broadly speaking, aesthetics has come to replace epistemology as the central preoccupation of educated Western people. One no longer inquires about what can be known; one is more likely to be concerned about what feels and looks good. Although there are serious problems with this move, which we will address, the perception of the significance of aesthetics is widespread and ought not be ignored.

Given this aesthetic and affective turn in culture, this question arises: What should Christians make of this turn of events? Here there is no consensus. Some simply refuse to accept this perception and continue to produce materials that support the truth claims of the Christian faith. These individuals would claim that it is the truth of Christianity and the Spirit of God working through this that moves people to faith in Christ. This approach may reach a certain segment, but it is not the path that I want to take. On the other hand, some would simply celebrate this empire of desire and seek to compose some version of the Gospel that, however obliquely, seems to answer these demands. If possible, I want to avoid this simplistic assessment as well.

In what follows, then, I intend neither to celebrate nor to lament these contemporary sensibilities, but rather to engage them as the necessary context of our Christian mission and our theological reflection. Such engagement is perilous, but no more so, I would argue, than ignorance of these sensibilities. For the so-called postmodern turn represented by these developments, like all cultural developments, is exceedingly complex. There are some aspects of it that demand critique — as I will argue in this chapter — but there are others that provide opportunities for Christian engagement and witness — indeed, that may betoken the attracting presence of God's Spirit.

I have said that this conversation falls into the general category of apologetic theology. That is, it will seek to develop theological categories, given to us by Scripture and tradition, in conversation with the contemporary cultural situation. It assumes that whether this is recognized or not, all living theology grows in this way. So I begin by developing a way of thinking about the contemporary situation that has developed in the last two hundred years, what I will call a post-Romantic sensibility. This will involve describing the new spiritual awareness that in many ways has replaced traditional religion.[7] But then I will address the larger question, which is this: How do these newly awakened sensitivities relate to the presence and purposes of God? The second question grows from the first: In the light of the current climate of heightened spirituality, how might the story of what God was doing in Israel and Christ be represented? How, today, might the Gospel be actually heard?

---

7. For the development of this, see Graham Ward, *True Religion* (Oxford: Blackwell, 2003), and more recently, Barry Taylor, *Entertainment Theology: New Edge Spirituality in a Digital Democracy* (Grand Rapids: Baker Book House, 2008).

Prelude to Aesthetic Theology

Why Aesthetics?

Let me begin by taking a stab at describing the sensitivities I have in mind — the so-called aesthetic turn in our culture. I have connected what I am calling "aesthetics" with the emotions, pleasure, and a search for style, and this needs further elaboration. I have pointedly avoided speaking about "beauty" because this term has become particularly problematic for many. But as a starting point, I can do no better than to adopt Frank Burch Brown's definition of *aesthetica:* "All those things employing a medium in such a way that its perceptible form and 'felt' qualities become essential to what is appreciable and meaningful."[8] This allows us to take into account a variety of forms and practices — consumer objects as well as paintings in art galleries, styles of fashion as well as architectural design, even, to a certain extent, sports and hobbies. I do not mean to imply that there are not significant differences among these activities — I will point these out from time to time. But in general I want to stress the kind of symbolic and affective intent that these projects share. I want to explore the way a broader understanding of aesthetics extends to all areas of our embodied and encultured life together. This allows us to consider a wider range of activities that humans pursue as they seek to fashion lives, objects, and spaces that they feel good about. But it also allows a consideration of the breadth of the contemporary art world, with its mixed-media installations and community art and public performances, in addition to the events and displays in museums, galleries, and concert halls.

So, the poetics that I will explore in these pages refers to the "poesis" (or making, by imitation) of which Aristotle spoke, which in my discussion will include creative activities of many kinds. Poetry itself is making sense by measured forms of language, but we construct meaning out of many things that do not have direct reference to language. Susan Stewart has defined such made things as "forms arising out of sense experience and producing, as they make sense experience intelligible to others, intersubjective meaning."[9] This definition helpfully adds the interpersonal dimension, for the images and practices

---

8. Frank Burch Brown, *Religious Aesthetics: A Theological Study of Making and Meaning* (Princeton: Princeton University Press, 1989), p. 22.

9. Susan Stewart, *Poetry and the Fate of the Senses* (Chicago: University of Chicago Press, 2002), p. ix. See Aristotle, *Poetics,* trans. S. H. Butcher (New York: Dover, 1997 [330 B.C.E.]). We discuss Aristotle's definition in the following two chapters.

that we address all reference connections among people, with the earth, and even with meanings that extend beyond these.

Recently our metropolitan newspaper, *The Los Angeles Times,* added a new section called "Image" that comes with the Sunday edition. Its purpose, like that of style sections in newspapers elsewhere, was to cover, in a single section, all matters of "fashion, beauty, style, and shopping." In spite of their need, in the light of declining advertising, to reduce their overall size, something has been happening in our culture that made such an innovation necessary for this and other daily newspapers. Sociologist Robert Wuthnow has studied these trends. Not only has he found the attraction of the arts increasing among our contemporaries, but, more importantly, he argues that this appeal is strongly connected to a rising interest in spirituality and religion. Among his respondents there was one clear finding: interest in and exposure to the arts has increased among those born more recently. Among those born in the 1970s, for example, 66 percent say they are creative, as opposed to 45 percent of those born in the 1930s and 16 percent of those born from 1910 to 1920. Wuthnow concludes, "Survey results are at least consistent with other data showing rising levels of exposure to and participation in the arts."[10]

In general, it appears that many people today want to be seen as "creative" or as having a "sense of style." Marketers are recognizing the importance of these trends. In a recent report, Daniel Yankelovich Associates urged advertisers and marketers to consider the importance of products that express an "aesthetic sensibility." In their surveys, more than half of respondents rate highly "using their imaginations," and this appears to be true across generations and genders. And the trend is increasing. Those who rated "having a sense of style" as extremely or very important increased from 29 percent to 36 percent in only five years (from 2001 to 2006); similarly, those wanting to express their creative side increased from 38 percent to 46 percent. The report goes on to make a recommendation to marketer clients: "In the retail world, consider one-of-a-kind retail environments that keep the consumer engaged by activating their artistic imagination."[11]

---

10. Robert Wuthnow, *All in Sync: How Music and Art Are Revitalizing American Religion* (Berkeley and Los Angeles: University of California Press, 2003), p. 66.

11. J. Walker Smith, "Monitor Minute," 5 December 2006. Smith is President of Yankelovich and Partners, the polling firm. I owe this reference to Robert K. Johnston. For a broader discussion of these trends in the larger culture, see Virginia Postrel, *The Sub-*

Prelude to Aesthetic Theology

There are serious theological objections raised against this kind of talk, and I will get to those in a moment. But here we acknowledge a common reaction of many people, especially religious folk: these trends reflect the increasing superficiality (and secularism) of our consumer culture. Since, they suppose, the pursuit of style and beauty must distract people from the deeper issues of life, it is something that ought to be opposed. But Robert Wuthnow's evidence implies that, even empirically, this judgment is untrue. Concern for style and aesthetics, his research shows, is correlated with *increasing* interest in, and even seriousness about, religious issues. If this is so, growing interest in the arts is something to be applauded rather than resisted.

But such responses show their own biases. The temptation to decry cultural trends, or the inclination to engage a particular cultural trend, reflects theological assumptions about God's presence (or absence) in the larger culture. If a cultural trend is simply another example of humanity's active hostility to God, surely it must be repudiated rather than engaged. But if, on the other hand, this thirst reflects a deeper longing for an encounter with God, it ought at least to be examined, if not welcomed. It seems that the question of God's presence in culture cannot be avoided, and it is to this question that I now turn.

Why Culture?

Here a more serious obstacle emerges. I have proposed engaging a sensitivity toward life that has come to prominence in the last two hundred years — I have called it post-Romantic. But there are important theological voices which argue that the discourse that has arisen in this time is completely mistaken, and therefore must be simply opposed. In the last half-century, there have been a series of attempts by Christians to emphasize the hostility of the contemporary age to God or the Gospel. In different ways, Christian leaders have not only warned us about the dangers evident in current trends, but have also sought to portray them as a decline from some previous period seen to be more congenial to Christian truth. Not incidentally, these previous periods were often believed to be more congenial to the production of great art. (Secular ob-

---

stance of Style: How the Rise of Aesthetic Value Is Remaking Commerce, Culture, and Consciousness (San Francisco: HarperCollins, 2003).

servers have made similar laments about modern culture, but I will focus here on Christian responses.)[12]

Early on, for example, my fundamentalist heritage insisted that the world had grown so corrupt — as represented by the cultural influences of Darwin, Freud, and, for the better educated, Nietzsche — that one needed to separate oneself entirely from the surrounding culture and prepare for the imminent return of Christ. Later I learned from C. S. Lewis that the medieval world constituted a bright vision from which we have fallen away in the modern period. In words that resonate with my argument, Lewis writes, "To understand this process fully would be to grasp that great movement of internalization, and that consequent aggrandizement of man and desiccation of the outer universe in which the psychological history of the West has so largely consisted."[13] Around this time Francis Schaeffer argued that modern thinking that derived from Kant and the Romantics promoted what he called an "upper-story" or mystical experience that was incompatible with the content of the Gospel.[14] Still later, some of the most important voices in mainstream Christian scholarship began to warn us against being co-opted by contemporary culture in our well-meaning attempts to engage it.[15] And even more recently a whole school of theology, called Radical Orthodoxy, has argued that the Reformation represents a fatal turn away from a more holistic understanding of God's involvement with the world, a turn that led to the Enlightenment and many of the pernicious qualities of modern life.[16]

Although proposing widely different timelines and a variety of factors for the "modern" falling away, these declinists all agree that we must understand our contemporary situation as *opposed* to God in fundamental ways — and, usually, opposed in ways that previous periods were not. Thus we must be suspicious of the trends we see around us,

---

12. For one example of a secular jeremiad, see Jacques Barzun, *From Dawn to Decadence: Five Hundred Years of Western Culture* (New York: HarperCollins, 2000).

13. See C. S. Lewis, *The Discarded Image: An Introduction to Medieval and Renaissance Literature* (Cambridge: Cambridge University Press, 1964), p. 42.

14. See Francis Schaeffer, *Escape from Reason* (Downers Grove, Ill.: InterVarsity Press, 1968).

15. See, for example, Stanley Hauerwas and William Willimon, *Resident Aliens: Life in the Christian Colony* (Nashville: Abingdon Press, 1990).

16. See, among others, John Milbank, *Theology and Social Theory: Beyond Secular Reason* (Oxford: Blackwell, 1990), and *Radical Orthodoxy*, ed. John Milbank, Graham Ward, and Catherine Pickstock (London: Routledge, 1999).

and alert to the subtle ways in which we are misled (and misshaped) by our culture. These are serious objections. If the descriptions of Brad and Lisa simply express a misshapen cultural formation, it makes no sense to engage them at this level. It certainly would be unwise to dismiss these worries out of hand — many have been helped, myself included, by these thinkers and their warnings. C. S. Lewis and Radical Orthodoxy have taught us much about what we have to learn from classical and medieval culture. Stanley Hauerwas's call for the church to return to its calling to conform itself to Christ has been essential reading for many seeking church renewal. These have all been helpful reminders that, as the Apostle Paul says, the human mind by its own wisdom does not — indeed, cannot — know God (1 Cor. 1 and 2). In this respect, every culture, like every person, displays a brokenness. But this is not the whole story even in the New Testament. Romans 1, for example, is equally clear that the presence and power of God are there for all to see within the created order, even if people often resist this witness.

The Lure of Contemporary Aesthetics

But we must not dismiss these objections too quickly — they call for a serious response. To focus on our particular interest, that of aesthetics, what can we say about the contemporary situation? Well, it is true that beauty has had a rough go of it during the last century. And surely the contemporary pursuit of pleasure is often not to be celebrated. But what is really at stake here? To answer this question, let us look more closely at some of the complaints made by theologians about the contemporary situation in the arts.

In an important article, John Milbank, a leading figure in the Radical Orthodox conversation, argues that the absence of beauty in modernity is symptomatic of a deeper problem. Beauty, he notes following Aquinas, is "what pleases the sight." This quality evokes a longing in the viewer which corresponds to a substantial depth in the object. So, Milbank believes, "to see . . . the beautiful is to see the invisible in the visible . . . the hidden divine source irradiating the finite surface."[17] In

---

17. Milbank, "Beauty and the Soul," in John Milbank, Graham Ward, and Edith Wyschogrod, *Theological Perspectives on God and Beauty* (Harrisburg, Pa.: Trinity Press, 2003), pp. 1-2.

the Middle Ages, people were used to looking through the visible, as it were, to the invisible. And they understood the ground of this invisible reality to be God. By contrast, the modern person, Milbank says, merely stands on the brink of the invisible, which is unknown. He concludes, "In modernity . . . there is no mediation of the invisible in the visible, and no aura of invisibility hovering around the visible. In consequence there is no beauty."[18]

The reasons for this are complex, Milbank believes, but may be reduced to two related failures of modern thought. Immanuel Kant, as the theorist of modern aesthetics, is the cause of the first of these. Kant argued that the ineffability that we recognize in beauty does not lie on the side of the object, but on that of the subject.[19] We experience this quality subjectively as "sublime," Kant believed, but not as an objective reality lying behind the experience. This lack of exchange or reciprocity between subject and object, Milbank argues, reflects a second and deeper disconnect between the person and God, which he sees as the more serious failure of modern thought: the denial of a real relation. Milbank sees this break as going back to William of Ockham, and infecting, especially, the thinking of the Reformation, which Milbank believes has contributed so much to this modern loss of depth.

The issues here are clearly theological. Much turns on the question of whether one needs to return to the medieval notion of "participation" — that fundamentally the human person, and creation in general, find their ultimate ground and being in God, and in what sense this is to be understood, in order to escape the flattening effects of modernity. And a related question is whether in fact the Reformation affirmation of everyday life, to put Milbank's concern in a positive way, *necessitates* the nefarious effects of modern life. In approaching these questions, I will argue that it is in the area of aesthetics in particular that these issues find their most telling expression, and, perhaps, their possible resolution.

Since we have begun with the challenge of Radical Orthodoxy, let me continue my argument with reference to a recent expression of this point of view. In an important discussion, Tracey Rowland argues that discussions during the Second Vatican Council (1961-1965) represent for the Catholic Church a wrong turning with respect to culture because

---

18. Milbank, "Beauty and the Soul," p. 3.
19. Milbank, "Beauty and the Soul," p. 4.

they were unconsciously contaminated by the modern thinking that Milbank described.[20] The failure of the leaders of the conciliar discussions, Rowland thinks, was to ignore how modernity forms people in ways that turn them away from their transcendent rootedness in God. This led the leaders of the council to unwisely celebrate the autonomy of modern persons — and, by extension, modern cultural forms — in contrast to John Paul II, who has subsequently characterized these developments as a "culture of death."[21] Since she focuses in particular on the notion of "formation" (nicely captured in the German word *Bildung*), it might be valuable to quote a section of *Gaudium et Spes* (the conciliar document on modern culture which she finds troublesome):

> When man works in the fields of philosophy, history, mathematics, and science, and cultivates the arts, he can greatly contribute towards bringing the human race a higher understanding of truth, goodness, and beauty, to points of view having universal value; thus man will be more clearly enlightened by that wondrous Wisdom, which was with God from all eternity, working beside Him like a master craftsman.[22]

Notice that the writers of the document, as indicated by the reference to Proverbs 8:30, clearly put this statement in the rich tradition of biblical wisdom. Rowland admits that this is consistent with treatments in the tradition, as well as Scripture, but worries that, if one ignores or is unaware of the Trinitarian ground of this, it becomes more evocative of the works of Wilhelm von Humboldt and Friedrich Schiller.[23] I find it significant that Rowland associates the danger of the document's ambiguity with these Romantic writers, who sought through aesthetic reflection to *overcome* the instrumental rationalism of the Enlightenment — to re-connect things which this rationalism had separated. But this move, for Rowland, is precisely the move that established the autonomy of the subject over against dependence on the transcendental (and Trinitarian) ground.

---

20. See Tracey Rowland, *Culture and the Thomist Tradition: After Vatican II* (London: Routledge, 2003). This book is part of the Radical Orthodox series edited by John Milbank, Catherine Pickstock, and Graham Ward.
21. Rowland, *Culture and the Thomist Tradition*, pp. 36-37.
22. Quoted in Rowland, *Culture and the Thomist Tradition*, p. 22.
23. Rowland, *Culture and the Thomist Tradition*, p. 24.

Thus several times in the book Rowland sets what she calls this Herderian view of culture, wherein each culture has its own uniqueness, over against a specifically Christian grounding of all cultures in God. She dismisses those writers who follow this positive thrust of Vatican II and seek a synthesis with modern culture as Whig Thomists who do not properly understand the danger of modern notions of *Bildung*.[24] The problems with modern culture are such that it simply cannot serve as *praeambula fidei*. Modern culture, she concludes, is "a hostile medium for the flourishing of Christian practices and beliefs."[25]

We will address the strategic question — What can be done about this situation? — in a later chapter. Here we are concerned with the theological assumptions being made about modern culture in this treatment, and in Milbank's claims that were quoted earlier. Is the turn toward immanence, and thus away from God, the only reading of our current situation? And, equally important, was some previous culture (for Rowland, classical culture) more open to its transcendent ground? Charles Taylor has recently proposed a different reading of the present situation. To focus our attention on the developments in the early nineteenth century, where Rowland saw a particular problem, Taylor sees there an expansion rather than a contraction.[26] True, the aesthetic moves of Schiller and Herder are made against a background of "fading . . . metaphysical beliefs, about the Great Chain of Being, the order of things, and the like" (354). Still, Taylor thinks, these poets and writers expand the options beyond the fixed frameworks that are no longer assumed; they develop what Taylor calls "a language of articulated sensibilities" (353). In the production of aesthetic objects, they move beyond a mimetic representation of external reality to a free-standing "semanticisation" (355), a creation of the essence of the response to the depths, without the story. Schiller, to whom we will pay particular attention in Chapter Four, explored these depths, even as he saw them in anthropological rather than religious terms (359). This new aesthetic territory became particularly significant for the arts. Taylor believes that music (Mozart), poetry (Mallarmé), and even non-representational art (Kandinsky) moved into this new space.

---

24. Interestingly, she sees this danger as constituting a Protestantization of Catholic views on culture since Vatican II. See p. 107 of *Culture and the Thomist Tradition*.

25. Rowland, *Culture and the Thomist Tradition*, pp. 41, 159.

26. Charles Taylor, *A Secular Age* (Cambridge: Belknap/Harvard University Press, 2007). Subsequent pages cited in the text refer to this work.

The basis of this, Taylor argues, lies in the affirmation of everyday life that comes from the Reformation, and that did so much to encourage the exploration of the world and, even in Romanticism, the expansion of creative options. For various cultural and historical reasons, the religious background was no longer assumed, but a substantive ethical notion survived: the idea that something outside oneself can be found and captured in art which can bring fulfillment to persons — can move them beyond simple human flourishing. Notice the new and enlarged place this gives to art and aesthetic practices. These writers believed that "Beauty is what will save us, complete us" (359). It is not hard to see the connection between Romanticism's exploration of personal creativity and the aesthetic turn that we have been tracing. In the terms of our argument, the Romantics recognized that practices and objects could draw the human person out of themselves toward a higher and fuller life.

The Theological Grounding of Desire

But a question still remains: How do we assess this aesthetic turn theologically? A common response to this situation, reflected in Rowland's treatment, is to see here a move toward Pelagianism. We moderns, so we are told, have found within ourselves the means of our own salvation — as if this had not been a persistent problem since the Garden of Eden. But I want to argue that this is not the only reading of these changes. Indeed, artists of the modern period pointedly do not seek something *within* themselves, but more often something *beyond*, hovering on the edges of their imaginations, drawing them out. Charles Taylor makes two critical points about this modern aesthetic framework (which he believes has come to define our contemporary understanding of the human quest). First, the enlargement of the spaces in which the imagination can function constitutes the ethical situation in which the modern person defines himself or herself. Whatever we think of it, there is no escaping this condition. Modern Western people cannot help reading their present situation through the lens of Romantic aesthetics. He acknowledges that this questing has "led great numbers into modes of free-floating, not very exigent spirituality," but asks, "Doesn't every dispensation have its own favored forms of deviation?" (512-13). More important, we simply cannot go back to some previous era. Even if we had a choice, Taylor thinks, it is "wiser to stick with the present dispensation" (513).[27]

The reason for this lies in the second point Taylor makes. The expanded territory for the creative imagination may well allow for readings of life and the cosmos that exclude God. Indeed, for the Romantics, Taylor admits, "the ontic commitments are unclear" (356). Unclear, but not closed. This means that art of this kind, while it can deny solid realities out there, can also "serve to disclose very deep truths which in the nature of things can never be obvious, nor available to everyone, regardless of spiritual condition" (356). If one believes that the Spirit of God is at work in the larger culture prompting and attracting people toward God, such an understanding of art opens up a new way of thinking about this activity. As an example of this possibility, Taylor discusses the poetry of Jesuit poet Gerard Manley Hopkins. As he sees it, Hopkins represents the great possibility opened up by the writers of the 1790s in their new understanding of poetics — indeed, Hopkins' work would have been inconceivable apart from them.

The key is found, Taylor believes, in their understanding of "symbol." That is the assertion that an object, event, or sound can become symbolic, that it can become "that whereby alone a domain was disclosed, we could say: that whereby alone certain meanings come to exist for us" (756). Here poetry takes on a performative function, opening up for us something that can be accessed in no other way. Even though words and objects cannot contain the infinite (the Protestant Reformers were clear about this), they can perhaps point to it and even open up contact with it. In this way, symbols can not only sustain or enrich; they can disrupt and challenge.

We will have a great deal more to say about the role of symbols in the next chapter, but at this point we might ask, What is at stake theologically in the symbolic possibilities that Taylor proposes? Here we will move beyond Taylor and advance two theological claims: that these

---

27. Although Taylor shows an appreciation for modern culture that is missing in Radical Orthodoxy and those who support it, in his epilogue he generously acknowledges their work and notes the similarity with what he is saying. He calls their view "the Intellectual Deviation story," which he says deals with theoretical understanding largely of the elites. He wants instead to explore how this emerges as a mass phenomenon, becoming what he calls a modern social imaginary. See *A Secular Age*, pp. 774, 775. In Chapter Nine we will explore the way in which Romantics allowed the aesthetic sphere to be separated from the whole of life, thus diminishing the value and role of the poetic.

symbolic possibilities reflect the structure and purposes of creation, which in turn can only be properly grounded within a Trinitarian conception of God. These theological convictions then provide a proximate and final ground for the symbolic potential of cultural forms. The proximate ground is the Reformation celebration of creation, as Calvin put it, as a theatre for the glory of God. Though the Reformers believed that the splendor and potential of created reality rest on God's creative and sustaining presence, they insisted the storied forms of creation had substantial importance in themselves. As Jeremy Begbie puts this: "Creation's beauty is not . . . something that lives in a land beyond the sensual or behind the material particular or beneath the surface, or wherever — *to which* we must travel. Creation's beauty is just that, the beauty *of creation.*"[28] This theological commitment opened the way for a deeper appreciation of the values of everyday life and the wisdom of cultural forms. For Calvin this meant that human meaning and even an encounter with God are not to be found in some realm beyond the created order; because of God's merciful condescension in Israel, in Christ, and in the means of grace, we can know God here in this order of things. The order of creation is specially revelatory of God. Calvin expressed it this way:

> The universe is ruled by God, not only because he watches over the order of nature set by himself, but because he exercises especial care over each of his works. It is indeed true that the several things are moved by a secret impulse of nature as if they obeyed God's eternal command, and what God once determined flows on by itself.[29]

Culture is always what we humans make of creation. That is, there is always something of the goodness of creation in human creation, however distorted this may be. In a later chapter we will note that this grounding in creation is fundamental to all Protestant aesthetics and,

---

28. "Created Beauty: The Witness of J. S. Bach," in *The Beauty of God: Theology and the Arts*, ed. D. J. Treier, Mark Husbands, and Roger Lundin (Downers Grove, Ill.: InterVarsity Press, 2007), p. 25, his emphasis. Begbie has done more than anyone else to develop this idea with respect to the theological potential of music. See his *Theology, Music, and Time* (Cambridge: Cambridge University Press, 2000).

29. Calvin, *Institutes of the Christian Religion*, Library of Christian Classics, vols. 20-21, ed. John T. McNeill, trans. Ford Lewis Battles (Philadelphia: Fortress Press, 1960), 1.16.4.

therefore, to how we can come to know and experience God. It also resonates with the Romantic conception of depth in human experiences with nature. I will argue that this particular Romantic tendency owes a great deal to the Pietist tradition. In reflecting on this, I have been especially attracted by the radical eighteenth-century German Pietist J. G. Hamann, on our construal of creation. His role is significant because he proposed that one only truly knows the world by trusting God. And when one trusts God, one has no occasion to doubt the world — one only sees when things are allowed (believed) to speak. Indeed, Hamann believed that trusting our senses allows us to see more about God in the depths of what we look at. So the delight and affection for what is there allow one to relate to the world poetically.

Consider the short piece on aesthetics that Hamann wrote, "Aesthetica in Nuce," what Hamann calls a "Rhapsody in Kabbalistic Prose."[30] Poetry, Hamann notes, is the mother tongue of the human race: "The senses and the passions speak and understand nothing but images. Imagery comprises the entire treasure of human knowledge and happiness." But the basis of this is always God's creation, which are words addressed to humanity: "Speak, that I might see you! — This desire was fulfilled in creation, which is an address to the creature, through the creature."[31] Sadly, we have mutilated nature through our unnatural abstractions and devious constructs; now only the poet is able to see and translate. And looking, the poet sees a reminder — more, a pledge — of what is fundamental: who the Lord is.[32] That is to say, if, by the creative, imitative Spirit, one sees what is there, one will raise "the extinct language of nature from the dead."[33] Then one hears the testimony of the unique name: Jesus, the glory of the Creator. "If you understand Christ," Hamann writes, "you will not only understand what you read but it will intoxicate you."[34]

This theological point needs special emphasis. Radical Orthodoxy locates the contemporary flattening of culture in the loss of its sense of

---

30. See the translation in Gwen Griffith Dickson, *J. G. Hamann's Relational Metacriticism* (Berlin: Walter de Gruyter, 1995), pp. 410-31. See also John Milbank, "Knowledge: The Theological Critique of Philosophy in Hamann and Jacobi," in *Radical Orthodoxy*, ed. John Milbank, Graham Ward, and Catherine Pickstock.
31. Dickson, *J. G. Hamann's Relational Metacriticism*, pp. 411-12.
32. Dickson, *J. G. Hamann's Relational Metacriticism*, p. 421.
33. Dickson, *J. G. Hamann's Relational Metacriticism*, p. 425.
34. Dickson, *J. G. Hamann's Relational Metacriticism*, pp. 426-27.

Prelude to Aesthetic Theology

"participation" in God. But Calvin in particular insisted that, while God sustains the world and works in it, the world has its own special goodness because of its created character — precisely because it is not God. Culture is a sphere in which God is at work; God's call is reflected in cultural products. But it is misleading to argue that culture either should or could participate in God in any ontological sense. Indeed, cultural practices as often reflect God's absence as his presence. They as often lead one away from God as toward him. But the forms and structures of creation are not completely separated from God, either; God continues to uphold them in Christ, and works by the Spirit to establish the purposes of creation.

Such a perspective on creation opens up new vistas of relationship with people and things of the earth. Jean-Luc Marion has argued that our response to this richness leads us to see it either as idol — something produced by my gaze — or as icon — that which opens to an infinite gaze. The former hides the invisible; the latter makes it visible. For this to happen, creation must be seen not as being but as gift, and a gift that always expresses the excess of the Giver. "Only agape can put things on earth," Marion says.[35] Despite his insistence on opposing being and gift, the claim he is making about the way things are has great implications. Because of the excess of creation, there is always potential in creation for more than meets the eye. We can enter into life-giving relationships with it, and we can make things out of it that give us meaning. Not only can we stand in awe under a canopy of stars, but we can also paint something called *The Starry Night* (Van Gogh) that gives us fresh eyes for this gift of the night.

To be sure, the gift character of creation does not guarantee the goodness of what is made of this. Like all gifts, this goodness can be squandered or misused. And culture reflects inevitably both the creative potential and the possible misuse. This brokenness suggests a further complication to our discussion of human making: We cannot simply assume a given cultural product reflects God's presence. But the order of desire which Hamann describes, grounded as it is on God, makes it possible at least for cultural products to direct one toward God.

But in what sense do we think of these things as possibly grounded in God? If the created goodness and potential of creation constitute the proximate ground for the symbolic potential of cultural forms, the Trini-

---

35. Jean-Luc Marion, *God without Being: Hors-Texte,* trans. Thomas A. Carlson (Chicago: University of Chicago Press, 1991 [1982]), p. 106.

tarian shape of God's work in creation constitutes the final ground for valuing the created order. God's presence may be described in terms of the intrinsic relationality both among the creatures of creation and between these and God's providential and redemptive work — all this defines the excess of the gift. This loving and active presence allows for a weaker, though still critical, sense of "participation" than that proposed by Milbank. I would suggest that creation "participates" in God in that God has committed to work in it, and, in Christ and by the Spirit, upholds and fulfills God's purpose of shaping creation into a vehicle of divine glory — all of which is reflected and summed up in the New Testament notion of *koinonia*.[36] This description of these relationships preserves both the priority of God's purposes in creation and the substantial value that God has placed in the created order, without seeking an ontological connection. This way of putting things also suggests that cultural products, especially aesthetic practices, may echo these relationships.

So, for the Reformers, the proximate valuing of creation rested on the larger grounds of God's Trinitarian presence. In particular, the notion of the symbolic potential of words and things, I believe, rests on the reality of the Incarnation, God's taking on *flesh* in Christ — a connection that the Reformers, for various historical and cultural reasons, mostly did not make.[37] God transforms creation through the life, death, resurrection, and ascension of Christ, and by the extension of this work through the giving of the Holy Spirit — what we call the economic Trinity. The significance of human culture lies in its being the arena in which God's work, especially as this is presented in Christ and through the Spirit, is recognized and embodied. God's participation in creation and creation's embrace by the Trinitarian presence of God — these together constitute theological grounds for the potential inherent in the symbolizing inclination of the poetic imagination, which Charles Taylor has described, and which I want to develop in these pages.

---

36. These issues are well laid out by Jeremy Begbie in "Created Beauty" in *The Beauty of God,* pp. 26 and 27, and by Alan Torrance in *Persons in Communion* (Edinburgh: T&T Clark, 1996), pp. 307ff. The issue, Torrance argues, is to allow our notion of participation to be controlled by the New Testament teaching of *koinonia* rather than Plato's idea of *methexis* (participation of particulars in the eternal forms). I have made a similar argument in *The Earth Is God's* (Maryknoll, N.Y.: Orbis Books, 1997), Chapter Two.

37. I have argued this point in connection with Calvin in William Dyrness, *Reformed Theology and Visual Culture: The Protestant Imagination from Calvin to Edwards* (Cambridge: Cambridge University Press, 2004), Chapter Three.

Prelude to Aesthetic Theology

Let this constitute an initial defense of our thesis. The affective response to the goods of creation, and to the symbolic practices humans make of these, finally has a personal reference. People are defined, as Augustine notes, not by what they know or achieve but by what they love. And in responding with affection, they are responding to the love that lies at the basis of the gift and giver of creation. The projects of Adam and Lisa spark their affection because there is something about creation that makes such responses appropriate.

Engaging the Romantic Inward Turn: A Positive Example

So I argue that it is possible to understand the post-Romantic sensitivities in a positive way. But what might this look like? Charles Taylor claims that the poetic imagination which the Romantics bequeathed to us can "serve to find a way back to the God of Abraham" (757). This broad stretching of the mental canvas can allow for other gods and spirits, of course, but there is no necessity for this Romantic turn to be understood in wholly subjectivist terms. The example Taylor advances in support of this, as we noted, is the poetry of Gerard Manley Hopkins. In Hopkins' poetry one can see a fusing of his embodied experience with something deeper, which, that poet believed, is God's action in the world.

In an article on Hopkins, Seamus Heaney points out that the modern notion of creativity, which we have traced to the German Romantics, can be understood in two ways.[38] One group, the symbolists (and, we might add, non-objective painters like Kandinsky and Pollock), saw poetry as a linguistic (or painterly) exploration, as seeking an end in its own uncovering. Heaney sees this creativity as a kind of birth.[39] A second way is to see creativity as incorporating an experience of something that precedes the poem (Heaney calls it an "idea") into the linguistic medium. Hopkins displays this second sort of creativity, Heaney claims. The poetic image combines the idea and the experience, Hopkins "alerts us to perceive."[40] Hopkins' poetry thus has a double

---

38. Seamus Heaney, "The Fire i' the Flint," in *Preoccupations: Selected Prose, 1968-1978* (London: Faber & Faber, 1980). See also Taylor, *A Secular Age*, p. 757.

39. Heaney, "The Fire i' the Flint," p. 81.

40. Heaney, "The Fire i' the Flint," p. 85.

source: his own experience and the connection of that to God. Heaney notes, "His idea of Divinity... underlay his poetic imagination and provided ... the ground-plan of the poetic act." Acknowledging the Christological basis of this, Heaney concludes, "Just as Christ's mastering descent into the soul is an act of love, a treading and melting, so the poetic act itself is a love-act, initiated by the masculine spur of delight."[41]

When Hopkins speaks in "The Windhover" of the falcon's flight of a morning, "the hurl and gliding," he can also say, "My heart in hiding/ Stirred for a bird — the achieve of, the mastery of the thing!"[42] Hopkins is here plowing the space the Romantic poets had staked out. The point is this: There is nothing in the deepening of the inner world that inescapably closes the creative imagination to the action of God. To return to Milbank's complaint, a tendency to expand the subject does not *necessitate* a turn away from the object. Indeed, in deepening the subject a possible way is opened to access something beyond the ordinary.

Contemporary Culture: The Aesthetics of Desire

So it is possible to understand the developments since Romanticism in a way that is consistent with God's presence and calling in culture. But it must be admitted that when one looks squarely at contemporary culture, one is not encouraged. What kind of use is being made of the new register of sensitivities that the nineteenth century opened up? One important way of parsing contemporary culture, I am suggesting, is to take notice of the wide range of longings, both physical and spiritual, for deeper and higher ways of being human. Our neighbors seek their fulfillment through travel, sex, work, family, and not infrequently by some faith in God (or gods). But in various ways, contemporary culture expresses deep-seated and restless hungers. People are, as Hans Walter Wolff put it in his description of the person in the Old Testament, "creatures of greedy need."[43] Whether in the shriek of delight or of suffering — they are creatures who cry out.

---

41. Heaney, "The Fire i' the Flint," pp. 92, 97.
42. Quoted in Taylor, *A Secular Age*, p. 762.
43. See Hans Walter Wolff, *The Anthropology of the Old Testament* (Minneapolis: Fortress Press, 1981 [1974]), p. 12.

Prelude to Aesthetic Theology

Because of the post-Romantic sensitivities, the contemporary person is mobilized by desire to pursue a good life. David Lurie, the protagonist of J. M. Coetzee's novel *Disgrace,* may be taken as a representative of this culture. Lurie, a college professor, has been found having an affair with one of his students. He is forced to leave the university and goes to live with his adult daughter. One day she asks him about what happened. "What is your case?" she asks. "Let us hear about it." Lurie answers, "My case rests on the rights of desire . . . on the god who makes even the small birds quiver." Then he thinks, *I was a servant of Eros.* That is what he wants to say, but does he have the effrontery? *It was a god who acted through me.* This sounds like vanity, he knows, but there is truth in it, he thinks. All through the sordid affair there was something good and generous, he believed, "that was doing its best to flower."[44] Earlier he had recalled Blake's dictum: "Sooner murder an infant in its cradle than nurse unacted desires."[45]

Clearly, Lurie's actions deserve all the anger and retribution that he receives. But what does one make of his rather plaintive feeling that there was surely something "good and generous" wanting to flower? The goodness and generosity seem to Lurie somehow prior to his experience. How does he make sense of this? Elaine Scarry thinks it has to do with the way beautiful objects seem specially designed to fit our perception. As a result, she says, we are not meant to be passive in their presence; we are drawn out by them. "It is as though beautiful things have been placed here and there throughout the world," Scarry writes, "to serve as small wake-up calls to perception, spurring lapsed alertness back to its most acute level."[46]

Desire represented by attractive things interrupts our lives; it calls us to seek our flourishing in something beyond the present experience. David Lurie seems to sense something like this, though he is not able to articulate it. He is not able to say who it was that placed these beautiful objects here and there, or why. Or what it is about his desire that is good and generous and what part is misshapen. And Lurie is not wrong in seeing that somehow desire relates to what he was after — his own fulfillment and flourishing.

---

44. J. M. Coetzee, *Disgrace* (New York: Penguin Books, 1999 [2000]), p. 89, his emphasis.
45. Quoted in Coetzee, *Disgrace,* p. 69.
46. Elaine Scarry, *On Beauty and Being Just* (Princeton: Princeton University Press, 1999), pp. 25, 81. She too faces the challenge of defending this experience without the metaphysical support provided by the existence of God.

Dangers Inherent in the Aesthetic Turn

So, even if there is no escaping the post-Romantic culture of inwardness, it cannot be embraced uncritically. There are too many David Luries out there. Our suspicion that God is at work in the ways that people hunger for a deeper encounter with reality should not blind us to the specific ways in which desire and its projects lead us astray.

Two such dangers come to mind. The first danger lies in reducing real religion to various aesthetic or mystical states. Once Romanticism discovered that aesthetic experience can transform people, it was a short step to understanding all religion as basically a feeling for God — a step that many contemporary writers on religion have taken. In late-twentieth-century sociology of religion, there was a persistent inclination to see in mystical experience the core of all genuine religion. Here scholars, in various ways, followed in the path that William James laid out in his Gifford Lectures of 1901-1902, published as *The Varieties of Religious Experience*. In one of his final lectures, James claimed that mystical states point in directions that all people aspire to:

> They tell of the supremacy of the ideal, of vastness, of union, of safety, and of rest.... The supernaturalism and optimism to which they would persuade us may, interpreted in one way or another, be after all the truest of insights into the meaning of life.[47]

In the conclusion, where he states his own "over-beliefs," James allows that the plunge into other dimension of existence, however you name it, is the true source and home of our ideals, to which we "belong ... in a more intimate sense than that in which we belong to the visible world."[48]

Mystical experiences, James noted, have profound, even transformative effects on human life, so that philosophers have no reason to call them unreal. But note the proviso that such experiences have no necessary connection to any particular creed — Hindus, Sufis, and Christians alike can boast of such mystical transformations. Such views have become common in recent sociology of religion, and they virtually

---

47. William James, *Writings: 1902-1910*, ed. Bruce Kuklick (New York: Library of America, 1987), p. 374. James connects these experiences to aesthetic appeal in pages 412-13.

48. James, *Writings*, p. 460.

colonized literature aimed at spiritual integration. Consider Robert Fuller, who recently has argued for the centrality of wonder in spirituality. He believes "a life shaped by wonder might... be the defining example of what 'being spiritual' means at its very best."[49] Fuller quotes Martha Nussbaum's belief that wonder is the only emotion that can lift the person above self-interest, which leads Fuller to suggest that if religion is to succeed, it "must ritualize experiences that provide a felt sense of this wider reality."[50] Notice that religion is not the goal, but a means, pressed into service to promote mystical experiences that constitute the aim of human life.

There is certainly no question that experiences which might be called "mystical" are to be found in many different religions and, indeed, among people with no religion at all. Nor is there any doubt that they might be useful in making people better or happier — an important factor for James, who is the father of American pragmatism. Indeed, a preoccupation with sports or fishing or the arts, as we have acknowledged, can bring a sense of fulfillment to people. This resonates with the widespread influence of Abraham Maslow, whose *Toward a Psychology of Being* promoted what he called positive psychology. Beginning with an optimistic view of human nature, he argued that humans reach their highest end in self-justifying and self-actualizing moments, what he called "peak experiences." During these experiences people actually are lifted above the relativities of history and culture into an absolute and universal realm — all secondary roles and associations fall away, and they become more truly and wholly human, and also more creative and more fully themselves. Maslow put it this way:

> If all people are different from each other in principle, they are *more* purely different in the peak-experiences. If in many respects (their roles), men [sic] are interchangeable, then in the peak-experiences, roles drop away and men become least interchangeable. Whatever they are at bottom, whatever the word "unique self" means, they are more that in the peak-experiences.[51]

---

49. Robert C. Fuller, *Wonder: From Emotion to Spirituality* (Durham: University of North Carolina Press, 2006), p. 15. Fuller later contrasts this spirituality, as "a distinct mode of apprehending experience," with obedience to transcendent authority (p. 147).

50. Fuller, *Wonder*, p. 66. The reference to Nussbaum is from p. 14.

51. Abraham H. Maslow, *Toward a Psychology of Being*, 2d ed. (New York: D. Van Nostrand Co., 1968), p. 108, his italics.

But *reducing* religious goals to such experiences, I would argue, denies both the historical and creaturely — and ultimately, the theological — context of human striving. Consider the historical and cultural context of such experiences. While it may appear that the mystical, or aesthetic, experiences are similar, there is increasing evidence that meanings are always culturally determined: what might satisfy as a peak experience in one place may be feared as a kind of possession in another. Moreover, we are becoming increasingly aware of the way our knowing, our feeling, and our aesthetic responses are impacted by our embodied nature. The deepest human experiences are not in spite of our bodies, but through and in terms of them.[52] In the light of the widely different social and economic situations in which people find themselves, then, it would be not only naïve but actually perverse to hold out such experiences as universal goals.

But there is a second related deviation to which our generation is inclined. The legitimate encounters with delight and beauty have in our time become so attractive that people are often willing to give up everything in their pursuit. The Romantic turn for many has led to various forms of narcissism and hedonism. Here we recognize a central problem with the Romantic focus on aesthetic contemplation. Because meaning and purpose can be given symbolic shape in works of art or ritual practices, it is possible not only to see these as ends worth pursuing, but also as final ends. They can not only be seen as goods; they can become idols. And even good things can control us. Pleasures that are a natural part of God's good creation can, over time, not simply season or enrich our lives — they can take possession of it. A culture that has increasingly focused on affirming and exploring desire has led, in many cases, to a frantic search for new and higher experiences of pleasure for their own sake. Psychologists have defined a new emotional disorder that is called "hedonic dysregulation," or more commonly "anhedonia."[53] In a familiar addictive process, the overstimulation of pleasure centers in the brain leads to higher and higher demands until only major pleasures can reach us. And over time the

---

52. See especially the work of Antonio Damasio noted earlier, and Mark Johnson, *The Body in the Mind: The Bodily Basis of Meaning, Imagination, and Reason* (Chicago: University of Chicago Press, 1987).

53. Archibald D. Hart, *Thrilled to Death: How the Endless Pursuit of Pleasure Is Leaving Us Numb* (Nashville: Thomas Nelson, 2007). He says, "Everything that gives us pleasure has the potential to become addictive when abused" (p. 98).

overload of pleasure centers leads to the situation in which the events of everyday life no longer give pleasure. Of course, addictions to drugs, gambling, and sex are well known. But many of us find ourselves caught up in more innocent-seeming cycles. We become so addicted to work, or a hobby, or a kind of consumption — all things that are not bad in themselves — that we become embroiled in a frantic multitasking search for a new high: another promotion, another deal to close, another event to plan, another thing to buy. The result is that we no longer have the capacity to enjoy the love of our family and friends, and we can no longer feel ourselves loved and cared for by God. The joys of everyday life no longer attract us.

A pattern is emerging. Notice how desire and its object are isolated from the larger human experience; they are pursued as ends in themselves. Rather than seeing experiences of this kind as contributing to a healthy life, they are held to constitute such a life. But perhaps there is a deeper framework that lies behind these deviations. All of the people who are pursuing pleasure would likely argue that they are looking for a life that is well lived — what we will frame as a beautiful or attractive life. In a recent discussion, Nicholas Wolterstorff has argued that the contemporary pursuit of such a life is frequently a modern form of the ancient Stoic idea of eudaimonism — the view that the goal of life is to live well or happily.[54] There will be many disagreements as to what activities should be included in a happy or well-lived life, but none as to this being the central aim of life. What is significant about such an aim, Wolterstorff points out, is the fact that it is invariably agent-oriented. That is, of the various candidates for action in one's life, the question is which "will contribute most to my living my life well."[55] Wolterstorff's argument in this book is that Augustine (and other Christian thinkers of that period) had to make a definitive break with eudaimonism in order for notions of human rights and intrinsic human dignity to emerge.

---

54. Nicholas Wolterstorff, *Justice: Rights and Wrongs* (Princeton: Princeton University Press, 2008), pp. 150-53. Wolterstorff thinks that this common view reflects an underlying utilitarianism (p. 146).

55. Wolterstorff, *Justice*, p. 153.

Constructive Engagement with Desire

We are going to engage Augustine's views of love and desire in the following chapter. But, meanwhile, this discussion has placed some serious roadblocks in the way of our poetic theology. If we have to give up the quest for a life well lived, then our entire project flounders. But is this what God asks us to do? Let me consider more carefully how desire works. Wolterstorff describes desire as "a mode of our investment in the occurrence of some state of affairs."[56] In other words, desire is directed toward some external event that will bring satisfaction. Adam plans his days at the football stadium, Sophia plans her visits to art galleries, and so on.

Notice, then, that it is possible to conceive of this movement of desire as the first step in the direction of something outside oneself. Octavio Paz puts this nicely. Desire, he writes, "is a shot fired in the direction of the world beyond."[57] Lisa believes that the thrill of the ski slope contributes to giving her a life that is somehow beyond the ordinary; it will allow a flourishing that fulfills something she longs for. She may be wrong about this, but she is surely not *completely* wrong. We might say that desire expresses, at least, the emotional connection with something outside ourselves; it may be the first indication that we are made for relationship. It is perhaps this which the character David Lurie sensed was "good and generous," seeking "to flower." And indeed, this movement of his soul, if I may use this phrase, might be read in a religious sense. St. Bonaventure goes so far as to say that desire is the movement of the soul toward God.[58] I think that G. K. Chesterton had something like this in mind when he spoke about what we should and should not enjoy:

> Do not enjoy yourself. Enjoy dances and theatres and joy-rides and champagne and oysters; enjoy jazz and cocktails and nightclubs if you can enjoy nothing better; enjoy bigamy and burglary and any crime in the calendar in preference to the other alternative; but never learn to enjoy yourself.[59]

---

56. Wolterstorff, *Justice*, pp. 185-86.
57. Octavio Paz, *The Double Flame: Love and Eroticism*, trans. Helen Lane (New York: Harcourt Brace, 1995), p. 13.
58. St. Bonaventure, *The Journey of the Mind to God*, trans. Philotheus Boehner (Indianapolis: Hackett, 1956).
59. G. K. Chesterton, *The Common Man* (London: Sheed & Ward, 1950), p. 252.

All these enjoyments, however imperfect they may be, move us to a focus that is outside ourselves. As Chesterton goes on to say, "Human beings are only happy so long as they retain the receptive power and the power of reaction in surprise and gratitude to something outside."[60] Or, as Octavio Paz puts this, "Eroticism is first and foremost *a search for otherness*. And the supernatural is the supreme otherness."[61] It is telling that all the spiritual exercises — of prayer, meditation, and reading of Scripture — involve focusing our enjoyment and our attention outside ourselves and, eventually, on God. In this process, those innocent loves, with which we began this chapter, are transformed into something higher and richer. But meanwhile, we can accept them for what they are: steps in this better direction.

But these initial desires, while they can be movements in a positive direction, in themselves are powerless to change us. What broke the hold of eudaimonism on Augustine, Wolterstorff notes, was his encounter with another person.[62] In other words, desire had to give way to love. He had to accept the claim of the other on him as a real responsibility, as compassion, and eventually as embrace.[63] Octavio Paz frames this in relation to the created and embodied context in which this movement occurs. Eroticism is movement in a potentially good direction, but it must become love: "Love is the attraction toward a unique person: a body and a soul. Without eroticism — without a visible form that enters by way of the senses — there is no love, but love goes beyond the desired body, and seeks the soul in the body . . . the whole person."[64] Thus desire moves toward the other and seeks communion, but this is a movement that can be misdirected — it can lead to exclusion as well as embrace.

Charles Williams' comments on Dante can help us avoid these contemporary dangers. In his study of Beatrice, he distinguishes a true and a false Romanticism. Dante's *Divine Comedy*, Williams notes, presents us with images of love. They are many, and they are often foolish. "But," says Williams in words that apply equally to contemporary desires,

---

60. Chesterton, *The Common Man*, p 252.
61. Paz, *The Double Flame*, p. 15, his emphasis.
62. Wolterstorff, *Justice*, p. 211.
63. I have been helped here by Miroslav Volf's *Exclusion and Embrace: A Theological Exploration of Identity, Otherness, and Reconciliation* (Nashville: Abingdon Press, 1996).
64. Paz, *The Double Flame*, p. 32. This resonates with what we said about *koinonia* earlier.

"they are apt also to have that kind of sincerity which may, one way or another, become fidelity to the image or the principle within or beyond the image. One way or another this state [of love] is normal; what is not yet normal is the development of that state to its proper end."[65] Beatrice, of course, is the central image of that love in *The Divine Comedy*. Dante's first encounter with Beatrice when she was nine years old was normal. His response, recorded in the *Vita Nuova*, recalls David Lurie's confession: "Behold, a god stronger than I who is come to rule over me."[66] Dante trembled when, years later, at the end of the Purgatorio, he recalled the experience. Her beauty fitted itself to his perception, as Scarry put it, and awakened him. But in itself this was neither a true nor a false Romanticism; it was merely innocent pleasure *(sollagia)*. But as we see in Dante's great poem, while it could become a symbol of something higher, it could also tend toward what Williams calls "lusuria" (or letchery). Like the love of Paolo and Francesca in *Inferno* (V), at whose story Dante is said to have fainted as though dead, the pleasantness of eros *(sollagia)* initially was not only permissible, says Williams — it was enjoined. The problem was that it became the end rather than a means; it was not followed to its source. As Williams says of these lovers, "Here all is still good except the very good itself; all is still valuable except value itself."[67] And as love is pursued *for itself* rather than for that which lies beyond and behind, it loses what good is left. The image is always in danger of extorting "from the glory its own satisfaction with the glory."[68] Then it is a false Romanticism.

Just as the encounter with Beatrice awakened Dante to love, so Dante had to be awakened to love's larger power. And this took the grace of illumination — represented in the *Comedy* by the role of Beatrice herself. Through the redirection of his desire, Dante comes to know the fullness of love "by grace," but then he not only has to experience it; he has to "*become* the thing he has seen in Beatrice," as Williams points out.[69] The lesson of Dante is inescapable: the force of eros will do its work. It opens up into the funnel that leads down to hell; but it can also draw us up to the dance and music of paradise.

65. Charles Williams, *The Figure of Beatrice: A Study in Dante* (London: Faber & Faber, 1963), p. 16.
66. Coetzee, *Disgrace*, p. 19.
67. Williams, *The Figure of Beatrice*, p. 118.
68. Williams, *The Figure of Beatrice*, p. 48.
69. Williams, *The Figure of Beatrice*, p. 37, his emphasis.

Conclusion

Grace is necessary. Apart from this, Adam will see that even great teams must lose; Lisa and Brad will be disappointed with their sport; and Sophia will find that art isn't everything. The question they all face is this: Does the love they have for these practices enlarge them? Does it stand for a love that lies beyond these practices but, strangely, creates a bigger and finer space for these — and beyond that, room to flourish?

Here is the positive theological point: the realization of God's loving embrace does nothing to undermine the meaning and enjoyment of these embodied pleasures. Indeed, if Adam and Lisa find in God their final ground, they are likely to enjoy their projects more deeply. Augustine, to whom I will turn in the next chapter, understood this larger context for desire very well. In his *Confessions,* he asks and answers a critical question:

> When I love you, what do I love? It is not physical beauty nor temporal glory nor brightness of light dear to earthly eyes, nor the sweet melodies of all kinds of songs, nor the gentle odor of flowers and ointments and perfumes, nor manna or honey, nor limbs welcoming the embraces of the flesh; it is not these I love when I love my God. Yet there is a light I love, and a food, and a kind of embrace when I love my God — a light, voice, odor, food, embrace of my inner man, where my soul is floodlit by light which space cannot contain, where there is sound that time cannot seize, where there is perfume which no breeze disperses, where there is a taste for food no amount of eating can lessen, and where there is bond of union that no satiety can part. That is what I love when I love my God.[70]

It is true that the aesthetic turn has led to a frantic search for mystical experiences of all kinds, and to addictive behavior and its accompanying levels of stress. But the abuse of goods underlines their indispensability; it should not lead us to deny their source in God and God's created purposes. What we cannot do, despite the deviations we prefer,

---

70. Augustine, *Confessions,* trans. Henry Chadwick (Oxford: Oxford University Press, 1992), X, 6, p. 183. Graham Ward, in his discussion of these things, notes that the patristic fathers understood the interconnection of spiritual and corporal senses in a way that we have lost. Cf. *Christ and Culture* (Oxford: Blackwell, 2005), pp. 99-100.

is ignore the turn to style and aesthetics that is so prominent. I have dealt with some of the theological reasons for the importance of this aesthetic turn in this chapter. In the next I will seek to develop this more fully into a poetic theology of culture, following which I will be ready to ask how we may take advantage of the opportunities our situation offers.

CHAPTER 2

The Historical Model: *Theologia Poetica*

Assuming that God is active in the work of creating culture, how is this to be understood? In this chapter I will put the theological conviction about God's presence in human culture in a particular historical framework that I am calling, for reasons that will soon be clear, a *theologia poetica* or "poetic theology." We began to lay out some theological parameters for this in the last chapter: describing creation as God's good gift and the ongoing project of God's Trinitarian presence in creation. Here we will look at this from the point of view of those situated in culture. This will involve shaping a particular understanding of cultural forms, and some suggestions about the way we can speak of God's presence in these forms.

To begin, let me return to the emphasis from the Vatican II document on culture, to which we referred in the last chapter:

> When man works in the fields of philosophy, history, mathematics, and science, and cultivates the arts, he can greatly contribute towards bringing the human race a higher understanding of truth, goodness, and beauty, to points of view having universal value; thus man will be more clearly enlightened by that wondrous Wisdom, which was with God from all eternity, working beside Him like a master craftsman.[1]

This statement recognizes that we all are born into the patterns of particular cultures, which, for better or worse, shape us. I have elsewhere

---

1. *Gaudium et Spes,* quoted in Tracey Rowland, *Culture and the Thomist Tradition: After Vatican II* (London: Routledge, 2003), p. 22.

argued in some detail that culture is what we humans make of God's good creation, and as such, culture is inherently moral and even theological. It is a dynamic and changing set of practices, objects, and commitments that, initially at least, constitute the limits of the possible for human activity.[2] It is within these patterns that we form traditions, shape institutions, raise families, and — what is the focus of this book — forge objects with aesthetic intent: things which call for a response of joy, or delight, or even horror. And — this was the argument of the first chapter — it is in these terms that we respond to God. But this influential statement from Vatican II puts this into a biblical category that I want to underscore. It recognizes that the best human work in any culture is an expression of what the biblical tradition calls wisdom, the human capacity to bring treasures out of the storehouse of the created order. This creative capacity expresses both the divine image in human activity and the general working of God's Spirit in culture.

So I want to describe this human activity in a particular way that I am calling "poetic," and I need to specify further what I mean by this. The fundamental way in which we humans respond to our cultural situation — and ultimately to God, who comes to us clothed in this situation — is by our doing and making — in other words, by our *praxis* and our *poesis* (Greek for "doing" and "making"). Humans make themselves and forge their identity through their doing and their making. As Graham Ward puts this, these activities, which are related, are "expressions by which the soul may arrive at truth."[3] But I want to argue that, spiritually, the category of "making" *(poesis)* is more important than "doing" *(praxis)*. We define ourselves not by the ordinary processes of living but by the larger symbolic activities by which we "make something" of ourselves. I want to call this larger sphere of imaginative and affective making our "poetics."

Within the products that make up our culture, I want then to focus on those range of practices, and those dimensions of our living, which have, broadly speaking, an aesthetic aim. I want to claim that these activities and these dimensions are more central to human identity and, whether believer or unbeliever, to one's religious life than the func-

---

2. William Dyrness, *The Earth Is God's: A Theology of American Culture* (Maryknoll, N.Y.: Orbis Books, 1996; reprint, Eugene, Ore.: Wipf and Stock, 2004). See Chapter Three, "Culture."

3. Graham Ward, *Christ and Culture* (Oxford: Blackwell, 2005), p. 231.

tional activities which fill up most of life. Moreover, I will argue that a kind of vernacular theology can be discerned in this arena that I am calling *theologia poetica* (poetic theology).

Medieval *Theologia Poetica*

Theologia poetica is a term derived from an important medieval conversation that I want to revisit. The term itself comes from Pico della Mirandola, a Renaissance humanist writing near the end of the fifteenth century. Pico sought, in his turbulent and uncertain context, to reconcile Christian thought with the classical tradition. He was retrospectively naming a tradition that began with Dante and stretched through Petrarch to the Renaissance humanists, a tradition which would eventually influence John Calvin. It might seem strange to retrieve this medieval notion as an instrument for contemporary cultural analysis, but it turns out that the late medieval world had much in common with the contemporary one. It was a period of a greatly enlarged sense of human achievement and potential, a time of focus on the human person (coming from Augustine) and the human capacity to shape the world, and finally, due to spectacular world-shaking events that included the Black Death and multiple wars, a time of widespread spiritual searching.[4] In many ways the developments represented by this tradition anticipated the innovations of Calvin and the Reformers and, by extension, the challenges we face in the modern period. New challenges were demanding new answers, to which the tradition, even — or especially — in its Christian (and Scholastic) form, seemed to provide no answers. For these writers and thinkers, the rediscovery of classical literature served as an impetus to reread the Scriptures with the new questions these sources raised.

The "poetic theology" which they suggested, and which we will explore, was not limited to poetry in the narrow sense. For Aristotle, who was the source of much of their reflection on art, we have noted that *poesis* was the art of making that consisted of an "imitation" (mimesis) of nature. It was a making, whether in language or in physical form, that

---

4. The standard treatment of the *theologia poetica* is Charles Trinkaus, *"In Our Image and Likeness": Humanity and Divinity in Italian Humanist Thought*, 2 vols. (London: Constable, 1970).

imitated nature with pleasing rhythm and harmony.[5] The humanists, building on this, came to define "poetry" in the broad sense of "whatever was figurative in imagery, elevated in form or language, or inspired in idea."[6] To their minds, the figures that best embodied these characteristics were the classical writers and artists. The idea was not that the ancient poets were inspired by God, but that God could use their stories to illuminate the depths of life, the final meaning of which was to be truly found only in the Christian Scriptures. Charles Trinkaus succinctly describes their goal: they sought the "reconciliation of human existence as they themselves experienced it — as primarily sensuous, affective, and voluntaristic — with the two intellectual traditions... the classical and the Christian."[7] Rather than speaking of a reconciliation of these worlds, I think it better to say that Dante and his followers read these ancient stories *in the light of the Christian story;* for these writers the Christian account was the key that unlocked those classical journeys. The stories of human striving that the classical writers told were best understood in the figurative recounting of history that Christianity represents, especially in the central symbolic activities of this story. One might say that Christians today face a similar challenge: How can we learn to read the deep longings of contemporary myths, and the resulting practices, in terms of the narrative and practices of the Christian faith?

I noted that the humanist stream was influenced especially by Augustine and anticipated the views developed further by Calvin, and I need to say a word more about these connections. Its sources in Augustine lie in three closely related emphases: his inward focus, his privileging of love over knowledge, and the embodiment of these in his idea of symbolism. In many ways these Augustinian ideas formed the basis for the development of medieval culture, and they clearly influenced the humanists — as they later influenced Calvin. First, Augustine, especially in the *Confessions,* turned inward in his search for God. Throughout his turbulent youth, in what he came to see as his

---

5. Aristotle, *Poetics*, IV. Aristotle believed that the attraction of this was the enjoyment persons feel in "recognition." An imitation that is successful causes one to say, "Ah, that is he!"

6. Stanley Meltzoff, *Botticelli, Signorelli, and Savonarola* (Florence: Leo S. Olshki Editore, 1987), pp. 6-7.

7. *"In Our Image and Likeness,"* pp. 651, 652. Trinkaus emphasizes the centrality of scriptural authority for these thinkers and writers.

long journey to God, he realized that the deep longings of his soul were in fact calls from God. As he put it, "I traveled very far from you, and you did not stop me. I was tossed about, spilt, scattered, and boiled dry in my fornications. And you were silent. How slow I was to find my joy!"[8] As he sought this source of love, he looked inward at the palace of memory and passed beyond this to God. "With you as my guide I entered into my innermost citadel, and was given power to do so because you had become my helper (Ps. 29:11). I entered and with my soul's eye, such as it was, saw above that same eye of my soul the immutable light higher than my mind."[9] There, through the mediation of Christ, he found God, his source and his home: "You stir man to take pleasure in praising you, because you have made us for yourself, and our heart is restless until it rests in you."[10] This inward quest reflected Augustine's Neoplatonic heritage, in which reality was understood to be a procession of all things from the One, or God, and the return to God by way of an inward process of ascent. As Peter Brown notes, this fundamental framework was as basic to Augustine's age as evolution is to our own — it "brought pagan and Christian thinkers together in a single horizon."[11]

But it was Augustine's development of this rich interior landscape that was to prove most influential. In the worldview he inherited, the ascent of the soul from the temporal to the eternal involved detaching oneself from earthly attachments. Augustine shows the influence of this, especially in his early work, by contrasting the love we should have for God with all other kinds of enjoyment. But as his thought matured, he came to see that one's love for God should orient rather than replace other sorts of loves. A properly focused love, Augustine believed, allows one to love others in and for the sake of God. In his treatise *On Christian Teaching,* he insists that only God is to be loved for himself. As he says, "If he [man] loves himself on his own account, he does not relate himself to God, but turns to himself and not to something unchangeable . . . so a person who loves his neighbor properly should . . . aim to love God with all his heart, all his soul, and all his

---

8. Augustine, *Confessions,* trans. Henry Chadwick (Oxford: Oxford University Press, 1991), II, 2, p. 24.
9. Augustine, *Confessions,* VII, 10, p. 123.
10. Augustine, *Confessions,* I, 1, p. 3.
11. Peter Brown, *Augustine of Hippo* (Berkeley and Los Angeles: University of California, 1967), p. 98.

mind."[12] But in a significant break with his classical heritage, he asserts that the central motivating force of the process is not the intellect, but love, centered in the will and often expressed in erotic terms. As he says in the final book of the *Confessions*, "Your works praise you, so that we may love you, and *we love you, so that your works may praise you*."[13]

In his great apologetic for Christianity, *City of God*, he develops his view of history around two kinds of love: the love of self, which ends in death, and the love of God, which leads to happiness.[14] It is the latter, Augustine believed, that all seekers of wisdom implicitly long for. Love can be well or poorly directed. As he says, "The love that is bent on obtaining the object of its love is desire, while the love that possesses and enjoys its object is joy.... These emotions are bad if the love is bad, and good if it is good."[15]

So Augustine insisted that the person is defined not by what she knows or can do — practices which engender pride — but by what she loves. And this love, provided it is well-directed — that is, centered in God — fulfills all that one desires, and allows one to make something attractive of life. The educated Roman felt that the basic problem was error — that is, misconceiving one's interests — but Augustine knew from Paul that our problem is prideful self-regard, the failure to love.[16] But the *City of God* shows that this notion of love can be properly ordered and experienced only when it is placed in the larger narrative of God's transcendent purposes for creation — human loves and purposes of creation are intertwined.

Augustine's description of the Christian life that was especially influential on the medieval period is found in *On Christian Teaching*. Here Augustine develops his view of signs — what we would call sym-

---

12. Augustine, *On Christian Teaching*, trans. R. P. H. Green (Oxford: Oxford University Press, 1997), I, 22.

13. Augustine, *Confessions*, XIII, 33, p. 302, emphasis added.

14. Augustine, *City of God*, trans. Philip Levine (Cambridge: Harvard University Press/Loeb, 1966).

15. Augustine, *City of God*. This quote is from IV, 7, p. 291: "Proinde mala sunt ista si malus amor est, bona si bonus."

16. Garry Wills, *Saint Augustine* (New York: Viking, 1999), pp. 93, 94. Wills argues that the idea of the will, as we understand it, was invented by Augustine. As we saw in the first chapter, it was this biblical notion of love that allowed Augustine to break with the classical idea of the (agent-oriented) good life. See Nicholas Wolterstorff, *Justice: Rights and Wrongs* (Princeton: Princeton University Press, 2008), Chapter Eight.

bols — which became fundamental to medieval understandings of the world. In this reinterpretation of his classical background, Augustine understood the process of faith not as an ascent but as a journey. "We are on a road," Augustine wrote. "We are on a road — in spiritual, not spatial terms — and one blocked as it were by thorny hedgerows."[17] The world is full of signs, he noted, to be used as means for the soul to reach its true homeland in God, who alone is to be enjoyed for himself. As he put it, "If we wish to return to the homeland where we can be happy, we must use this world . . . to derive eternal and spiritual value from corporeal and temporal things."[18] But symbols don't function only as a means of insight; they operate in the dynamic conflict of desires in which the soul journeys to (or away from) God. These signs attract or repel.

Thus the world speaks to the one who travels toward God, but only if the journey is grounded in and driven by love that is directed to God — defined as a will that is focused on God. Augustine developed this notion of the self more fully in his treatise on the Trinity. The person, composed of memory, understanding, and will, becomes an image of the Trinitarian character of God. And Augustine believed that it is from this understanding of the person, grounded in God, that one moves to comprehend the world. This theologically grounded self came to be fundamental for the humanists, and, later, for Calvin, who in fact may be said to have re-interpreted humanism in a way that prepared for its modern development.

Historian William Bouwsma has distinguished two streams of Renaissance humanism, one influenced by the Stoics and the other by Augustine. He describes the difference incisively: "With the Stoics we must begin with the cosmos, and this in turn implies a certain view of man. But with Augustinianism we must begin with man, and from here we reach a certain view of the cosmos."[19] For the latter tradition, reason by itself cannot bring persons to their true end; grace alone can do this.

---

17. Augustine, *On Christian Teaching*, I, xvii, p. 15.
18. Augustine, *On Christian Teaching*, I, iv, p. 11.
19. William Bouwsma, "The Two Faces of Humanism: Stoicism and Augustinianism in Renaissance Thought," in *A Usable Past: Essays in European Cultural History* (Berkeley and Los Angeles: University of California Press, 1990), p. 45. The discussion in this paragraph is dependent on pp. 45-50. Bouwsma includes Calvin as an example of Augustinian humanism. He acknowledges that these streams are ideal types, but significant in their influence nevertheless.

THE METHOD OF POETIC THEOLOGY

Rather than seeing the glory of the human in their independence, Augustinians stressed the dependence of the person on God. While the Stoics denigrated the passions, and so advocated withdrawing from the world to calm the passions, Augustinians had a more positive view of the passions and thus of the body. Most important, while seeking a reconciliation of Christian and pagan traditions, Augustinians, following the Bishop of Hippo's famous treatment in the *City of God,* emphasized as well the tension between these traditions.

Against this background I want to return to the medieval development of the *theologia poetica.* We have mentioned that the tradition finds its earliest (and most original) expression in Dante's great *Divine Comedy* (1310-1320). There Dante is taken on a journey through hell and up into purgatory by the classical writer Virgil, whom he addresses in the *Inferno:* "Now go; a single will moves both of us:/you are my Guide, my governor, my master."[20] Because of that "single will," Dante believed that Virgil could be his guide. Dante also believed that whatever truth was written by Virgil came from God. But there is a further parallel that has implications for our own treatment of culture, and which will be expanded in much that follows. In the *Comedy,* Dante is taken on a journey that is a metaphor for the journey of life. For Dante, it is a journey to God and the final vision of God in heaven. In order for Dante to reach this true homeland, however, he has to journey through hell and purgatory. That is, he is made to see those whose conflicts of love and desire led them away from God; and he has to pass through his own experience of purgation to be prepared to see God.

This image of the journey toward God (or the fall away from God) embodies the basic premise of a *theologia poetica.* For Dante, there is an analogy between the figuring imagination of the ancient poet and the story of the soul's journey to God as described in the *Comedy;* the figurative logic of the one resonates with the underlying story of the other. Dante, like others in the tradition of the *theologia poetica,* had a high view of Scripture. Indeed, the *Comedy* is filled with scriptural references, which grow in number as Dante nears the vision of God at the end of the Paradiso. But if, as Dante believed, that story is rooted in the reality of God's (and our) history, then gifted people ought to be able to catch glimpses of this figuring within creation and culture. For Dante,

---

20. Dante, *The Divine Comedy,* trans. Allen Mandelbaum (New York: Knopf, 1995), II, 139-40. Subsequent citations by canticle, canto, and line will be given in the text.

only the Bible makes this clear, but the intimations of story are there for Virgil and others to "perceive" — just as the reality of God's presence was there for Gerard Manley Hopkins to capture in his poetry.

Toward the end of the Paradiso, the Apostle John asks the pilgrim Dante how it is that he came to seek this good he so earnestly pursues. "What inclined you," John asks, "to aim your bow at such a high target?" (XXVI, 25). Dante answers that "the good, once it is understood as such, enkindles love" (XXVI, 28, 29). But John presses Dante: "Tell me, too, if you feel other cords/draw you toward Him?" (XXVI, 49, 50). Dante's answer is significant. The poet decribes the range of attractions that serve as "teeth by which this love grips you" (XXVI, 51): the world's existence, his own existence, the death of Christ on the cross, and the hope of eternal life. All these, Dante says, "set me on the shore of right love" (XXVI, 55-65). When Dante has finished this confession, all heaven resounds with sweet singing: "Holy, Holy, Holy" (XXVI, 69). As Dante emphasizes in the next canto, his journey is a counter-journey to Ulysses' "mad course" (XXVII, 83). And this pilgrimage to God is, in large part, a journey through and beyond that adventure. It fulfills that quest just as it satisfies the lure which "nature or art has fashioned" (XXVII, 91). And it leads to praise.[21]

For Dante, the significance of this convergence of attractions is larger than his desire to tell a good story. The story he tells becomes an embodiment of his own praise to the God that draws him upward; his making (his poetics) ends up with aesthetic *and* liturgical import. As David Ford and Daniel Hardy argue in their excellent discussion of these things, Dante has captured the essential logic of the Christian faith: "This sees praise and adoration of God, and, in appropriate ways, of people, as the essence of every person's vocation, and constitutive of right relationships."[22] For Dante, then, the aesthetic vision leads him — and the reader — toward their proper orientation toward God. That is, it leads to truth, but one that is embodied in song and praise.

Further along in the medieval tradition of the *theologia poetica,* Francesco Petrarch argued for the importance of cultural wisdom for people of faith. When (in 1362) he heard that his friend Giovanni

---

21. For Dante, even the beauties of heaven are still somewhat shadowy. The defect, however, lies in Dante, "whose sight is not yet sublime" (XXX, 78).

22. David Ford and Daniel Hardy, *Living in Praise: Worshiping and Knowing God* (Grand Rapids: Baker Book House, 2005 [1984]), p. 64.

Boccaccio had determined to get rid of his books, having been told by a monk that, since death was near, he should give up poetry, Petrarch was alarmed and wrote to his friend: "I know of many who have attained the highest saintliness without literary culture; I don't know of any who were excluded by culture. . . . The road to virtue through ignorance is level . . . but fit for lazy souls."[23] Boccaccio heeded Petrarch's advice and later became the leading interpreter of Dante and of the *theologia poetica*. In his *Life of Dante* (1370-1375), he describes the relation between theology and poetry. Scripture teaches theology, he writes, by acts, "so that being thus taught, we may attain to that glory which he by his death and resurrection opened to us."[24] Boccaccio proceeds to give a classic expression to Dante's attitude toward ancient poetry: "In like manner do poets in their works . . . sometimes under fictions of various gods, again by the transformation of men into imaginary forms, and at times by gentle persuasion, reveal to us the cause of things, the effects of virtues and vices, what we ought to flee and what follow; in order that we may attain by virtuous action the end that they, although they did not rightly know the true God, believed to be our supreme salvation."[25] If you deny this, Boccaccio argues, how can it be that Scripture itself uses visions and fictions (parables) to describe the truth?

The writer who named the tradition more than a century later was Pico della Mirandola, the Renaissance humanist. His treatment of the role of imagination is an instructive example of the workings of this poetic vision. In his treatise *On the Imagination,* Pico seeks to discern the proper role for this important human capacity.[26] He sees the imagination as a power of the mind *(phantasia)* to receive from the senses material that the mind *(intellectum)* in turn fashions into universal principles (25, 29). The role of the imagination in this process is to animate the soul, moving it as directed by the mind — the variety of fantasy's

---

23. Boccaccio, in *The Decameron of Giovanni Boccaccio,* ed. Mark Muse and Peter E. Bondanella (New York: W. W. Norton, 1977), p. 174.

24. Boccaccio, *The Earliest Lives of Dante,* trans. James Robinson Smith, Yale Studies in English no. 10 (New York: Henry Holt, 1901), p. 51.

25. Boccaccio, *The Earliest Lives of Dante,* p. 51.

26. Giovanni Francesco Pico della Mirandola, *On the Imagination,* trans. and ed. Harry Caplan (New Haven: Yale University Press, 1930 [1500]). Subsequent pages will be cited in the text. Pico, of course, anticipates the modern preoccupation with "imagination," but note that for him it was largely a receptive faculty; for moderns it has been creative, often in an absolute sense.

movement reflecting the various human temperaments, and the "ministrations of good and bad angels" (51). Here Pico harvests much from his contemporaries' wisdom of knowing and imagining. Toward the end a problem emerges: How does one protect against false imaginings, which, Pico believes, are the cause of all our troubles? The remedies are to be found only in the Christian faith (85). We escape the darkness of the imagination by the light of Scripture, but also, Pico believed, by the lesser lights "of the learned men, and saintly, lamps which they, ever watchful and supremely zealous for the splendor of this light, formerly kindled for themselves and us" (93). As Aristotle says, we need to reject the merely bestial, and avoid the "slippery impulse of appetite" (91, 95), remembering that the phantom of the world is fleeting. Pico concludes with a Christological focus: because our powers are weak, we "implore the aid of God above. . . . His aid will always be present, if for its attainment we pour out prayers to Christ, who is God, and Mediator between men and God; who is most often present even when not invoked; who continually knocks at the door of our heart" (95). For it is through such prayer that we "foster the imagination" (95).

Interestingly, for Pico, problems arose not from the workings of the imagination — the humanists had a positive view of this faculty — but from the temptations and failings of the person. In the theological terms that Calvin would develop, problems arose from depravity and sin, which since the beginning have infected cultural forms. The solution to this, Pico believed, was not to be found in scholastic disputation, which the humanists despised, but in the devotional practices of prayer, praise, and confession. So the praise of Dante, following the practices of severe penitence, and the devotional practices of Pico suggest the way to become properly oriented along the perilous journey to God. And it is frequently — especially for our modern contemporaries, as it was for Dante — in poetic forms, what is figurative in imagery, that this way to God can be encouraged.

One can argue that much of the substance of this humanist vision, if not the emphasis on its aesthetic form, was embodied in the thinking of Calvin.[27] The great Reformer, in his *Institutes,* carried forward the

---

27. This is assumed by Bouwsma, who places Calvin along with those who constitute Augustinian humanism. Bouwsma argues elsewhere that Calvin especially followed the humanist tradition in his rhetoric to move and persuade the hearer (reader). See William Bouwsma, *John Calvin: A Sixteenth-Century Portrait* (New York: Oxford University Press, 1988), pp. 114-16.

conviction that "there is within the human mind, and indeed by natural instinct, an awareness of divinity." This awareness reflected the active presence of God: ". . . ever renewing its memory, he (sc. God) repeatedly sheds fresh drops."[28] Notice, as with Augustine, that this awareness manifests itself in an inner sense: "For each one undoubtedly feels within the heavenly grace that quickens. Indeed, if there is no need to go outside ourselves to comprehend God, what pardon will the indolence of that man deserve who is loath to descend within himself [*in se descendere*] to find God?" (1.5.3). Even atheists, Calvin observed wryly, "from time to time feel an inkling of what they desire not to believe" (1.3.2). But Calvin knew all too well that we do not follow up on these inklings; in fact — and here a suspicion of the imaginative faculty enters — we are prone to fashion images of false gods. "All," Calvin says, "degenerate from the true knowledge of him. . . . They do not . . . apprehend God as he offers himself, but imagine him as they have fashioned him in their own presumption" (1.4.1).

Calvin rejected aspects of the medieval vision, as we will note later. But there is a profound continuity between the medieval humanist vision and Calvin's theological method. This represented a continuation of the humanists' insistence that, on the one hand, God used human forms to express divine meaning, and that, on the other hand, language could be shaped so as to persuade hearers.

Consider first Calvin's adoption of the humanist sense of accommodation. The humanist tradition assumed that the world provided a lens by which God could be known, but it was a lens that was clarified only when this was read in the light of Scripture. Similarly, Calvin believed that the world and Scripture invite careful observers to see God. In the presence of these teachers, the Holy Spirit invites followers to a lifelong process of learning, a journey, if you will, to God.[29] To this end, God must accommodate himself — that is, descend into human forms — so that humans may be drawn up to heaven. Cornelis van der Kooi describes Calvin's method in this way:

---

28. *Institutes of the Christian Religion,* Library of Christian Classics, vols. 20-21, ed. John T. McNeill, trans. Ford Lewis Battles (Philadelphia: Fortress Press, 1960), 1.3.1.

29. This is the argument found in Cornelis van der Kooi, *As in a Mirror: John Calvin and Karl Barth on Knowing God: A Diptych,* trans. Donald Mader (Leiden: Brill, 2005), p. 27. Van der Kooi acknowledges that interpreting Calvin in this way departs from the idealistic perspective that has dominated Calvin studies.

The Historical Model

> Human knowledge of God exists thanks to accommodation. Accommodation describes what happens structurally in this descent. In his coming down, in all his acts and words, God accommodates himself to our human measure and human capacity for understanding.[30]

In the created order and in Scripture, God leans down to allow something of his glory to be seen.

Calvin is heir to the humanists in a second critical way. He continues their commitment to the importance of rhetoric, to the appropriate use of language to persuade the listener. Calvin enjoyed and highlighted the figures of Scripture and knew that his own language needed a deliberate and skillful adaptation to the audience through decorum. But seeing this as an expression of accommodation, Calvin knew this had a theological ground to it. As William Bouwsma says, "Rhetoric . . . had, for Calvin, some mysterious affinity with divinity. God's creation of the world was a magnificent expression of rhetoric."[31] Significantly, God seeks in the arrangement of objects and colors to draw people to himself. "According to Calvin," van der Kooi notes, "in many manners, through a colorful palette of means, God entices, draws, invites, and encourages man to acknowledge his Maker."[32]

We know that not everyone appreciated or understood Calvin's humanist method because of the defense of this method by Philip Sidney a generation later. During that century, an emphasis on literal truth led to a suspicion of poetry as somehow devious — a suspicion that Calvin certainly would not have shared. Led by Peter Ramus, a kind of logic developed that sought to order all of knowledge into a plain and simple structure. To those following Ramus, poetry seemed to be a kind of sleight of hand that befuddled the clarity represented by this logic. Ramus, writing in 1569, had this to say about the work of poets:

> This is what the poet does as a major part of his tactics, when he sets out to sway the people, the many-headed monster. He deceives in all sorts of ways. He starts at the middle, often proceeding thence to the

---

30. Van der Kooi, *As in a Mirror*, p. 42.
31. Bouwsma, *John Calvin*, p. 117.
32. Van der Kooi, *As in a Mirror*, p. 26.

beginning, and getting on to the end by some equivocal and unexpected dodge.³³

Writing later in the century, Philip Sidney, speaking from the perspective of the humanist movement, mounted an impressive defense of the poetic imagination that is still worth reading.³⁴ Sidney believed that poetry, far from promoting confusion, is in fact the first light-giver to ignorance, after which one can feed on tougher knowledge (74). Poetry does not deflect understanding so much as nurture it. How else could we "see" the divine majesty if we did not have it pictured for us in David's poetry? (76). Thus, poetry does not simply instruct; it moves the soul toward what it shows. Sidney contrasts this poetic work with the "sullen gravity" of the moral philosopher who teaches by precept, and with the historian who teaches by examples — which are, Sidney noted, mostly bad examples (83). By giving the mind "an image," poetry carries more weight in instruction than either precept or example, which is why, Sidney says, Aristotle places poetry over history (88). Because poetry moves the reader, it is of a "higher degree than teaching" (91), for, after all, one must desire to learn. Poetry, whether in the form of comedy or tragedy, "entices" one to virtue and so is "the most excellent workman" (94).

A Culture of Desire and a Contemporary *Theologia Poetica*

Much separates our modern world from the world in which this *theologia poetica* developed, so we must be careful not to claim that anything like this is possible for us. We have a very different picture of imagination and the cosmos than did Pico or Dante; our scientific understanding of cultures adds dimensions that were not understood then. In the first chapter we considered and rejected the suggestion of

---

33. Ramus, quoted in Walter J. Ong, *Ramus, Method, and the Decay of Dialogue: From the Art of Discourse to the Art of Reason* (Cambridge: Harvard University Press, 1958), p. 253. I discuss the development of this logic and its impact on the Protestant imagination in *Reformed Theology and Visual Culture* (Cambridge: Cambridge University Press, 2004), Chapter Four.

34. Philip Sidney, "A Defense of Poetry," in *Miscellaneous Prose of Philip Sidney*, ed. K. Duncan-Jones and Jan van Dorsten (Oxford: Clarendon, 1973). Subsequent pages will be cited in the text. See page 63 for the influence of continental humanism on Sidney.

The Historical Model

Radical Orthodoxy that we need to recover the notion of "participation" found in patristic and medieval sources. Perhaps the most important difference lies in the resolutely immanent frame in which modern people face the world: How do openings to a world beyond, to engagement with God, take place in such a world? Here is a challenge that medieval Christians knew nothing about.

Still, they suggest that in the conversation between the Christian tradition and what we might call, following the biblical precedent, cultural wisdom, a contemporary *theologia poetica* might be possible. (Interestingly, the humanists received their share of criticism from their contemporaries, which recalls the cultural despisers today, as Sidney's defense indicates. Throughout the early Renaissance, critics of Augustinian humanism worried about its openness to classical culture — in the century after Dante, many monasteries forbade their novices to read the *Comedy*.) But their openness to a vital conversation between classical and Christian culture, continuing a wisdom tradition that is rooted in Scripture, provides an important lesson for Christianity's struggle with modern culture.

Daniel Hardy and David Ford, in their discussion of the Greco-Roman background to the early and medieval church, suggest what this lesson might be. The two main cosmologies struggling for mastery, they note, were the Stoic focus on the immanence of the divine, and the Platonic stress on God's transcendence. They explain why both were deficient: "The notion of God's action could not appear in either, and neither could radical newness."[35] Yet *both* were pressed into service when they were put into conversation with the biblical understanding of God's creation in time and the continuing action of God in Christ and the work of the Holy Spirit. In a sense, Paul confronted both views on Mars Hill (Acts 17), and transformed both by preaching the resurrection of Christ — which, despite their culture's supposed openness to transcendence, the people pointedly did not want to hear about. Our challenge today may be put in similar terms: How do we confront the autonomous search for human flourishing by the account of God's raising Jesus by the power of the Spirit?

What is the lesson we learn? It was only against the backdrop of one or another of these worldviews that the genuinely new element in the Christian faith could appear. While it is wrong to see any period of his-

---

35. Ford and Hardy, *Living in Praise*, p. 77.

tory as more open to receiving God's intervention than any other,[36] the *newness of the Gospel can be made to appear only against the backdrop of the cultural wisdom of one's day.* As in the parable of the sower, the good news grows up out of that wisdom, which it challenges, confirms, and corrects. Dante had to show Virgil's wisdom, so that the readers of his day could properly grasp the splendor that Dante saw in Paradise.

A Contemporary Theology of Symbolism

But how does this happen today? It is clear that contemporary artists, unlike medieval writers, no longer work from any shared vision of God or God's future, but they do continue to shape objects of desire and of hope. They still gesture toward something beyond the ordinary. Artists of all kinds still seek to present the unpresentable — to make visible a possible world. As Philip Sidney put it, some people do things with nature; the poet "doth grow in effect another nature." He makes things better or new, "freely ranging within the Zodiac of his own wit."[37] That is, the poet's work will put forward via its own formal qualities a possible world, and invite perception and move the emotions.

So here is the challenge for a contemporary poetic theology: In a world that has given up any shared faith in God (or gods), how can our projects provide any echo of a Presence beyond what we see? What would a poetic theology look like today? I will seek to address this on two levels, first by recalling the common human hunger for a human flourishing that moves beyond the ordinary world, and developing a theory of symbolism that accounts for this impulse; and second, by remembering that God has not left us alone but continues to use such impulses to move people toward the light.

First, recall my argument of the first chapter: that desire, in part, is the impulse to reach out beyond oneself, form relationships, make

---

36. This is where we parted company in the first chapter with Tracey Rowland, *Culture and the Thomist Tradition: After Vatican II*, pp. 46, 47. She argues for a special role for Latin in preserving mystery (see pp. 48, 49). See also Hans Boersma's discussion of the dichotomy between the culture of the New Testament period, which is open to transcendence, and our own modern culture, which is closed to it. "Accommodation to What? Univocity of Being, Pure Nature, and the Anthropology of St. Irenaeus," *International Journal of Systematic Theology* 8, no. 3 (July 2006).

37. Sidney, "A Defense of Poetry," p. 78.

promises, and even praise what is good and beautiful. And, motivated by this desire, people struggle to make something of their lives — what I will later describe as seeking to build a beautiful life — for themselves and their families. But nothing like this would be possible by simply pursuing self-interest, or even reproducing culturally defined repertoires. People want to make something *new* of their lives, and this means that they are capable of making moral commitments and shaping practices which represent these commitments. In the first chapter I argued that this is because of the human connection with each other, with the stability and goodness (and excess) of the created order, and ultimately with God. Not only are people capable of making moral promises; they are capable of being loved and respected for who they are, as ends and not merely as means. All of this reflects a theological situation that people can ignore but cannot escape, because it reflects the way God has put the world together.

As a result of this theological situation, people are not satisfied with a life that just works well — with simply doing things, as we put it earlier; they want to *make* things that speak of who they are and what they find worth celebrating. This means that they are interested in the look and feel of their lives and projects. Sociologist Margaret Archer expresses it this way: "When we seek to be loved, regarded, and respected, not only are these things not for sale, but also they are something like a terminus in that they do not lead on to further ends which could be achieved by ... instrumental rationality."[38] The practices that embody this "terminus" — work, family, community — are constituents of human flourishing; they are ends, not means. Further, as Archer goes on to say, it is the feel of their work that moves people to "devote" themselves to their concerns, to give "devotion" to them. Whatever their specific religious views or lack of them, people invest themselves in rituals of dedication.

Recall Adam and his football games, Lisa and her skiing, Brad and his fishing, and Sophia and her artistic activities. For these people, these activities have become more than simple diversions. They have become what they "live for"; the practices have become what I will call symbolic — that is, they are invested with personal and emotional con-

---

38. Margaret Archer, *Being Human: The Problem of Agency* (Cambridge: Cambridge University Press, 2000), p. 79. Archer echoes Antonio Damasio (*The Feeling of What Happens* [New York: Harcourt Brace, 1999] when she says, "Our emotions are essential adjuncts to the pursuit of the morally good life, not in terms of emotivism but by way of vision and commitment."

tent. These things, insofar as they are pursued in terms of intrinsic ends, reflect the basic human impulse toward making symbols of what is finally meaningful for us. Symbolism, in the sense I am using it, involves *discovering* meaning in what is given in creation, which is the theological condition for this process, *ascribing* significance to objects and actions, and being moved to *pursue* these as ends in themselves. And it is the motivation to pursue — the affective attraction — that constitutes the aesthetic element.

Since this understanding of symbolism is central to the argument of this book, let me develop the notion in more detail. While much literature on symbolism focuses on objects and images, I have come to believe that symbolic practices — involving both objects and ritual practices — are more often the central motivating factor for people.[39] These practices provide structure and meaning for people; they are instruments of orientation. In the terms we are using, they are the way we "make something" of our lives. And they do this by capturing the vitality of our connections to the earth and other people (and potentially with God). As W. J. T. Mitchell says in his study of visual culture and images, these constellations should be seen as "'go-betweens' in social transactions, as a repertoire of screen images or templates that structure our encounters with other human beings."[40] My point is that they not only reference these relations but also give them life, and they vivify them in such a way that people are moved by them. I could go on to distinguish various kinds of aesthetic projects from constructed objects, and the symbolism appropriate to each, perhaps distinguishing an intransitive symbolism from a transitive symbolism. But this is not necessary for my purposes here — it is work for another time.

My claim is that in symbolic practices, we have an everyday aesthetic of attraction at work. I have been helped by Roberto Goizueta's

---

39. I believe this is because much of the discussion of symbolism is overly allied with semiotics. In my research I found that, in the experience of worship, people often were not able to isolate particular objects or images as sources of meaning, but more often found meaning in more holistic experiences that I am calling symbolic practices. See *Senses of the Soul: Art and the Visual in Christian Worship* (Eugene, Ore.: Cascade Books, 2008), esp. Chapter 7.

40. W. J. T. Mitchell, *What Do Pictures Want?* (Chicago: University of Chicago Press, 2005), p. 351. Interestingly, Mitchell goes on to say that visual culture finds its "primal scene" in what Emmanuel Levinas calls the face of the other. He thinks the slogan for our time is not "things fall apart" but "things come alive" (p. 172).

The Historical Model

discussion of aesthetics in relation to justice. Influenced by the Mexican philosopher José Vasconcelos, Goizueta sees the central core moment of aesthetics as an "empathic fusion." Aesthetics draws us into relationships that are affective, which means that this movement is allied with love. Goizueta elaborates this point:

> Play, recreation, and celebration are the most authentic forms of life precisely because, when we are playing, recreating, or celebrating, we are immersed in, or "fused," with the action itself, and those other persons with whom we are participating. Thus, we are involved in and enjoying the living itself.[41]

These central symbolic activities have a certain precedence, we are claiming, even with respect to issues of truth and morality. They are our way of gaining access to what the world is about.[42] While the symbol has to have some cognitive purchase to be effective, it is not centrally a way of knowing. A symbol better represents what we might call understanding rather than knowledge — reflecting a kind of wisdom about life and the world. Moreover, while there are moral dimensions to these activities, they are not primarily about goodness. But to say this does not diminish the importance of truth or goodness; rather, giving priority to aesthetics of this sort increases their influence — it ramps up the energy of these values in our lives. As Goizueta argues, the fundamental problem with liberation theology (and, I would add, with much discourse on social justice) is that it is overly functional, that it has lost touch with basic human values, which Goizueta sees as fundamentally aesthetic. He argues, "The aesthetic dimension of human action is *mediated* by the ethical-political; it is encountered and lived out *within* ethical-political action, as the deepest meaning and significance of the ethical-political. The aesthetic is not a final stage beyond the ethical but the fullest sense *of* the ethical."[43] This way of thinking implies a dy-

---

41. Roberto Goizueta, *Caminemos con Jesus: Toward a Hispanic/Latino Theology of Accompaniment* (Maryknoll, N.Y.: Orbis Books, 1995), p. 94.

42. Cf. Mitchell, *What Do Pictures Want?:* "There is no getting beyond pictures . . . to a more authentic relationship with Being. . . . Pictures are our way of gaining access to whatever these things are" (p. xiv).

43. Goizueta, *Caminemos con Jesus*, p. 128, emphasis his. However, this way of putting these mediated relationships suggests to me that "fusion" may not be the best word to describe the aesthetic experience.

namic and holistic understanding of the relationships among these values, which, I would argue, is best understood in terms of the meaning of God's good creation and God's Trinitarian presence there.

The fact is that humans cannot live without symbolism. While one often hears that people are more scientifically oriented today and, as a result, less likely to have deep relationships with objects and images, I do not believe this is so. W. J. T. Mitchell and David Freedberg have both argued compellingly that images still have the power to move people. Mitchell says, "New media have made communication seem more transparent, immediate, and rational than ever before, at the same time that they have enmeshed us in labyrinths of new images, objects, tribal identities, and ritual practices."[44] I believe that humans inevitably shape symbols of their environment by a particular extension of their calling, as God's image, to name creation. They bring flowers and candles to mark a spot where someone has died; they put out yellow ribbons to remember someone who is kidnapped. In a sense, when Adam was asked to name creation, it was not only a matter of ordering and arranging it, but also of investing it with significance — without names, people and things cannot have any real consequence. Humans not only use creation in doing things; they separate out parts of it, reshape them, and ascribe special meaning to them. Built into the human character is the impulse to move beyond praxis to poesis — that is, they invariably make symbols.[45] And it is in naming things and shaping them so they come alive that humans construct and find their identity. These "symbolic" creations then become benchmarks, pointers of something beyond the merely natural.

Now the problem that John Calvin saw all too clearly is that we are also rebels against God and the order God has given to creation, so we invariably use this naming capacity to shape idols. Sooner or later, we give more attention to the work of our hands than we give to God and the works of God. But this familiar tendency does not necessarily make

---

44. Mitchell, *What Do Pictures Want?* p. 26. And see David Freedberg, *The Power of Images: Studies in the History and Theory of Response* (Chicago: University of Chicago Press, 1989). Freedberg notes that the whole idea of aniconism is impossible and, in fact, that our inclination to adornment of images and practices increases their efficacy (pp. 54, 135).

45. I will argue later that the Protestant tradition has had difficulty understanding this impulse, perhaps seeing God in creation, but unable to contemplate meaning in aesthetic objects more generally — often, not even in the sacraments.

our symbolic proclivity evil or irredeemable. After all, languages of any kind can be used either to praise or to blaspheme. We inevitably shape objects of our world symbolically because we cannot live with a purely instrumentalist view of objects in the world — this is part of being created in God's image.

Biblical Reflections on Desire

At this point I want to pick up the theme of creation that I introduced in the first chapter. This is important, because the view of symbolism that I am developing is a unique expression of the human capacities within the morally and spiritually charged created order. Central to the Genesis account of creation and human disobedience are the notions of attraction and affection, of expulsion and withdrawal — that is, of eros and agape. Preachers often appeal to the third chapter — where the tempter persuades the woman to look again at the forbidden fruit — to warn about the dangers of seduction (and of the visual in general). The writer of Genesis says, "So when the woman saw that the tree was good for food, and that it was a delight to the eyes, and that the tree was to be desired [Heb., *chamad*] to make one wise, she took of its fruit and ate" (Gen. 3:6). Similarly, the last commandment in Exodus 20:17 uses the same word in warning: "You shall not covet [Heb., *chamad*] your neighbor's house, you shall not covet your neighbor's wife, . . . or anything that belongs to your neighbor."

So the connection is often made between seeing and desiring, and things that are forbidden. In the Christian tradition this connection has become the starting point for a negative theology of desire. The eye especially is not to be trusted. But, taken in their larger context, the Genesis narrative and the Exodus account clearly do not want us to draw that conclusion. We note that in the second chapter of Genesis the very same combination of words is used for *all* the trees of the garden: "Out of the ground the LORD God made to grow every tree that is pleasant to the sight and good for food, the tree of life also in the midst of the garden" (2:9). *All* the trees are made to delight the eye and spark desire. It was the tempter's strategy to ignore this general designation and focus perversely on the tree that was forbidden. In a sense this strategy involved ignoring the breadth of God's gifts and grace — the excess of creation — and narrowing the focus precisely to impugn God's goodness.

The desire which may properly be fixed on all the trees and, presumably, on all that is one's own household is not wrong, but it may be misplaced when it is directed at that which is forbidden.

Indeed, the proper value of desire is recognizing the goodness that God has placed all around, as Paul tells Timothy: "For everything created by God is good, and nothing is to be rejected, provided it is received with thanksgiving; for it is sanctified by God's word and by prayer" (1 Tim. 4:4-5). Here desire for the goods of creation leads to specific acts of worship — thanksgiving and prayer. This theological movement is consistent with the notion of symbolism I am developing. The order of creation is made in such a way that humans experience it as a field of moral forces — they are placed in creation not just to keep it but also to enjoy (or sometimes resist) its attraction. It is created to spark affection and response — the moral and the aesthetic are bound up together. The Apostle John makes this fundamental law of the affections clear when he says that we love because we are loved: "In this is love, not that we loved God but that he loved us and sent his Son to be the atoning sacrifice for our sins. Beloved, since God loved us so much, we also ought to love one another" (1 John 4:10-11).

Especially striking in these accounts is the way that images — what is seen and what delights the eye — function within this morally charged framework. As Augustine wrote in *On Christian Teaching,* they become "signs" along our spiritual journey. Biblical notions of the symbolic must be understood in this larger context. This is especially clear in the Song of Solomon, the part of the wisdom literature of the Hebrew Scripture that makes generous use of erotic imagery. There we find a clear connection of erotic desires with "what is good and generous," even, the church teaches, with our love for God. Robert O'Connell discusses this in connection with Augustine's view of cupidity (desire). He notes, "What draws us upward and away from bodily sex is this spiritual 'appetite' for 'beatitude,' beatitude which is only the more attractive for embodying, on a higher level, all the allure of sexual union."[46] Cupidity, in other words, must be transformed, not removed.

In the New Testament, James, a leader of the Jerusalem church, understood the importance of human desires. He claimed that all our disputes and conflicts come from the cravings that are at war within us. He

---

46. Robert O'Connell, "Augustine and Sexuality," in *Augustine Today,* ed. Richard John Neuhaus (Grand Rapids: Wm. B. Eerdmans, 1993), p. 76.

writes, "You want something and do not have it; so you commit murder. And you covet something and cannot obtain it; so you engage in disputes and conflicts.... You ask and do not receive, because you ask wrongly, in order to spend what you get on your pleasures" (James 4:2-4). Though James is working with a somewhat different notion of desire, his focus on the human craving for what one does not have strikes a very contemporary note.

In the Epistles of John, the author adds a further theological dimension that is important to any Christian symbolism. John connects the life we long for with what can be touched and seen, particularly with the coming of Christ in physical form. John opens his letter this way: "We declare to you what was from the beginning, what we have heard, what we have seen with our eyes, what we have looked at and touched with our hands, concerning the word of life" (1 John 1:1). His love for Christ, grounded in what can be touched, seen, and heard, produces in the believer a longing that will one day be fulfilled in a final visual experience — what the medieval Christians called the beatific vision. As he writes in the third chapter, "Beloved, we are God's children now; what we will be has not yet been revealed. What we do know is this: when he is revealed, we will be like him, for we will see him as he is" (1 John 3:2). Augustine believed that this verse pointedly *endorses* our desires, as he makes clear in his commentary: "Because you cannot at present see, let your duty be in desire. The whole life of a good Christian is a holy desire.... God by deferring our hope stretches our desire; by the desiring stretches the mind; by stretching making more capacious."[47] So unacted desires, far from being the ugly thing that William Blake suggests, may be part of a fundamental human process of spiritual growth. In any case, they cannot be ignored.

The shape of this life resonates in important ways with Plato, who sought — indeed, longed for — a kind of justice that lay at the core of all life and thought. But what he was seeking, the Christian believes, is best represented not as a timeless form but as a "logos" that animates and lightens the world — not an object to be known, but a person to be loved. This mediator and sustainer of creation is the eternally begotten and beloved Son of God, who for us and for our salvation became human. This

---

47. Augustine, *Ten Homilies on the First Epistle of John*, in vol. 7 of *The Nicene and Post-Nicene Fathers*, Series I, ed. Philip Schaff, 14 vols. (reprint: Peabody, Mass.: Hendrickson, 1994), IV, 6.

enfleshment of Deity has critical aesthetic implications. Because of the divine invasion of creation, the Christian sees the world not as illusion, as Plato did, but as figure — the visible and concrete shape of actuality. Moreover, since creation is both disordered by human disobedience and rebellion and restored by the life and work of Christ, it too is subject to longing. As Paul says, "The whole creation has been groaning in labor pains until now; and not only the creation, but we ourselves, who have the first fruits of the Spirit, groan inwardly while we wait for . . . the redemption of our bodies" (Rom. 8:22-23). So desire, both of the creature and of the person, is intrinsic to the present shape of creation. These together long for a future of fulfillment and sight — "now we see in a mirror, dimly, but then we will see face to face" (1 Cor. 13:12). This longing and this hope constitute, centrally, the figure (or shape) of the present. For many of our contemporaries, desire provides a potential opening for the Spirit of God, because desire directs us beyond ourselves; it seeks connection with other people and with the goodness of the world. And finally it reflects, so the Bible claims, something of God's own yearning for us. As James says when he answers the questions we quoted above: Don't you know that God desires you? "God yearns jealously for the spirit that he has made to dwell in us" (James 4:5).

Human desire, then, is responsive to the created order, but beyond this it is responsive to a personal ground of that order. As I argued in the first chapter, the creation order is held and brought to life by the Trinitarian presence of God. Later, in the chapter on the aesthetics of church, I am going to argue that the theological practices of worship are key to understanding (and fully enjoying) the symbolic practices that enrich human life. But here I want to claim that the theological grounds of creation and Trinity provide the content of all meaningful symbolism. As Jesus tells Satan, we do not live by bread alone, but by that which grounds all symbolic activity — namely, every word that proceeds from the mouth of God (Matt. 4:4). To elaborate this injunction from the beginning of his ministry, Jesus, on his last night, took this bread and gave it a new name — "This is my body." Here is Jesus the incarnate God, as the new Adam, demonstrating this special symbol-making calling, drawing a connection between his continuing presence with the believers and the materiality of creation in the form of bread. This bread now becomes a living connection between the believer and Christ — "This you will do in remembrance of me," Christ says. To underline the new meaning of this bread as constructing a concrete connection with the end of time, Paul adds, "As often as you eat this bread . . . you proclaim the Lord's death until he comes" (1 Cor. 11:26). In a world where we struggle not to "lose touch" with one another, Christ has given us this image of himself to hold on to, and by which we orient ourselves, which theologically and strategically is the center of our understanding of symbolism.

Contemporary Aesthetics and God

But how can we apply these reflections, now, to the contemporary world of art and aesthetics, where theological or religious references are mostly missing?[48] I think that Jacques Maritain, who understood the modern aesthetic situation better than any other theologian, can help us make a connection between the theological claims we just advanced and the contemporary aesthetic situation. Although it is the case that the experience of God is a supernatural event, he believed that there are experiences in the natural world which resonate with that event. He described two such experiences, what he called two different ways of knowing. The first are moral judgments. Moral judgments, he says, are common to people everywhere. Such judgments and the virtues they represent are one of the ways people come to orient themselves in the world. But, Maritain argues, their significance transcends this world. These judgments, he thinks, "create a certain affinity in the soul with the spiritual order."[49] The second way of knowledge is found in activities of artists and poets. As I will argue below, artists work to create spaces for contemplation. Maritain thinks that the activity of contemplation, turning toward an object in love and appreciation, is a "distant image of mystical contemplation" (281). Echoing Philip Sidney, Maritain believes that if anyone enters a "conspiracy," even unconsciously, with God, it is the poet rather than the philosopher. The poet's art is the "grandchild of God" (in Dante's phrase). This is because the artist's "proper task" is

---

48. See James Elkins, *On the Strange Place of Religion in Contemporary Art* (New York: Routledge, 2004).

49. Jacques Maritain, *Distinguish to Unite; or, The Degrees of Knowledge*, trans. G. B. Phalen (New York: Charles Scribner, 1959), p. 280. Subsequent pages will be cited in the text. We will explore Maritain's notion of "connaturality" in more detail in Chapter Five below.

to create an object that brings joy to the spirit in which the brilliance of form shines through. He perceives in things and brings forth a sign, weak though it may be, of the spirituality within them; he is connaturalized, not with God himself, but with the mystery that is scattered in things and which has come down from God, the invisible powers at play within the universe. (282)

Maritain believes that in the creative process, the artist's spirit joins the natural elements (a process he calls "connaturality") to create something new, and thus participates in God's creative work. He acknowledges that art gives only a "savor" of these powers, that our hunger for these is satisfied only by the God who is the creator. Still, he believes that "in this fallen and redeemed world wherein grace presses in on every side, human life tends toward the Christian life, since every man belongs by right to Christ, the head of the human race" (259).

Maritain's reference to Christ, human and divine, is significant. In an earlier work he had given the outline of an argument wherein Christ is understood as the key to a theological interpretation of art history. In *Creative Intuition in Art and Poetry,* comprised of lectures given at the National Gallery in Washington, D.C., he argued that Western art cannot be understood apart from Christ. In the patristic period, ideas of creativity rested on the understanding of the human self, grasped as object, "in the sacred examplar of Christ's divine self" as this was defined at Chalcedon. This prepared for the development of the fully human self, which appeared in the medieval period (especially, he thinks, in the work of Giotto). Finally, in the modern period we have sought to explore the self as subject "in the creative subjectivity of man himself, man the artist or the poet."[50] Again, the secret to understanding this aright, Maritain argues, is Christ present as Spirit. Although Maritain does not explicitly say this, he implies that just as Christ was the means by which the Western tradition understood what it means to be human, so Christ is also the way in which, in our era, our post-Romantic subjectivity can be properly assessed.

As far as I can tell, Maritain nowhere developed these suggestions

---

50. Jacques Maritain, *Creative Intuition in Art and Poetry* (Cleveland and New York: Meridian Books, 1954), p. 20. And John Zizioulas makes a similar argument in *Being as Communion: Studies in Personhood and the Church* (Crestwood, N.Y.: St. Vladimir's Seminary Press, 1985), wherein the notion of the human self in the West cannot be understood apart from patristic theology.

further, but they provide pointers that ought to be followed up.⁵¹ Maritain is unique, not only in recognizing the fundamental shift represented by modern art (which we explored in the first chapter), but also in seeking to understand it theologically. We will return to this discussion below, but here it is enough to recognize what Maritain assumes: In the modern period, the human self is not an object to be depicted but the *mode* by which the artist performs his work. By making something into which the heart can pass, as Maritain puts it, the artist is instigating a movement of the affections, which resembles the movement in the direction of love — of compassion and embrace — that we described in the first chapter. Human making resembles this — perhaps for the Christian, it calls for it — but it is not necessarily the same movement.

The Artistic Calling: Making Symbols

How then do we understand poetics in this era of subjectivity? We noted earlier that the Romantic poets' rediscovery of the symbol has been important in the development of modern aesthetics. Of course, the Romantics did not invent the notion; in fact, one could argue that their musings were influenced by previous (medieval) understandings that derive, I would argue, from Augustine. In Christian tradition, symbolic times and places mapped out human life and the world in figures and patterns. The highest human goods, love, and God have always been referenced indirectly by symbols (or, as they are called in the church, sacraments). As we saw in the first chapter, this notion of symbolism was significantly advanced during the Romantic period. As Charles Taylor notes, in the nineteenth century it was believed that "Through language in its constitutive use (let's call it poetry), we open up contact with something higher or deeper (be it God or the depths of human nature, desire, the Will to Power, or whatever) through language."⁵² Or, we might add, through paint, figured shape, or dance we can open up contact with something deeper. What is significant is the way, in that century, cultural artifacts could become "signs" that

---

51. I have tried to do this in "Subjectivity and Modern Art: Theological Reflections on Jacques Maritatin and Charles Taylor," in "Arte, Fede, Suggettivita," ed. Stefanie Knauss (Bologne: Centro per le Science Religiose, forthcoming).

52. Charles Taylor, *A Secular Age* (Cambridge: Belknap/Harvard University Press, 2007), p. 758.

moved people to develop a particular sensibility. Scholars of culture have noted, for example, the role of the mass-produced novel in the development of this inner sensibility. Gordon Lynch points out the significance of the novel during this period, "which was not only used as a tool for the cultivation of deep emotional and aesthetic experiences but also whose pages themselves often contained celebrations of such sensibility."[53]

Similarly, in our time the symbolic spaces created by and for our communities reflect the unspoken and sometimes unspeakable longings that lie hidden there. They can also uncover the structure of people's lives. The dilemma of contemporary aesthetics is that, while it frequently ignores or denies this deeper reality, some artists want to hold on to the reality of symbolic depth, or, at the very least, the role of the aesthetic encounter in human flourishing. Art cannot do without the surplus of meaning, what we are calling the symbolic. And though artists like J. M. Coetzee are hesitant to recognize this, they invariably load their most important work with a moral charge. Artists need their work to either attract or repel. My argument is that this need reflects the fact that the moral and aesthetic meanings are built into the created order — they call out. Our relations to each other, to the creation, and ultimately to God are not inert or passive; they are always characterized by charged distance and difference. And, as Graham Ward has pointed out, distance and difference are always relational, and always mediated through actions which alter them. This is seen most clearly, he thinks, in our sexuality, in which responsive bodies interact such that relationships with other people invariably have an erotic component. He says, "Difference, to the extent that it treats the bodies of other responsive beings, is always erotic and therefore sexually charged to a greater or a lesser degree."[54] As Augustine argued, everything created has the capacity to become a sign for the affections. Even if they have lost sight of the transcendent ground of their work, artists understand this intuitively. Their goal is to create objects, or environments, that move viewers — they want to make their work into signs that are emotionally charged. In order to lay hold on our imaginations, whether corporately

---

53. Gordon Lynch, "Film and the Subjective Turn," in *Reframing Theology and Film*, ed. R. K. Johnston (Grand Rapids: Baker Book House, 2007), p. 116. Lynch cites in particular the work of John Mullan.

54. Ward, "Divinity and Sexual Difference," in his *Christ and Culture*, p. 153.

The Historical Model

or individually, the hoping and the longing that keeps a person going must take some symbolic shape. It must be made into a practice or an object that is figurative and resonant.

The modern aesthetic question, says Thierry de Duve, is not "What is beautiful?" but "What is said to be art (and literature)?"[55] Jean-François Lyotard, who quotes Thierry's insight, goes on to argue that art is central today precisely because it does not follow the rules — indeed, in its radical figuring of reality, it *produces* the rules. But artists cannot escape the wish to have their work matter, to seek in it some kind of transformation — even if this is in a religionless way. As Thierry says elsewhere,

> The best modern art has endeavored to redefine essentially *religious* terms of humanism on a *belief-less* way. In 1913, when Malevich painted his *Black Squares on a White Ground* ... who could then have understood that he was inoculating the tradition of the Russian icon with a vaccine capable of preserving its human meaning, for a period which faith in God could no longer keep alive?[56]

The turn to the subject has at times meant a turn away from the object, as we noted earlier. Yet even in that refusal, there can be a revelation of the human situation. This is true in two ways: both for art's sense of (and rebellion against) human limits and death, and for its longing to transcend this and find some place of meaning beyond the ordinary. The first may be illustrated by Matthew Barney (b. 1967), and the second by Mark Rothko (1903-1970). Barney, a contemporary New York artist, has been called a one-man Baroque revival, and has captured something of the contemporary sensitivities in his images and videos. His figures are parodies of the human pursuit of desire, beautiful bodies distorted or distended — he exhibits what one writer calls "the emptiness inside of excess."[57] The ever-present "beautiful women" of contemporary advertising are subverted by Barney, who as artist simultaneously gives and takes away these objects of desire. Un-

---

55. Thierry de Duve, quoted by J. F. Lyotard in *The Postmodern Condition: A Report on Knowledge*, trans. G. Bennington and B. Massumi (Minneapolis: University of Minnesota, 1979), p. 75.
56. Thierry de Duve, *Look: One Hundred Years of Contemporary Art*, trans. Simon Pleasance and Fronza Woods (Brussels: Ludion, 2000), p. 14.
57. Anonymous article on Eyestorm.com/Barney. Accessed 7/14/04.

like Coetzee, who seems to show the endless pursuit of desire actually stumbling across something "good and generous," Barney argues that these discoveries cancel each other out. In *Drawing Restraint 7* (1993), Barney shows two satyrs (images of lust) wrestling, uncontrollable desire against desire, where no one is a hero and everything is a vehicle of driving and uncontrollable forces.[58]

Barney's images become powerful symbols of the endless — and apparently fruitless — search for new experiences of "fulfillment." Along the way, their form presents a further reason why symbolism is critical for the human imagination. Symbols that are effective, that "work," possess a beauty, or at least an allure, that attracts — or sometimes repels — us. They literally *move us* to change things — symbols propel, impel, or bring us up short. Barney's formal violence repels *and* attracts the viewer at the same time. These images demonstrate the role that symbols play in setting up the moral field in which human actors live. Symbols like Barney's may awaken the awareness of the restrictions of human desire, their ability to promise more than they deliver. But Christians believe that symbols play a constructive role as well. Can they not spark deep longings which remind them of — even attract them toward — the future glory that is to be revealed in Christ? In any case, symbols always reflect the ambiguity of the human situation: they can be images of hope, but they can also be powerful images of human rebellion and unfulfilled longings.

An example of the more positive role is to be seen in the work of Mark Rothko, a major twentieth-century abstract expressionist. Rothko's best-known work consists of large monochromatic images that refuse simple analysis. In 1971, fourteen of his works were installed in an octagonal chapel in Houston that was originally designed as a Catholic ecumenical chapel but became a multi-religious space. Upon entering the quiet space, one is immediately surrounded by these deep black-purple images. As one spends time in the space, the tactile surface of the paintings seems to deepen, inviting one to enter the space that Rothko creates, to complete the work. And as one looks, the works gradually educe an emotional sense of presence. And this reflects the artist's intent. In an important article, Rothko describes the history of art in terms of the struggle between appearance and the tac-

---

58. See "Matthew Barney and Beyond." Supervert/com/essays/art/Barney.html. Accessed 7/14/04.

Matthew Barney, *Drawing Restraint 7*, 1993.
Courtesy of the Gladstone Gallery, New York.

tile.[59] Rothko's choice of the tactile and the sensual, he believes, allows plasticity its greatest freedom, and its most expansive symbolic potential. "Plasticity," he says, "is the quality of the presentation of movement in a painting" (55). People today lament the loss of "myth," which Rothko notes is a sense of unity, or of an integrating narrative (37, 104). Modern art carried this lack of unity to its logical conclusion in Dada, which displayed not only a philosophical but also a "plastic" skepticism (60). But isn't it possible, Rothko wonders, to appreciate modern developments for what they affirm rather than what they deny? Rothko believes that at its best, perhaps modern art "is not a wanton act of destruction, but part of a process for the evolving of more comprehensive synthesis" (61). In this synthesis the tactile presence of the work embodies its own meaning; it is, in Charles Taylor's term, "semanticized." When it is successful, the plastic media and the message fuse: the plasticity *is* the message, and all the factors produce delight or emotional exultation — which, Rothko believes, is the response to beauty (63, 77).

The relevant question is this: How does Rothko's work continue to exercise such emotional power over viewers? In a very different context,

---

59. Mark Rothko, *The Artist's Reality*, ed. Christopher Rothko (New Haven: Yale University Press, 2004), p. 49. Subsequent pages will be cited in the text.

Mark Rothko, the Rothko Chapel — a sacred space open to all, dedicated to art, spirituality, and human rights — in Houston, Texas; dedicated in 1971.
Source: Art Resource/NY.

Sarah Coakley has argued that the allure of gender liberation "has fascinated the late twentieth century mind, [offering] the prospect of an escape from stereotype, the hope of an elusive personal transformation beyond normal human expectations and restrictions."[60] But, she asks, to what eschatological end are these expectations raised? A similar question arises in the analysis of Rothko's work. It invariably raises the possibility of an experience of flourishing beyond normal human limitations — but to what eschatological end?

Here Rothko cannot be of help, for the experience with his work, like the experience with much contemporary art, is inherently unstable, even volatile. It suggests, to use C. S. Lewis's term, a "spilled religion," which one might follow to its source. The experience of this sensuality can replace the experience of God — it certainly does for many people — but it can also lead one down the dark hallway where one stumbles

---

60. Sarah Coakley, *Powers and Submissions: Spirituality, Philosophy, and Gender* (Oxford: Blackwell, 2002), p. 161. Coakley is referring in particular to the work of Judith Butler.

The Historical Model

upon Someone who was always there. Indeed, it will probably do one or the other, eventually. But notice that it does this by sparking desire, and a vision, not by proposing clear and distinct ideas.

But it would be a mistake to read Rothko as continuing the rejection of meaning that is represented by Marcel Duchamp and Dada, as is often done. There is a loss of a previous myth, Rothko admits: "Who would not rather paint the soul-searching agonies of Giotto than the apples of Chardin, for all of the love we have for them?" (104). His work, like that of the Romantic poets, is carried out in a world of diminished metaphysical commitments. But even in the reduction to the tactile, affirmation is still possible — indeed, one might argue that it is inescapable. The material, Rothko believes, is a "substantial basis for the evolution of symbols which could bring to life, in terms of pictorial symbols, human interaction in relation to [a] new myth" (102). Here is the point: Artists still seek the universal (and new myths) because the call of God is unquenchable. But they now gesture toward the ineffable in the encounter with the tactile. In pronouncing materiality good, did not God suggest that an affirmation of material values brings with it a meaning that transcends the material? And in the Incarnation, the ascension, and Pentecost, did not God re-affirm this materiality within the context of the Myth that lies behind all myths? A long exposure to Rothko's work suggests that, while it does not intend the supernatural in any traditional way, it elicits experiences that point beyond the immanent — it proposes a kind of secular mysticism and even hints at a kind of eschatology. In other words, it encourages devotional practices that gesture toward . . . what? As David Summers argues, the Rothko Chapel could not have taken the form it did "without embodying traditional forms of religious observance . . . a use of historical forms at a remove from historical traditions."[61]

So, at the conclusion of this chapter, let me return to my original claim. The practices that promote this process of insight are a kind of meditation on the forms — they are in fact secular devotional practices that for many contemporary people have replaced religious practices. They might even be described as a sort of secular prayer, opening oneself in quiet to something that is beyond. The point at which the Christian might best engage the devotee of Rothko, then, is not at the level of

---

61. David Summers, *Real Spaces: World Art History and the Rise of Western Modernism* (New York: Phaidon, 2003), p. 651.

intellectual argument — insisting, for example, that the emptiness of his forms reflects the general bankruptcy of modern culture — but at the level of suggesting an alternative and more deeply satisfying form of such devotional practices: the praise of Dante or the prayer of Pico.

CHAPTER 3

Poetic Stewardship of Life

Earlier I took issue with the perennial impulse of Christians to distrust their cultural context and, not infrequently, to see it as a falling away from some previous period of righteousness. I promised to advance both theological and strategic reasons for this rejection. The theological issues I discussed in the first two chapters; in this one I will turn to the strategic concerns. The point is, even if theologically the currents swirling around are conflicting (when haven't they been?), the pressing concern for most people is this: What do we do about things? What strategy do we adopt as God's people?

The Moral and Spiritual Situation

The argument of this chapter is that cultural warnings, however understandable they may be in general, provide no positive guidance for our poetic interaction with our world. Worry has never been a stimulus for creative living. Let me recall the conclusion of Tracey Rowland about the cultural situation we face in late modernism. She thinks we face a putative "universal culture" which has supplanted the universality of Greco-Latin classical culture. "This culture," she concludes, "far from being a *praeparatio evangelii* in the manner of Classical culture, is actually a hostile medium for the flourishing of Christian practices and beliefs."[1] Having challenged the theological assumptions of

---

1. Tracey Rowland, *Culture and the Thomist Tradition: After Vatican II* (London: Routledge, 2003), p. 159.

this conclusion, I will ask now: What is one supposed to do about the current hostility toward Christianity? Rowland's answer appears to be that Christians must pick and choose those elements from their culture that "already carry with them an openness to theism and to created natures."[2]

A more positive approach has been recently outlined by Kevin Vanhoozer.[3] He and his colleagues in that book encourage Christians to become "cultural agents" by discerning the worlds within and behind the cultural artifacts of our day, and by responding appropriately. He says,

> Culture is the environment and atmosphere in which we live and breathe with others. We are surrounded by cultural texts of all kinds, bombarded with messages, solicited by visions of the good life. To understand just what a cultural text is proposing, one must take time and pay attention.[4]

Vanhoozer understands that our response is, in part, an act of self-creation and that immersion in the values of our culture is, in some sense, inevitable. But in the end he insists that our Christian identity is basically countercultural. Our goal, he says, is "to create forms of life that correspond to the biblical text in contemporary cultural contexts," using biblical terms to shape our message.[5] He calls this process "excorporation," taking something from the hegemonic culture to use in speaking (and acting) Gospel truth.

Although Vanhoozer is careful to insist that we first listen to cultural texts before we rush to judgment, the approach to culture that he proposes is, in the main, oppositional. Culture shapes us over time according to its own agenda; it is a nurture that corrupts nature — and we must discern and subvert this agenda. Although he acknowledges the contribution of cultural studies (and cites Michel de Certeau), his focus is still on what culture does to us rather than what we do with (and at times to) culture. There is a great deal of overlap between Vanhoozer's

---

2. Rowland, *Culture and the Thomist Tradition*, p. 154.
3. See his lengthy introduction to *Everyday Theology: How to Read Cultural Texts and Interpret Trends*, ed. Kevin J. Vanhoozer, Charles A. Anderson, and Michael J. Sleasman (Grand Rapids: Baker Academic, 2007).
4. *Everyday Theology*, ed. Vanhoozer, Anderson, and Sleasman, p. 53.
5. *Everyday Theology*, ed. Vanhoozer, Anderson, and Sleasman, pp. 55-56.

approach and my own. But his analysis focuses a bit more on the interpretation of texts; in what follows, I want to focus more on reception and engagement with cultural forms more generally.

Of course, in a sense, Rowland and Vanhoozer are both right: culture does shape us. But even if this formation is not always benign, it is inevitable; we cannot escape our encultured situation. But neither can we escape, as I see it, the theological reality of God's active presence in culture, especially within what I am calling cultural wisdom. Moreover, this Presence is also a voice which speaks deep within each person, often in the form of longings and desires that seek to move the soul. No cultural arrangements can keep creation and culture from constituting a theatre in which God's glory is somewhere to be seen and where the Spirit everywhere is active.

I will have more to say about how to discern this presence, but for the moment, I will leave to one side the question of how one determines, as Vanhoozer puts it, which elements are open to theism or proper biblical teaching — for which his book provides some very helpful guidance. The more immediate question is this: Whatever its weaknesses, how does one go about living in this world? What does one *do?* Or, to put this question in terms of my larger argument: Given that one lives in culture as a purposeful agent pursuing certain values, what does one *make* of things? The answer implied in treatments like Vanhoozer's is that one thinks about things and forms clear opinions about what is appropriate or not appropriate in given cultural patterns. Then one forms a strategy of response. Let's call this the ideological approach to culture: one reflects on culture, and then one responds in appropriate ways.

There is nothing wrong with careful reflection on culture, of course; it is a good thing as far as it goes. But I would propose that an overly strong focus on making cultural judgments risks mischaracterizing both cultural products and the situation of the interpreter.

Let's start with the admonition to reflect on the artifacts of culture. The problem we face when construing the meanings of cultural products is that these are not fixed — they are constantly negotiated, contested, and often revised. This is true of larger cultural trends as well. As Vanhoozer acknowledges, cultures have porous boundaries — I would go further and say that today they are mostly hybrids. More and more this is true of cultural products as well — the pop singer Sting borrows from the sixteenth-century composer John Dowland; exhibitions display the influence of African art on the art of Mexico; and so on. This dynamic situation makes cultural analyses highly complex. Even cultural trends emerging from hostile situations can serve good purposes, and the reverse is true as well. In the areas of both popular culture and high culture, works of art and the various media are constantly reshaping themselves and being reassessed. Vincent Van Gogh didn't sell a single painting during his lifetime; now he is among the giants of modern art. Television was once blamed for all the evils of contemporary life; current critics are describing the new age of smart television. And so the list goes on.[6]

The interpreter faces an analogous problem. What I am calling the ideological approach to culture seems to assume that the interpreter is standing somewhere apart from the culture making careful judgments about what is or is not "biblical" or "open to theism." Whenever I read descriptions of "cultural hermeneutics," a term that has been expanded to describe the active interpretation of all forms of life, and not simply texts, I can't help thinking that the operative — if unexamined — model is still an isolated scholar sitting alone in her/his office grappling with a written text or, in this case, an isolated cultural product.

There is a certain irony here. Scholars arguing that we must take account of modern culture and resist its pull are making an assumption about the way culture works that is itself thoroughly modern. This modern notion of culture sees cultures as unified entities that are held together by shared values and common practices. Christian reflection on such entities often implies that a kind of objective appraisal can be made of this entity called "modern culture." But again this assumes that Christians can inhabit a space somehow removed from their cultural surroundings. The truth is, of course, that they are already formed by their culture long before they begin any critical reflection on it. "Culture" is not out there waiting to be examined; it is already a part of who they are. Furthermore, contemporary studies of culture have shown that cultures are not fixed entities but increasingly are composed of multiple elements whose boundaries are open to immigrants. More and more cultures are interacting to such a de-

---

6. For contrasting views on television, see Neil Postman, *Amusing Ourselves to Death: Public Discourse in the Age of Show Business* (New York: Penguin, 1985), and Steven Johnson, *Everything Bad Is Good for You: How Today's Popular Culture Is Actually Making Us Smarter* (New York: Penguin, 2005).

gree that all cultural encounters have cross-cultural elements.[7] So to describe Christians as sitting in judgment on the situation around them is unrealistic, but also — the point I want to develop — it is strategically unwise.

I want to suggest, further, that such analytic approaches to culture not only misunderstand the product and the interpreter, but also seriously misconstrue the interpretive situation. Much of the time, and for most people almost all of the time, elements of culture do not come at them separately, available for quick labeling and appropriate response. Indeed, they rarely stand still long enough for close examination. Most of the time, things come in complex relationships and multifaceted situations to which one has to respond — often quickly. Moreover, cultural situations come laden with layers of interpretation and response — our coworker describes a movie that deeply upset her, a family member is offended by a book someone had loaned him, and so on. But the more important point has yet to be mentioned: What is often most prominent in this interpretive situation is not the ideological components but what I am calling its aesthetics — more generally, what we might call (after Graham Ward) the economy of response.[8] That is, what matters is what this state of affairs does to me, how I feel about it, and how I need to respond to it — what I am drawn to or repelled by, and what I make of this.

Let me try to describe a better way of thinking about what I am calling the "interpretive situation." In the first chapter we described briefly the encultured situation of people. People are shaped by the cultural patterns into which they are born. This includes ideas about life and the world, but even these are mostly embodied in expected behavior and ordinary language. Most of the values in all of this are implicit — we often cannot even describe the moral implications of much of our inherited practices. Of course, education — especially Christian growth — is a process of becoming aware of these implications and seeking to respond to them in appropriate ways. But even for educated people and for mature Christians, much of our knowledge is what Michael Polanyi calls tacit knowledge. Charles Taylor has recently called this set of circumstances a "social imaginary," which he describes as "repertory . . .

---

7. This point is helpfully argued in Kathryn Tanner, *Theories of Culture: A New Agenda for Theology* (Minneapolis: Fortress Press, 1997).

8. See Graham Ward, *Christ and Culture,* Part One (Oxford: Blackwell, 2005).

including the ensemble of practices which [a group] can make sense of." The important element is that this imaginary is embodied not in ideas but in images, stories, and sets of practices; it is carried by actors who already know what to do and tacitly agree on what the practices are.[9]

It is in such a cultured world that the person is called on not to think about things but to respond, to *do* things and *make* new things. Of course, one must not respond unthinkingly, but one's response to culture usually takes the form of habitual practices which embody his or her beliefs. He or she is called to construct a life that embodies Christian (or secular) assumptions. Christians, for their part, do a wide variety of things that reinforce or contest their cultural situation. Miroslav Volf describes the situation as one of seeking a Christian difference. This, he notes, "is always a complex and flexible network of small and large refusals, divergences, subversions, and more or less radical alternative proposals, surrounded by the acceptance of many cultural givens."[10] The reason for this diversity of tactics is that culture itself, as we have noted, is a dynamic complex of factors. So, Volf argues, "there is no single correct way to relate to a given culture as a whole, or even to its dominant thrust; there are only numerous ways of accepting, transforming, or replacing various aspects of a given culture from within."[11]

The multifaceted response to a given situation does not excuse actors from responsibility, to be sure. People, by virtue of their creation in God's image, are inevitably moral agents. Their actions are invariably in pursuit of what they perceive to be overriding goods. Nor is moral agency limited to large moral issues (Should I have an abortion? Should I move in with my girlfriend? Should I misstate fourth-quarter earnings?); moral agency is inherent in all we do as human beings, even in the small projects. Moreover, it arrives in the form of what we might call affective signs (to use Augustine's term) that pique my interest and arouse my desires or my fears. The moral charge cannot be separated

---

9. Charles Taylor, *A Secular Age* (Cambridge: Belknap/Harvard University Press, 2007), p. 200. And see Michael Polanyi, *The Tacit Dimension* (New York: Routledge & Kegan Paul, 1967).

10. Miroslav Volf, "When Gospel and Culture Intersect: Notes on the Nature of Christian Difference," in *Pentecostalism in Context: Essays in Honor of William W. Menzies,* ed. Wonsuk Ma and Robert P. Menzies (Sheffield, U.K.: Sheffield Academic Press, 1997), p. 233.

11. Volf, "When Gospel and Culture Intersect," p. 233.

from the attraction (or disgust) I feel in the circumstances. I find myself at every moment in situations in which I must respond, and inevitably, this response has a moral, aesthetic, and even religious dimension. That is, in the end, I will surely respond in ways that issue in praise or honor of whatever gods (or God) I serve.

Of course, people do not ordinarily think about their situation in this way. They think more narrowly of their immediate and practical goals: getting the shopping done, stopping at the cleaners, applying for a job, and so on. That is, the situation takes on a particular embodied character, and people respond to it in terms of what I have called praxis. In fact, one can argue that life, from putting blocks into a pile to planning for retirement, is a series of interconnected projects. It is just in this context that I want to return to the notions of "art" and "aesthetics." David Summers has proposed a definition of art that he describes as "post-formal." Art, he argues, is best understood as "fashioning distinctive human social spaces and artifacts."[12] Although these fashionings typically respond to some human need, since they are human projects, they are often done — indeed, if we understand aesthetics in the broadest sense, almost always done — with a view to their aesthetic contour, even if, Summers asserts, things are often aesthetic "after the fact." To place this in the context of my argument: If Summers is right, we can claim that the projects of life arise and find their meaning amid the narratives we are seeking to construct out of the materials of our world. In addition, one of the aspects of these stories, one that matters deeply to humans, is their shape and splendor — their figure, and the feelings this is meant to arouse.

Our lives (and our cultures) are a complex arrangement of many little stories. Some of them — the way we select our clothes, arrange our furniture, or set the table for guests — have specific aesthetic purposes. But I would argue that all of them, in some sense, serve aesthetic *and* religious purposes. How is this so? It is so because our projects are constructed with a view to our enjoyment, but beyond this, because they are, ultimately, shaped to praise or honor what we think is important. Everything that humans do with purpose has, eventually, the intention of celebration. In our more cynical moments, we might call this "spin" or "promotion," but in any case it is an echo of our determination to

---

12. David Summers, *Real Spaces: World Art History and the Rise of Modernism* (New York: Phaidon, 2003), p. 40.

praise or commemorate what we value. We do this without thinking, because it comes naturally to us. We celebrate our football games, our children's accomplishments, our work, not simply because, if we are lucky, we enjoy these endeavors, but because we are creatures made to praise — remember the accounts of Adam, Brad, Lisa, and Sophia. This is a very important aspect of what it means to be human. As I argued in the last chapter, and as David Ford and Daniel Hardy point out, "praise and adoration of God, and, in appropriate ways, of people [and, we might add, of our projects is] the essence of every person's vocation, and constitutive of right relationships."[13] Finally, then, it is not proper thinking that makes us good people — that was the mistake of Greek philosophy — but rightly oriented and embodied praise. Although this surely includes thinking, it is better understood, in a more holistic sense, as the dynamically and aesthetically shaped response to the stories of our lives (and our cultures).

Aesthetics and Contemplation

The argument that I am making is consistent with that of Nicholas Wolterstorff; indeed, it has been influenced in many ways by his classic discussion of art. Wolterstorff believes that art ought to be a dimension of the whole of life — we seek to live our lives aesthetically. An important criterion of aesthetics, he argues, is its "fittingness" to our own values and to the cultural values that surround it. Wolterstorff thinks that the separating out of art into separate spaces and institutions undercuts this more holistic understanding of aesthetics as a part of life well-lived, and he calls on Christian artists to think more holistically about art.[14]

This comports well with the argument I want to make. But let me speak briefly about what Wolterstorff calls the institution of high art, which has stipulated that the purposes of art should be narrowed down to "perceptual contemplation."[15] Now Wolterstorff would not want to deny the importance of this newly drawn sphere for art, but he wants to

---

13. David Ford and Daniel W. Hardy, *Living in Praise: Knowing and Worshiping God* (London: Darton, Longman & Todd, 2005), p. 64.

14. Nicholas Wolterstorff, *Art in Action: Toward a Christian Aesthetic* (Grand Rapids: Wm. B. Eerdmans, 1980). Wolterstorff develops the notion of fittingness in Chapter Two.

15. Wolterstorff, *Art in Action*, pp. 18, 24.

call attention to the way this separates the activity of enjoying art from the other activities of art and life. He notes, "To one who contemplates, life is a distraction."[16] But in the sense that I have been employing aesthetics, I want to insist that the projects of life and contemplation are not as far apart as Wolterstorff sometimes makes them appear. Contemplation may in fact *prepare* one for life; and life in turn yearns for contemplative moments — in contemporary parlance, "kicking back" or "chilling." I believe that there is a deep human need for contemplation in the sense of standing in the presence of great beauty, whether it is embodied in a great work of art or in a stunning sunset. This is true because, fundamentally, we are creatures shaped for contemplation, whether this means listening with rapt attention to a concert or sitting alone quietly in the presence of God. In fact, I will argue in a later chapter that being struck dumb by an experience of great beauty is not unrelated to (and in fact may prepare one for) falling before God in worship.

The cultural situation that this call to contemplation responds to is the inward turn of Romanticism that I described in the first chapter, which itself was, for better or worse, a further development of the inward turn of the Reformation (and of Augustine before that). This inward turn is frequently maligned, and its Reformation roots ignored, when it is blamed for fostering the autonomous individual of the Enlightenment. According to this argument, the rise of art galleries, museums, and concert halls, separated from the noise and bustle of life, reflects the privatization of aesthetic experience (and the parallel privatization of religion), all of which reflects the triumph of the autonomous individual. From this point of view, we may regret these developments, but this is not the only way to think about these things. When understood in terms of the deep longing of human beings for communion with God, these developments provide spaces in which the human spirit may be opened to something larger, even to something transcendent. For many people, these concert halls, galleries, and darkened movie houses provide a space and create expectations which make possible, even call for, deep experiences which in our commercial culture are otherwise unavailable. Indeed, Robert Wuthnow argues that the growing private sphere, rather than being a turn away from God, provides a new and expanding frontier for a deepened — and often serious — spirituality.[17]

---

16. Wolterstorff, *Art in Action*, p. 27.
17. Robert Wuthnow, *All in Sync: How Music and Art Are Revitalizing American Religion*

Poetic Theology — Again

So the special spaces of galleries and concert halls are, or at least can become, particular instances of the larger call of culture to celebration and praise. In the last chapter we developed this view of culture in terms of the medieval humanist notion of "theologia poetica." I have described this as, on the one hand, the impulse in human culture to fashion our "little stories" with attention to their figure and splendor, and, on the other hand, the inclination to explore the best efforts of contemporary (and classic) writers and artists for signs of grace.

From time to time I have made reference to the lively conversation about hermeneutics, the art of interpretation as applied to culture, that is currently underway. For some time now, cultural critics have sought to apply methods originally applied to interpreting Scripture to our larger life in the world. Ever since Schleiermacher shaped what he called a general hermeneutic, theologians have begun to construe cultural products and life in general "interpretively" — that is, in terms of a given set of values and commitments. But what I am calling poetic theology takes this one step further. This method asks whether it is possible to find ways of using culture to provide lenses for understanding Scripture. Certain theologians of culture have referred to this process of interpretation as reversing the hermeneutical flow. That is, rather than, in every case, reading Scripture to shed light on our world, these interpreters argue that we should, temporarily at least, seek to use the best light from contemporary culture to illumine the human situation and even help us understand Scripture.[18]

I find this project congenial to my own because it seeks to embed

---

(Berkeley and Los Angeles: University of California Press, 2003), pp. 13, 14. Bryan O'Doherty even thinks that the space of the art gallery recalls the medieval church, where art replaces religious verities outside of time. See *Inside the White Cube: The Ideology of the Gallery Space* (Santa Monica: Lapis Press, 1976; 2d ed., 1999), pp. 7-9.

18. The most prominent exponent of this position is Larry Kreitzer, who in a series of books seeks to show how contemporary film and fiction shed light on parts of Scripture. See his most recent book, *Gospel Images in Fiction and Film: On Reversing the Hermeneutical Flow* (Sheffield: Sheffield Academic Press, 2002). My colleague Robert K. Johnston seeks to apply this method to his study of film in *Reel Spirituality: Theology and Film in Dialogue* (Grand Rapids: Baker Book House, 2000; 2d ed., 2006). For a critique of this view, see William Romanowski and Jennifer L. VanderHeide, "Easier Said Than Done: On Reversing the Hermeneutical Flow in Theology and Film," *Journal of Communication and Religion* 30 (March 2007): 40-64.

the interpretive process within the larger context of everyday life. Moreover, this openness to cultural wisdom resonates with biblical instances in which, for example, Jesus adopts common narrative motifs in his parables, and Paul uses contemporary poetry to frame his presentation of the Gospel, and the writer of Proverbs borrows heavily from Egyptian wisdom to help elaborate the fear of the Lord. Insofar as it is appropriate to speak of "flows," however, rather than emphasizing the reversed flow of hermeneutics, I would prefer to say that our goal is, within the overall commitment to the authority of Scripture, to discover ways in which Scripture and our contemporary culture mutually illumine one another.

More broadly, I would prefer in fact to put the process in rather different terms. Instead of a "hermeneutical flow" in either direction, or in both, I want to hold out for a hermeneutical situation in which we are called not simply to understand or interpret, but to respond. I have argued that the call of culture, and of particular elements within a culture, is morally and aesthetically charged. Therefore, the challenge thrown up by culture is not evaluation or understanding primarily, though it will include these; it is in the end a *call* to live faithfully before the face of God. This call appeals to what the Bible calls the heart, or the center of the personality, which issues in our desire to praise and honor what we hold dear. And biblical faithfulness, as cultural wisdom, emerges in the interaction between the construction of our stories and the demands of culture (and God's presence in these). Like music, faithful living happens, so to speak, between the notes.[19]

Rather than assuming that, because of the obvious defects of our culture, God is absent (a strange assumption in any event), this approach assumes that God is present, actively calling people, in and through the forms of culture and its products, to respond to what is good, and to God's call through this. This call has traditionally been understood as the general call, as opposed to the particular call which comes through Scripture. But I want to argue that these, finally, cannot be separated. Our faithful and Spirit-guided study of Scripture will pre-

---

19. I owe the description of music happening "between the notes" to Nicholas Cook in his wonderful *Music: A Very Short Introduction* (Oxford: Oxford University Press, 2000). I have argued that this emphasis on obedience rather than reflection influences how we understand the authority of Scripture. See "How Does the Bible Function in the Christian Life?" in *The Use of the Bible in Theology: Evangelical Options*, ed. Robert K. Johnston (Richmond: John Knox Press, 1985; reprint: Wipf & Stock, 1997), pp. 158-74.

pare us to respond as we should, but this preparation will take place as often in schooling our desires and emotions as it will in training our minds and intellect — and this schooling is just as often a process of discerning cultural wisdom as it is one of applying biblical truth. Indeed, these together constitute our obedience to God.

Early in the twentieth century, Martin Heidegger spoke of the "call" to which authentic human life is a response. One can dismiss this as empty, as Tracey Rowland does,[20] or one can insist that what Heidegger intended is what theologically is the general call of God, which is implanted deeply within the human situation, and is the experience of all people everywhere, whatever their faith convictions. This active call of God makes possible the dynamic setting in which people find themselves and which sets the stage for what I am calling a poetic theology.

Let me return to Paul's sermon on Mars Hill, where he gives the classic example of this theological dynamic at work, quoting an ancient poet in the process: "[God] made all nations to inhabit the whole earth, and he allotted the times of their existence and the boundaries of the places where they would live, so that they would search for God and perhaps grope for him and find him — though indeed he is not far from each one of us. For 'In him we live and move and have our being'" (Acts 17:26-28). In other words, a major purpose for God's creating the potential (and limitation) of human cultures was so that in these places, people would be moved to seek him. Paul then makes use of this pagan poet with a Christian difference (cf. Miroslav Volf), suggesting that the presence of God is not simply an inert fact but an active and searching presence who seeks us out.

Paul Ricoeur: Creating a Beautiful Life

I have noted that discussions of "hermeneutics" have been expanded to include the value-laden interaction between humans and their environment. Hans-Georg Gadamer articulated this process in terms of the merging of the horizon of our world, and its effective history, with the

---

20. Rowland, *Culture and the Thomist Tradition*, pp. 13, 14. Martin Heidegger's classic article "The Origin of a Work of Art" is translated and included in *Philosophies of Art and Beauty*, ed. Albert Hofstadter and Richard Kuhns (New York: Oxford University Press, 1964).

world of the Bible and, in particular, proposed seeing the former as an asset rather than a liability in the process of understanding.[21] And Charles Taylor, we have seen, has argued for a similar conversation between Christian faith and the culture of modernism. But to develop further my notion of poetic theology, I turn more specifically to the work of Paul Ricoeur.

Throughout his work, Ricoeur has acknowledged the importance of the poetic. He develops this in particular in the first volume of *Time and Narrative*. There he describes the tendency to make sense of one's life as a kind of poetic activity. By this he means the inclination that we have to put the events of our lives into a narrative order, an activity he calls "emplotment." He describes this as "the activity that produces plots in relation to every sort of static structure."[22] This fits with what I have called the figurative and striking, since what attracts and engages us, extended over time, is what Ricoeur calls "emplotment." This way of putting things suggests that we are a collection of little stories, which are impacted by other stories.[23] This accumulating narrative includes small things, like a visit to the art museum, and large things, like one's heart transplant five years ago. Often our story merges with that of a particular church, which becomes a part of our story and which in turn encompasses our story in the stories that it tells. In a larger sense, the Kingdom of God is itself a collection of little stories. Those stories, of course, center on a particular series of events, the life and work of Christ, but when that story is thickly told, it consists of many little stories, from Rahab the harlot to the stoning of Stephen.

What is poetic, Ricoeur says, is the active process of emplotment, which makes a figural whole out of the little events, the sequences of scenes of our lives. I sit down to watch a movie, and afterward I accompany my wife to the store to buy clothes that she suggests I need. From one point of view, these appear to be isolated and disconnected events, but seen from within, I (and my wife) know that they make up a part of my overall project of creating a more "poetic" — or one might say

---

21. Hans-Georg Gadamer, *Truth and Method*, trans and ed. Garrett Barden and John Cumming (New York: Seabury Press, 1975). And see the more recent application of this in James K. A. Smith, *The Fall of Interpretation: Philosophical Foundations for a Creational Hermeneutics* (Downers Grove, Ill.: InterVarsity Press, 2000).

22. Paul Ricoeur, *Time and Narrative*, trans. Kathleen McLaughlin and David Pellauer (Chicago: University of Chicago Press, 1984/1990), Volume 1, p. 33.

23. Ricoeur, *Time and Narrative*, p. 80.

"beautiful" — life.²⁴ It seems to me that the project of cultural engagement is better described in light of these larger human pursuits than in terms of "interpreting" isolated artifacts or works of art. What human beings do is shape their lives, and their use of culture, of its arts and popular culture, is invariably subordinated to this larger project.²⁵

I have said that going to an art gallery is itself a little story. How is this so? It is an episode in a larger narrative with its own structure and goal. In the broadest sense, it can provide diversion and entertainment on a Sunday afternoon, pleasures which are not to be belittled. But it may also provide stimulation for a process of reflection that began with a conversation with a friend yesterday, and was stimulated by something I came across in a novel I am reading. Clive Marsh has studied the experience of people going to movies. His findings are relevant to the point we are making. He found that though people often say they go to a movie to "escape," in fact "they often get more than they expect." His study leads him to conclude that going to movies, and entertainment more generally, "is taking the place of religion as a cultural site where the task of meaning-making is undertaken."²⁶ Going to movies and other kinds of entertainment becomes part of the way that people make something of their lives.

Here is where Ricoeur's description of the process of emplotment of stories becomes helpful. When in *Time and Narrative* he describes the work of making a figural narrative out of disparate scenes, he builds on understandings of time and narrative derived from Augustine and Aristotle respectively. In the last sections of the *Confessions,* Augustine discusses the problem of experienced time. Augustine struggles with the discordant nature of human desires, the *distentio animae,* the rest-

---

24. This resonates with some recent attempts to discuss theology in terms of a dramatic presentation. See Michael Horton, *Covenant and Eschatology: The Divine Drama* (Louisville: Westminster Press, 2002), and Kevin Vanhoozer, *The Drama of Doctrine: A Canonical-Linguistic Approach to Christian Theology* (Louisville: Westminster John Knox Press, 2005). As will become clear, however, I want to broaden the category of "drama" to include visual and even kinesthetic dimensions.

25. This process is similar to what veteran video gamers call "telescoping," wherein gamers "probe new environments for hidden rules and patterns [and] . . . build telescoping hierarchies of objectives." See Johnson, *Everything Bad Is Good for You,* p. 56. This may explain something of the fascination with video games.

26. Clive Marsh, "On Dealing with What Films Actually Do to People," in *Reframing Theology and Film: New Focus for an Emerging Discipline,* ed. R. K. Johnston (Grand Rapids: Baker Book House, 2007), pp. 147, 150.

less exploring of the soul, which is experienced as a tension between expectation, memory, and attention. This rugged landscape of the soul, this distention, is properly tended only in the intention *(intentio)* of the soul — that is, in the passing of the soul beyond itself and its becoming one with God.[27]

Aristotle, while he does not deal with time, wrestles with the tension between the discordant and concordant factors in drama and concludes that only in the form of dramatic narrative can these elements be resolved. The satisfaction which the viewer feels in the reversal and denouement, and in the recognition of the action, corresponds to his or her own sense of what is right and possible. But beyond this, Ricoeur notes, the "spectator's emotional response is constructed in the drama, in the quality of the destructive or painful incidents suffered by the characters themselves."[28]

In this sense, going to an art gallery or a movie can become an exercise in distention, a part of the restless searching. But it may also portend the intentional aspect of the person as well: the claim that life includes a dimension of something deeper — "more than meets the eye." So Ricoeur argues that an encounter with a work of art, and the pleasure and discipline derived from this little story, can become practice for constructing the figurative shapes of our life.[29] This experience can become a shaping experience that helps us develop a sense of contour and proportion, just as, more directly, Christians believe that devotional and worship practices train the imagination to live well before God.

In a sense, so I am claiming, all the little projects, or stories, provide the material out of which we seek to construct a good life. The individual events are like so many notes, which we struggle to compose into a melody. Aristotle held that the fundamental impulse in the poetic imagination was "mimesis" or imitation. Dramatic action, what we are calling the figuration of our lives, may then be called creative imitation in the form of action. Imitation, which Aristotle says is, like desire, natural to us as humans, speaks of the charged character of the situation in which we live our lives. But it also indicates the work of bricolage that makes up the figuring action of our lives, in which pieces and events are brought together into some aesthetic order.

---

27. Ricoeur, *Time and Narrative*, vol. 1, p. 26.
28. Ricouer, *Time and Narrative*, vol. 1, p. 26.
29. Ricouer, *Time and Narrative*, vol. 1, p. 40.

Ricoeur goes on to describe the emplotment process in terms of three aspects — prefiguration, configuration, and refiguration. We will examine these briefly to see how they might apply to the interpretive situation that we are defining as poetic stewardship.

Prefiguration

Part of the problem with traditional hermeneutics, as Gadamer pointed out (and Bultmann before him), was that it ignored the way that one's horizon of expectation influences the reading of texts (and of culture). Gadamer was significant for pointing out, however, that, far from obstructing meaning, the tradition of hopes and dreams one brings to interpretation *enables* one to find meaning. In the terms we are using, the processes of cultural interpretation are part of the larger project of constructing a life. The person or persons are caught in the midst of a multitude of projects (the little stories) that they are seeking to fuse into a coherent and attractive narrative. Notice that it is not as though they "bring their stories with them" to this experience; rather, they are made up of these stories, *that is who they are:* the situation catches them red-handed in the middle of scrabbling together a plot ("mythos"). The values that drive this storytelling, we have argued, are also values that they learned from their cultures; the patterns of the former derive from the patterns of the latter. So again, it is not as though they wonder, from some Olympic height, what they should make of this modern culture. No. They are caught out in the midst of their enculturated situation. They seek to put themselves together out of materials their culture has provided. This is not to suggest some kind of cultural determinism, as though they can do nothing about this situation. Of course they are moral agents who are responsible for what they do with their cultural inheritance. But the materials they use and the symbols they shape are, for better or worse, through and through cultural. And since, as I have argued, these materials are always ambiguous, forever changing shape before our eyes, there is always the possibility of making something new (and better looking!) out of the stories that our culture hands out.

Of course, there is always the possibility that one will destroy or misuse something that he or she is given. This represents a further problem with the distrust of specific cultural formations. This attitude both undermines the ability to "make good" out of difficult circumstances, in the way that God also redeems bad situations and persons, and overlooks the way in which, theologically, the fundamental issues are with the person and the disordered desires that result from human sin and not just with the culture around them. Evil can reside in structures, of course, and cultural products can promote vice, but they do so only because the evil they embody answers to the sinful desires of people who created the structures and are influenced by them.

Configuration

So cultural materials are not inert. They often come in forms that have a particular quality and a direction that pushes, attracts, or repels us. In the case of works of art, like Picasso's *Guernica* and Cormac McCarthy's *The Road,* they offer us a possible world that opens out of the world that we start with. They have to include the patterns of our culture in some form if we are to enter them at all, but once inside, there is no telling where they might lead. Ricoeur calls this second step the world of the "as if,"[30] or better, "what if." That is, we are to suspend disbelief and give ourselves to the experience in such a way that we ask ourselves, at a very deep level, What if the world were like this? If we are successful, and the artistic symbols are strong enough, we can *feel* what it was like to live in a village bombed by the forces of Franco (Picasso), or *imagine* making our way through a post-nuclear landscape with dread and hope (McCarthy). Ricoeur's contention is that this can happen only when the parts are put together in a particular way. This process of assemblage, Ricoeur says, "extracts a configuration from a succession."[31]

The plot or story, then, can attract our attention in a way that the various elements, however splendid they are in themselves, cannot. But why do stories attract us in this way? They do this because, when successful, they resonate with our own tentative attempts at emplotment. They shame our incompetence, or fire our hope, or sometimes they do both together. But why story? Why not simple aesthetic display? Spectacle? Here recall the theological point that the Augustinian humanists understood: that cultural wisdom taps into something beyond itself. The little stories speak to us of Story. Ricoeur in fact admits that the very

30. Ricouer, *Time and Narrative,* vol. 1, p. 64.
31. Ricoeur, *Time and Narrative,* vol. 1, p. 66.

idea of emplotment, as we know it in Western culture, is the heir of Hebrew and Christian stories.[32] If this is so, we can advance the claim that stories which attract, which pique our desire, contain glimmers of a deeper narrative that resonates with our feeble figurative efforts; they propose what Tolkien has called "deep magic."

The story of God's love told through Israel and Christ and evident in the founding of the Christian church is proposed as a possible world by the announcement of the Gospel, but also, more tellingly, by the example of specific Christian communities. Here let me make two observations about the category of configuration as it relates to our general promotion of poetic theology. First, the Gospel is important for people today, and not only because it is true and historical and therefore demands assent — as though belief could ever be coerced in this way. Christians believe, of course, that the story of the Gospel is true and historical, but even for most of them, these qualities are not why they believed it in the first place. No, the story of the Gospel is attractive to people today because it arouses their desire for love, grace, and hope for something beyond ordinary human flourishing (in this life and beyond). It is a story that radiates a splendor that answers to their deepest longings. In a later chapter I will argue that these images of glory constitute a vital component of Scripture that readers have too often overlooked.

The second observation is that modern culture, in spite of its pretensions and poses, awakens longings and sparks hopes that it is not able to satisfy. This wisdom in its many forms has much to contribute to Christian understanding both of Scripture and of the Christian life. Often the light shines out where one least would expect it: among the slaves in the American South and the favelas of Rio there has arisen music that has captured the imagination of generations. Science and technology, though subject to abuse, have also contributed to raising living standards for millions. These gifts are also little stories that are capable of being integrated into the narratives that we seek to construct, and we would be ungrateful not to allow them to have their impact on our lives. But in the end, such wisdom, by itself, is not enough. For this we need, as James says, a wisdom that is from above (3:17),

---

32. Ricoeur, *Time and Narrative*, vol. 1, p. 69. Here Ricoeur also cites Erich Auerbach, *Mimesis: The Representation of Reality in Western Literature* (Princeton: Princeton University Press, 1953); Auerbach has argued this point in terms of the whole development of Western literature.

even if this will always be shaped in terms of (and will reshape) stories that make us what we are.

Refiguration

What do we do with these glimmers of grace? That, of course, depends on us. Nothing is predetermined; all options are on the table. In this phase, which Gadamer calls application, we can choose to enter one or another of these possible worlds. In this sense, every cultural text — all serious art, whether or not it claims to be literally or historically true — is "fiction" — that is, it embodies a *possible* world. It is possible for us to enter it, or not. Of course, things are never as wide open as I am making them out to be, because our stories necessarily influence what we can and cannot enter. But one thing is certain: one's world will invariably be shaped by the stories he or she explores. One way or another, we will be shaped by what we have seen and loved. As Ricoeur says, the world, for him, "is a set of references opened by every set of descriptive or poetic text I have ever read, interpreted, or loved."[33] Notice that what has shaped him is finally what he has loved. This brings us back to Augustine's suggestion that what brings us to the fullest life is shaped by what we love.

It would be a mistake to see this process simply in individualistic terms, for just as we are invariably embedded in a cultural situation, so we are also shaped by our social relationships. Graham Ward has argued that the work of cultural interpretation issues in what he calls a shared "theological standpoint" that is analogous to the project of emplotment that we have described. This is not a "natural" or "objective" point of view (he rejects perspectivalism); this is an achievement of "shared knowledge; an understanding of the world that, in being articulated, is recognized and held to be a better account of the world than others available."[34] Note that a standpoint necessarily arises through social interaction — that is, the person is not only formed by this pro-

---

33. Ricoeur, *Time and Narrative*, vol. 1, p. 80.
34. Graham Ward, *Cultural Transformation and Religious Practice* (Cambridge: Cambridge University Press, 2005), p. 76. Ward thinks that the embodied and corporate nature of this standpoint and the projects in which this results escape Ricoeur's continuing captivity to the Cartesian self, and moves beyond Gadamer in allowing contesting and negotiating between horizons rather than simply merging them.

cess but is an agent in shaping its direction. Moreover, it is from within this situation that people join together in various social and, eventually, institutional projects. Though encountering (and negotiating with) other equally strong standpoints (agnostic, Muslim, etc.), "the contemporary cultural imaginary," Ward believes, "is . . . already fertile with Christianity in a manner not available in the climates of positivism and atheism that followed the Second World War."[35] But what role does the poetic play in this shared knowledge?

Breaking Through to the Poetic and to God

In the process that I have briefly described, we see ways in which people, in their encounter with each other and with various cultural goods (and potentially with God), move beyond praxis to poesis. The process suggests that, little by little, people are able to rise above a merely functional way of living in order to "make something lovely" of their homes or their families — or at least they hope to do so. In the first chapter we saw that the impulse to move beyond the immediate situation in which we find ourselves is built into what it means to be human. My larger claim is theological: This movement that is embodied in our desires and fears, that is in our feeling for what is around us (cf. Antonio Damasio), reflects something of God's purposes for us, and finally is meant to move us to love and worship God. By virtue of their creation in God's image, I am arguing, human beings are responsive agents. In fact, Emil Brunner describes the "image of God" in which Genesis says humans are created in terms of "responsibility" or, literally, their "respond-ability."[36] That is, our very ability to feel emotions that move us toward or away from people and situations is part of an intricate set of dispositions that make up the fundamental structure of our spiritual lives.

But these responses are appropriate and effective because they answer to the way the world around us is constituted. We are drawn toward people and situations for a wide variety of reasons, of course, but we are especially attracted to those things which are textured in attrac-

---

35. Ward, *Cultural Transformation and Religious Practice*, p. 166.
36. See Emil Brunner, *Man in Revolt: A Christian Anthropology*, trans. Olive Wyon (Philadelphia: Westminster Press, 1947).

tive, figured ways. Human life is lived, so to speak, in a charged field of moral and aesthetic values to which we respond and, finally, in terms of which we forge our identities.

But how does one break out of the merely practical level of life toward what I am calling the poetic sphere? Here M. M. Bakhtin can be of help. He describes the way the novel has developed in the modern period as that genre of literature which takes the temporality of human life seriously.[37] Within this zone of the here and now, the discourse of the novel has emerged. In the storied context of the novel, the individual is faced with inconclusive events and radical contingency, and the reader wonders what the protagonist will make of all these disparate events and situations. According to Bakhtin, he is called to acquire "the ideological and linguistic initiative necessary to change the nature of his own image" (38). But the problem is that the poetics of the situation is locked away; Bakhtin says it is subordinated to what he calls the "bounded image" (50).

People, in other words, become stuck in routines and roles which are intrinsically unsatisfying, but which, in many ways, they seem powerless to change. The career waiter had always hoped to break into acting or return to school, but never manages to do so. How does such a person break through to the poetic? Bakhtin argues that there are two factors which have been decisive in the development of the novel and which are essential to creating the dialogical situation in which this change in image becomes possible. These are laughter and polyglossia. Laughter allowed people to parody every genre, which in turn "freed consciousness from the power of the direct word" (60). Laughter, in other words, becomes a weapon against the world as taken-for-granted. In the latter, polyglossia — struggles between and within languages, high and low, foreign and domestic — made it possible for different languages to "mutually illuminate one another" (76). Bakhtin believes that this dynamic situation of parody and the clash of voices decenters everyday life and makes change possible. He concludes, "The dialogic orientation of word among other words (of all kinds and degrees of otherness) creates new and significant artistic potential in discourse . . . which has found its fullest and deepest expression in the novel" (275).

---

37. M. M. Bakhtin, *The Dialogic Imagination: Four Essays,* ed. Michael Holquist, trans. Caryl Emerson and Michael Holquist (Austin: University of Texas, 1981), pp. 7-11. Subsequent pages will be cited in the text.

Notice that it is in the exchange between the various languages, an openness to which was made possible by laughter, that change can take place. But note further that it is not simply any alternate voice, but voices, as Bakhtin puts it, which have been canonized — that is, shaped into artistic images — that truly make change possible (417-22). These images, in the form of artistic classics, grow and develop over time and continue to do their work on the imaginations of subsequent generations. Such classics embody parody and dialogic encounters that enable and stimulate a change in images.

This suggests that novels, as well as other embodied images, can provide alternative narratives, which can open up the experience of the reader in a way that makes change possible. In the very clash, or dialogue, of languages one can "see" some new way of making a life. But does seeing a new way to live imply that a new life is really possible? It turns out that this is precisely the claim that Scripture makes about all of life's little stories: Change is possible, but not guaranteed. Seeing oneself in terms of the alternative voices of Scripture suggests that one might actually become something different, perhaps something better and more attractive. Scripture includes the dialogue of voices that add to its power and influence. Moreover, it is clear that part of the attraction of Scripture is its figural and narrative form — its images and stories. Augustine recognized the power of these intertextual dimensions of Scripture when he noted that it "is much more pleasant to learn lessons presented through imagery, and much more rewarding to discover meanings that are won only with difficulty.... It is a beneficial thing that the Holy Spirit organized holy scripture so as to satisfy hunger by means of its plainer passages and remove hunger by means of obscurer ones."[38] All of this contributes to the promise of Scripture that transformation of the reader is what God intends and works to accomplish.

But how does this relate to the goods that cultural wisdom has handed down, specifically the classics of literature and art, to which Bakhtin is referring? Here I will make two interrelated claims. First, because of the way the world is made and God's continued presence in that world, and because human agents are made in the image of God, cultural products, when they are good and true, can move people toward God. They can, as it were, echo and even facilitate the movement

---

38. Augustine, *On Christian Teaching*, trans. R. P. H. Green (Oxford: Oxford University Press, 1997), p. 33.

of the soul toward God that is described in the Christian narrative. But second, because of the broken nature of that creation and that agency, a simple encounter with an alternate voice, or even the imaged dialogue of voices, cannot result in any genuine transformation. Even the freedom from a life-taken-for-granted that laughter allows and the attraction of alternate stories do not, in themselves, make people better.

Or do they? This is the question which poetic theology must answer. There are those, of course, who would argue that this is precisely the role of beauty and of great art and literature: to create a more humane and gentle people. But Christians disagree about whether this is possible. In the remaining part of this chapter I want to discuss two possible responses that Christians might make to this claim and, along the way, outline a Christian poetics that I will develop in more detail in later chapters.

In the recent past, theologians have been actively seeking to reassert the priority of beauty in theological conversation. It is no accident that in the triumphant secularism of the twentieth century, beauty had a hard go of it, and efforts to establish the importance of art and aesthetics similarly suffered setbacks. But recently theologians such as John Milbank and Hans Urs von Balthasar have recovered the medieval argument that beauty is a transcendental form of God's presence, and therefore that experiences of beauty can be understood, by analogy, as experiences of God. In Chapter Seven I will discuss in some detail these and other attempts to describe beauty in relation to God.

While there is an obvious affinity with the argument that we are making in this book, there are important differences as well. Justin Klassen has laid out these difference recently in describing the distinction between what he calls rhetorical and dialectical theology.[39] Balthasar and Milbank develop a strategy that Klassen calls rhetorical, in that they make a direct claim on the basis of God's objective presence in historical forms. As Klassen puts it, rhetorical theology seeks "to persuade its reader directly into a 'participatory' way of living by virtue of its narrative of the church's historical 'participation,' instead of throwing its reader into a dialectical opposition between faith and despair"

---

39. See Justin D. Klassen, "Truth as 'Living Bond': A Dialectical Response to Recent Rhetorical Theology," *International Journal of Systematic Theology* 10, no. 4 (October 2008): 431-46. Subsequent pages will be cited in the text. Klassen's terms recall David Tracy's distinction between analogical and dialectical imaginations, but refer more to forms of discourse than do Tracy's more comprehensive categories.

(435-36). Rhetorical theology believes that readers may be persuaded of God's presence through the assertion of "rhetorically compelling content" (433); their eyes may be captivated by the spiritual reality of God's presence, and so they may believe and live in the truth thus seen.

According to Klassen, the problem with such a direct appeal is that there are various "compartments" possible to these elements — namely, faith and despair (433). In other words, one has the option of responding in various ways to this call, as Paul makes clear in Romans 1. Here Klassen makes use of Kierkegaard's method of despair, which allows one to respond to truth by "forgetting the self *as the activity of becoming a self*" (437, his emphasis). Kierkegaard argued that direct appeals to history and objectivity overlook the approximation that all historical materials imply. They must therefore be accepted by faith, via "the uncertainty of historical becoming" (437). "Such an existence," Klassen argues, "can only be *lived* by virtue of a faith that can never be 'certain' of its success in so living" (438, his emphasis).

Taking our cue from Klassen, let's suggest two theological elements that become critical to the development of our theological aesthetic. First, even though it is true, as Scripture claims, that God's beauty shines through the created order and that Christ upholds that order, we do not have direct access to God through this beauty — in the first chapter I challenged the notion of participation that Radical Orthodoxy endorses. Powerful works of art, just like other objects of desire, can move us toward God, can become a step in the journey that leads to God — but they do not constitute a witness that is unambiguous. The reason for this can be found in Paul's assertion that though the very heavens declare the glory of God, we humans suppress and distort the truth we feel and do not honor the one to which this witnesses (Rom. 1:18, 21). Later, in Romans 7, Paul, from his own experience, testifies that when he tried consistently to live a beautiful life, he found that he was unable to do so. This does not make the perception or even the attraction of beauty (and the figural shape of poetry) less important, but it does mean that its role must be incorporated into a larger narrative of journey and conversion.

Second, the problem is not only the nature of the brokenness of our vision and the world, but also the historical and progressive nature of faith. It is always possible to relate to the claims of objective beauty "despairingly," Klassen reminds us. That is, we are inclined to forget that the self is a call and a process of becoming, through time, by faith in

God's grace and leading. At the end of the first chapter, we saw that the contemporary deviations in the pursuit of aesthetics seem to specialize in celebrating an essentialized self in the aesthetic moment, forgetting that the self is formed over time by a process that necessarily involves faith in some form or another. The Christian life of faith is not simply an event or an illumination;[40] it is a growing up into Christ in all things (Eph. 4:14-15), through the historical exigencies that a person necessarily encounters. It is a breaking through to a larger shared knowledge about things that is lived out and not simply observed. This, as we will see in a later chapter, marks the uniqueness of the Protestant and Reformed view of aesthetics that underlies my notion of poetic theology.

---

40. In this way Gerhard Nebel's description of the Protestant tendency to understand aesthetics as an event rather than a fixed entity is misleading, and therefore Balthasar's dismissal of it is premature. See *The Glory of the Lord: A Theological Aesthetics*, trans. Erasmo Leiva-Merikakis (Edinburgh: T&T Clark, 1982), vol. 1, pp. 64-70. Aesthetics must be understood as incorporated into a larger process of becoming like Christ.

Building Blocks for a Poetic Theology: How Did We Get Here?

CHAPTER 4

Re-reading the Nineteenth-Century Romantic Heritage

Nietzsche anticipated much twentieth-century criticism against Christianity, and, at the same time, embodied much of that century's preoccupation with aesthetics. In the process, he renounced a desiccated Christian faith that appeared unconnected with the depths of human feeling. In "the Anti-Christ" he insisted,

> Christianity has sided with all that is weak and base, with all failures; it has made an ideal of whatever *contradicts* the instincts of the strong life . . . it has corrupted the reason even of those strongest in spirit by teaching men to consider the supreme values of the spirit as something sinful.[1]

However unfair his assessment of Christianity may have been in general, this particular charge — that Christianity and the passions of life are enemies — has enough merit to call for some response. After all, if Nietzsche is right about this, a project of poetic theology would not appear promising.

From one perspective, this seems like a strange complaint. Didn't the Reformation, following from Augustine, represent an inward turn in which faith was made a personal (and inward) decision? How is it that Nietzsche (and others) could accuse Christianity, especially the Protestant Christianity of his time, of ignoring the deepest human longings?

---

1. Friedrich Nietzsche, "The Anti-Christ," in *The Portable Nietzsche*, ed. Walter Kaufman (New York: Viking Press, 1954), p. 571, his emphasis.

The Christian Roots of Romanticism

Whether or not there were grounds for this charge in the church of Nietzsche's day, it cannot be doubted that the tradition provides some traction for his complaints. Calvin was not opposed to the poetic — we have seen that he belonged in the tradition of late medieval humanism that valued this part of life. He believed art was a gift of God. But he also believed that art appealed primarily to the emotions, and this constituted a weakness that made it incapable of teaching and edifying believers. At the same time, Calvin believed that the events of creation and redemption constituted a drama of the highest order in which humans were invited to participate as players. Creation itself was, he believed, a theatre for the glory of God. These emphases suggested new ways of reflecting on art and its relation to theology, but they also excluded ways favored during the medieval period. Here Calvin departed from his Augustinian heritage in critical ways. He would certainly not have denied Augustine's claim that we are on a journey of the affections, and that the will (and feelings) need to be schooled in the awareness of a life lived in the presence of God — which was Calvin's great image of "piety" (Latin, *pietas*). But he denied Augustine's description of the world as filled with signs which, when "used" rightly, can lead us to God. The over-rich flowering of medieval symbolism and sacramentals led Calvin to deny any religious role to symbols beyond the word and table.

Calvin's aesthetic was to a great extent illustrated in the dramatic narrative of John Bunyan, which I will explore later. Like Calvin before him, Bunyan denied any substantial role to external signs as leading the affections toward God; indeed — in anticipation of Nietzsche's concern — the life of feeling was subordinated to the will in Christian's journey to the heavenly city. While morality did not supplant aesthetics entirely, it clearly upstaged and colonized it.

Still, despite Nietzsche's charge, the inward turn represented by the Protestant Reformation and its celebration of everyday life clearly prepared the way for the transformation represented by the Romantic movement. Since this has proven so influential on twentieth-century aesthetics, and on popular life generally, I will pick up the conversation about Romanticism that I started earlier.

In the seventeenth century, the Reformed tradition developed in two quite distinct directions. One was more influenced by Peter Ramus and focused on rational order; the other — to my mind truer to Calvin

Re-reading the Nineteenth-Century Romantic Heritage

himself, and more open to the Holy Spirit — gave important place to feeling and personal experience.[2] In the eighteenth century a similar split occurred in Lutheran-influenced areas, manifesting itself in the growing rationalism in the universities and the dominant orthodoxy on the one hand, and in the various Pietist groups on the other. Other social and historical influences were at play, obviously, but it is crucial to point out that currents widely seen as secularizing — the development of autonomous individualism and of Romantic mysticism — themselves had religious (and Protestant) roots.[3] Rather than disparaging developments in the nineteenth century, then, one should note ways that the religious impulses lying behind them were misused and how they might be recovered.

The critical influence here was the Pietist stream of Protestantism which was seeking to keep alive medieval mystical traditions. Already in 1606, Johann Arndt published *True Christianity*, which W. R. Ward calls the most successful devotional work of Protestant history. This book was essentially a Lutheran reworking of medieval mystical texts.[4] The Pietists that sprang from Arndt sought to replace rational polemics with an intense and emotion-filled spiritual life. The influence of medieval mystics often put them at odds with the dominant Lutheran orthodoxy in a way that recalled the struggle between the medieval humanists and Scholastic theologians. Later in the century, Philip Spener, anticipating Charles Wesley, gathered serious Christians together in "Pietist colleges" so that they could encourage each other in the life of prayer and devotion.

These developments would have a deep impact on the nineteenth century. Especially important for that century was the radical Pietist Johann Georg Hamann, whom we met previously.[5] Over against the grow-

---

2. I have described these sides of Reformed thought and practice in William Dyrness, *Reformed Theology and Visual Culture* (Cambridge: Cambridge University Press, 2004), Chapter 5. In this I am dependent on the work of Janice Knight.

3. This is now widely recognized. See, for example, Michael Buckley, *At the Origins of Modern Atheism* (New Haven: Yale University Press, 1987).

4. A useful summary of this movement is found in W. R. Ward's article "Pietism," in *Global Dictionary of Theology*, ed. W. Dyrness and V. M. Karkkainen (Downers Grove, Ill.: InterVarsity Press, 2008).

5. See especially Hamann, "Aesthetica in Nuce," trans. Gwen Griffith Dickson in *Johann Georg Hamann's Relational Metacriticism* (Berlin: Walter de Gruyter, 1995). See also the helpful discussion in John Milbank, "Knowledge: The Theological Critique of Philos-

ing rationalism of his day, Hamann insisted that our response to the world must be religious rather than simply intellectual; we must act in it with the whole person. In his "Aesthetica in Nuce," Hamann refers to Pontius Pilate's famous question "What is truth?" which was also the Enlightenment question of Hamann's day. But like many of his contemporaries, Hamann believed that Pilate's connection with reality was only a superficial one, and so he was unable to *see* Christ enthroned in his suffering. Only those connected by faith to the depths of things are able to see in reality its unfathomable depths. The Enlightenment gaze could not reach to this place. Hamann sought to recover these regions by recognizing the role of what he called poetry in the process of human knowing. Here is how he begins his aesthetics: "Poetry is the mother tongue of the human race, as gardening is older than farming; painting than writing; song than declamation." To bring the voice of creation to clarity is "the part allotted to the Poet."[6] Pietists like Hamann so trusted God that they had no occasion to doubt their senses, and by trusting these, they believed, they learned more of God.

By our ineradicable connection with the creator and sustainer, Hamann believed, we not only see what is before us, but also know it as a sign disclosing the depth below it. For Hamann, then, aesthetics was more than an emotional connection to what is there; it was an ability to see things as they speak to us; as he said of God's creation, "Speak, that I might see you!"[7] Proper hearing, however, does not come naturally to us. Faith in things and their depths was, for Hamann, an extension of his saving faith in Christ — his was a "knowledge by faith" following on his "justification by faith." This knowledge was only possible by faith — that is, indirectly. But the more deeply we comprehend our creation in the image of God, the more deeply we can discern God in creation. Hamann writes, "The more vivid this idea of the image of the invisible God is in our minds; the more able we are to see and taste, to contemplate and feel with our hands his friendliness."[8]

---

ophy in Hamann and Jacobi," in *Radical Orthodoxy: A New Theology,* ed. John Milbank and Catherine Pickstock (London: Routledge, 1999), pp. 23-29, on which I am dependent for this section.

6. Hamann, "Aesthetica in Nuce," pp. 411-12. The "Aesthetica" was first published in 1762.

7. Hamann, "Aesthetica in Nuce," p. 412. Cf. "Nature works through the senses and the passions" despite our having "mutilated" it by our abstractions (p. 420).

8. Hamann, "Aesthetica in Nuce," p. 421.

Re-reading the Nineteenth-Century Romantic Heritage

There is little doubt that this stream of Christianity played a major role in the transformation of sensibility that took place around 1800. Kant and Schleiermacher both owed much to their Pietist heritage; artist Caspar David Friedrich, arguably the most important Northern Romantic artist, cannot be understood apart from his Pietist upbringing.[9] Hamann was a great influence on J. G. Herder, his close friend and protégé. But there is another dimension to this Pietist influence that is critical. Just as modern readers often read medieval texts outside their context of liturgical and devotional practices, so the Pietists have often been read outside the context of their communal practices. But the rich awareness of God which Hamann championed was a product of the devotional life of prayer, mutual confession, and Bible reading, even of the hymn singing, for which these groups were so well-known — and which came to have such a critical influence on Schleiermacher. It was the set of affective practices that served as the lived-out rhythm of their beliefs.

These influences, among others, converged in European culture at the end of the eighteenth and the beginning of the nineteenth centuries; they provide the context for Nietzsche's famous accusation which begins this chapter. Philosophers and poets of that period began to place questions of aesthetics and feeling at the center of their discussions, and in doing so raised issues that have occupied theologians up to the present. These discussions are critical for our project of developing a poetic theology, and so I will review them briefly in this chapter. The question I ask in this chapter and the next is this: What theological resources should one develop, and which should one resist, in the service of a poetic theology?

Romanticism, Art, and Theology

Hamann's thinking is a critical precursor of that of the German Enlightenment philosopher Immanuel Kant (1724-1804). Kant, though deeply influenced by Pietism, abrogated a significant component of it and thereby initiated what has been called a Copernican revolution in philosophy. His innovation lay in proposing that knowledge is con-

---

9. On this, see William Dyrness, "Caspar David Friedrich: The Aesthetic Expression of Schleiermacher's Romantic Faith," *Christian Scholar's Review* 14, no. 4 (1985).

structed based on two elements: what is given in our experience through our senses, and the shaping power of our imagination. For Kant, as for the Pietists, the criteria for meaning lie within our minds, not in the world outside. But unlike these thinkers, he did not connect this sense experience to its creative grounding in God, or to the communal life that celebrated this. He drew two conclusions from this that influenced how subsequent theologians thought about art and theology. First, since God does not appear in our experience, we cannot have true knowledge of him. For Hamann (and later, Kierkegaard), our experience of God, though mediated through the historical life of faith, is formative for human existence. For Kant, it is the moral life that humans experience directly; God's existence is postulated in order to give meaning to this moral life. Second, for Kant, humans' experience of art and beauty is not part of their holistic sensual experience in the world, which ultimately connects us with the Creator; it is merely a matter of taste, which is an expression of feeling *(Gefühl)*. Thus, at the beginning of his *Critique of Judgment,* Kant wrote that judgments of beauty are a matter of the imagination as this is stimulated by desire. Such judgments are not logical but subjective, even if we mean them to have a universal validity. But in preserving, as he thought, a space for faith, Kant separated sense experience of the world from anything real beneath it. Individuals could not go deeply in their "listening" to the creation, because they could not assume that God was speaking there. For Kant, the noumena that stands behind experience (the phenomona) was forever out of reach. If this is so, in the end, as Feuerbach and Nietzsche would later conclude, the noumenal (or God) is essentially nothing at all.

It is hard to overemphasize the importance of Kant's revolution. Isaiah Berlin has called this "the greatest single shift in the consciousness of the West that has occurred."[10] In the realm of visual art, for example, the transition implied a shift from holding up a mirror to nature to expressing the artist's self — art was transformed, in M. H. Abrams' famous expression, from a mirror to a lamp.[11] As I noted in the first chapter, the focus of the creative process, and thus of the nature of

---

10. Isaiah Berlin, *The Roots of Romanticism,* ed. H. Hardy (Princeton: Princeton University Press, 1999), p. 1.

11. See M. H. Abrams, *The Mirror and the Lamp: Romantic Theory and the Critical Tradition* (New York: Oxford University Press, 1971).

beauty, now lies not on the side of the object but on the side of the subject. A great deal of the discussion in the first chapters of this book revolved around the tension between those who want to resist this revolution and those who want to explore the world Kant proposed. I followed Charles Taylor in insisting that even if we could, we would not want to go back before the subjective turn of modern art and aesthetics. So I want to argue that both the religious inheritance of these thinkers and the understanding of poetics that resulted provide positive resources for a contemporary poetic theology.

The philosopher who applied Kant's thinking, especially his language of form, most directly to aesthetics was Friedrich Schiller in his famous series of letters *On the Aesthetic Education of Man*.[12] These letters, originally written in 1795 for a Danish prince, became a basic text for a generation of Romantic writers and authors who sought to be liberated from what they saw as the tyranny of arid rationalism. The key, Schiller argued, is to train the sensibilities by the fine arts so that the truth of philosophy becomes a force, a spiritual energy. Here the role of the creative artist — and, by extension, the role of the creative "person" — takes on an importance that would only grow during the nineteenth century. Through the creative process, this spiritual energy flows from the artist: "From the pure ether of his daemonic nature, [it] flows forth from the well springs of beauty, untainted by the corruption of the generations" (52). This godlike capacity springs, in Kantian fashion, from two impulses, the sensuous and the formal: the one arouses, and the other brings harmony. These impulses operate in combination in the impulse of play (German, *Spieltrieb*, 75). Only in play does the person become complete, Schiller believed: "One is only wholly man [sic] when he is playing" (80). Only in this way does the person achieve a balance between the external necessity and internal freedom: "On the wings of imagination man leaves the narrow bounds of the present . . . in order to strive forward to an unbounded future" (116). Only in this way does one move toward the good and the true. Because contemplation is one's first free relation to the universe — here the influence of Kant is apparent — it allows the freedom of the spirit, in a leap of aesthetic play, to adorn oneself and all one does and makes, until society is united by beauty, "like," Schiller concludes in a paean of praise, "the pure Church" (140).

---

12. Friedrich Schiller, *On the Aesthetic Education of Man*, trans. Reginald Snell (New Haven: Yale University Press, 1954). Subsequent pages cited in the text refer to this work.

What is striking is the religious tone that pervades these letters. It is hard to imagine Schiller apart from the Pietist discourse which preceded and prepared for it. Schiller describes, he says, the path to divinity (*Weg zu Gottheit,* 63). One pursues this path by seeking within the power of creativity — though he acknowledges that the materials for this must come from without. This power of creativity forces nature to serve its interests; as Isaiah Berlin says, it crushes nature to its "beautiful unfettered morally directed will."[13] One can see here the path that Nietzsche will take. But still, Schiller is close enough to his Pietist influence to urge his readers to seek a relationship with the universe (a term that Schleiermacher will later use for God), mediated through beauty, which is also seen as grace (132). Moreover, play for Schiller is a kind of devotional practice, which makes possible a reconciliation of sense and reason, of freedom and necessity. In the final letters the tone evolves into a feverish (and evangelical) exhortation. Readers are urged to seek the highest level with an active imagination. Indeed, while Schiller appears to have lost the conscious sense of God's presence, the process of imaginative focus he proposes resonates with what the medieval mystics spoke of as "active prayer."

This devotional impulse had two important outcomes in the nineteenth century. One was to suggest that the objects created by this play could stand for something new. Notice that the signs of one's experience do not reveal the deep connection of experience with the creator, as in Hamann; they are a revelation of a new world altogether. As Charles Taylor put this, the highest objects of thought and feeling — God, love, and devotion — were "made objects of thought and consideration for us through expression in symbols."[14] The Romantic poets felt that "poetry" or works of art in general could constitute symbolic forms of the highest reaches of the human imagination. It is not far from this to the contemporary search for experiences which generate meaning — whether symbolic objects or practices. We take this for granted. We have all come to assume that some art exhibit, some trip or experience can be a carrier of some higher meaning for us. In this respect we are heirs of the Romantic conception of symbolism deriving from Schiller.

---

13. Berlin, *The Roots of Romanticism,* p. 79.
14. Charles Taylor, *A Secular Age* (Cambridge: Belknap/Harvard University Press, 2007), p. 756.

But the second innovation is equally important for subsequent reflection on aesthetics. The Romantic poets further developed a new range of experience that they called variously the depths or wellsprings of potential within the human spirit, an idea which they clearly inherited from the Pietists, and before them, the medieval mystics. That is, not only could Romantic poetry make new things exist for us, but it could do so in a new arena of experience. Charles Taylor sums up the Romantic achievement: "Through language in its constitutive use (let's call it poetry), we open up contact with something higher or deeper (be it God or the depths of human nature, desire, the Will to Power, or whatever) through language."[15] While this achievement was often misused, its impulse was not wrong, as Augustine knew: it is through the constitutive use of language, through its "poesis" (making), especially in the form of prayer and praise, that the human person can encounter God.

The Aesthetics of Schleiermacher

The theologian who first followed up these Kantian and Romantic insights in thinking about aesthetics and theology was Friedrich Schleiermacher (1768-1834). Raised in a strong Moravian environment, Schleiermacher had come to understand faith in a deeply emotional way. When he came to Berlin in 1796, while he was dismayed at the loss of faith among the artists and writers he knew, he was struck by their deep sense of the possibilities of creativity and language, which Schiller had described. But at the same time he was surprised by their assumption that this had no necessary connection with the Christian tradition. His response was published in 1799 in his famous *Speeches on Religion,* in which he sought to show that these artists' understanding of beauty was a kind implicit faith in God, if they could only see things properly. He may well have had Schiller's letters in mind in the Third Speech. Consider your experience, he says to these "cultured despisers." You know a kind of conversion when you encounter a great work of art: "By an immediate, inward illumination, the sense for the highest comes forth and surprises . . . by its splendor." Understanding that a great work of art could accomplish this, "you may perhaps be met by such a

---

15. Taylor, *A Secular Age,* p. 758.

beam of your own sun and turned to religion."[16] Perhaps, he tells these "cultured despisers," since religion and art stand together as kindred beings, you are "unintentionally, the rescuers and cherishers of religion."[17] Because your imaginative treatment of the outer world reflects the reality of a divine inner world, he wrote, this creation can itself be a sign of God's presence.

Creative art can reflect God, Schleiermacher believed, because the highest work of art is humanity itself:

> The greatest work of art has for its material humanity itself, and the Deity directly fashions it. For this work the sense must soon awake in many, for at present, He is working with bold and effective art. And you will be the temple servant when the new forms are set up in the temple of time. Expound the Artist then with force and spirit.[18]

Schleiermacher's claim recalls Hamann's view of our sense experience as a sign of a deeper presence, except that, for Hamann, this experience was a *result* of faith in the Crucified One rather than being a pre-reflective and intuitive experience of everyone.

Still, it was obvious that Schleiermacher's Moravian background played a critical role in his developing theological method. In particular, he spoke lovingly of their Singing Hours *(Singstunden)* in which verses from various hymns are strung together and sung so as to "make a tremendous religious effect.... Such a service is worth more than many beautiful sermons." And later in life he spoke of "that mystic tendency... which has been of so much importance to me, and supported and carried me through all the storms of skepticism."[19] Philip Stoltzfus has argued that these experiences together with his own musical inclination led Schleiermacher to use the notion of *Stimmung* or "the consciousness of a shared sense of mood" as key to the way one comes to experience God.[20]

Schleiermacher later broke with this Romantic circle because his

---

16. Friedrich Schleiermacher, *On Religion: Speeches to Its Cultured Despisers*, trans. John Owen (New York: Harper & Row, 1958 [1799]), p. 139.
17. Schleiermacher, *On Religion*, p. 141.
18. Schleiermacher, *On Religion*, p. 142.
19. Quoted in Philip Stoltzfus, *Theology as Performance: Music, Aesthetics, and God in Western Thought* (New York: T&T Clark, 2006), p. 52.
20. Stoltzfus, *Theology as Performance*, p. 244.

notions of individuality and of creativity were always religiously grounded. Still, as he later developed these ideas, it became clear that his aesthetic method was much more than an apologetic strategy for him. The fundamental impulse to knowledge, he was to argue in his *Dialektik* (1814), was aesthetic in nature. Though, following Kant, he believed that God could not be simply an object of knowledge, this transcendent reality must be assumed as the basis of all thinking and willing.[21] But how does this come to expression? He argued that the basic shaping power of knowledge was an "artwork" *(Kunstwerk)*, and that the basic picture we draw of the world is "art" *(Kunst)*.[22] Even before knowledge there is this prior human impulse which is reflected in what Schleiermacher called an "image" *(Bild)* that stimulates deep feeling, even before it passes over into language and becomes "signs" *(Zeichen)*.[23] For Schleiermacher, the basic impulse behind knowing and willing was aesthetic in character in that it was based on a sense of dependence on unconditioned reality that issues in feelings and perceptions. Moreover, the feeling response to the world, which Schleiermacher saw as active rather than passive (as it was in Kant) — what he called *Gefühl* — belongs to the essence of art. As Stoltzfus notes, "This move maintains the autonomy of art as a free production — a self-activity of self-consciousness, while at the same time affirming that this autonomy arises out of an active 'willingness to be affected.'"[24]

When Schleiermacher comes to write his systematic theology, the *Glaubenslehre (The Christian Faith)* (1830-31), he includes no discussion of the arts or even of music. But still he maintains that *Gefühl* or one's immediate self-consciousness forms the basis of all religion and ecclesiastical communion: his musical aesthetic method has become wholly theological.[25] For Schleiermacher, the very essence of religion was this "sense" of absolute dependence on God. Because of his Moravian back-

---

21. Though earlier he was influenced by Schelling's identity philosophy, he later broke with this implicit pantheism, arguing that God could not be the absolute source of thought without being transcendent over the world. See Friedrich Schleiermacher, *Dialektik*, ed. Ludwig Jonas (Berlin: G. Reimer, 1839), p. 186, and Martin Redeker, *Schleiermacher: Life and Thought*, trans. John Wallhausser (Philadelphia: Fortress Press, 1973), pp. 105-6.

22. Schleiermacher, *Dialektik*, p. 12.

23. Schleiermacher, *Dialektik*, p. 41 (from Schleiermacher's 1822 notes).

24. Stoltzfus, *Theology as Performance*, p. 89.

25. See the discussion in Stoltzfus, *Theology as Performance*, p. 92.

ground he was able to restore feeling to a central role in theology and to connect this with the aesthetic impulse to lay hold of the world through feeling. In light of this, one can appreciate Schleiermacher's attempt to resist arid rationalism and adopt an expressivist language for theology. But this also proved problematic. With his focus on interiority, the question inevitably arose as to whether there was any objective reference to this experience, or precisely how an experience of God was mediated through aesthetic experiences. Put another way, since religious awareness of God can be expressed in aesthetic categories, how is the experience "of God" different from that of listening to music?[26]

Knowledge, then, begins with an aesthetic sense, but for Schleiermacher it also finds its highest expression in aesthetic objects. He understood human consciousness to be a kind of organ by which the absolute comes to expression. Specific individuals in their creativity could become mediators of divine reality, just as the unified system of nature is a kind of "symbol" of God — this became the basis for his understanding of the Incarnation. These ideas come to their highest (early) expression in his *Christmas Eve Dialogue* (1805). Here the happy company of celebrants recognizes that they are bound together in the joy they share over the birth of the Redeemer. This led Schleiermacher to the conviction that human life could become, both individually and communally, a kind of ethical work of art, displaying the Christian life in its purest form.

This early work of Schleiermacher is especially important because the feelings of piety, expressed, in Moravian fashion, most purely in music, are not buried in the interior life of these figures — they are portrayed in their active and convivial life together. They are, as Stoltzfus argues, a kind of performed theology.[27] Schleiermacher understood that our dependence on God has to do in a fundamental way with our affections, and he also saw that our aesthetic experience provides a key to understanding this dependence, since our basic orientation to the world is affective. But he was unable to show how these relationships

---

26. Stoltzfus notes three related problems with Schleiermacher's project: his language of interiority; the relationship of discourses of receptivity and action; and the notion of theological writing as pure expression. See *Theology as Performance*, pp. 102-6.

27. See the excellent discussion in Stoltzfus, *Theology as Performance*, pp. 100-105, to which these comments are indebted. Stoltzfus points out that Schleiermacher needs to be understood in his Enlightenment context and his desire to move beyond theology as expressed in subject/object polarities.

were also fundamentally different. Further, Schleiermacher seems to imply that one appropriates this natural experience of God "directly" rather than indirectly, through the historical and embodied life of faith, as Kierkegaard would argue.

Nevertheless, Schleiermacher, stimulated by his Romantic context, advanced the discussion by arguing that creativity is fundamental to human knowing and willing, and that these in turn are evidence of God's presence. Though he often referred to this sense as "feeling" *(Gefühl)*, he did not mean emotions in the narrow sense but in the pre-theoretical sense of being dependent on God — something that would seem to resonate well with Augustine's use of the affections. Indeed, it might be said that Schleiermacher recovered the great Augustinian tradition of relating to the world by love and affection.

Here Schleiermacher could be said to anticipate twentieth-century developments that seek to understand the human processes of knowing and willing in a holistic way. His view that the creative response to the world is the basis for all knowing and doing has come to be widely accepted. Sociologist Margaret Archer is just one example. When she argues that the key to differentiation between self and the world "lies in human powers of sight and movement,"[28] she could be developing Schleiermacher's fundamental orientation. Sight and movement as we intuitively experience these are fundamental to theory and practice respectively. On this basis we can say that ritual activity, our making something of the world, may be fundamental not only to religious belief but to any fully human life in God's creation. In this respect, Schleiermacher, despite his views of God and the work of Christ, has much to teach us about a faith that is deeply grounded in the whole person, especially as this can be developed within a Trinitarian framework.

The Heritage of Schleiermacher: Paul Tillich

If Schleiermacher could be said to have a twentieth-century heir in his views of art in relation to God, it would surely be Paul Tillich (1886-1965), probably the most important theologian reflecting on art during

---

28. Margaret S. Archer, *Being Human: The Problem of Agency* (Cambridge: Cambridge University Press, 2000), p. 179. In addition, one could mention, among others, the work of Pierre Bourdieu and Antonio Damasio.

the twentieth century. This connection suggests that it is worthwhile to consider him here. If Schleiermacher sought an analogy between our dependence on God and an understanding of art and creativity, Tillich moved firmly from reflection on the meaning of art to seeing its relation to God. In part this reflected their different biographies. Schleiermacher went from a background of deep faith to a later exposure to art and artists; Tillich's experience with modern art during World War I was seminal in the development of his theological ideas. As he says later of this period,

> The visual arts became my hobby in the trenches of the First World War as an antidote against the enormous ugliness of life near the Front. But soon they became for me a realm of human creativity from which I derived categories both for my philosophical and for my theological thought.[29]

The way he proceeded initially to develop these categories was by beginning with a more general analysis of culture. In an important early article titled "The Idea of a Theology of Culture" (1919), he argued that a normative theology of culture had replaced what was formerly called theological ethics, in that it relates to all cultural forms — and not simply to what we call moral issues.[30] He defined religion as the "experience of the unconditioned . . . of absolute reality founded on the experience of absolute nothingness."[31] What is actual in religion is the meaning that comes to expression through symbols of culture, not some particular divine being.[32] Since art, at least potentially, expresses human meaning, it is an indicator of the spiritual situation of a given culture, and therefore it is intrinsically religious. Here is how Russell Manning explains this:

---

29. Paul Tillich, *On Art and Architecture,* ed. John and Jane Dillenberger (New York: Crossroad, 1987), p. 126.

30. Paul Tillich, "On the Idea of a Theology of Culture," in Victor Nuovo, *Visionary Science: A Translation of Tillich's 'On the Idea of a Theology of Culture' with an Interpretive Essay* (Detroit: Wayne State University Press, 1987), p. 22.

31. Tillich, "On the Idea of a Theology of Culture," p. 24. He later came to define this experience famously as "ultimate concern about the ground and meaning of being," which he admits is "rather near" to Schleiermacher's "feeling of absolute dependence." See Paul Tillich, *Systematic Theology,* vol. 1 (Chicago: University of Chicago Press, 1951), p. 42.

32. Tillich, "On the Idea of a Theology of Culture," p. 25.

"Since religion is that which participates in and reflects the unconditioned ground, its meaning comes to clearest expression in human self-interpretive activities, of which art is the best example."[33]

Tillich's experience was in many ways the archetypal experience of the twentieth-century person of nominal Protestant faith. As he looked at Botticelli's paintings in the Berlin museum, he saw what had once been "actual" in religion but was no longer accessible — these symbols had lost their impact. Meanwhile, many around him went into empty churches and agreed with Nietzsche that a desiccation had taken place. Tillich saw what Nietzsche had only felt: Whatever we believed about the history of art and religion, contemporary religion seemed to have lost its affective power. To fill this empty space, Tillich proposed his famous notion of "symbol." Unlike "signs," which point to reality, symbols participate in the power of what they represent. As Tillich put it, "They open up dimensions of reality which cannot be grasped any other way."[34] Art, then, is important to religion, but more particularly to the person of faith. Art that becomes symbolic of the ground of being can help people understand that they are grasped by the power of being, in a way parallel to the way that symbolic statements like "Christ is the Savior" function for believers.

But notice how Tillich's study of art gave him important vocabulary to express this. In his analysis of cultures, he came to believe that the notion of "style" was key to understanding these artistic symbols. For an encounter with style is "an encounter of man with his world, in which the whole man in all dimensions of his being is involved."[35] Tillich understood that religious symbols involve people in all their social and cultural interactions. In his day he saw in the progression from naturalism to idealism and finally to Expressionism a growing freedom from the encountered reality. The last of these is higher in that the artist shows something that cannot be expressed in any other way and is not limited by representational concerns. This began, he believed, with Cézanne, whose still lifes "embody a cosmic power which is religiously far superior to sentimental Jesus portraits."[36] Of all styles, Tillich pre-

---

33. Russell R. Manning, "Towards a Critical Reconstruction and Defense of Paul Tillich's Theology of Art," *Arts: The Arts in Religious and Theological Studies* 16, no. 2 (2004): 33.
34. Tillich, *On Art and Architecture*, p. 133.
35. Tillich, *On Art and Architecture*, p. 129.
36. Tillich, *On Art and Architecture*, p. 133.

ferred Expressionism, because he saw in it a "strong religious passion . . . striving . . . after expression."[37] Tillich's claim resonates with Jacques Maritain's assertion that the subjective turn in modern art increases the significance of art. Art's capacity for moral and even religious exploration is increased rather than diminished, but only as it is able to express some theological grounding, which Tillich found in the absolute and Maritain found in the person of Christ.

Thus Tillich believed that artists have a particular sensitivity to the spiritual situation of culture and can bring this to expression. Interestingly, he saw even in Cubism a kind of Expressionism that revealed a deep truth about its culture. Artists working in this mode had the awareness that the world "was falling to pieces. Its structure is disrupted, its meaning is lost. On the other hand, there is the tendency to uncover the basic elements of this world, and start, with their help, building something new."[38]

Although he often got his stimulus from thinking about secular art, Tillich did not neglect religious symbols — the speech and objects that are used in worship. He sees the process of forming separate religious symbols as a kind of psychological necessity in order for one to experience what is truly religious, both in the liturgy and in the culture. The production of specifically religious symbols becomes a counterweight to seeing culture as simply secular. These symbols resonate with a religious meaning that is found in the art of a culture. But in both cases what should be held on to is the religious meaning, not the religious — or symbolic — form.[39]

This final claim indicates both the strength and the weakness of Tillich's program. On the one hand, no one has done more to underline the "religious" dimension of culture, the idea that cultural forms inevitably express deep concerns that are ultimately religious in nature. Tillich believed that to understand the art of a particular period, one has to know as much as possible about the values and commitments of that time. In this sense, he believed that it was meaningless to speak of "secular culture," as though cultural forms could exist apart from the value commitments of the people who make up that culture. Further,

---

37. Tillich, "On the Idea of a Theology of Culture," p. 30.

38. Tillich, *On Art and Architecture*, p. 137. He admits that this portrays best the God-man who was crucified, but without resurrection or glory (p. 138). One might argue that in Cubism the Protestant iconoclastic tradition was finding expression.

39. Tillich, "On the Idea of a Theology of Culture," pp. 35-36.

he saw that the meaning of these commitments is often expressed most clearly in symbolic forms. Yet Tillich's concern to privilege the meaning over the forms, though reflecting his (very Protestant) concern with idolatry, seems to undermine the deep meaning he wants to express. As Michael Horton puts it, Tillich's symbolic language is finally "indicative" rather than "disclosive." Are statements like "God is the ground of being" and "Faith is ultimate concern" merely symbolic, or are they claims about the way things are? Horton is right to suggest that "without a non-symbolic referent, there can be no symbolic efficacy. . . . There must be some cognitive purchase for symbols and metaphors."[40] One might conclude, as with Schleiermacher, that if Tillich's sense of the connection between culture and spirituality is sound, why should we sever the connection between the meaning and its historical form — does this not undermine the cultural depth that these theologians celebrate? Symbolic practices are surely reflective of underlying commitments, but not any absolute commitment will do. For Christian believers, the reality of God's presence in Christ by the Holy Spirit provides the interpretive key to the poetic forms. Although we may start and learn from the poetic formations of artists, we must, like Dante, have recourse to Scripture to discern their full meaning.

Two further comments about Tillich will move our discussion forward. First, Tillich's views on art reflect his experience with a new set of institutions — museums, galleries, art auctions — all components of what we have come to call "the art world." Tillich can take his starting point from his visits to museums of modern art because, since Schleiermacher, these venues for art had come to represent a new and very powerful social world. The very emergence of this world is significant. During the course of the nineteenth century, the rationalism and necessity which Romantic poets repudiated came to be institutionalized in what is known as the Industrial Revolution. While it raised the standard of living in a way unprecedented in human history, those schooled in the Romantic tradition saw the noise and grime of industrial cities as an affront to human sensitivities. Influenced by John Ruskin (who, interestingly, was raised in a conservative Protestant envi-

---

40. Michael Horton, *Covenant and Eschatology: The Divine Drama* (Louisville: Westminster John Knox Press, 2002), pp. 60, 61, 64. One might make a similar criticism of the important work of Sallie McFague, who has stressed the importance of metaphoric language in theology. See *Speaking in Parables: A Study in Metaphor and Theology* (Philadelphia: Fortress Press, 1975).

ronment), intellectual leaders in the late nineteenth century came to define the realm of "culture" over against a burgeoning and unsavory "society" they saw developing around them. Ruskin defined this realm in terms of what he called vital beauty, "the felicitous fulfillment of function in living things, more especially of the joyful and right exertion of perfect life in man."[41] Museums and art galleries were to become the institutional setting for this new sphere of "culture." It was in this world that Tillich discerned the religious strivings he celebrated.

This provided Tillich with both an opportunity and a challenge, which leads to my second observation. Tillich employed the discourse favored by this world — style, Expressionism, Cubism, and so on — which tended to influence (or even shape) his theological claims. A common complaint lodged against Tillich's theological method, which he called "correlation," is that the questions he brings to theology tend to determine, rather than simply influence, the response from the side of the Gospel. As with his mentor, Schleiermacher, it sometimes appears that a new word from God cannot be spoken against the word of the culture. One can see this dynamic at work in the role Tillich gave to religious symbols. We noted that he believed that the production of specifically religious symbols could become a counterweight to seeing culture as simply secular. The importance of these symbols lay not in their intrinsic meaning, but in the way they resonated with a religious meaning that he had already found in the art of his culture. The danger is that the temporary reversal of the hermeneutical flow, which we considered earlier, here becomes permanent. God's word in Scripture has been displaced and resituated in the discourse of culture.

I noted earlier that Tillich described the way that religious symbols, such as "Christ as Savior," function like artistic symbols, which can help people understand that they are grasped by the power of being. But what if we turned this order around? What if artistic symbols derive their power from a deeper religious source that is represented by the Christian confession that Christ is the Savior? It is this claim that I will develop when we come to the contribution of Jacques Maritain below.

But it would not be fair either to Tillich or to our own project to leave things here. Tillich's concern to listen to cultural forms as a legiti-

---

41. From John Ruskin, *Modern Painters,* quoted in Raymond Williams, *Culture and Society, 1780-1950* (New York: Penguin Books, 1963), p. 145. Williams' book remains the best description of the split between culture and society that occurred during this period.

mate sphere of theological exploration must be applauded — it is as necessary as it is unusual. The fact is that the discourse arising in the art world bears significant overtones of the human hunger for God and, often, of deep insights into the human situation. I have already pointed out the religious sources of some of these impulses, but one might go further to explore the religious, even devotional nature that artistic practice has come to embody. It is these impulses and this nature that I want to highlight in these chapters. The issue again rests on the question of how God is at work in cultural forms, and how this is to be determined. We turn now to more recent thinkers influenced by Romanticism to see what we might learn from them.

Neo-Romantic and Neo-Medieval Views of Art and Creativity

Both Schleiermacher and Tillich saw aesthetic language as essentially theological in that — either as aesthetic impulse or as symbol — it is grounded in God's being. The thinkers we explore in this section also believe that aesthetics has a theological dimension, in a somewhat weaker sense, in that it draws one toward God. I refer to these as Neo-Romantic or Neo-Medieval in that they continue the Romantic quest to participate in the transcendent, and they frequently revisit much of the medieval discussion of God and beauty. Rather than privileging the experience of the symbol or impulse, as Schleiermacher and Tillich did, these will privilege the personal subject to which the symbol or story draws us, and who is the active source of its power. And in contrast to those theologians, the Neo-Romantics we look at may not think of the art object, and the practice of art, as theological in any direct sense. What is important is the joy and beauty these objects might evoke, an evocation which may move us toward (or away from) participation in God.

Clive Staples Lewis (1898-1963), though he was not a theologian or a philosopher of art, was arguably the most widely read and influential writer on these topics in the last century. And he would have resisted the designation as Romantic, which he believed represented "either the enjoyment of nature . . . or else the indulgence of a *Sehnsucht* [longing] awakened by the past, the distant and the imagined, but not believed, supernatural."[42] Lewis's own experiences of longing were more fleeting

---

42. C. S. Lewis, "Christianity and Culture," in *Christian Reflections,* ed. Walter Hooper (Grand Rapids: Wm. B. Eerdmans, 1967), p. 16.

and elusive, perhaps because, unlike the Romantic poets, he had a greater sense of the transcendence of the object longed for than of its immanence.[43] But in the end Lewis can say of his own experiences of longing, "I still cannot help thinking . . . that the experiences themselves contained, from the very first, a wholly good element. Without them my conversion would have been more difficult."[44] Although these experiences prepared the way, it was his conversion that finally mattered.

But what are these experiences to which he refers? And in what sense were they aesthetic? Or religious? To get at their importance, listen to Lewis describe the first such experience he remembers, when he was about six:

> As I stood beside a flowering currant bush on a summer day there suddenly arose in me without warning, as if from a depth not of years but of centuries, the memory of that earlier morning at the Old House when my brother had brought his toy garden into the nursery. It is difficult to find words strong enough for the sensation which came over me . . . [an] "enormous bliss" of Eden . . . of desire; but desire for what?[45]

This was followed by other such experiences — with the Green Hills of his childhood, an enchanted island, music which ravished the soul, stories of faeries — which could all carry this unspeakable desire. With his conversion Lewis came to believe that this desire was ultimately for the vision of God. Lewis addresses the relationship between these experiences in his famous essay "Transposition." He explains that what has

---

43. These differences are emphasized in the comparison of Lewis and Wordsworth in Daniel Kuhn, "The Joy of the Absolute," in *Imagination and the Spirit: Essays in Literature and the Christian Faith Presented to Clyde S. Kilby*, ed. Charles Huttar (Grand Rapids: Wm. B. Eerdmans, 1971), pp. 189-91. Although Kuhn believes that Lewis's sense of the immanent presence developed later, Owen Barfield has said that Lewis "in his theological utterances always emphasized the chasm between the creature and creatures, rather than anything in the nature of participation." See *Owen Barfield on C. S. Lewis*, ed. G. B. Tennyson (Middletown, Conn.: Wesleyan University Press, 1989), p. 111.

44. Lewis, "Christianity and Culture," p. 23. The footnote to this passage contains Lewis's famous reference to *Sehnsucht* as "spilled religion." "The unconverted man who licks [these drops] up . . . begins to search for the cup whence they were spilled."

45. C. S. Lewis, *Surprised by Joy: The Shape of My Early Life* (London: Fontana, 1955), p. 19.

happened in experiences of this kind is that this higher desire (for God) has been "transposed" onto lower ones. He believes that art, like sex, can convey a joy that cannot be explained merely by the aesthetic or erotic character of these experiences, even if, as embodied humans, our present desire for the "Beatific Vision" simply cannot outweigh our desire for beauty, sex, or food. But what, he asks, if every transposition is the reverse side of a higher fulfilling? What if all this provides a background for understanding the theological virtue of hope, so that, he concludes tellingly, our present embodied life may be the diminution, the symbol of something higher.[46]

Although at first glance Lewis might appear to be an ally in our search for a poetic method, in the end he is suspicious of such attempts. It is true that for Lewis the human experiences of longing or hunger can serve as the starting point of a religious journey. He was convinced, however, that if the experiences of this world give rise to longings which nothing in this world can satisfy, what satisfies these must lie *outside* the world — these longings are "news from a country we have not yet visited."[47] So the images and stories he shapes are meant to be bearers of this "quest," but they could just as easily serve other gods and other quests — there is nothing intrinsically religious about them. As he liked to say, stories in themselves are neither high nor low — they are good, as he put it, only as God's hands are on the reins.[48] What is important is that these images, replete with their aesthetic attractions, participate in the higher program of God's drawing people to himself, just as our lower feelings find their fulfillment in their participation in higher ones.[49]

Lewis by no means disparages the role of the image or the power of the aesthetic, just as he does not belittle the emotions linked to sex, food, and even mirth. Corbin Scott Carnell argues that unlike T. S. Eliot, Lewis seems to exult in the pleasures of the senses.[50] And so Lewis trea-

---

46. C. S. Lewis, "Transposition," in C. S. Lewis, *Screwtape Proposes a Toast, and Other Pieces* (London: Fontana, 1965), pp. 86-90.

47. Lewis, "Transposition," p. 98. He goes on to say that our desire for paradise is an indication that such a thing exists, not that we will necessarily inhabit it.

48. Lewis, *The Great Divorce*, quoted in Corbin Scott Carnell, *Bright Shadow of Reality: C. S. Lewis and the Feeling Intellect* (Grand Rapids: Wm. B. Eerdmans, 1974), p. 128.

49. Lewis actually calls the participation of lower emotions in higher ones "sacramental" in "Transposition," p. 83.

50. Carnell, *Bright Shadow of Reality*, pp. 129-30.

sures the images that he uses; he believed that myth was one of the only ways that the fallen imagination could be healed. But he believed that the aesthetic *quality* of stories — not their substance — is their most important feature. In his essay "On Stories," he insists that it was not the simple story-line that attracted him to his favorite stories but their "atmosphere." It was the danger, even the trappings of the story that drew him to reread his favorites. As he says of dramatic moments, "It is the quality of unexpectedness, not the fact, that delights us." He believed that this quality best portrays "regions of the spirit," an otherness, which resonates with a quality of our own soul. But these qualities are not sought as ends in themselves; they have no intrinsic symbolic role. They serve a single end: to pierce the reader's imagination.[51]

But do these objects have no religious end in themselves? Is it only the atmosphere and not the narrative that draws one beyond the ordinary life? In suggesting that the stories are shadow rather than figure, Lewis breaks with the Romantics' conception of "symbolism" that I have described, and with Augustine before them, because Lewis could not bring himself to see symbols as having any specifically religious (or Christian) content. It is symptomatic of this dichotomy that Lewis did not give much attention to his work as "Christian art"; he frequently said that he was a writer who happened to be a Christian. The Christian part came in naturally, as he would say. So he intended to make no contribution to "Christian aesthetics" — something he doubted even existed. But, at the same time, he felt his myth-making was getting at something that was really there. But this something, this longed-for paradise, existed on the *other side* of the door, somewhere beyond this world; meanwhile, we live in the world of diminution, the symbol. This "knobbly" world is not necessarily an illusion, as Plato would say (though one sees the distant echo of Plato in Lewis's work); it is a figure of paradise, but somehow other and separate from it. Art can speak of this region — even, like sex, stimulate our desire for it — but in the end it cannot participate in it.

If Schleiermacher and Tillich make too much of the dependence of aesthetic experience on God, Lewis appears to make too little of it. Indeed, the experience itself is of no intrinsic importance. Its value lies only in its incorporation into the properly theological realm of God's

---

51. C. S. Lewis, "On Stories," in C. S. Lewis, *Of This and Other Worlds,* ed. Walter Hooper (London: Collins, 1982), pp. 35-42; the quotation is from p. 42.

general call, but it cannot be seen to participate in that call. Apparently our project of poetic theology would have little attraction for Lewis, despite his recognition of the power of poetry.

More helpful for our purposes is the recent work of David Bentley Hart, an Orthodox writer on aesthetics. Like Lewis, Hart believes that art, beauty, and image speak of something that is really there, but he wants to draw a stronger connection between the image and the divine reality. While he is no Romantic, he also believes, with Lewis, that desire is constitutive of our being: "Desire is the energy of our movement, and so of our being."[52] He also agrees with the argument I am making that at a deep level this desire corresponds to the call of God. But, unlike Lewis, he would insist that beauty speaks directly of God because it expresses the participation of all things in God. (Early in his book Hart acknowledges his debt to Radical Orthodoxy, whose views on beauty we discussed in the first chapter.) Hart has relatively little to say about the practices and objects of art; but he shapes a framework with large implications for art-making as well as for the larger practices of Christian living.

Hart's argument centers on the question of beauty — widely appealed to, he avers — and its place in the Christian tradition. Beauty is important, he believes, because it "adheres to every moment of the Christian story" (4) and is one with its truth. Notice the way he wants to connect beauty directly with the narrative — that is, the aesthetic substance — not simply with its quality, as Lewis does. In fact, he believes that the Christian faith is ethical because it is first aesthetic, which for him means that it opens up being to love and knowledge only within the context, the ordering of beauty. It invites a desire that is moral because it is not disinterested (15), and that is poetic before it is rational (132, 133).

The designation of desire as moral and not disinterested provides an opening into Hart's treatment of beauty, as well as a sharp contrast with the modern tradition of disinterested beauty. For Hart, beauty is always interested because it is intimately related to God as its source and end. As a result, it is objective, since it is given in creation and thus has phenomenological priority; it is the true form of distance, filling

---

52. David Bentley Hart, *The Beauty of the Infinite: The Aesthetics of Christian Truth* (Grand Rapids: Wm. B. Eerdmans, 2003), p. 190. Subsequent pages will be cited in the text.

and embracing intervals with the plenitude of love and peace, which have their source in God; and therefore beauty evokes desire, eros, and agape together, a desire that "delights in the distance of otherness" (20). I find this particularly significant. Because beauty draws and attracts (ultimately toward God), for the Christian, otherness and distance are not problems to be overcome, as they are in much contemporary philosophy.

This connectional view of beauty leads Hart to develop a unique view of symbolism, one with great significance for art and faith. He wants to resist a reductive symbolism that abstracts from the particularity of things. While he does not dismiss a symbolism that captures the immediacy of splendor, radiance, and mystery, as these are made manifest in the particularity of created things, he proposes a symbolism that arrests the surface force of the aesthetic in order to disclose the depths in which it participates — one that is more important for what it does than what it is (24, 35). By contrast, he notes, Tillich's symbolism does nothing to clarify the concrete but reduces it to abstractions — for example, to "the ground of being," which Hart suggests is no less idolatrous than the belief that God's gracious acts in history are really acts (27). "The content of Christian faith abounds in particularities, concrete figures, moments like the crucifixion, which cannot simply be dissolved into universal truths of human experience.... The 'symbol,' extracted from the complexities of its many contexts, is ... the paralysis of beauty" (27-28). Here is a fruitful notion of events, and presumably artistic re-interpretations of these events, that open the way to God, providing imaginative doors through which one can walk. And here is a helpful explication of symbols which represent the connections which beauty illumines. Moreover, Hart's focus on relationality and distance allows us to think about symbolism in ways other than ontological participation, which we rejected earlier, and opens the way to a symbolism deriving from the Trinitarian life of God.

Hart seeks an alternative rhetoric and a fuller vision than that which has resulted from the abyss — which, he believes, Kant opened. That philosopher's opening made possible a variety of other kerygmas — of obligation, of difference, of the will to power, and so on — all of which deny the gift of love expressed in God's creative and redemptive work. But this work constitutes a particular narrative, with hard edges: "The Christian story," Hart writes in words that Lewis would approve, "is the true story of being, and so speaks of that end toward which all human thought and every natural human act are originally oriented" (31). In contrast to Lewis's story, this story constructs meaning *on this side* of the wardrobe door.

In this substantial work, Hart proceeds to sketch a systematic theology that is grounded in God's works, both internal and external to his being, which are "perfectly expressive signs of [his] delight" (131). Christ is the form that persuades, made visible in the resurrection and brightened by the Spirit (147, 335, 203). The Trinity is a perichoresis of love, infinite and — contrary to much recent discussion of God — apathetic, precisely so that God can be "the fullness of love dwelling within our very being" (166). These sketches suggest that a focus on a theology of beauty might allow us to rethink systematic theology in new ways, a project to which I will return in the conclusion of this book.

Still, Hart's project raises questions. Over against typical Protestant theology and unlike Lewis, it is the gaze, vision, that controls his theology. Although indebted to Plato, Hart's gaze is not a controlling scrutiny, as Foucault feared. Rather, he wants to reverse Kant's revolution. He wants to turn away from the subject toward the "sun of the good."[53] He wants a gaze that positively embraces the splendor of God's gifts. "And what one sees and hears, if desire seeks it, is the creature's participation in God, the fountainhead of being" (144). While resisting the claim that creatures participate in God, we can appreciate Hart's insistence on the symbol affirming the particularity; adhering, as he says, to "every moment of the Christian story" suggests an alternative way of understanding the "symbolic participation" that we are pursuing in these pages.

But Hart's project has a further limitation. Lewis and Hart both do well to rehabilitate the role of desire in theological reflection. But desire cannot be simply affirmed without qualification, because it can seek the wrong object; the gaze, after all, can *become* controlling. A weakness of Hart's bracing vision is that the creature seems always drawn toward the light as an incontrovertible fact rather than a broken possibility. For Hart, sin is merely the suppression of the gift, something which dulls the senses (268), rather than any active disobedience or rebellion. But if this is so, how do we account for the evil so visible on

---

53. Hart, *The Beauty of the Infinite*, p. 137. Hart says of Kant's revolution: "Now the phenomena would revolve around the unyielding earth of apperception; again, we would stand at the center" (p. 137).

every hand? And what is its aesthetic potential? As we have noted, a simple appeal to beauty is insufficient — God's presence cannot be directly discerned in a fallen world; it must be appropriated through the uncertainties and struggles of living by faith.

Still, in a sense Hart is doing what no other theologian in this chapter has been able to do: connect a rigorous aesthetics with a strong theological framework. Writing early in the twenty-first century, Hart is able to make use of the revival of Trinitarian theology that marks the last half of the twentieth century, which is the subject of the next chapter. In one sense we might propose that the nineteenth century rediscovered a sensibility and developed a discourse that subsequent discussions of art and theology must employ. These writers show ways in which aesthetic experience is fundamental to human life in the world and the substantive role that symbolism can play in human flourishing. But what they were unable to do was to adequately connect this with a sufficient account of the presence and activity of God. One might put it this way: While they restored the importance of the affections and devotion, they were unable to properly direct that devotion theologically. While they recognized the role of spiritual practices, they overlooked the need to recover the ground of these in the Triune God. In the following chapter I want to explore the possibilities for this recovery more fully.

CHAPTER 5

Twentieth-Century Aesthetics: In Search of a Theological Voice

The nineteenth-century developments, especially those that go under the name of Romanticism, are varied and complex. But I have argued that the fundamental sensibility developed there is both consistent with and, in some ways, a development of important aspects of the Christian tradition. There were many besides Nietzsche who were anxious to argue these developments invalidated traditional Christianity. Others, like Ralph Waldo Emerson, believed that the newly awakened hungering depths, detached from any specific account of Christ or God, were religion enough for the modern person. But while it produced its typical deviations, which we reviewed in Chapter One, it fashioned, like it or not, the discourse by which the contemporary person, whether religious or not, defines himself or herself.

The challenge I want to face in this chapter is this: How can we frame this discourse in a way that is consistent with the Christian tradition? I have engaged previously with those who deny that this is possible, and some of them will reappear in this chapter. But first let me restate my thesis: This sensibility of affections and inwardness resonated with significant aspects of the Christian tradition — specifically, its long mystical and liturgical tradition and its impulse to engage cultural wisdom, what we are calling the *theologia poetica*. But, initially at least, this was not accompanied by the theological framework that had sustained and developed these earlier movements — it kept the practices of devotion, but lost their object and ground. In this chapter, then, I will propose theological parameters in which an adequate poetic theology may be recovered and sustained — in the process making use of resources from both Catholic and Protestant theological traditions.

BUILDING BLOCKS FOR A POETIC THEOLOGY

Modern Catholic Theologies of Aesthetics

David Bentley Hart, whom we met in the last chapter, makes a great deal of use of Thomas Aquinas. He is able to do this, in large part, because of the revival of Thomism in the twentieth century. Neo-Thomist thinkers sought to make these medieval resources available for modern persons. Rather than focusing on the beauty and joy that we desire, as Hart and Lewis did, these thinkers, taking their cue from Christological and Eucharistic formulations, focused on the object of beauty itself — on the work, as carrier and extension of God's presence. The discourse of these thinkers is what we might call sacramental. In the object itself, the form, the visible and the invisible are fused in a way that can, potentially, mediate the presence of God — the object itself can be a bearer of God's presence in a special sense that none of the previous modern writers proposed.[1] And their starting points in understanding what we might call sacramentals were the liturgical practices and sacraments of the church as these were understood in the medieval period.

In the Middle Ages, the arts existed as "craft" *(ars)* or as the liberal arts taught at the university. Nevertheless, discussions of beauty and what we call aesthetics were prominent, and they followed directly from the fundamental theology of that period. Thomas Aquinas held that goodness and beauty are related. He wrote, "Goodness expresses perfection, which is something desirable, and hence it expresses something final."[2] Note the role that desire plays in connecting with what is "final." Beauty and goodness fundamentally are identical, Aquinas went on to say, in that they are based upon the same form of the good, but they differ logically:

> Goodness properly relates to appetite (goodness being what all things desire). . . . On the other hand, beauty relates to a cognitive power, for those things are said to be beautiful which please when seen (Lat. "id quod visum placet"). Hence beauty consists in due proportion, for the senses delight in things duly proportioned, as in what

---

1. The most obvious exception from the last chapter would appear to be the role that the icon might play for Hart, who is Eastern Orthodox. Interestingly, however, Hart does not engage in any extended discussion of icons in his book.

2. Thomas Aquinas, *Summa Theologica*, Question 1, Part 5, Reply to Objection 1, in *Basic Writings of Saint Thomas Aquinas*, ed. Anton C. Pegis (New York: Random House, 1945), p. 43.

is like them — because the sense too is a sort of reason, as is every cognitive power.³

In this famous definition, Thomas connects the good (and thus morality) with desire and appetite, but, unlike Kant, designates the perception of beauty as a cognitive power. Consistent with Aquinas's empiricism, seeing colors, shapes, and forms is recognized as a kind of knowing, involving a cognitive process in its own right. As Umberto Eco explains this: "Aesthetic knowledge has the same kind of complexity as intellectual knowledge, because it has the same object, namely, the substantial reality of something."⁴

The most substantial modern exponent of these medieval ideas — which provide such a contrast with Kant's aesthetics of feeling — is the French philosopher Jacques Maritain (1882-1973), whom we introduced earlier. In his early and influential essay *Art and Scholasticism* (1920), Maritain points out how wide-ranging (one might say holistic) medieval discussions of beauty were, for they included references to shipbuilding and cabinetmaking as well as painting and sculpture. In contrast to modern ideas of art, in the Middle Ages art belonged to the practical order; it was a making ordered to a particular practical end. "The sphere of making is the sphere of Art, in the most universal sense of this word."⁵ The end of this is inherent in the work; everything done is done for the sake of the work. With an eye on the twentieth-century's pursuit of pleasure, Maritain notes that the ennui of living and willing ceases at the door of the workshop (9). So, although art belongs, as Thomas has said, to the intellectual order, it is "a habitus of the practical intellect" (12) — what Maritain calls a kind of prudence.⁶ Following certain fixed rules, what Maritain calls a "lived participation in logic" (49), the artisan of that day created more beautiful things, while "he adored himself less" (22). This beauty was an object of intelligence, but

---

3. Aquinas, *Summa Theologica*, Question 5, Part 1a, p. 47.

4. Umberto Eco, *Art and Beauty in the Middle Ages,* trans. Hugh Bredin (New Haven: Yale University Press, 1986), p. 73. Although he differs with Maritain's designation of this as "intuition," Eco believes aesthetic perception to be a dialogue with its object, which must be "won" (p. 82).

5. Jacques Maritain, *"Art and Scholasticism" and "Frontiers of Poetry,"* trans. Joseph W. Evans (New York: Scribner's, 1962), p. 8. Subsequent pages will be cited in the text.

6. On this, see Ralph McInerny, *Art and Prudence: Studies in the Thought of Jacques Maritain* (Notre Dame: University of Notre Dame Press, 1989).

it was also a reflection of divine beauty; though made out of the creation, it drew the soul beyond the created order. Although Maritain recognized the spiritual power of the poetic, he also saw the necessity for it to be grounded in God — something he recognized the Romantic sensibility did not always appreciate. As he said,

> Poetry (like metaphysics) is spiritual nourishment; but of a savor which has been created and which is insufficient. There is but one eternal nourishment. Unhappy you who think yourselves ambitious, and who whet your appetites for anything less than the three Divine Persons and the humanity of Christ. It is a mortal error to expect from poetry the super-substantial nourishment of man. (132)

His focus on the habitus or craft of art, and its responsibility to its human and divine context, made Maritain's work immediately influential. Eric Gill in England and Georges Rouault in France were among the many influenced by the thinking represented in this early work.

In a later book, Maritain developed some of the implications of this early work.[7] Art, he noted, is "the creative or producing, work-making activity of the human mind" (3). He defined poetry in the more general sense that resonates with the argument we are making: it is "that intercommunication between the inner being of things and the inner being of the human Self which is a kind of divination" (3). So poetry is the "secret life" of all the arts. When there is a genuine interaction between humanity and nature, beauty is involved, and poetry is the result (4, 5). But this is true, Maritain claims, only when humanity is illuminated by the incarnation of God in Christ. The self emerges in Western art only in relation to theological formulations of the person of Christ. Humanity first saw the self as object in the revelation of Christ's divine self (especially in the great councils that defined Christ's nature); then humanity came to understand the self as subject; and finally it came to see the creative subjectivity of the person as poet or artist (20).

Working from this Christological basis, Maritain is able to develop a high view of human subjectivity. The self is represented not merely in the flux of superficial feelings, but in a deep ontological sense, in "the substantial totality of the human person" (82). This is embodied in po-

---

7. Jacques Maritain, *Creative Intuition in Art and Poetry* (Cleveland and New York: Meridian Books, 1954). Subsequent pages will be cited in the text.

etic creation: "In a way similar to that in which divine creation presupposes the knowledge God has of his own essence, poetic creation presupposes . . . a grasping, by the poet, of his own subjectivity, in order to create" (82). And in God's own bonding with creation in Christ, the personal depths of creation are revealed. So even in the modern promotion of the self, the artist cannot escape the influence of Christ. Thus modern art brings with it a new potential by which the inner meaning of things is grasped through the interaction with the artist's self — both are manifest in the work (25). Referring to the giants of modern art, Maritain says, "At the root of the creative act there must be a quite particular intellectual process without parallel in logical reason, through which Things and the Self are grasped together by means of a kind of experience or knowledge which has no conceptual expression and is expressed only in the artist's work" (29).

This theological grounding of the artist's work, both in creation and in the selfhood of Christ, makes possible a striking view of the process of art-making. Working with the disciplined human capacities (what the medievals called habitus), the artist ferrets out the inner workings of nature, which is "in its own way the labor of divine creation" (50). Maritain called this knowledge-with-things "connaturality." That is, the soul of the artist seeks itself by "communicating with things," effecting knowledge through "affective union" (83). Here Maritain builds on his medieval sources by integrating them with a modern understanding of the self. Maritain can acknowledge here the developments of the Romantic period even as he discerns the fundamental theological error of Romanticism. By the person, he means "subjectivity in its deepest ontological sense, the substantial totality of the human person, a universe unto itself, which the spirituality of the soul makes capable of containing itself through its own immanent acts" (82). But this also rests on a clearly Christian view of creation as revealed in the Incarnation, which always contains more than it shows.[8]

For Maritain, beauty emerges out of this "connatural" knowledge of the self and things. It "spills over or spreads everywhere, and is everywhere diversified" (124). Notice that beauty emerges from the work — from below, as it were, not from above. Even if it reflects the radiance of

---

8. See the excellent discussion of this in Rowan Williams, *Grace and Necessity: Reflections on Art and Love* (London: Continuum, 2005). Williams rightly notes that Maritain has not received the recognition that he deserves for his insights on modern art.

the transcendent, as Thomas would say, it is a spontaneous product of the affective union of self and nature which comes to expression in the work. This allowed modern art to have great potential, but also exposed it to great dangers. Modern art's temptations were, Maritain believed, to favor the anti-rational rather than the super-rational, to seek beauty at the expense of the beauty of the human form, or to choose the self over the thing seen — all distortions that have been visible in the subsequent history of modern art.

Maritain makes a critical contribution by framing the medieval discussion in ways that contribute to contemporary thought. He has been criticized for promoting an uncritical modernism, especially in connection with Vatican II.[9] But he pointedly avoids the modern dichotomies by locating art in the larger arena of human work, and in the medieval idea of knowing by making, which, he argues, continues the divine work of creation. Still, he is also able to embrace modern developments, especially notions of the self, by arguing for their Christological grounding. In other words, he claims that this connatural knowledge, possible because of the artist's creation in the image of God, is finally only understandable in Christological terms — that is, in the actuality of God's union with the creature.

Here Maritain makes a claim with profound implications for our understanding of modern art. We have seen that the Romantic poets developed further the inward turn of the Reformation and the Pietists. They were able to formulate their aesthetic symbols within a new register of subjectivity. This development is often lamented as the origin of both contemporary hedonism and the autonomous self. But I believe this oversimplifies these developments. Whatever its dangers, the modern exploration of subjectivity is a cultural reality of enormous significance. And it is in the arts where this is seen most clearly. Precisely at this point Maritain suggests a constructive way of understanding these developments. In his later book he calls the modern period the fourth phase of the sense of the human self. Here "the process of internalization through which human consciousness has passed from the concept of the Person to the very experience of subjectivity comes to fulfillment: it reaches the creative act itself" (25). This provides a revelation not only of the subjectivity of the artist, but of what Maritain calls the "inner

---

9. See Tracey Rowland, *Culture and the Thomist Tradition: After Vatican II* (London: Routledge, 2003).

meaning of things." These, he says, "are grasped through the artist's self and both are manifested in the work together" (25).

As we noted earlier, though he does not develop this in the detail we might wish, and while we might resist the implicit notion of progress, Maritain's description of a work of art is especially suggestive for our project of poetic theology. A work of art — indeed, any creative project or practice — brings together the perception of the person with the deep meaning of things made. This provides a model for an understanding of participation that avoids the ontological dilemmas of Plato's notion of *methexis* (participation in eternal forms) — the central problematic of Platonic thought. The artist's work is best understood on the analogy of incarnation rather than participation. It also suggests a way of understanding Romantic notions of the creative self not simply as a reduction but as a deepening of human experience, and an understanding of the artwork as symbolic of this consciousness. For Maritain, the artist's participation in the work echoes God's own participation in the created order, so that art becomes an embodiment of human perceptions as these are joined with the material, producing a form of knowledge that is not expressible in any other way.

Let me try to put this into my more general argument. Given a kind of symbolic fusion, one could argue that people's aesthetic (even their recreational) projects express their connaturality with the created order. They express themselves, as we say, through these. And it follows that if we are to have any real knowledge of Adam or Lisa, whom we met in the first chapter, we must take their projects seriously, not simply as expressive of their commitments but as signs of openness to whatever meaning may lie beyond this.

There is clearly more work to be done here. If we grant that art-making echoes God's presence in the created order, how is this active presence understood? Further, how is it possible for God to be present (or referenced) in the art object? The Catholic perspective, we have seen, assumes a more direct connection and tends to see the object sacramentally. The focus on *form* as carrier of deep and theological meaning is advanced by the best-known of the twentieth-century Catholic writers on aesthetics: Hans Urs von Balthasar (1905-1988), to whom we now turn.[10]

---

10. See his seven-volume work titled *The Glory of the Lord: A Theological Aesthetics*. It was first published in German (from 1961 on); English translations began appearing in 1982.

While Hart acknowledges his dependence on Balthasar,[11] he does not give the beauty of form the centrality that it has for Balthasar, nor does Hart share with Balthasar the latter's admiration for Karl Barth. In fact, Balthasar takes as the starting point of his discussion of beauty Barth's treatment of "Glory" in *Church Dogmatics,* II/I.[12] One can see in this great passage the central themes of Balthasar's work. Barth says that God's being is eternal in glory. And it is his dignity "to make himself conspicuous and everywhere apparent as the One who is" (640). God's glory is "the inner essential objective which a man has and which expresses itself in the force of his appearance and activity, in the impression that he makes on others. *Kabod* is light, both as source and radiance" (642). Barth goes on to stress that this radiance "reaches all other beings and permeates them" (646), though he adds — characteristically — that we must wait for the revelation of this. "The creature has no voice of its own" (648). Beauty is the unique form and "explanation" that this glory takes, which awakens joy. If this is missing, Barth asks, "what becomes of the evangelical element of the evangel" (655)? In words that particularly anticipate Balthasar, Barth stresses that the persuasive, convincing form of God is to be seen in Jesus Christ. "What is reflected in this determination of the relationship between the divine and human nature in Jesus Christ is the form, the beautiful form of the divine being (664)," and the Son in his relation to the Father is the "eternal archetype and prototype of God's glory in his externalization" (667).

In the end, Barth's Protestant reticence keeps him from recognizing the significance of this form for the spiritual life. For him, the form of beauty is not self-evident; it is only given to us via the cross and the Resurrection (665, 666). The form is mediated further by the life of faith. Moreover, Barth knew that the danger of aestheticism was real; the study of beauty is, after all, a parenthesis to the study of theology (653, 666).[13] And Barth's reserve is eschatological as well as ontological. As we await the final revelation of beauty, we are surrounded by the

---

11. Hart calls his own work "marginalium on some pages" of Balthasar. See David Bentley Hart, *The Beauty of the Infinite: The Aesthetics of Christian Truth* (Grand Rapids: Wm. B. Eerdmans, 2003), p. 29.

12. Karl Barth, *Church Dogmatics: The Doctrine of God,* ed. and trans. G. W. Bromiley and T. F. Torrance (Edinburgh: T&T Clark, 1957), II/I. Subsequent pages cited in the text refer to this work.

13. See the helpful discussion of this in Richard Viladesau, *Theological Aesthetics: God in Imagination, Beauty, and Art* (New York: Oxford University Press, 1999), pp. 26-29.

earthly form of beauty, the church (676). But beyond this tribute to the earthly form of the Bride of Christ, Barth gives us no help in developing an aesthetics of church — something I will attempt in a later chapter. In fact, he betrays his continuing iconoclastic temperament in another place when he says, "Images and symbols have *no place at all* in a building designed for Protestant worship."[14]

Balthasar finds inspiration in Barth's theology, but corrects his Protestant reserve by pointing to what is for him the fundamental weakness of that tradition: its denial of the analogy of being. In fact, Balthasar's work is intended, in part, to correct Protestant asceticism, which involves "the expulsion of contemplation from the act of faith, the exclusion of 'seeing' from 'hearing' . . . and the relegation of the Christian to the old age which is passing away."[15] He too recognizes the dangers of aesthetics (which had become secularized, he thinks, due to Romanticism and Idealism [80]), but he argues that when this discussion is placed in the larger perspective of Christian theology, that danger is avoided. For this reason he insists that one needs to read the first volume of *The Glory of the Lord* in light of subsequent volumes, where it becomes clear that theology culminates in the event and drama of the play of redemption in which we are involved.[16]

Balthasar begins his reflection by recovering a comprehensive (Thomist) doctrine of being. That is, the form appears beautiful only because the delight it arouses is "founded upon the fact that, in it the truth and goodness of the depths of reality itself are manifested and bestowed" (118) — beauty is what gives goodness its attraction. Moreover, the beauty of this form is particularly visible in the epiphany of God in salvation history, and supremely in the incarnation of the form of God in Christ (124). Balthasar develops this theological aesthetics in two ways. One is a theory of vision, which is a "theory about the perception of the form of God's self-revelation"; the other is a theory of rapture,

---

14. Karl Barth, "The Architectural Problem of Protestant Places of Worship," in André Biéler, *Architecture in Worship*, trans. Odette and Donald Elliot (Philadelphia: Westminster Press, 1965), p. 93, his emphasis.

15. Hans Urs von Balthasar, *The Glory of the Lord,* vol. 1: *Seeing the Form,* trans. Erasmo Leiva-Merikakis (Edinburgh: T&T Clark, 1982), p. 70. Subsequent pages will be cited in the text.

16. See also Hans Urs von Balthasar, *Theo-Drama: Theological Dramatic Theory,* vol. 4: *The Action,* trans. Graham Harrison (San Francisco: Ignatius Press, 1994 [1980]). And cf. Viladesau, *Theological Aesthetics*, pp. 30-32.

which is a theory about the incarnation of God's glory and "the consequent elevation of man to participate in that glory." The former is fundamental theology; the latter is dogmatic theology (125). This venturing forth of God and the human return to God, reminiscent of the medieval procession and return, constitutes the very core of Balthasar's theology and is reflected in the major sections of volume 1: "The Subjective Evidence" and then "The Objective Evidence." The former describes perception as a fully human act of encounter through the senses; "in Christianity God appears to man right in the midst of worldly reality" (365); the latter describes the revelation in Christ precisely in its quality as form as "the perfection of the form of the world" (432).

Balthasar's consistent focus on biblical material — here too he follows Barth — disciplines his dependence on the Greek philosophical tradition, but both contribute to his theology. From these materials he fashions an aesthetic theory — the power of beauty speaks of the divine beauty in which it is grounded — and a theological aesthetics: the highest art is the revelation of God in history, especially as seen in the form of Christ. Whereas Maritain focuses on the act of creative intuition, Balthasar believes that the beauty of God is discovered in the act of reception and adoration, which for Balthasar is not only the center of theology but "also the heart of the individual's existential situation."[17] In other words, Balthasar wants to locate the center of aesthetics in worship. While both Balthasar and Maritain depend on modern conceptions of the self, Balthasar's contribution is to an aesthetic theology rather than to theological aesthetics. It is in the form of God's revelation, especially as this is visible in Jesus Christ, that the glory of God's being is glimpsed, and this constitutes the goal of the human search. While there are important implications here for the project of poetic theology, Balthasar makes no direct attempt to contribute to the question of how the process of human creativity participates in the aesthetic form of revelation — indeed, he has surprisingly little to say about the actual process of art-making.

But there is a further reservation about Balthasar that a Reformed project of aesthetics must register. We noted above that Balthasar, in part, is seeking to counter a Protestant asceticism, which, he says, banished contemplation from the act of faith. There is certainly some truth in this charge (and this will be the subject of a later chapter), but still, I

---

17. Balthasar, "In Retrospect," quoted in Viladesau, *Theological Aesthetics*, p. 33.

would claim, human brokenness has resulted in such diminished spiritual capacity that direct appeal to a vision of glory is problematic. The project I want to encourage is the integration of contemplation into the process of walking and living by faith. For contemplative practices — practices and objects that spark joy and affection — not only represent an endeavor which most readily connects with the contemporary imagination; they are, I want to argue, important as (potential) theological sites in their own right.

Non-Western Aesthetic Sensitivities

Here we need to return to nineteenth-century conversations to pick up an element that, to this point, we have not touched on: cultural and ethnic diversity. Much of what we have said might be construed to mean that the Western trajectory of aesthetics is privileged. And many in this tradition would have assumed that it is. Balthasar and others like him are continuing a conversation that began in classical Greco-Roman culture and that has continued to shape Western thinking on aesthetics up to the present. But already in the nineteenth century Karl Wilhelm von Humboldt and Johann Gottfried Herder were beginning to explore the possibilities and potential of cultural difference. Herder in particular, employing an organic model, proposed an internally related social entity that develops over time and becomes conscious of itself as a people *(Volk)* through the use of a common language; much of this he had learned from Johann Georg Hamann.[18] Modern anthropology works from a more strictly empirical basis, but the idea of cultural and ethnic diversity, however porous the boundaries among these entities, has become a commonplace in cultural reflection.

In one sense, recognition of ethnic diversity continues the Kantian project, in which our experience of the world is shaped and organized by factors we bring to experience, these factors now understood to include a variety of cultural values and practices. Theologians still are apt to worry that the empirical differences entail a kind of relativism that

---

18. See F. M. Barnard, *Herder's Social and Political Thought: From Enlightenment to Nationalism* (Oxford: Clarendon Press, 1965). Herder believed that "language is the medium through which man becomes conscious of his inner self, and at the same time it is the key to the understanding of his outer relationships" (p. 57).

precludes universal norms. Tracey Rowland, whose discussion of Vatican II we considered in the first chapter, seems to feel that any recognition of cultural diversity risks what she calls an "explosive problematic" which implies that because each culture is unique and possesses intrinsic merit, one is barred from introducing Christian ideas into them. In this sense, she argues, Western culture is privileged because it was built upon classical Greco-Roman culture, which was more open to the Gospel because of its capacity for self-transcendence. Thus, Rowland claims (echoing Joseph Ratzinger — now Pope Benedict XVI), the Greco-Roman heritage of Christendom is "indispensable."[19]

We have already challenged this easy dismissal of the substantial issues raised by the Romantic writers. There is much about Herder's views of culture that would be subject to revision, even to serious critique. Twentieth-century thinkers have trouble with the organic model of development that nineteenth- century philosophers favored, with its teleological reading of history — subject as it was to so much abuse during the Nazi period. Still, one has a certain sympathy with Isaiah Berlin when he says of Herder's views, "By enabling this doctrine to emerge, Herder did plunge a dagger in the heart of European rationalism, from which it never recovered."[20] While it denied a universal rationality, Herder's doctrine made two constructive moves that are suggestive for a theology of culture. First, Herder suggested that people are related not simply through institutional arrangements but through what he termed internal relations — all that comes to expression in their language and religious practices. This suggests an understanding of culture as a common human project defined by its relationships, which for Christians include the underlying involvement with the redemptive actions of God. Second, Herder proposed a unifying notion of power *(Kraft)* as the basic idea of his theological cosmology, which was for him the manifestation of the continuing presence of God.[21] One does not have to accept the full Hegelian and developmental implications of this idea to suggest that what Herder sought to express is better understood as the continuous working of the Trinitarian presence of God through

---

19. Rowland, *Culture and the Thomist Tradition*, pp. 23, 46, 47. She acknowledges that there may be other cultures which embody these good qualities, but that modern culture is not one of them!

20. Isaiah Berlin, *The Roots of Romanticism*, ed. H. Hardy (Princeton: Princeton University Press, 1999), p. 67.

21. Barnard, *Herder's Social and Political Thought*, pp. 51-53.

the Holy Spirit, working to bring creation to its perfection, a framework providing critical resources for Christian views of art and aesthetics, which I will explore below.

While I cannot present any lengthy reflections on cross-cultural aesthetics, let me return to an example of someone reflecting on aesthetics from a different cultural setting — one that has been influential on the arguments of this book. Hispanic-American theologian Roberto Goizueta proposes a view of aesthetics that may help us see the difference that Herder suggested not in terms of opposition but in terms of enrichment. As a Jesuit working in the broad tradition of liberation theology, Goizueta argues that the true nature of the person is a "praxis" whose end is internal to itself and whose nature is intersubjective.[22] But when asking about what is foundational to this praxis, Goizueta parts company with the liberation theologians. The key category for understanding this experience, Goizueta proposes, is not social transformation but aesthetic fusion — the former is a by-product, while the latter is of the essence of human action. Here Goizueta makes use of the Mexican philosopher José Vasconcelos, who argued (over against the positivism of Auguste Comte) that true understanding involves the "empathic fusion" between subject and object in order to enjoy and celebrate the object (91-92). Real relationship is fundamentally aesthetic — it involves, as Augustine said, what we love and not just what we know. We are to work out the oneness that we share with God (and which God shares with the world) by exploring those forms of life in which we are fused with the action — those practices motivated by love, which Goizueta calls the law of aesthetics (92). Rather than dealing with the general and abstract, the artist deals with particularities of these relations. As Vasconcelos argued, only this aesthetic sense is capable of expressing the unity between persons. Moreover, this orientation is not only theologically grounded; it also resonates deeply with Latin culture — its character as open, fused, heterogeneous, and mestizo (94-96).

In subsequent chapters of his book, Goizueta goes on to show how this is embodied in the religious popular culture and its aesthetic products. These are the forms in which Latinos express their religiosity. Pro-

---

22. Roberto S. Goizueta, *Caminemos con Jesus: Toward a Hispanic/Latino Theology of Accompaniment* (Maryknoll, N.Y.: Orbis Books, 1995), pp. 81-85. Here he works in the tradition of Aristotle and his modern interpreters like Maritain. Subsequent pages will be cited in the text.

cessions and images connect these people with the aesthetic dimension of life, as an end and not simply a means to other ends. The goal is that all human action should take on the character of a liturgical celebration in which affective and domestic life — and the marginalized and "useless" persons who inhabit this world — are affirmed. "In daily life we learn to value human relationships as ends, and therefore as liberating and empowering" (113). Notice how the aesthetic dimension in all of its concrete particularity is central to cultural formation — liberation follows as a by-product.

Here is a rich and subtle application of important themes of the Catholic tradition — of the theological and aesthetic nature of human relations and the priority of love — in a new setting that reflects the changing and diverse nature of the contemporary world. One sees the Catholic imagination at work in the impulse to celebrate the quotidian and popular expressions of faith, which are seen as intrinsically aesthetic. Protestants might wonder whether this does not risk diluting a particular presence of God — in his word and in the Eucharist — and the special narrative shape of this presence. But Protestants themselves need to answer the question Goizueta's work implies: How might our communal life and its aesthetic practices reflect the presence of God? What connection do these have to the narrative of the Gospel?

Neo-Reformed Aesthetics: Creation and the Historical Life of Faith

Protestant reflection on aesthetics, which has experienced renewed life in the last generation, has gone some way in proposing a theological framework for aesthetics and even a poetic theology. These thinkers would tend to endorse Balthasar's concern to focus on the particularity of God's special work of salvation, though they prefer a focus on the substance rather than the form of that revelation. In general, the Protestant concern is not with the positive connection of aesthetics and theology (they too want to root aesthetics in the good creation and gracious acts of God) but with the human ability to apprehend this. Protestants' convictions about sin and evil lead them to believe that one cannot simply read God's purposes from the world as it is. Indeed, they worry — as Barth suggested — that one could be led astray by the splendors that are seen there.

The recent contributions of Protestants to this discussion have come in two related ways. On the one side are those who continue more directly the Reformed creational focus of John Calvin, and on the other side are those who seek to understand art and aesthetics in terms of the newer appreciation of the Trinity. These are discussed together because they both work from the Reformation emphasis on the separation of God and creation, however modified by the Incarnation and the presence of the Spirit. And both, therefore, see art in its materiality as fundamentally metaphoric and illuminating of, rather than transparent to, the divine presence.

The major concern of Calvin and the other Reformers was to recover the power of the Gospel narrative, which, they believed, had been silenced in the medieval period. As a result, Calvin focused on the priority of the preached word, which he believed was uniquely able to convey the transformative power of God's actions. For Calvin, preaching was connected to the work of God by the Spirit in a way that images and ritual practice could not be. Interestingly, while he denied images any role in mediating God's presence, Calvin had a robust sense of the power of imagery in preaching and of the dramatic course of God's redemptive working in creation and history — which he often called a theatre for the glory of God. We have already seen, in earlier chapters, ways in which these emphases have continued to influence thinking about aesthetics.

Earlier I described the two emphases of the Reformed tradition — the one focusing on a rational order and the other more open to fresh working of the Spirit. The clearest example of the second of these streams was the eighteenth-century American theologian Jonathan Edwards. Edwards placed the language of beauty at the center of his theological project — language which, he felt, best expressed the inner nature of God. Edwards believed that central to the loving nature of God is the desire to communicate the excellencies of God's being. Creation itself is an expression of this fullness and beauty, and therefore the elements of creation are types of the higher, spiritual excellencies of God.[23] The excellencies, or beauty, which reflect God's inner being are of two kinds: primary and secondary. The latter is the larger and more general category that consists in various kinds of beauty which are seen

---

23. See Sang Hyun Lee, *The Philosophical Theology of Jonathan Edwards* (Princeton: Princeton University Press, 1988). "Created existence . . . is the spatio-temporal repetition of God's inner Trinitarian fullness" (p. 52; cf. p. 81).

in creation, or the works of artists and architects, or even the righteous rulers of nations. These objects "consent" or agree with each other in the sense that they reflect the harmony and proportion appropriate to them. As Edwards says, "When one thing sweetly harmonizes with another, as the notes in music, the notes are so conformed and have such proportion one to another that they seem to have respect one to another, as if they loved one another. So the beauty of figures and motions is, when one part has such consonant proportion with the rest as represents a general agreeing and consenting together."[24]

The higher or primary beauty is based on actual consent or "love." Edwards writes, "The highest excellency . . . must be the consent of spirits one to another. But the consent of spirits consists in their mutual love one to another, and the sweet harmony between various parts of the universe is only an image of mutual love."[25] This mutual love is ultimately to be found in the Triune God and the love between members of the Godhead, but it is communicated to the creature whose continued existence depends on God. The basic structure of being, then, is relational, and thus reflects, in its being, this primary beauty — and the Trinitarian activity of God.[26] We naturally delight in secondary beauty, but those whose eyes are opened by the Spirit, in a way similar to that proposed by Hamann, can see in this the deeper beauty of God.

The relational character of divine beauty and its expression in loving mutuality are attractive, but their value is undermined by Edwards' dichotomy between spiritual and material beauty. On the basis of Edwards' Platonic idealism, spiritual beauty is necessarily higher; natural beauty has meaning only as it participates in and communicates the higher spiritual beauty. But for Edwards there is a further problem that intervenes in our human attempt to capture this beauty. In his writings on the revival, he stressed that there can be no pure spiritual experience because such experiences, in our fallen condition, are always mixed with impure and carnal elements.[27] Even the spiritual experience of

---

24. Edwards, "The Mind," in Jonathan Edwards, *Scientific and Philosophical Writings*, ed. Wallace E. Anderson, vol. 6 of *The Works of Jonathan Edwards* (New Haven: Yale University Press, 1980), p. 380.

25. Edwards, "The Mind," pp. 337-38.

26. See Louis J. Mitchell, *Jonathan Edwards on the Experience of Beauty*, Studies in Reformed Theology and History, no. 9 (Princeton: Princeton Theological Seminary, 2003), p. 7.

27. Jonathan Edwards, *The Great Awakening: A Faithful Narrative*, ed. C. C. Goen, vol.

Christians, Edwards thinks, has layers of impurity that must be discarded. While this certainly reflects the Reformed conviction about human sin, it also seems to imply that corruption is inherent to our *bodily* lives. Such a dualism does not give confidence to someone setting out to make art, for Edwards warned that the imagination, dependent as it is on the constitution of the body, tends to tarnish the spiritual affections and exaggerate fanciful elements so that the spiritual part is lost. The devil also enters and encourages pride and self-confidence. So dangerous is this imaginative capacity that when Edwards considered the accounts of many converts, he concluded that it is not the opinion of any of us "that any weight is to be laid on anything seen with bodily eyes."[28]

So, we are left with a dilemma: while there is a deep and lively sense of the beauty that is resident in God and that is communicated to the creature, Edwards leaves us with an experience of beauty that is, in the end, entirely spiritual. This experience may result in a new and lively sense for the beauties of creation for those with regenerate eyes. For the rest, only an echo of beauty remains, and for these at least, the project of shaping the created order into reliable images of this beauty is not encouraged. It is not clear whether Edwards actually supposes the beauty that God has communicated to the world is actually invisible to those without faith, or that these merely fail to attribute the beauty to God. In any case, it seems that Edwards would not encourage the project of seeing any religious significance in the unbeliever's sense of beauty.

The Dutch theologian and politician Abraham Kuyper (1837-1920) was perhaps the first person in this tradition not only to think about God and aesthetics, but also to directly address the project of making art as a serious human calling. In his *Lectures on Calvinism* (1931)[29] he recognized that art has an important role to play in human life; it is, Kuyper writes, "a most serious power in our present existence." Since this is so, he asks, can such a power be independent from "the deepest root which all human life has in God"? (151). But what would an art properly rooted in God look like? Taking his cue from Calvin, Kuyper

---

4 of *The Works of Jonathan Edwards* (New Haven: Yale University Press, 1972), p. 459. For the discussion which follows, see pp. 461-67.

28. Edwards, *The Great Awakening: A Faithful Narrative*, p. 188.

29. Abraham Kuyper, *Lectures on Calvinism: The Stone Foundation Lectures* (Grand Rapids: Wm. B. Eerdmans, 1931). The lectures were given at Princeton Seminary in 1898. Subsequent pages cited in the text refer to this work.

notes that any art that "does not watch the forms and motions of nature nor listen to its sound" is in danger of deteriorating into fantasy (154). An art that does this sensitively will "discover in those natural forms the order of the beautiful . . . reminding us in its productions of the beautiful that was lost, and of anticipating its perfect coming luster" (154-55). We notice here both an allowance for the role of sin and an appreciation of art's eschatological role, something that characterizes Protestant reflection on art.

Kuyper believes that modern developments in the arts, which we have referenced, were actually made possible by the Reformation. Kuyper claims that in making the clean break from medieval religious art, the Reformers actually *advanced* the development of art in two senses. First, in releasing art from its religious guardianship, it freed art to explore the common lot of humanity, resulting in the "emancipation of our ordinary earthly life" (166) — a point that has been emphasized more recently by Charles Taylor. Rather than focusing attention on a crucifix — the "Man of Sorrows," for example — "some now began to understand that there was a mystical suffering also in the general woe of man" (166). But second, in discovering the joys and sorrows of the people and their lives, art could reflect a religion that has "graduated from the symbolical into the clearly conscious life" (146). Kuyper here betrays his nineteenth-century context when he describes the Reformers' rejection of medieval symbolism as a kind of enlightenment — with none of the Romantic appreciation for symbolic depth. Because they have come to clarity in their religion, Kuyper says, Protestants should not lament the emptiness of their churches, bereft as they are of images and symbols, for in maturity a person does not return to "the playthings of . . . infancy" (149).

Many in the Reformed tradition have found inspiration, and some caution, in the work of Kuyper.[30] One might describe the emphases of this Neo-Reformed tradition of reflection on the arts as falling under two headings: those who stress an antithesis and those with a more positive reading of culture. First, because Calvinism insists that all of life flows from the principle of faith, it introduces a strong sense of "antithesis" between those whose faith rests in God and those whose faith

---

30. These developments are surveyed in Graham Birtwistle, "H. R. Rookmaaker: The Shaping of His Thought," in H. R. Rookmaaker, *The Complete Works of Hans Rookmaaker* (Carlisle, U.K.: Piquant, 2002), vol. 1, pp. xv-xxxiii.

rests elsewhere. While Kuyper, as Calvin before him, was clear that all of life lies open before God and shares the common blessing of God (what Kuyper famously called "common grace"), this modern Calvinist, like Edwards, insisted more strongly than Calvin himself on the antithesis that faith creates. At least that is how I read him. This has led some thinkers in this tradition to stress the *difference* between Christian and secular worldviews, and to look, for instance, at the development of modern art and culture as displaying this antithesis. The famous Dutch philosopher Herman Dooyeweerd, for example, followed up on Kuyper's suggestion that reality displayed an order, which Dooyeweerd described as "law-spheres." These spheres express the legitimate development of the multifaceted goodness of creation — what he called the opening up of creation. The modal moment of the law sphere of aesthetics he proposed was "harmony in its original sense," and it is displayed by those gifted by God to create great works of art.[31] What is done by the artist happens in every other sphere as the virtuosi "open up" the good creation of God. But at the basis of every cultural product, Dooyeweerd believed, lies a religious ground motive. Moreover, there is a fundamental antithesis between the Christian ground motive — creation, fall, redemption in Jesus Christ — and all others.[32] Though Dooyeweerd was clear that Christians cannot break off engagement with these other world views, their distortions will surely show themselves in the cultural products they produce.

The person who applied Dooyeweerd's (and Kuyper's) views most consistently to the history of art was Hans R. Rookmaaker (d. 1977). His most famous work was a Christian critique of the rise of modern art in the last two centuries.[33] What is involved in modern developments in the arts, he argued, "is a whole way of thinking that leaves out of account . . . vital aspects of our humanity" (9, 10). He traced this loss through the loss of ideals in the nineteenth century, through Expressionism and Dada in the twentieth century. Like Tillich, Rookmaaker saw German Expressionists as searching for a universal unity that tran-

---

31. Herman Dooyeweerd, *A New Critique of Theoretical Thought*, 4 vols. (Philadelphia: Presbyterian and Reformed Publishing Company, 1969), vol. 2, p. 128.

32. Herman Dooyeweerd, *A New Critique of Theoretical Thought*, 4 vols. (Philadelphia: Presbyterian and Reformed Publishing Company, 1969), vol. 1, pp. 114-15.

33. Hans R. Rookmaaker, *Modern Art and the Death of a Culture* (Downers Grove, Ill.: InterVarsity Press, 1970; reprint, Crossway Books, 1994). Subsequent pages cited in the text refer to this work.

scended the particular and a reaction against the positivism of the previous century (110-12). But in the course of this quest, especially for those like Picasso, who was influenced by Expressionism, the human and the personal were lost — lost to the extent that Marcel Duchamp could say "Man is dead" (129). Rookmaaker concludes, "Modern art ... puts a question mark against all values and principles. Its anarchists' aims of achieving complete human freedom turn all laws and norms into frustrating and deadening prison walls" (161). Rookmaaker helped give Christians, who had never thought about art, tools to reflect on what they were seeing. As Rookmaaker liked to say to his students, when looking at art, "you do not know what you see, but you see what you know." But the continuing influence of Kuyper's antithesis made it difficult for him to constructively engage with these modern artists and with the project of poetic theology more generally.

A second, more positive contribution of Reformed reflection, which we tried to develop in this book, might be termed a humble aesthetic of our common life in a good creation. We have noted that since Calvin, this tradition has taken its starting point from the goodness of the created order. Tracking down the grace of this order, what Dooyeweerd called "opening up creation," offers the surest way of discerning God's purposes in the arts. Rookmaaker, in spite of his pessimism about modern art, could at times express this aesthetic of everyday life in winsome terms. He closed his book by pointing out that the real challenge is to live a life of meaning and fulfillment, and that art needs to be understood in these larger terms. "The aesthetic can never be realized in its fullness without these other elements [of the whole of life], and the other elements only get their artistic meaning because they are brought together in an artistic way" (132). Rookmaaker also claimed that "Christian art is nothing special. It is sound, healthy, good art. It is art that is in line with the God-given structures of art, one which has a loving and free view on reality, one which is good and true" (128). But if this is so, cannot others also make art that resonates with these structures, and which is good and true?

Although Dooyeweerd and Kuyper had spoken of beauty in the classical terms of harmony and proportion, these last quotations imply a wholly different way of thinking about aesthetics and beauty, one that takes its start from everyday life. This "aesthetics of the whole of life" has been developed further by Calvin Seerveld and Nicholas Wolterstorff. Seerveld wanted to escape any transcendental reference to art, such as that represented by Maritain.[34] Rather, he believed that art, like all other Christian callings, has the modest task of moving all things, from politics to sex, under the leading of the Holy Spirit, toward what Seerveld called a "saved normality" (90). But what is it that makes art different in its quality as "aesthetica"? Its focal moment, Seerveld believes, is what he calls "allusiveness": a disciplined making that stimulates the senses and emotions with its free play of suggestions (126-35). Philosopher Nicholas Wolterstorff proposes a similar way of thinking about art-making by locating it within the larger world of purposeful human action.[35] When modern art is studied from this point of view, Wolterstorff concludes, what seems to have come into its own is not art but aesthetic contemplation. But by being taken out of its natural context within the fullness of life, this rarefied encounter has achieved a rather more narrow meaning (36). This specific experience of contemplation certainly has its role to play, but it can distract one from a larger sense of responsibility. Artists have the same calling as everyone else: to serve their neighbor and to praise God in their special vocation of promoting human livelihood and delight (77). This leads Wolterstorff to propose the notion of fittingness as an aesthetic norm: Good art reflects a world that suits the context, and that reflects something of the goodness and health that God intends the world to exhibit.

These themes have encouraged many to think about and participate in the arts in helpful ways. Taking their cues from God's good creation and God's final purposes of shalom in that creation, artists, by carrying on a deep and careful conversation with their materials (as Wolterstorff puts it), can discover something about themselves and the world that is worthy, perhaps even transformative — art in this sense, contrary to Kant and Schleiermacher, can be a form of knowledge. But the prior emphasis on antithesis (which Wolterstorff avoids) has dis-

---

34. Calvin Seerveld, *Rainbows for the Fallen World: Aesthetic Life and Artistic Task* (Toronto: Tuppence Press, 1980), p. 122. Subsequent pages will be cited in the text. See also his *A Christian Critique of Art and Literature* (Toronto: Association for Reformed Studies, 1968).

35. Nicholas Wolterstorff, *Art in Action: Toward a Christian Aesthetic* (Grand Rapids: Wm. B. Eerdmans, 1980). Subsequent pages will be cited in the text. Wolterstorff's ideas in some ways anticipate those of art historian David Summers, who wants to rethink the categories of art history in terms of formats within "real spatial circumstances." See David Summers, *Real Spaces: World Art History and the Rise of Western Modernism* (New York: Phaidon, 2003).

couraged some from venturing into this world or from working together with others on worthy cultural projects. Perhaps these handicaps are the reverse of the strengths of this tradition. If the norms of everyday life control the process, the impetus for creative innovation and production can be lacking and the contribution of poetic knowledge overlooked. But these weaknesses may also reflect a deeper theological weakness in the tradition: an absence of reflection on the active presence of God through the Holy Spirit. The question that this tradition has frequently overlooked may be framed in these terms: How can we understand the processes and objects of art-making not simply as Christian practices, but as a theological locus?

A Relational and Trinitarian Aesthetics

Some Protestant writers on aesthetics have worried that the Neo-Reformed dependence on the structures of creation could be understood in a legalistic way, as confining rather than liberating.[36] But a deeper concern reflects the desire to understand art-making as itself a (potentially) theological practice. In this sense these writers want to follow up on Jacques Maritain's suggestion that a work of art is a fusing of the perceptions of the artist and the materials in a creative entity that reflects (and continues) God's own creative work. Although none expressly acknowledge his influence, they do in fact take further Maritain's suggestion of the Christological basis of this process.

These theologians want to begin the reflection on art not with creation, but directly with the Trinitarian activity of God. One of the pioneering voices in this conversation was that of Colin Gunton. In *Yesterday and Today*, published in 1985, he seeks to use aesthetics to understand the dual nature of Christ. He begins, interestingly, by noting that our experience is overly dominated by visual patterns of perception.[37] This encourages us to see objects as mutually exclusive. Music, he suggests, helps us to see the way in which two accounts of an event can be juxtaposed without one precluding the other. Gunton claims that this has im-

---

36. For this critique and a constructive proposal, see Jeremy S. Begbie, *Voicing Creation's Praise: Towards a Theology of the Arts* (Edinburgh: T&T Clark, 1991), pp. 142-63.

37. Colin E. Gunton, *Yesterday and Today: A Study of Continuities in Christology* (London: SPCK, 1997 [1985]), p. 114. Subsequent pages will be cited in the text.

plications for the way the world is (116). Understanding these interpenetrating presences, as two or more musical sounds can make up a single chord, helps us overcome a pattern of epistemology inherited from Plato and allows us to see the world in a way more consistent with modern physics — recognizing that objects can exist simultaneously in different modes and places.[38] Later Gunton develops this relational ontology, grounded in God's Trinitarian reality, in ways that are highly suggestive for understanding God's presence and purposes in art, and in culture more generally.

In his 1992 Bampton Lectures, Gunton sought to understand the particularly modern issue of unity and diversity in terms of a Trinitarian ontology.[39] The challenge, as he defines it, is to find meaning in human cultural products that affirms human worth and respects the particularity of creation — in the terms I have been using in this chapter, to reconcile the subjective process of creativity and the value and meaning of the created object. Gunton believes that the loss of faith in a Christian God as the ground of cultural activities has led to a clash of unitary theories. Ironically, the Reformers' concern to clear superstitions out of the house of culture has provided space for a multitude of faiths to rush in. Many are recognizing that art calls for a transcendent reference, because art, as Wittgenstein said, is the object seen *sub specie aeternitatis*. But not just any *aeternitas* will do, Gunton insists. Rather, he says,

> A God conceived Trinitarianly, a God who contains within himself a form of plurality in relation and creates a world which reflects the richness of his being, can surely enable us better to conceive something of the unity in variety of human culture.[40]

This claim enriches the Reformed starting point of God's good creation by insisting that this goodness, both in its nature and in its history, reflects above all the loving mutuality of the Triune God.

This too makes possible a deeper understanding of "participation" which is grounded not simply in the *presence* of God upholding all things in Christ, but in the relational *activity* of God bringing the cre-

38. Gunton, *Yesterday and Today*, pp. 116-17.

39. These lectures were published as Colin E. Gunton, *The One, the Three, and the Many: God, Creation, and the Culture of Modernity* (Cambridge: Cambridge University Press, 1993).

40. Gunton, *The One, the Three, and the Many*, p. 177.

ated order through Christ and by the Holy Spirit to its God-ordained perfection.[41] In this way one can actually speak of a work of art participating in God *in the sense that* it becomes part of the historical dynamic of God's activity. The poetic can be understood as taken up into the process of redemption that God is bringing about in Christ. In a later book Gunton says, "All true art . . . is . . . the gift of the creator Spirit as he enables in the present anticipations of the perfection that is to come at the end of the age." Art is redemptive in the sense that "it is an activity which enables the creation to reach towards the perfection that is its destiny."[42] Gunton here highlights the eschatological implications of art-making that we have hinted at previously. Art is an echo of eschatological gifts that the Spirit has poured out on the church. When speaking in these terms, we must avoid an over-realized eschatology of God's presence in works of art, with which both Schleiermacher and Tillich may have flirted. But, Gunton reminds us, we must at the same time avoid an under-realized eschatology in which art is a purely human affair that plays no role in the future that God is bringing about.

Borrowing from Gunton, then, I would like to insist that art represents a symbolic participation in the program of renewal, and in the struggle with the forces of evil, in which God is engaged in Christ and through the Holy Spirit. Thus poetic practice, when it is successful, echoes this active presence of God in bringing about renewal and wholeness. And if the personal engagement of the artist, so critical in the modern period, is understood in the Christological sense that Maritain proposes — that the artist by the gifting of the Spirit is moving toward the human flourishing that Christ makes possible and to which God calls us — then we can appreciate the human depths that the Romantic poets opened as terrain in which the Spirit is working. In this way we can say, again echoing Maritain, that art is not simply an expression of the human spirit, or simply of nature, but of both together as God also is at work in them to bring about his great work of performance art.

Elsewhere Gunton argues that in a real sense creation takes form — is made real — in great art. Art enables the world to take meaningful form; the world and its structures speak "words" in the arts. This ech-

---

41. Gunton calls this a Trinitarian analogy of being. See *The One, the Three, and the Many*, p. 140.

42. Colin E. Gunton, *The Triune Creator: A Historical and Systematic Study* (Grand Rapids: Wm B. Eerdmans, 1998), p. 234.

oes Hamann's (and Augustine's) suggestion that our sense perception, when it is grounded in faith, allows us to see the world as signs of a deeper reality. The Gospel as the greatest dramatic story helps us see that truth and beauty take shape not by escaping from the world but by acting within it to bring about shalom.[43] This process is to be distinguished from the classical understanding of natural theology, in which various attributes of God are visible in creation. Rather, we are claiming that the Triune God is present — speaking and acting — in creation. Moreover, this presence accounts, ultimately, for the lure that sparks human desire — in particular, through aesthetic objects and practices. To use Lewis's analogy, when these experiences are good, God's hands are *already* on the reins. They are grace-filled.

Jeremy Begbie develops further this model of art-making in his *Voicing Creation's Praise,* published in 1991.[44] Tellingly, he intends there a "philosophy of art" rather than a study of aesthetic contemplation (xviii); Protestant reflection on art is quite consistently about art objects and art-making, and rarely about contemplation (a failing that we will explore later). When he asks what bearing theology has on the arts, he too finds the understanding of the Trinity crucial. "The metaphor of Christ as the agent, sustainer, and goal of creation has in fact considerable potential to illuminate both the acts and the eternal being of God as triune, and, by extension, the nature of the created world" (170). Taking his cue from the mutuality embodied in the Trinity, which is reflected in God's creative work, we find that we are involved in a common history with the world; its redemption and ours are vitally connected. Through the human voice, the inarticulate nature can speak (177). Human creativity, then, is about sharing through the Spirit in the "creative purpose of the Father as he draws all things to himself through his Son" (179).

This emphasis on the Trinitarian mutuality and exchange has proven to be a fruitful model for thinking about the arts, especially when this is connected with the earlier idea of art participating in God's good creation. This is explored in a later book edited by Begbie. There Trevor Hart asks an important question: Given the Promethean claims

---

43. Colin E. Gunton, "Creation and Re-creation: An Exploration of Some Themes in Aesthetics and Theology," *Modern Theology* 2, no. 1 (1985): 8, 14, 17.

44. Begbie, *Voicing Creation's Praise*. Subsequent pages cited in the text refer to this work.

of modern artists like Arnold Schoenberg and Wassily Kandinsky, how can the application of human imagination enhance the good of creation? Here the model that is most helpful, Hart believes, is the Incarnation, especially as Paul develops this in Galatians 4:4-7. There the free response of the incarnate Jesus, who by the power of the Spirit expresses his intimacy with the Father by calling "Abba," models the way in which the artist can offer the gifts of creation back to God by the Spirit. As Christ takes our flesh, with all of its flaws, and through Spirit-inspired artistry transfigures it and offers back to us to the glory of the Father, so the artist can take the goods of creation, however flawed they may be, and transform them into images that glorify God.[45] Here Hart draws out implications from the perichoretic mutuality of the Godhead to help us understand something of the koinonia and mutual giving that human activities are meant to reflect.

For these thinkers, art objects function metaphorically, proposing a dynamic juxtaposition into which we are drawn as in a game. In exposing ourselves to the best art, we are also ourselves "put into play," and we come out of this process changed. Begbie, like Gunton, proposes that music best expresses "the temporal morphology of creation as we encounter it,"[46] an insight that is greatly expanded and elaborated in Begbie's later work *Theology, Music, and Time*.[47] In this book Begbie reiterates his goal not of understanding art via theology, but of reaching a revitalized understanding of theology through the arts. Art, in the form of music, advances theology by "enacting theological wisdom" (5). Music as a socially embedded and bodily practice, by its temporal and material character, makes important claims about the world (55). In particular, music shows the created order to be temporally limited but meaningful. It displays an interpenetrating, layered quality that is characterized by delay/patience, by promise/fulfillment, and by resolution

---

45. Trevor Hart, "Hearing, Seeing, and Touching the Truth," in *Beholding the Glory: Incarnation through the Arts*, ed. Jeremy Begbie (Grand Rapids: Baker Book House, 2000), pp. 2-25. A theologian who has developed the role of the Spirit in this process is Patrick Sherry, *Spirit and Beauty: An Introduction to Theological Aesthetics* (Oxford: Oxford University Press, 1992).

46. Begbie, *Voicing Creation's Praise*, p. 245. Begbie cites Gunton here and repeats Gunton's concern that "the tendency to appeal chiefly to visual models in theology of art has done little to help" (p. 225).

47. Jeremy Begbie, *Theology, Music, and Time* (Cambridge: Cambridge University Press, 2000). Subsequent pages cited in the text refer to this work.

prefigured/delayed. All these, Begbie argues, are central traits of God's saving activity. A central claim of the book, which marks a genuine advance in the discussion and which features the notion of participation that I am proposing, is that art in this form gives insight into the world but also reorders our sympathies; it is involved in the very salvific processes of God in worship and witness (127). In music, the "process of salvation can be conceived . . . as an ongoing healing of our time through participation in the temporality established in Jesus Christ" (150, 151). The experience of music gives us a deeper insight into, for example, the advent of the Eucharist and its repetition over time, but it also displays its "potential to be taken up into the process of shaping a mature Christian identity" (169, 152).

Interestingly, though Begbie admits that other forms of music may have different theological capabilities (7), and that his project is limited to exploring the temporality of music (19), he cannot see how music by the Russian Orthodox composer John Tavener may be engaged in a different but equally legitimate theological project from his own. While admitting that Tavener appeals to people who are distracted and driven, Begbie feels that Tavener's transcript of eternity negates time and fails to allow God a creative engagement with the created world (144, 145). This criticism may reflect a limitation of Begbie's own tradition and of the Neo-Reformed tradition more generally. True, Begbie offers a helpful discussion of music as providing the conceptual tools to explore the temporal and interpenetrating dynamics of God's creation (271); it even helps us to see ourselves as shaped by and in this temporality. Nevertheless, on this view, music is still only metaphor; it is a giver of insight. But perhaps the Orthodox believer Tavener wants to say that it can be something more. Can it perhaps be a kind of icon, transparent to its eternal ground? Can it perhaps stop us in our tracks and make us aware of a Presence before which we may be transformed? These questions may embody the fundamental challenge to the Protestant tradition of reflection on the arts: How does one understand aesthetic practice to mediate God's presence?

What have we learned from this brief survey of recent discussions of theological aesthetics? The difference between a Catholic and a Protestant imagination has issued in a spectrum of views, though with two similar poles. Some, such as Tillich and David Bentley Hart, want to see the objects as, in some sense, revelatory of God's *being*. These of the Neo-Reformed and Trinitarian bent prefer to speak of God's presence in terms of a common (and more or less deeply shared) *project*. The first wants to understand participation in terms of ontology; the second wants to understand participation in terms of relation and activity. The first emphasizes immanence; the second, transcendence. While there is much to be learned from Tillich and Schleiermacher, at the end of the day the second group, in my judgment, does a better job of preserving the materiality and, potentially, the freedom of the artistic process. A focus on art as activity allows a better integration with the full life of Christian obedience, and of the history in which God is at work. A helpful way of reflecting on these differences, it seems to me, is in terms of Alasdair MacIntyre's notion of traditions.[48] Schleiermacher and Tillich reflect a continental tradition of philosophy whose idealism has been nourished by Plato and the Neoplatonic tradition. The others, especially those in the Anglo-Saxon world, in various ways trace their lineage to Aristotle, especially to his focus on the practice of virtue. The latter tends to see art as an instrument of human action but struggles to see this as a theological locus; the former risks a mysticism that loses the particular responsibility of the artist and her community. Overlying these traditions are the continuing relevance of Protestant and Catholic readings, and of the contributions of other cultural groups, like those represented by Goizueta. The conversation is a rich one.

In the next chapter we will continue our particular project of refining a Reformed perspective on aesthetics that has listened and learned from these voices, framing it in particular over against a Catholic sacramental reading.

---

48. See Alasdair MacIntyre, *Whose Justice? Which Rationality?* (Notre Dame: University of Notre Dame Press, 1988), and *Three Rival Versions of Moral Inquiry* (Notre Dame: University of Notre Dame Press, 1990).

CHAPTER 6

Dante, Bunyan, and the Search for a Protestant Aesthetics

In this chapter I want to turn my attention to the particular theological tradition I represent, what might broadly be called Reformed Protestantism. What, if anything, I want to ask, does this tradition have to offer our project of poetic theology? I began to answer this question at the end of the last chapter in terms of recent Trinitarian discussions, and in Chapter Three by describing what I called a dialectical theology. In this chapter I will seek to describe this in some detail — sympathetically, I trust. In the next chapter I will offer some critical comments about what I believe is missing from this tradition.

Although Protestants — especially of the evangelical variety — have often been on the defensive when it comes to art and aesthetics, I want to argue that they need not be. I will propose that Protestants have inherited a particular aesthetic framework that is different from — if less obvious — than that of the Catholic and Orthodox traditions. While it would seem to be difficult to generalize about the disparate and frequently quarrelsome group that goes under the name of "Protestant," there is a growing recognition that in the sixteenth and seventeenth centuries, especially in England, a uniquely Protestant way of reading and writing developed that reflected the fundamental insights of the Reformation. Building on the work of John King and Barbara Lewalski, scholars have begun to describe a broadly Protestant tradition that issued in particular patterns of writing and interpretation.[1] These patterns were widely shared by Protestants of that

---

1. See John N. King, *English Reformation Literature: The Tudor Origins of the Protestant Tradition* (Princeton: Princeton University Press, 1982), and Barbara K. Lewalski, *Protes-*

and subsequent periods, even by groups that were divided over other (non-literary) issues. At the end of the chapter I will seek to show the importance of this practice of reading for a Christian poetics.

To approach this issue, I will first look briefly at what might be regarded as paradigmatic works of the Catholic and Protestant traditions — Dante's *Divine Comedy* and John Bunyan's *Pilgrim's Progress* — as a way of describing two contrasting approaches to life that, following David Tracy, we might term analogical and dialectical, respectively.[2] Then I will attempt to outline the elements of an aesthetic framework derived from this Protestant form of life. For purposes of this discussion, I will continue to assume Frank Burch Brown's definition of aesthetic phenomena or aesthetica, to which we referred in an earlier chapter: "All those things employing a medium in such a way that its perceptible form and 'felt' qualities become essential to what is appreciable and meaningful."[3] Let me examine, then, two contrasting ways in which such phenomena can be construed and appreciated.

Dante and the Politics of Desire

One influential way of framing aesthetics is represented by Dante Alighieri in *The Divine Comedy,* written while Dante was in exile from his native Florence during the first two decades of the fourteenth century. Dante represents, we recall, the classic example of the medieval *theologia poetica* which we described in the second chapter. The *Comedy* is cast in the form of a journey undertaken by Dante through the circles of hell, and by way of purgatory, to a beatific vision of God in heaven. According to medieval exegesis, this journey was intended to be read on four levels. It is first of all an account of a "literal" journey that Dante recounts, beginning on the Thursday before Easter, 1300, guided first by Virgil and then by Beatrice, to a vision of God. Second, read on a moral level, the poem represents the progressive recognition of the evils attendant upon the human condition, and Dante's growing

---

tant *Poetics and the Seventeenth-Century Religious Lyric* (Princeton: Princeton University Press, 1979).

2. See David Tracy, *The Analogical Imagination: Christian Theology and the Culture of Pluralism* (New York: Crossroad, 1981).

3. Frank Burch Brown, *Religious Aesthetics: A Theological Study of Making and Meaning* (Princeton: Princeton University Press, 1989), p. 22.

Dante, Bunyan, and the Search for a Protestant Aesthetics

awareness of his iniquities in particular, and the possibility of their purgation and final removal. Third, it represents a mystical quest — in the words of St. Bonaventure — of the Soul's journey to God. And finally, it embodies the anagogical level — that is, the understanding of life as seen in anticipation of the glories of heaven.[4]

The world which Dante describes, under the influence of Augustine, is filled with "signs." The persons and events that Dante encounters along his journey are all pointers that assist him in moving him toward his goal. St. Augustine had earlier described the pilgrimage of life in his work *On Christian Teaching*, which we discussed earlier. This work defines in many ways Dante's medieval worldview. Dante's journey is a transcript of Augustine's road of the affections. He writes, "We are on a road — in spiritual, not spatial terms — and one blocked as it were by thorny hedgerows."[5] The world is full of signs, he noted, to be used as a means for the soul to reach its true homeland in God, who alone is to be enjoyed for his own sake. As Augustine put it, "If we wish to return to the homeland where we can be happy, we must use this word . . . in other words, . . . derive eternal and spiritual value from corporeal and temporal things" (I, iv, p. 11). Dante's narrative is framed, then, as a symbolic journey toward this true spiritual homeland.

There are obstacles along this road of the affections. We are blocked, Augustine had said, by these hedgerows "through the evil influences of our earlier sins" (I, xvii, p. 15). In the introductory Canto, Dante's way is blocked by a leopard, representing lust; a lion, depicting pride; and, worst of all, a wolf, picturing greed — this progressive order of sins is reiterated in the levels of hell (and of purgatory) that Dante will pass through and represents all that hinders the soul's journey to God. But just at the moment of Dante's worst fear in the dark forest, Virgil, the pagan Roman poet, appears and encourages him to "climb up the mountain of delight, the origin and cause of every joy."[6] Note that it is not Scripture or a trusted saint but a pagan poet whom Dante calls "my

---

4. Dante himself describes these levels of meaning of his poem in his letter to Can Grande, his host in Verona, probably written from Ravenna in 1319. See *Dantis Alagherii Epistolae: The Letters of Dante*, trans. and ed. Paget Toynbee (Oxford: Clarendon Press, 1920), Letter X, p. 199.

5. Augustine, *On Christian Teaching*, trans. R. P. H. Green (Oxford: Oxford University Press, 1997), I, xvii, p. 15. Subsequent pages will be cited in the text.

6. Dante, *The Divine Comedy*, trans. Allen Mandelbaum (New York: Knopf, 1995), *Inferno*, I, 77-78. Subsequent references will be made in the text.

master and my author" (*Inferno,* I, 85); Virgil directs Dante to take a way that bypasses the wolf. Dante's sins will be faced and gradually effaced in purgatory, and Virgil's leadership will finally give way to that of Beatrice, who represents divine love. But meanwhile, Virgil has been commissioned by Beatrice to lead Dante through the inferno and up through purgatory; Beatrice sponsors Dante's journey in the same way as the saints who appear with medieval donors on altarpieces. But it is Virgil who directs Dante's journey through hell and purgatory. Dante's very affection for Virgil's gifts, which he recognizes as rooted in God, can be used to move Dante toward God. This too reflects Augustine's views. Since the love of God is central, Augustine recognized that all loves must flow into this love. We love ourselves and others in God, and for the sake of God (I, xxxvi, p. 25).

Significant on the journey are the liturgical markers by which Dante is made to reflect on his sins and move toward God; indeed, the medieval liturgy is a critical structuring element, especially of the middle canticle, the "Purgatorio." The journey of life is both a gradual purgation of one's besetting sins and a progressive attachment to those things in which God can be seen and loved.[7] The latter is frequently celebrated in song, dance, and visual forms in the *Comedy.* But this way of finding God through the goods that God has made is best seen in the role of Beatrice, who on the literal level was the girl representing the perfection of beauty that Dante had seen and loved in Florence, but who in the *Comedy* is transformed into the human image of divine love. Beatrice becomes central at the end of the *Purgatorio,* where she takes over for Virgil (though she has already played a role at the beginning by explaining Virgil's role to Dante). The Roman poet is forbidden to enter the spheres of paradise, but Beatrice, as the image — almost the incarnation — of divine love, leads Dante toward the light which is God.

This journey of affections is possible, Beatrice insists in Augustinian terms, because God has made us for himself. She explains this to Dante:

---

7. A professor from Thailand, Satanun Boonyakiat, has pointed out that Dante's journey of *attachment* stands in stark contrast to the symbolic journey of the Buddha, which represents a progressive *detachment* from the goods of this world. See his article "The Divine Comedy" in *Global Dictionary of Theology,* ed. W. Dyrness and V. M. Karkkainen (Downers Grove, Ill.: InterVarsity Press, 2008).

> Your life is breathed forth immediately
> by the Chief Good, who so enamors it
> of his own Self that it desires Him always.
>
> *(Paradiso,* VII, 142-44)

Meanwhile, this world shines with a borrowed beauty, which we, our vision clouded by our sin, see at one remove — through a glass darkly, as the Apostle Paul put it in 1 Corinthians 13.

Near the end of the *Purgatorio,* the Three Virtues appear, "dancing to their angelic measure," and describe Beatrice's assignment with Dante:

> "Turn, Beatrice, O turn your holy eyes
> upon your faithful one," their song beseeched,
> "who, that he might see you, has come so far.
> Out of your grace, do us this grace; unveil
> your lips to him, so that he may discern
> the second beauty you have kept concealed."
>
> *(Purgatorio,* XXXI, 133-38)

This second beauty is the very splendor of the eternal light of God, which Dante will see with unveiled eyes in the final canticle. But this vision is both enabled and anticipated by the unveiling of the smile of Dante's guide, Beatrice. And the final vision of God in turn illumines all that had led Dante toward the light. As he says in the final Canto,

> O grace abounding, through which I presumed
> to set my eyes on the Eternal Light
> so long that I spent all my sight on it!
> In its profundity I saw — ingathered
> and bound by love into one single volume —
> what, in the universe, seems separate, scattered.
>
> *(Paradiso,* XXXIII, 82-87)

For Dante, the scattered lights of grace and beauty are testimonies to God's own splendor, and in the final vision of God they are gathered into a single volume bound by love. It is love that draws the soul toward God, and the response it elicits is that of penitence (in the *Purgatorio*) and finally of praise and song (in the *Paradiso*). So, for Dante, the right ordering of the person, as we also argued in the first chapter, is brought about by the disciplines of worship: confession, prayer, and praise.

Bunyan and the Hermeneutics of Suspicion

A very different picture of the world, and of art and beauty, emerges in John Bunyan's *Pilgrim's Progress,* written in the middle of the seventeenth century. The two authors' contexts illumine the contrast of the works: the former written by an honored writer and cultural hero, the latter by a poor, self-taught preacher languishing in Bedford Jail; the one a refugee of honor, the other an exile of disgrace. Bunyan's pilgrim is also on a journey: toward heaven and God. There are even echoes — probably accidental — of the *Comedy* as he begins his journey:[8] "As I walked through the wilderness of this world, I lighted on a certain place where was a den, and laid me down in that place to sleep.... I dreamed a dream."[9] If Dante's journey represents a disciplining of the affections, Bunyan's is a schooling of the will, or, as Bunyan would put it, of the heart. Like Dante, Bunyan's pilgrim, named Christian, at once faces obstacles. One is the great burden (of sin) on his back, which causes him to weep and tremble. But the other sets his imagination apart from that of Dante: his certainty, which he explains to his wife and children, "that this our city will be burned with fire from Heaven; in which fearful overthrow, both myself, with thee my wife and you my sweet babes, shall miserably come to ruin" (5-6). His journey, then, is one of escape and deliverance rather than of purgation. In Christian's anguish, Evangelist appears to him and points out the way that he must go: "Keep [yonder shining light] in your eye and go up directly thereto..." (7). And so Christian begins to run, not heeding the cries of his family to return, crying, "Life! Life! Eternal life" (8), recalling the

---

8. Probably these are unintentional. "Attempts to identify an underlying medieval or Renaissance model have failed. Bunyan had but the most meager historical knowledge and interests; and it is far more probable that the work owes everything to his own originality." See *The Oxford Dictionary of the Christian Church,* 2d ed., ed. F. L. Cross et al. (Oxford: Oxford University Press, 1974), p. 1091.

9. John Bunyan, *The Pilgrim's Progress from This World to That Which Is to Come, Delivered under the Similitude of a Dream* (Chicago: Moody Press, n.d. [1678/84]), p. 5. The den is a reference to his prison cell. Subsequent pages cited in the text are from this edition.

words of Christ: "Whoever loves son or daughter more than me is not worthy of me" (Matt. 10:37).

Unlike the *Comedy,* where the world is full of signs that, used rightly, can lead the soul toward the light, Christian's way is beset with various temptations and trials that threaten to mislead him. If Dante suggests a hermeneutics of discernment whereby one is encouraged to discern what is good and love the good for the sake of God, Bunyan fashions a hermeneutics of suspicion, where the goods of this world are mostly distractions. The figures that Christian encounters frequently seek to dissuade him from his journey and belittle its goal: the goods of this world are not signs of God but burdens to be cast off in favor of the higher good that heaven will provide. The response of Atheist to Christian's journey is typical of the skepticism he encounters. When Atheist hears of the object of Christian's journey, he responds, "[I] have been seeking this city these twenty years, but find no more of it than I did the first day I set out" (157). And so, he tells Christian, "I am going back again, and will seek to refresh myself with the things that I then cast away for hopes of that which I now see is not" (157). But for Christian, the goods of this world offer a false allure from which one must resolutely turn away.

Early on, Christian sees that his journey will be fruitless if he is not relieved of the burden of sin that he carries with him. A longing for deliverance and a fear of judgment, rather than love, motivate Christian's journey. Near the beginning of it, Interpreter introduces Christian to one (unnamed) who was likewise burdened with the pleasures and profits of this world, and who dreamt of judgment. In his dream he saw himself left behind as many were carried up into the clouds, where a Judge sat upon the cloud and kept his eye on him and called to the man's mind all his sin. "Keep all things so in thy mind," Interpreter tells Christian, "that they may be as a goad in thy side, to prick thee forward in the way thou must go" (40). Soon Christian comes upon a cross, and as he approaches it, "his burden was loosed from his shoulders, and fell from off his back . . . and I saw it no more" (41). For Christian there is no painful process of purgation, but simply a deliverance — his sins disappear into a dark sepulcher.

Christian stands for a time before the cross, weeping in wonder, and then proceeds on his way with a merry heart: "Then Christian gave three leaps for joy, and went on singing" (41). Although liberated from sin — indeed, *because* he is forgiven — Christian is not at home in the world. Mostly that which appears pleasant and attractive proves to be a snare for him. In the midst of a difficult way, he comes upon a pleasant arbor "made by the Lord of the hill for the refreshment of weary travelers" (46). But as he relaxes in that place, he falls into a deep slumber and forgets himself. When he wakes, he realizes that it has grown late, and he rushes off, leaving behind the scroll — Bunyan's image of the Bible — which he has to go back later to retrieve. In the course of his journey, he passes through Vanity Fair, where all the goods of the world are displayed along with "jugglings, cheats, games, plays, fools, apes, knaves, and rogues, and that of every kind" (100). Of this image of the collected goods from all the countries of the world, Bunyan notes, "The way to the Celestial City lies just through this town where this lusty fair is kept" (100). Indeed, the Prince of princes himself was invited here by Beelzebub to "buy his vanities, yea would have made him Lord of the fair" (100-101). As that One refused these temptations, so must the pilgrim. The great commotion that pilgrim and his companion (Faithful) cause issues in their arrest — because they "cared not so much as look upon" all the goods there displayed and refused to define their lives in terms of (or as consumers of) these goods.

It would be wrong, however, to say that the goods of this world have no value for Christian. He can turn the goods and experiences of this world to good account (although not in the same way that Dante did in the *Comedy*). It is not all deferred gratification. The most striking image of this is Christian's arrival at Palace Beautiful. After various trials, Christian "lift[s] up his eyes and behold there was a very stately palace before him, the name of which was Beautiful, and it stood just by the highway" — Bunyan's image of the church.[10] Although he arrives there late in the evening — due to his having slept too long in the pleasant arbor — he is admitted. He enjoys pleasant discourse with Piety, Prudence, and Charity, after which they dine together (where Bunyan inserts clear Eucharistic references); then Christian is shown his room, "a large upper chamber whose window opened toward the sun-rising" (57-58). From there, significantly, in the morning, his hosts show him the Delectable Mountains of heaven. "He saw a most pleasant mountain-

---

10. See Gordon Wakefield's description of the church for Bunyan — "The fellowship of believers... is everywhere, and it is inescapable" — in "To Be a Pilgrim: Bunyan and the Christian Life," in *John Bunyan: Conventicle and Parnassus*, ed. N. H. Keeble (Oxford: Clarendon Press, 1988), pp. 124-25.

ous country..." (61). This is Immanuel's Land, which, for Bunyan, is clearly visible only from within the fellowship of the church.

It is not surprising that Bunyan reserves his most expressive (and emotional) language for the arrival of the pilgrims at the country of Beulah — on the borders of heaven. "In this country the sun shineth night and day... the reflection of the sun upon the City was so extremely glorious that they could not as yet with face behold it, but through an instrument made for that purpose" (that is, its light cannot be seen directly but must be reflected via temporal things; here Bunyan echoes 2 Cor 3:18; see 179, 181). Still, the pilgrims have to cross the river (of death) to reach this city, and ministering spirits arrive to help them through. In Bunyan's version of the beatific vision, faith becomes sight in a final vision of God's beauty: "the beauty and glory of [the city] were inexpressible.... [You] enjoy the perpetual sight and visions of the Holy One for 'there you shall see him as he is' (1 John 3:2).... There your eyes shall be delighted with seeing, and your ears with hearing the pleasant voice of the Mighty One" (185-86). The pilgrims enter and are transfigured, and Bunyan gives what has become the normative image of heaven in the Western imagination: their raiment shines like gold; they are given harps to praise, and crowns in token of honor, in a city paved with gold that shines like the sun, that is eternally praising the divine glory: "Holy, Holy, Holy is the Lord!" (189). The words of the classic hymn capture the movement of Bunyan's pilgrim: Although grace teaches Christian's heart to fear, that same grace (finally) will lead him home.

Bunyan and a Protestant Poetics

Both of these classics reflect a common tradition of Western Christianity, of course. This world does not carry its own meaning, but points beyond itself to the world of God, where resides humanity's true home and end. The human journey has a meaning that is moral, not just eschatological. One cannot journey alone; helps, companions are necessary, and, eventually, the redemption of Christ alone suffices to lead one to the light. But amid these similarities there are contrasts. Indeed, when taken on their own terms, there is a gulf fixed. And it is precisely within questions of aesthetics where these differences appear most clearly.

Here we recall the definition of Frank Burch Brown that we are using to describe aesthetic objects as employing a medium in which the "form and 'felt' qualities become essential to what is appreciable and meaningful."[11] Clearly the form and qualities are essential to both of these works. But surely, someone will ask, though both *The Divine Comedy* and *The Pilgrim's Progress* are literary classics, they are not intentionally "artistic" in the same sense. Using them to develop alternative aesthetics is therefore unfair to the intentions of, at least, Bunyan. Leaving aside the question of which is better or higher art, few critics today would accept the notion that Bunyan's work is intentionally artless.[12] In fact, in his "Author's Apology," Bunyan defends his use of dialogue and metaphor, almost as if he too had read Augustine. Typically, he makes his defense (in verse!) by an appeal to Scripture:

> I find that Holy Writ in many places
> Hath semblance with this method, where the cases
> Do call for one thing to set forth another.
> Use it I may then, and yet nothing smother
> Truth's gold beams; nay, by this method may
> Make it cast for its rays as light as day.[13]

The aesthetic form, while not despised, is designed to enhance the matter thus expressed. This is especially evident in the two authors' different uses of symbolism. Dorothy Sayers points out that Bunyan's images are more like *personified abstractions* — portraying anger, envy, and chastity; Dante's figures are often mythical or historical (and these side by side!) personages "who are [also] *symbolic images* of the qualities they represent."[14] The latter can be richer and more compelling because they represent something higher and deeper, in part, by being what they are (what Sayers calls natural symbolism). This is what also allows, say, Beatrice and Virgil to be read on several levels. Bunyan's

---

11. Brown, *Religious Aesthetics*, p. 22.

12. See Beatrice Batson, *John Bunyan's "Grace Abounding" and "Pilgrim's Progress": An Overview of Literary Studies: 1960-1987* (New York: Garland, 1988), pp. xiv-xv. Still, Batson argues that Bunyan's ultimate purpose is to move the reader in a spiritual sense.

13. Bunyan, "The Author's Apology for His Book," in *The Pilgrim's Progress* (London: Marshall, Morgan & Scott, n.d.), p. ix.

14. Dorothy L. Sayers, *Introductory Papers on Dante* (London: Methuen & Co., 1954), pp. 5-7; the quotation is from page 7.

images have the more narrow purpose of portraying a single virtue or vice. Bunyan is less interested in the poetic form than the theological meaning.

But the fact that Bunyan's form does intend to call attention to itself does not keep it from embodying a specific aesthetic contour. Indeed, I will argue below that this indirection is one of the characteristics of the Protestant aesthetic form. Here Bunyan is heir to important developments in the seventeenth century, especially evident in Richard Sibbes and Richard Baxter, where sensible images are put in the service of edification.[15]

Nor is it fair to say that Bunyan's purpose is edification while Dante intends a broader illumination and delight. Dante in fact describes his purpose in writing the *Comedy* in his Letter to Can Grande in ways that Bunyan himself would have endorsed. The aims of the work, Dante says, are many, but "it may be stated briefly that the aim of the whole and of the part is to remove those living in this life from a state of misery, and to bring them to a state of happiness."[16] So both have a moral and spiritual purpose, one that each intended to be furthered by the "form and qualities" that characterize the media. The difference, I believe, was the kind of reader and the act of reading that each was seeking to encourage. Dante sought a reader who saw in the classical literature of Homer, Virgil, and Statius elements of Christian truth that are most clearly articulated in the Christian faith and its liturgy; Bunyan sought readers grounded in Scripture who would respond to its substance but also to its unique "poetics."

While Bunyan's starting point was the medieval pilgrimage allegory, his readers were not encouraged to practice the kind of mystical and devotional reading that Dante sought. In a word, Bunyan wanted Protestant readers. Barbara Johnson describes Protestant readers as those who took their interpretive and aesthetic cues from the reading of Scripture, which they saw as a liberating agent, and subsequently they

---

15. On Bunyan's dependence on Baxter and Sibbes, see U. Milo Kaufmann, *"The Pilgrim's Progress" and Traditions in Puritan Meditation* (New Haven: Yale University Press, 1966), pp. 133-50. He notes that for these, images are used subject to the authorization of Scripture and the rational control of its truth. On Sibbes's influence more generally on Protestant aesthetics, see William A. Dyrness, *Reformed Theology and Visual Culture: The Protestant Imagination from Calvin to Edwards* (Cambridge: Cambridge University Press, 2004), pp. 166-71.

16. Dante, *The Letters of Dante*, Letter X, p. 202.

applied this orientation to all of their reading and writing. In fact, Johnson believes that the "Protestant reader emerges full-blown in the figure of John Bunyan and his book *The Pilgrim's Progress*."[17]

One way of addressing these distinctions is by describing the role of sight or vision in both. For Dante, the traveler is moved by desire that is frequently kindled by sight. Although it is love that draws all things to God, as we have seen, seeing its embodiment in temporal forms sparks Dante's desire. Beatrice, the earthly figure whose beauty struck Dante when she was nine, stirs up Dante's love for God; Matilda awakens Dante's awareness of the beauty of creation (*Purgatorio,* XXVIII); Piccarda Donati encourages Dante's submission to God's will (*Paradiso,* III). These images constitute *symbolic personages* which carry multiple meanings. Dante often goes to great lengths to describe their visual aspects, which carry meaning in their own right. Bunyan's *personified abstractions,* by contrast, are described notionally rather than visually; it is their instruction rather than their image that is meant to move the traveler.[18] Even when Christian's interest is engaged, this is sparked not by seeing images but by "reading" a text. In Bunyan's work, the scroll that Evangelist gives Christian at the very beginning plays a critical role in his journey. This scroll instructs Christian to "Flee the wrath to come" (7).

Whereas the dominant trope for Dante is seeing light, for Bunyan it is reading a text. This difference leads to engagement with the world in vastly different ways. For Bunyan, as Thomas Luxon points out, "looking at *things* is presented under the metaphor of reading and interpreting them."[19] Reading and rightly interpreting these living words stand in contrast to Dante's practice of seeing things as images of divine love. The former sheds meaning, Bunyan believed, while the latter obstructs it. We must be careful not to imply that reading engages the rational faculties while looking is emotional. The trope of reading does nothing to diminish the emotional impact of what is read and understood. If anything, this impact is increased. "Words, we see, are to be preferred

---

17. Barbara A. Johnson, *Reading "Piers Plowman" and "The Pilgrim's Progress": Reception and the Protestant Reader* (Carbondale, Ill.: Southern Illinois University Press, 1992), p. 3.

18. In addition to the discussion noted in footnote 14, see Dante, *The Divine Comedy: Hell,* trans. Dorothy L. Sayers (London: Penguin, 1949), p. 13.

19. Thomas H. Luxon, "Calvin and Bunyan on Word and Image: Is There a Text in Interpreter's House?" *English Literary Renaissance* 18, no. 3 (1988): 441.

to images," Luxon argues, "but faith in the word plants a new image on the heart, a lively image that speaks far more clearly than mere words notionally understood."[20]

As Luxon's term "lively image" implies, the priority of word and language in the Protestant tradition does not necessarily eclipse the role of visual images, nor, as I will argue, the appropriation of cultural wisdom, though it surely changes the way these are understood. The supposed contrast between word and image that Walter Ong described is surely an oversimplification.[21] Word and image have always gone together in various dynamic combinations, and even the supposed triumph of the word during the Reformation merely altered rather than displaced the role of image and imagination.

This "lively image" I intend to track down in what follows. But first let me make an additional comment on language. The fact that Bunyan's "reading" replaces Dante's "seeing" involves language in a way that will become important to Protestant aesthetics. It is a commonplace that, in general, an emphasis on language replaces an emphasis on image in Protestant art. This is seen in the fact that "art" in this tradition has been displayed most prominently in literature and music, which arguably is a temporal or narrative art analogous to literature. But there is a deeper and more fundamental reason for this priority of language to Protestant aesthetics that is often overlooked. Language, Protestants believe, corresponds better to the historical facticity that lies at the basis of faith, which I highlighted in Chapter One: Protestants believe that language, particularly scriptural language, is a unique and necessary carrier of those facts.

Dante could trust the images of desire that God had put in his way, and these images moved him toward God; Bunyan's pilgrim, on the other hand, needed Interpreter (and later, Faithful) to be sure that he had the story right. And having the story right was crucial to Christian for the very important reason that it was this story that he had to live out. Here, I believe, lies an additional difference between Dante and Bunyan, and between Catholic and Protestant aesthetics. Dante's own journey is ultimately not what the "story" of the *Comedy* is about. It is a literary conceit that serves to highlight the just judgment of

---

20. Luxon, "Calvin and Bunyan on Word and Image," p. 451.
21. Walter Ong, *Orality and Literacy: The Technologizing of the Word* (London: Methuen, 1982).

God, the possible purgation of sins, and the eventual vision of God in heaven. Dante is a privileged witness of these realities who is sent back as another apostle to reveal God's purposes.[22] In the terms we borrowed from Justin Klassen earlier, Dante's discourse is rhetorical, appealing directly to the imagination. For Bunyan, Christian's journey *is* the drama; he is in constant danger of losing his way. Knowing the correct version of the story is the all-important criterion for his keeping to the way — when he loses the scroll at the Pleasant Arbor, he must retrace his steps until he finds it. Interest in the story is not merely academic; it is of vital spiritual — even eternal — importance. Pilgrim must know the story so that he can himself follow its plot. This suggests that a critical aesthetic category of a Protestant aesthetic is dramatic action. In terms of Frank Burch Brown's description, the perceptible form and felt qualities of a Protestant art are essentially dramatic. Bunyan's discourse, then, is dialectical, drawing much of its force from its opposition to the lure of the world and requiring appropriation in terms of living by faith, not by sight. To develop this claim, I will suggest three categories that illuminate the aesthetic framework that follows from this orientation: brokenness, hidden character, and the prophetic.

Brokenness

All Christians believe that the world as it exists is fallen and in need of redemption. But how this fallenness is understood has important consequences for the process of evaluating and making art. In his discussion of religious images, Catholic theologian Karl Rahner has claimed,

> Against all attempts to safeguard religious knowledge by detaching it from other kinds of knowledge, traditional Christian anthropology has always clearly insisted that sense knowledge and spiritual knowledge constitute a unity, that all spiritual knowledge, however sublime it may be, is initiated and filled with content by sense experience.[23]

---

22. Peter Hawkins argues that Dante believed that the *Comedy* was itself a form of Scripture, and that he was an apostle, another "John," whom Jesus loved. See *Dante's Testaments: Essays in Scriptural Imagination* (Stanford, Calif.: Stanford University Press, 1999).

23. Karl Rahner, "Theology of the Meaning of Religious Images," in *Theological In-*

Rahner here articulates the classical Catholic view of sense knowledge that is consistent with Dante. Since there is fundamental unity between sense knowledge and spiritual knowledge, we can trust our experience — sense knowledge does not deceive us. Like Dante, Rahner believes that the goods of this world can direct us to God. In this sense, Rahner's method is rhetorical: he wants to persuade readers directly of this participatory way of living.

But it is just this unity that Protestants during the Reformation came to deny, or at least distrust. This distrust, the Reformers believed, had theological and biblical roots, but it also sprang from a particular cultural and religious situation. Calvin in particular denied the ability of persons to truly seek God on their own, something that the proliferation of medieval devotional practices seemed to assume. Only the pure preaching of the Word of God, received in faith, was felt to adequately communicate saving truth; only this was the proper vehicle of the Spirit.[24]

Here I believe that one can argue that Calvin was right in seeking to recover the centrality of the proclamation of Scripture, but mistaken in limiting such proclamation to verbal preaching. Because it turns out that denying the religious use of imagery — and other external mediations of spiritual truths (the labyrinth, pilgrimages, and the like) — and insisting on a radical disjunction between God and the world had the unintended consequence of suggesting an almost unbridgeable gulf between the inner and the outer ways of coming to truth and, more importantly, to God.[25] Since Reformers believed that truth had to be appropriated internally through the hearing of the word, what is grasped inwardly by the working of the mind came to have more authority than what was experienced through the bodily life in the world, and accordingly, intellectual life came to be valued above the affective life. The part this played in the development of devotional practice I explore below, but here I want to underline the importance of this for aesthetics.

What might be the aesthetic implications of this split? Since the world is broken, the connection between any beauty resident in the

---

vestigations, Volume 13, 1992, quoted in Richard Viladesau, *Theological Aesthetics: God in Imagination, Beauty, and Art* (New York: Oxford University Press, 1999), p. 77.

24. See Dyrness, *Reformed Theology and Visual Culture,* Chapter Four.

25. In the next chapter I will suggest that Calvin may not have felt that this limitation, so important for his day, was necessary for all time.

world and the beauty of God is severed. This rupture, of course, is grounded in Calvin's view of sin and the disruption it caused, but it had its cultural impact through the apparent denial of any direct religious or spiritual meaning to the world around us. Again, it is unclear whether Calvin intended to stress the antithesis in the way that the tradition has come to emphasize this — I rather doubt it. Indeed, he could argue that sparks of God's beauty and glory are still to be seen in the world and that they provide a dramatic stage for God's glory. But for most of Calvin's followers, these things in themselves cannot lead one toward God. Paul Ricoeur explains the meaning of this rupture between the world of God and our world: "Any project of making a continuous whole of one's existence is ruined."[26] One becomes a disciple of Jesus only by uprooting oneself — like Bunyan's pilgrim, one must make a clean break with things, even with one's family, when one sets out on the journey to God.

Not that the Christian has to go out of the world altogether. The rupture implies not so much flight from the world as a deep mistrust of it. Throughout his journey, the pilgrim's critical faculties are fully engaged in a kind of hermeneutics of suspicion. What beauty exists, judged by whatever standard one may erect, is flawed, broken. Moreover, its seduction has to be carefully assessed and, often, resisted. The brokenness of the world is such that one cannot simply read off God's purposes from the perfection of a rose or the good intentions of a neighbor. As John Walford argues in his study of the seventeenth-century Dutch landscape painter Jacob van Ruisdael, the best interpretation of the "vanity" of Ecclesiastes — which van Ruisdael frequently evokes — is "brokenness."[27] This interpretation of sin lends a depth to the beauty of van Ruisdael's landscapes that they would not otherwise have — and that is absent, for example, from the work of one of his contemporaries, Claude Lorraine. For van Ruisdael, the evident beauty of the created order has been fatally compromised by the inescapable brokenness — portrayed by the fragment of a wagon wheel or a disintegrating house.

At first glance, the trees and the lake in *Oak Trees on the Lake with*

---

26. Paul Ricoeur, *Figuring the Sacred: Religion, Narrative, and Imagination*, trans. David Pellauer, ed. Mark I. Wallace (Minneapolis: Fortress Press, 1995), p. 59. The reference in the next line to uprooting oneself is on p. 57.

27. E. John Walford, *Jacob van Ruysdael and the Perception of Landscape* (New Haven: Yale University Press, 1991).

Dante, Bunyan, and the Search for a Protestant Aesthetics

Water Lilies, from late in the painter's life, appear completely natural — naturalness was highly praised in seventeenth-century Dutch art. But a closer look indicates that it is a "selected naturalness": a dead beech tree leans out from the shore, autumnal colors tell of the coming winter, and dark clouds threaten. Still, at the far left, the shepherd cares for his sheep — going out to his labor until the evening, as Psalm 104:23 puts it — and there is light in the sky; these elements remind the viewer of the sustaining presence of God. As the Netherlands Confession has it: "The world is before our eyes as a beautiful book... like letters which give us the invisible things of God." But the beauty is threatened; the contrast of dead and living vegetation speaks of the transience of life and the need for grace.

Brokenness does not lead either to world flight or to despair, because God did not leave the world in this situation. Brokenness, on the Christian account, has been addressed in the life and work of Christ. For the Protestant, the cross of Christ is not simply a reminder of the folly of human hubris or a symbol of self-denial — it is in many ways the central reality of the Christian life. Catholic aesthetician Richard Viladesau, for example, can write, "The message of 'the cross' is the symbolic epitome of the wider message of self-denial, 'death' to self, in Christ, as the means to new life."[28] In this he echoes Dante's view, and it is true as far as it goes, but for the Protestant, it does not go far enough. The cross is not simply a symbol of the human existential situation — which, after all, was on display in the Garden of Eden before the Fall; it was a historical intervention by God to address that situation. And it is the key to the story that Christians believe they are living, a reality that engages their emotions as well as their intellect.

The Protestant emphasis on brokenness, and on the pervasive influence of human sin, calls into question the medieval notion of "participation," as we argued earlier. But it suggests another possible way of thinking about our participation in God — one based on the dramatic narrative of the Gospel rather than on the medieval notion of the analogy of being. That is, our fellowship *(koinonia)* with God and each other is based on our being taken up into the life of God as this was realized in the person of Christ, by the power of the Holy Spirit, so that we are enabled to live out in the world the reality of the Gospel. This means that the "aesthetics" of the cross is not evident directly from the narrative of

---

28. Viladesau, *Theological Aesthetics,* p. 190.

Jacob van Ruisdael, *Oak Trees on the Lake with Water Lilies,*
c. 1670, Berlin, Staatliche Museum.
Source: Art Resource/NY.

Christ's death. The response to this is necessarily ambiguous — one can still either wash one's hands, as Pilate did, or recognize the Son of God, as the Roman centurion did. That is, its "beauty" is seen indirectly, as it is lived and practiced as a form of life in the world.

This dramatic uncertainty lies at the heart of Calvin's conception of creation as a theatre for the glory of God — here in this order of things God's dramatic reversal of a broken order is becoming visible. But, notice, it is the drama, not God, which is visible. It is a common criticism of Calvin's Christology that it seemed to deny the substantial healing of creation through the Incarnation that is featured, for example, in Eastern Orthodox theology. This certainly precludes certain uses of the Incarnation, as I will argue later. But something important may also be preserved by this emphasis. Calvin insisted on the theological significance of the ascension, as underlining the reality of Christ's physical absence. This absence, of course, is bridged by our participation in the

Eucharist, wherein we are joined with Christ by the Spirit, but it also speaks of this present time of waiting for Christ's return. This opens the way for us to understand our "spiritual" participation in God through our being drawn into the Trinitarian life of God, as we are joined with Christ by faith, and our living out that life by the power of the Spirit *in this time and place*. This extends our "participation" in God to our worldly discipleship, thus elevating everyday life to a new spiritual (and aesthetic) importance.

Aesthetically, then, this dramatic and narrative emphasis implies a particular notion of "image" and "imagination." The image that reflects the story embedded in the life of Christ and that embodies this dynamic between life and death takes the form of a parable, or a maxim. It challenges the viewer (or hearer) to take up a position with respect to this story. Christ's own ministry fully affirmed the life and joy of life in creation. But it was a creation threatened by storms and accidents, and by hunger and disease. And his death is a powerful encounter with this brokenness, which we in our own way are meant to live out — we are to "take up our cross" and follow him. It is this death that gives our lives their special dramatic quality. And the perceptible form of Protestant aesthetics will tend to bear this cruciform mark.

For all the importance the cross has for Protestants, they have spent little time focusing on the actual event of the cross — the Catholic imagination evident in Mel Gibson's movie *The Passion of the Christ* has traditionally been alien to them. It is more important for Protestants to *interpret* the cross, to see their lives as cross-shaped — it is to influence their practices of reading, which in turn is to impact their everyday life. In his *Institutes,* for example, Calvin spends barely a page describing the actual event of Christ's death. But he writes a long chapter on what this death means for Christians — that since Christ suffered this way, we should not expect our lives to escape such hardship; that our lives should be characterized by this willingness to suffer for Christ; and so on (this is to say nothing of the great sections he uses to develop the theological meaning of that event).[29] The event of the cross finds its real meaning in this typological extension in the life of the believer, who in this way "participates" in God (and in God's work).

---

29. See John Calvin, *Institutes of the Christian Religion,* Library of Christian Classics, vols. 20-21, ed. John T. McNeill, trans. Ford Lewis Battles (Philadelphia: Fortress Press, 1960), 4.8: "Bearing the Cross: A Part of Self-Denial."

Hans Holbein, *The Entombment of Christ,* 1521, Basel Museum.
Source: Art Resource/NY.

When the brokenness is understood in the light of the Christian story, even what is ugly or deformed can be infused with a depth and power — it can be what is "appreciable." We can understand and express in our poetic figuration something of the absence of God as well as of the presence of God. But brokenness and absence do not have the last word. In Jeremy Begbie's words, Christians can see the world in terms of a "redeemed brokenness."[30] Fragility, suffering, and even death can be symbolic of the larger Christian drama, something to be faced and overcome. Hans Holbein, who publicly sided with the reform in June of 1529 and moved definitively to England in 1532, worked for most of his life within the framework of Reformation thought. His earliest painting, before his formal alliance with the reform, shows the influence of Grünewald and Dürer. *The Entombment of Christ* (1521), which is in the Basle Museum, portrays Christ after he was taken down from the cross and before he was prepared for burial. In 1867 Dostoyevsky visited the Basle Museum on his way to Geneva. His wife later described his reaction to Holbein's painting:

> [Dostoyevsky] stood for twenty minutes before the picture without moving. On his agitated face there was the frightened expression I often noticed during the first moments of his epileptic fits. He had no fit at the time, but he could never forget the sensation he had experi-

---

30. See the conclusion of Jeremy Begbie, *Voicing Creation's Praise: Towards a Theology of the Arts* (Edinburgh: T&T Clark, 1991).

enced in the Basle Museum in 1867: the figure of Christ taken from the cross, whose body already showed signs of decomposition, haunted him like a horrible nightmare.[31]

What struck Dostoyevsky so deeply may have impacted his portrayal of Prince Myshkin in *The Idiot*. Beauty is not that which, being seen, pleases, but that which reflects the deep reality of the world we live in; indeed, it reflects the story that informs our lives — and it determines the felt qualities of authentic art. But it does more: in and through these qualities it makes a claim on us.

Hidden Character

This leads us to a second theme of a Protestant aesthetic, what I will call its *hidden character*. We discussed above the literary character of Bunyan's work as an art that calls attention not to itself but rather to the matter it seeks to express. In this way Protestant aesthetics is often hidden or enigmatic and its method indirect.

A common description of Bunyan's prose is that it seeks edification rather than art. Roger Sharrock has said, "Donne and Milton recognize an aesthetic category; Bunyan does not. He accepts only the category of edification."[32] But this should not be taken to mean that he gave no thought to style, as we have seen. Rather, he sought edification through the art — his unique blend of colloquial and biblical styles were pressed into higher service. As Monica Furlong puts it, "[Bunyan's] beliefs were so thoroughly assimilated that they did not clash with the artistic purpose of the book, in fact they gave it its passion and energy."[33] In other words, Bunyan's call to pilgrimage is essential to what is appreciable in the form — to the lively image.

A major characteristic of Protestant aesthetics is often referred to as "simplicity" or "silence." Peter Auksi uses these terms and notes sug-

---

31. From the translator's introduction to *The Idiot*, quoted in John De Gruchy, *Christianity, Art, and Transformation: Theological Aesthetics in the Struggle for Justice* (Cambridge: Cambridge University Press, 2001), p. 99.

32. Roger Sharrock, quoted in U. Milo Kaufmann, *"The Pilgrim's Progress" and Traditions in Puritan Meditation*, p. 7.

33. Monica Furlong, *Puritan's Progress* (New York: Coward, McCann & Geoghegan, 1975), p. 94.

gestively that the Reformers left us "a body of incidental aesthetic theory which, while it does not constitute a seemly whole, has nevertheless influenced deeply attitudes toward the world of matter and the arts in the historical culture of reformed religions."[34] I think a better term for this is its "hiddenness" — that is, the art that results from works influenced by this tradition may often be misunderstood; its beauty may be missed — just as Jesus' parables are told only for those with ears to hear. This characteristic has led the most prominent aestheticians writing in this tradition to discard the notion of beauty altogether. Nicholas Wolterstorff, for example, develops the notion of "fittingness" to describe the beauty of, say, a New England meetinghouse.[35] Similarly, Calvin Seerveld has developed extensively the notion of "allusiveness" that he believes should replace the traditional — and now widely misunderstood — notion of beauty. "Peculiar to art," he says, "is a parable character, a metaphoric intensity, an elusive play in its artifactual presentation of meanings apprehended."[36] Both of these notions express something of the hiddenness that is central to Protestant aesthetics.

Consider the painting *The Potato Eaters* (1885) by Vincent van Gogh. On one level, van Gogh's painting is a simple recollection of a peasant meal — what Kathleen Erickson has called "the first truly realistic peasant painting in Western art."[37] Although it does not adhere to classical or contemporary standards either of style or of subject matter, at a deep level it confronts serious issues of life and death. As Vincent said in a letter to his brother Theo (in May 1885), "We must continue to give something real and honest. Painting peasant life is a serious thing and I should reproach myself if I did not try to make pictures which will rouse serious thought. . . ."[38] Erickson has argued that van Gogh did not give up his deep Christian faith when he left the institutional church

---

34. Peter Auksi, "Simplicity and Silence: The Influence of Scripture on the Aesthetic Thought of the Major Reformers," *The Journal of Religious History* 10, no. 4 (1979): 363, 364. The silence relates to the necessity of listening carefully (and internally) to the preached word. See also Auksi, *Christian Plain Style: The Evolution of a Spiritual Ideal* (Montreal: McGill University Press, 1995).

35. Wolterstorff, *Art in Action: Toward a Christian Aesthetic* (Grand Rapids: Wm. B. Eerdmans, 1980), pp. 114-19 and p. 186.

36. Calvin Seerveld, *Rainbows for the Fallen World: Aesthetic Life and Artistic Task* (Toronto: Tuppence Press, 1980), p. 27.

37. Kathleen Powers Erickson, *At Eternity's Gate: The Spiritual Vision of Vincent Van Gogh* (Grand Rapids: Wm. B. Eerdmans, 1998), p. 88.

38. Erickson, *At Eternity's Gate*, p. 88.

Dante, Bunyan, and the Search for a Protestant Aesthetics

Vincent Van Gogh, *The Potato Eaters*, 1885, Van Gogh Museum, Amsterdam.
Source: Art Resource/NY.

around 1880; rather, he sought it more deeply — as something embedded in life. He continued to read his beloved *Imitation of Christ* and, interestingly, *The Pilgrim's Progress.* As a result of his continuing faith, this simple meal takes on the depth of a Eucharist in which each serves the other, or even the significance of a last supper where the betrayer breaks bread with Christ. Erickson argues that when God touches us, our most mundane acts convey this presence "with far more poignancy than the traditional subjects of cross and cathedral."[39] In the midst of the difficult journey of life, there is the light of God — symbolized by the lamp and the hope of heaven, symbolized by the crucifix on the wall. The perceived form takes on a charged beauty, though it is one that may be missed.

A good description of this characteristic, and arguably one of its historical sources, is to be found in Puritan William Perkins' influential treatise *The Art of Prophesying,* written as an instruction for preachers early in 1592. The art of preaching that Perkins sought to encourage was

---

39. Erickson, *At Eternity's Gate*, p. 88.

a "simple and plaine speech," expounding and applying Scripture so that its power would be made available to the listener. Perkins allows that a preacher may well study the best thinkers and commentaries in sermon preparation. Perkins does not deny the value of the cultural wisdom that we have described. The preacher may develop elaborate rhetorical strategies, but when he (there being no women preachers in Perkins' day) mounts the pulpit to preach, "he ought in publike to conceale all these from the people and not to make the least ostentation." Perkins goes on to quote a Latin expression: "*ars etiam est celare artem*" ("It is also a point of art to conceal art").[40] Of course, by art Perkins does not mean what we do (*ars* might better be translated as "craft" or "skill"), but his notion that the best art conceals its art in order to better accomplish its rhetorical purpose might nevertheless be taken as a watchword for Protestant aesthetics.[41]

Perkins' concern was to avoid any display that would call attention to the preacher (and lead to pride), but even more he wanted to ensure that whatever art might exist would serve the end of God's call in the sermon. I noted above that for Christian in *The Pilgrim's Progress*, getting the narrative right was critical to his finding his way to the heavenly kingdom and that this privileged the trope of reading and hearing over seeing and vision. In this respect his stop at Interpreter's House was an essential part of orienting himself for the journey. Interestingly, it is in Interpreter's House that Christian sees the only actual "picture" that appears in *The Pilgrim's Progress*. Interpreter leads Christian into a private room, and Christian is shown "the picture of a very grave person [hung] against the wall; and this was the fashion of it: it had eyes lifted up to Heaven, the best of books in its hand, the law of truth written upon its lips, the world was behind its back; it stood as if it pleaded with men, and a crown of gold did hang over its head." When Christian asks the meaning of this, Interpreter tells him this picture is the only one the Lord has authorized to "be thy guide, in all the difficult places thou mayest meet with in the way."[42] Christian is meant to have this lively

---

40. William Perkins, "The Art of Prophesying," in *Works of That Famous and Worthy Minister William Perkins* (London: John Legatt, 1631), vol. 2, p. 670. The Latin expression can be traced to Ovid, *Ars Amatoria*, Book II, l. 313 (c. 1 B.C.E.): "If art is concealed, it succeeds."

41. This is an argument that I develop at length in *Reformed Theology and Visual Culture*, especially in Chapter Five.

42. Furlong, *Puritan's Progress*, p. 31.

image on his heart, one that directs him in the journey he is taking. This interpreter can assist in forming this lively image. Indeed, as implied by the "picture," the viewer could actually *become* this image.

In early New England, John Foster's famous print of Richard Mather would have hung in many godly homes. Images of righteous preachers, especially of first-generation settlers in New England, took the place of medieval images of saints — precisely because they were the ones who could rightly interpret the parabolic nature of scriptural teaching. They point us to the word, and illumine for us this lively image, as Richard Mather does in Foster's print.

The Prophetic

This brings us to a final category that I will call *prophetic*. A Protestant reading of the world leads not only to a mistrust of the allure of the world but also to a protest against its brokenness. If Christian's world cannot simply be enjoyed, it surely must be engaged, even opposed. Since the order of the world, even (or especially) in its brokenness, is morally charged, it must be resisted — indeed, this resistance lies at the core of the biblical drama. As Christian soon learned, one must resist the temptations that present themselves — the world demands moral discernment and a politics of resistance. For Dante, the aesthetic side of events and individuals — dancing, singing, and so on — could be fully embraced and enjoyed; for Christian, persons and situations had an aesthetic dimension to them, but this could not be separated from the deeper moral and spiritual struggle in which he (and they) were engaged. And for those determined to pursue this struggle, there was clearly a price to be paid — they would suffer for their pursuit of righteousness. (The comparison between Dante's image of martyrdom and Bunyan's image of martyrdom would be illuminating here.) Brokenness and absence here cannot be evaded — this is not yet the time for music and dancing.

The role that "interpretation" plays, I have suggested, is central to a Protestant aesthetics, and it signals its prophetic character. Those forms and stories function best that encourage viewers and hearers to reconstrue the pattern of their lives, to re-interpret or *re-read* that pattern in accordance with the biblical truth, and, more importantly, to direct their lives in accordance with what is seen and heard. In the Chris-

John Foster, Print of Richard Mather, c. 1670.
Reproduced by permission of The Huntington Library, San Marino, California.

tian tradition since Augustine, there is the conviction that the proper interpretation of Scripture leads to the correct view of one's life in the world. Another way of saying this is that reading skills developed to interpret Scripture can be applied — one might even say that they *are necessarily applied* — to the interpretation of life.

Dante, Bunyan, and the Search for a Protestant Aesthetics

Bunyan's narrative style intentionally employs conflict and struggles that illumine the reader's own life in the world. Christian's passage through Vanity Fair, for example, is a powerful reflection on the vacuous pursuits of commercial culture. Kathleen Swain describes the way that Bunyan's "symbolic power struggles" engage the reader in interpretive activity. His allegory, she writes, is meant "to initiate a process of gradual enlightenment and progressive self-discovery."[43] This process is personal without being individualistic. The experiences of Christian in his life before God progressively define his sense of himself. Indeed, for Christian the meaning of the self is progressively uncovered (especially in his frequent retelling of the story of his journey) through the historical process of living by faith.

Paul Ricoeur sees this reflected in Christ's parables. As he puts this, parables "invite the reader to continue, on his or her own account, the Bible's itineraries of meaning."[44] The word of the Gospel is meant to draw the hearer into its conflicted world — which, the Bible claims, involves seeing the world in a new and more truthful way. So imagination, like beauty, does not play an independent role but is implicated in this dramatic re-ordering of things. An excellent example of this is to be found in the world that van Ruisdael creates in his landscapes. This world seems to embody all the goodness and joy that the Creator intended. There are a peaceful river, a grouping of trees, a flock of birds, perhaps some laborers returning home after work, and an apparently prosperous home in the middle distance. But a closer look changes all this; indeed, one might say that van Ruisdael deconstructs this complacency. The river is peaceful, but it also echoes the path the men are taking alongside it, and speaks of the flowing of life toward its inevitable death. The trees are lovely, but they are also broken, injured perhaps by some strike of lightning. The birds fly through a sky that is darkened by ominous clouds. On closer examination, the prosperous burgher's home is clearly falling into ruins. And so on. What is given in creation is also threatened — it can be lost. But beyond all this, the viewer is invited to take a position with respect to this panorama: Is this a proper

---

43. Kathleen M. Swain, *Pilgrim's Progress: Discourses and Contexts* (Urbana: University of Illinois Press, 1993), pp. 20-21. Swain borrows the phrase "symbolic power struggles" from Angus Fletcher. She discusses the "narrative self" in pp. 135ff. I am dependent on her description in this paragraph.

44. Ricoeur, *Figuring the Sacred*, p. 149. Ricoeur goes on to argue that this way of reading reflects the original function of imagination.

way of seeing things? If so, how must she live out her own time in the world?

Dependence on the narratives of Scripture has engendered within Protestantism a temporal logic that is best seen in the interpretive practice of "typological" reading. That is, earlier parts of Scripture are understood to anticipate later events that elaborate and fill out the implications of what came before, and, in turn, events of Scripture are seen as informing events of the believer's life in the world — indeed, to prepare one for the world to come. In spite of the fallibility of God's human followers, Scripture develops — in various ways, and in a diversity of genres and circumstances — an unfolding narrative that comes to its climax in Jesus Christ, but that will not reach its true goal until the arrival of a resurrected creation, coming down, John says, from heaven and from God. Moreover, Christians are encouraged, in this typological view of things, to read their lives as an extension of this biblical narrative — as a pilgrim's progress toward the heavenly kingdom.

Given its temporal logic, Protestant aesthetics has consistently located its full comprehension (and experience) of beauty toward the future. From the top of the Palace Beautiful, Christian could look into the distance and see the Delectable Mountains. "At a great distance, he saw a most pleasant mountainous country, beautified with woods, vineyards, fruits of all sorts, flowers also with springs and fountains, very delectable to behold."[45] Beauty is from God, but its reference is not above, but ahead. And the imagination is best employed to see the joys of this world as anticipations — as types — of the fuller reality that Scripture says awaits the believer. As Lutheran Gerhard Nebel explains, beauty — for Protestants — is more an event than a state. It is "the revelation of the paradisal and eschatological possibilities present in the midst of a sinful world."[46] Art, on this view, is able to provide anticipations of that future — though not in isolation from the narrative that leads to that place.

---

45. Bunyan, *Pilgrim's Progress*, p. 61.
46. Gerhard Nebel, quoted in Hans Urs von Balthasar, *The Glory of the Lord: A Theological Aesthetics*, vol. 1: *Seeing the Form*, trans. Erasmo Leiva-Merikakis (Edinburgh: T&T Clark, 1982), pp. 64-70; quotation is from p. 64. Nebel's views are expounded at length in this volume.

Dante, Bunyan, and the Search for a Protestant Aesthetics

A Protestant Pedagogical Reading

A particular focus on reading has emerged in the course of our exposition of a Protestant aesthetic. First we saw that Protestants, because of their special formation in the reading and hearing of Scripture, have come to understand their encounter with the world in terms of the metaphor of reading and interpretation. Second, the particular way in which they have understood Scripture has led them to a typological understanding, not only of Scripture itself, but of the meaning (and "beauty") of life in the world. They discern life in terms of the narrative of the Gospel, which finds its full meaning not above in the realm of God, but ahead in the eschatological goal of life and the world.

Graham Ward, in discussing Christian notions of reading, describes the way these lead to a particular spiritual pedagogy.[47] He proposes an understanding of allegory (what we are calling typology) that is dynamic over against the usual static discussions of symbolism. Taking his cue from the Gospels (and a doctrine of creation), he proposes a narrative of participation and disclosure (221). When these stories and parables are read and retold, the "telling itself participates in [the disclosure of God] and produces a divine pedagogy" (224-25). Ward notes that since the world is substance, God's good creation, and not simply shadow (as in Plato), we can trust our perceptions (231). And, as a result, human action motivated by this reading and re-reading of the Gospel can lead to a doing (praxis) and making (poesis) in which the latter becomes more fundamental. Social action can be finally oriented toward creative action.

Through an innovative reading of Gregory of Nyssa's *Life of Moses,* Ward develops a theology of representation and reading that gives Moses' life a universal reference, which, like scriptural texts, discloses "the nature of the world" (235). But this only happens as the reader is trained to read the world theologically — that is, when human desire and the operation of the Spirit in creation are placed in dialogue. But, consistent with the imagination that we are exploring, this appeal is indirect rather than direct, dialectical rather than rhetorical. It creates and pre-

---

47. See Ward, "Spiritual Exercises: A Christian Pedagogy," in *Christ and Culture* (Oxford: Blackwell, 2005), pp. 219-47. Subsequent pages will be cited in the text. While Ward does not identify this pedagogy with a Protestant reading, his notion of reading and indirection is consistent with the argument we are developing.

serves a dislocation (and eventual resolution) through a process of intertextuality (236). Our hunger is satisfied by reading (and re-reading) Scripture as this is embodied in the reading (and living) of our lives. The ancient devotional practice of *lectio divina* continues as a central moment of Christian poetics. This makes possible the reorientation of the secular rituals which express, even against our will, the soul's longing for God, who alone is desirable.

But this dialectical imagination also seeks to draw an important distinction between these two kinds of practices — praxis and poesis. It does not forget that humans live in a broken world where human poetics works with borrowed light. Its sight is partial, enigmatic, and capable of misleading. The fact that we are moved by some aesthetic object is, by itself, not enough. The larger question is, How does it move us? And, more importantly, what does it move us toward?[48] Beyond this, something else is necessary. As Eberhard Jüngel says, "In the meantime, special revelatory events are required for something to appear and shine in its own light in our world."[49] And Scripture is the privileged place where these events are recorded and interpreted, and the meditation, praise, and prayer they spawn are what properly orients our poetic theology. It is there that we are taught both how to read and how to (properly) enjoy what we read.

The Modern Imagination

We are now in a position to return to our original question: Why is it that Protestants are put on the defensive when it comes to art and aesthetics? I have hinted that part of the problem lies with limitations within Protestantism itself — something we explore in the next chapter. In the remainder of this chapter, however, I want to suggest a way

---

48. For development of these questions, see Cecilia Gonzalez-Andrieu, "Lorca as Theologian: The Method and Practice of Interlacing the Arts and Theology," Ph.D. dissertation, Graduate Theological Union at Berkeley, 2007. I owe this reference to John Handley. I regret that I saw this important work too late to take full advantage of it.

49. Eberhard Jüngel, "Even the Beautiful Must Die! Beauty in the Light of Truth: Theological Observations on the Aesthetic Relation," in *Theological Essays*, vol. 2, trans. J. Webster and A. Neufeldt-Fast (Edinburgh: T&T Clark, 1995), p. 76. Jüngel goes on to say that although this revelation is also an aesthetic event, it is ultimately subordinate to truth.

in which the problem lies not with Protestant Christianity but with the way the arts have come to be seen and understood in the modern period.

For Christians, clearly, art and aesthetics do not in and of themselves contribute what is necessary to human flourishing. I have argued that they are important to the degree that they play a role in opening us up to a larger narrative and dramatic enactment going on around us. For many modern people, this claim that art ultimately feeds on religion is deeply repulsive — and this may account for some of the defensiveness that Protestants feel. For many of our neighbors, art is perhaps the last human project that offers the possibility of promoting human flourishing. This point of view might be traced back to Friedrich Nietzsche, who wrote *The Birth of Tragedy* precisely to propose the "aesthetic interpretation and justification of the world."[50] As we have seen, Nietzsche recognized the enemy to this proposal as Protestant Christianity. Notice Nietzsche's interpretation of the aesthetic themes we have developed:

> From the very first, Christianity spelled life loathing itself, and that loathing was simply disguised, tricked out, with notions of an "other" and "better" life. A hatred of the "world," a curse on the affective urges, a fear of beauty and sensuality, a transcendence rigged up to slander mortal existence, a yearning for extinction, a cessation of all effort until the great "sabbath of sabbaths" — this whole cluster of distortions, together with the intransigent Christian assertion that nothing counts except moral values, had always struck me as being the most dangerous, most sinister form the will to destruction can take.[51]

An awareness of brokenness becomes, in Nietzsche's mind, a loathing and hatred of the world; a hidden beauty betrays a fear of sensuality; an anticipation of heaven involves the cessation of all effort; and, worst of all, the insistence on moral values becomes dangerous and sinister. Again I will leave to one side for the moment to what degree Nietzsche's diatribe may have been justified in the light of the culture-bound Chris-

---

50. Friedrich Nietzsche, *The Birth of Tragedy*, trans. Francis Golffing (Garden City, N.Y.: Doubleday/Anchor, 1956), p. 10.

51. Nietzsche, *The Birth of Tragedy*, pp. 10-11.

tianity current in his day. It is enough to recognize that Nietzsche's construal of Christianity has entered into the mainstream of aesthetic conversation, and its tone is very much alive in our own generation.

But there is an unrecognized element in Nietzsche's characterization of Christianity which may reflect his own Protestant heritage.[52] One way of reading Nietzsche is to see this diatribe as a protest against an art, and by extension a religion, which had become puerile and unconnected with the deepest emotions of life. The reference to Dionysius developed extensively in *The Birth of Tragedy* reflects his effort to revivify art and return it to its ancient alliance with the forces of magic. At the climactic moment of the Dionysian ritual, god makes himself present. Nietzsche writes, "The satyr chorus is . . . a vision of the Dionysian mass of spectators, just as the world of stage, in turn, is a vision of this satyr chorus. . . . In this magic transformation the Dionysian reveler sees himself as a satyr, and *as a satyr, in turn, he sees the god.*"[53]

In other words, Nietzsche wants his aesthetic experience to be "disturbatory," as Arthur Danto has put it — to disrupt life and transform it.[54] Here Nietzsche is borrowing an ancient theory of "dramatic representation" in which images present and embody the power and reality of their divine source — a theory that strongly influenced the development of modern art, from Wagner's operas to the performance art of the later Picasso — indeed, much of contemporary art. Nietzsche was quite right in seeing the art of his day as facile — unconnected with the emotional and mythical depths he wanted to experience. And perhaps he was not wrong in connecting this with a thin, moralizing Christianity, and with Protestantism in particular.

The iconoclasm of the Reformation was one of the causes of disconnecting art from these primitive sources. And this diminishes them in a way, as Arthur Danto explains: "Once we perceive statues as merely designating what they resemble, where resemblance explains

---

52. Nietzsche's father was a Lutheran minister who died in 1849 when Nietzsche was five.

53. Nietzsche, *The Birth of Tragedy,* trans. Walter Kaufmann (New York: Random House, 1964), pp. 63-64, his emphasis, quoted in "Painting as Performance: The Case of Picasso," in Betsy G. Fryberger et al., *Picasso: Graphic Magician: Prints from the Norton Simon Museum* (Palo Alto, Calif.: Iris and B. Gerald Cantor Center, Stanford University, 1998), p. 92.

54. Arthur Danto, *The Philosophical Disenchantment of Art* (New York: Columbia University Press, 1986).

their form, rather than containing their form, a certain power is lost to art."[55] Calvin and the other Reformers did seek to disconnect images from this ancient magic. But remember what they felt was at stake: Calvin despised these images not because he did not believe in the stories they told; he despised them precisely *because* he believed them. He did not deny drama because he did not accredit the Greek myths. In fact, Belden Lane has argued that drama lies at the heart of Calvin's conception of theology. In his commentary on John 13:31, Calvin wrote the following:

> For in the cross of Christ, as in the splendid theatre, the incomparable goodness of God is set before the whole world. The glory of God shines, indeed, in all creatures on high and below, but never more brightly than in the cross, in which there was wonderful change of things — the condemnation of all men was manifested, sin blotted out, salvation restored to men; in short, the whole world renewed and all things restored to order.[56]

It was jealousy for the true dramatic character of reality that led Calvin to despise other dramatic claims. As J. R. R. Tolkien famously argued,

> The gospel contains a fairy story . . . which embraces all the essence of fairy stories. . . . The art of it has the supremely convincing tone of Primary Art, that is, of creation. Because this story is supreme, and it is true. Art has been verified. . . . Legend and history have met and fused.[57]

So it turns out that Nietzsche merely replaced one means of dramatic self-discovery — the Christian — with another: the Dionysian.[58] He

---

55. Danto, *The Philosophical Disenchantment of Art*, p. 128.

56. Calvin's New Testament Commentaries, vol. 5, p. 68, quoted in Belden Lane, "Spirituality as the Performance of Desire: Calvin on the World as a Theatre of God's Glory," *Spiritus: A Journal of Christian Spirituality* 1, no. 1 (Spring 2001): 11.

57. J. R. R. Tolkien, "On Fairy-Stories," in *Essays Presented to Charles Williams*, ed. C. S. Lewis (New York: Oxford University Press, 1947), pp. 83-84.

58. See Jean-Luc Marion, *God without Being: hors-texte*, trans. Thomas A. Carlson (Chicago: University of Chicago Press, 1991), p. 38: "Freed from moral idolatry, the gods nevertheless remain subject to another unique instance of which they are the function,

sought to revivify the ancient mythology that Christianity had long since dethroned, and in the process he overthrew the other truly dramatic possibility. But Picasso was right in supposing that images could convey the urgency of this dramatic situation. He knew that images could do more than simply convey ideas; they could connect us with God (or gods). Where else could this have come from if not the influence of his Catholic childhood and its sacramental imagery?

We have admitted that, for most Christians, art and aesthetics have no independent role to play in leading to human felicity. The experience of art plays a part, large or small, in a larger drama that is being played out around us. This drama, which includes responding to the call of God that comes to us, is one that, Christians believe, engages everyone. To this extent, "nothing counts except moral values," as Nietzsche claimed. Except we would put it this way: nothing counts but this moral (and theological) situation — or, better, only those things count which are taken up into this situation. It is this situation, God's program of redemption, that finally is beautiful or ugly, that attracts or repels. Other things should be discarded if they distract from or obscure this dramatic reality. But the reverse is true as well: these other gifts should be treasured to the degree that they resonate and draw one in the direction of this drama. As Kierkegaard understood, we are not in the theatre watching the play; we are on the stage, and the time for saying our lines has come.[59] In many ways the world of the drama, to say nothing of our destiny, hangs on whether we will play our part at this critical dramatic moment.

But does the Protestant imagination we have sketched really allow for events or objects to carry this dramatic weight? Does it allow for God to be at work in the lure of culture, outside of the preached word? We will address this central question for a Protestant poetic theology in the next chapter.

---

the will to power. . . . Thus one idolatrous apprehension succeeds another." In neither case is God free.

59. Søren Kierkegaard, *Purity of Heart Is to Will One Thing*, trans. Douglas W. Steere (New York: Harper & Row, 1956), pp. 180-81.

CHAPTER 7

Calvin, the Locked Church, and the Recovery of Contemplation

I argued earlier that poets and artists during the Romantic period recovered a vocabulary of feeling and beauty that they identified with particular (creative) practices. These practices and the associated discourse — of creativity, imagination, and self-discovery — have, in the subsequent two centuries, come to define what we now call art, especially as this is embodied in "the art world." But beyond this, for many of us, poetic practices have become building blocks of our personal and group identity. Moreover, the activities that play this role represent a wide variety of practices in addition to formal aesthetic practices — various kinds of sports (even extreme sports) and, for many, popular music, movies, and video games. All these — what we might call affective practices — represent a place where delight is possible and self-discovery takes place.[1]

Moreover, it is increasingly evident that, for many educated people in the West, these aesthetic and recreational practices have come to replace religion: a game of Sunday-morning soccer or a visit to an art exhibition not only supplants but *stands in for* church attendance. I want to ask, in this chapter and the next, if something like this is true. Is there something about the current expression of Christianity — and I have in mind Protestant Christianity in particular — that lessens its appeal in

---

1. One might argue that something similar is true for events that undermine a person's self-image. Jeffrey G. Murphy comments, "One reason we so deeply resent moral injuries done to us is not simply that they hurt us in some tangible or sensible way; it is because such injuries are also *messages* — symbolic communications" (Murphy's emphasis). See Jean Hampton and Jeffrey G. Murphy, *Forgiveness and Mercy* (Cambridge: Cambridge University Press, 1988), quoted in Wolterstorff, *Justice: Rights and Wrongs* (Princeton: Princeton University Press, 2008), p. 296.

the face of these competitors? Or, alternatively, what do these activities seem to provide that Christianity, apparently, does not? Before addressing these questions, and in order to prepare for them, I need to make some historical comments.

Romanticism and Its Precedents

I am claiming, along with Charles Taylor, that Romanticism developed a discourse and a register of feeling that has come to define the modern self. But I don't want to suggest that what these writers and poets were saying was altogether new. In an important sense, Romantic authors were simply retrieving (and elaborating) a tradition of feeling and associated practices that were indebted to the German Pietists and, beyond these, to the medieval mystics. The role of the former is more widely acknowledged, but the longer-term precedents call for elaboration as well. The medieval mystics of the twelfth and thirteenth centuries developed Augustine's journey of the affections into a multi-stage mystical journey to God. We have noted that Augustine had come to favor the will, or the power to love, over the intellect. During his Neoplatonic period, he assumed that the intellect was the highest human faculty. But his reflections on Paul's letters to the Romans and the Galatians had convinced him that God's will as "loving love" was fundamental to the divine being — an idea that he elaborated in his great treatise on the Trinity.[2]

I have earlier described Augustine's influence on the development of humanism in the Middle Ages. In the twelfth century, as Sarah Coakley points out, there "emerged a new fascination with the Augustinian faculty of the will, reworked in terms of the affections and of erotic desire."[3] These developments were made possible by an awakening individualism that allowed new patterns of interior piety and love for God to emerge.[4]

---

2. See Garry Wills' description of this in *Augustine* (New York: Viking Press, 1999), pp. 93-94. He attributes the idea that Augustine invented the idea of the will (which was not developed in classical thought) to Albrecht Dihle.

3. Sarah Coakley, *Powers and Submissions: Spirituality, Philosophy, and Gender* (Oxford: Blackwell, 2002), p. 79.

4. See Colin Morris, *The Discovery of the Individual, 1050-1200* (London: SPCK, 1972), pp. 158-60.

Calvin, the Locked Church, and the Recovery of Contemplation

The Cistercian monk St. Bernard, in his multi-volume commentary on the Song of Solomon, celebrates this newly awakened sense of love as the privileged way of access to God. He pictured the erotic imagery of marital love found in the Song as a sanctuary where one might find the "gift of holy love, the sacrament of endless union with God."[5] For Bernard, love is the primary way in which we can come to God. "Love is the only one of the motions of the soul, of its senses and affections, in which the creature can respond to its creator"; it is, he thinks, the only way we can repay the favor of God's love for us.[6] And it is the only way to true self-discovery as well. It is only when we love God with our whole heart, Bernard says in the fiftieth sermon on the Song, that God "is indeed experienced, although not as he truly is, a thing impossible for any creature, but rather in relation to your power to enjoy. Then you will experience as well your own true self."[7]

This union of love is accomplished through Christ, the Word made flesh, to whose humanity we humans are drawn. Bernard acknowledges that the love of the human heart is always in some sense carnal. And this is why, he thinks, God became human. God "wanted to recapture the affections of carnal men who were unable to love in any other way, by first drawing them to the salutary love of his own humanity and then gradually to raise them to a spiritual love."[8] In the mid-thirteenth century, St. Bonaventure laid out this process in terms of a mystical itinerary in his *Journey of the Mind to God.*[9] There the famous Franciscan theologian describes the six stages by which the soul moves gradually from contemplating the vestiges of God in the world, to seeing the image of God in the mind, to seeing God as "He who is," and finally to experiencing him as the final Good, self-communicating love. For Bonaventure, the intellect is surrounded and nourished by love, which alone moves the soul toward God. The role of human desire is prominent in this

---

5. St. Bernard, *Sermons on the Song of Solomon,* vol. 1, trans. Kilian Walsh (Kalamazoo, Mich.: Cistercian Publications, 1971), Sermon 1, p. 2.

6. St. Bernard, *Sermons on the Song of Solomon,* vol. 4, trans. Irene Edwards (Kalamazoo, Mich.: Cistercian Publications, 1980), Sermon 83.4, p. 184. Unlike his colleague William of St. Thierry, however, he saw love as a way of knowing.

7. St. Bernard, *Sermons on the Song of Solomon,* vol. 3, trans. Kilian Walsh and Irene Edwards (Kalamazoo, Mich.: Cistercian Publications, 1979), Sermon 50.3, p. 35.

8. St. Bernard, *Sermons on the Song of Solomon,* vol. 1, Sermon 20.5, p. 152.

9. St. Bonaventure, *The Journey of the Mind to God,* trans. Philotheus Boehner (Indianapolis: Hackett Publishing Co., 1990 [1956]).

mystical journey. Here he develops Augustine's dictum that we are to love God in all things, and all things in God. Desire, he argues, is the movement of the soul:

> Human desire . . . seeks whatever it seeks only because of the highest Good, because what it seeks either leads to the highest Good or has some likeness to it. So great is the power of the highest Good that nothing can be loved by a creature except through the desire for that Good, so that he who takes the likeness and the copy for the truth errs and goes astray.[10]

Significantly, in the prologue, Bonaventure describes the starting point for this journey in terms of a vision of the Seraph that he had on Mount Alverno, where St. Francis had often retreated for prayer. The six wings of the angel stand for the six steps of the itinerary in three pairs: two steps in which we travelers are to pass through things external, the whole of God's creation, after which two steps lead us through our own interior selves made in God's image, until finally two steps lead upward to the vision of the goodness and beauty of God in the heavenly Jerusalem. This movement of the soul is profoundly aesthetic: Bonaventure discovers the divine meaning of created things through their beauty.[11]

Reading these medieval texts in isolation from the communal and monastic setting in which they were written, modern readers are apt to look at this process as a detached and purely spiritual (and usually individual) affair. But such assumptions are seriously misleading. For medieval mystics, the nurture and stages of the love of God involved particular practices of obedience, penance, and prayer. The life of monks was ordered by strict rules of liturgical practice. Colin Morris comments, "At Cluny, the greatest monastic centre of the tenth and eleventh centuries, the liturgy was so expanded in length and complexity that it swallowed up much of the time originally allotted to study and manual labor."[12] They insisted on this elaboration because they believed that the practice of the liturgy — the prayers, readings, and litanies — were the privileged means by which the inward journey to God was facilitated.

---

10. St. Bonaventure, *The Journey of the Mind to God*, III, 4, p. 21.

11. See James Fodor's discussion titled "The Beauty of the Word Re-membered," in *The Beauty of God: Theology and the Arts*, ed. D. J. Treier, Mark Husbands, and Roger Lundin (Downers Grove, Ill.: InterVarsity Press, 2007), pp. 173-75.

12. Morris, *The Discovery of the Individual*, p. 27.

Calvin, the Locked Church, and the Recovery of Contemplation

Implicit in the levels, or stages, of spiritual growth — which was often pictured in medieval art as a stairway to God — was the wide variety of possible experiences and responses, and thus of intimacy with God. As in the New Testament itself, Sarah Coakley points out, the responses to the risen Christ in early and medieval spirituality were wide-ranging. Her description of this variety is worth quoting at length:

> Not all responses are equally deep; and the closest recognition (involving dark "esctasy" in Nyssa or actual mingling with the word in Origen) will often ... involve long years of moral and spiritual preparation, prolonged *practice* in "sensing" the presence of Christ. . . . This approach also indicates how seeking and recognizing the resurrected Christ require a *process* of change.[13]

The point that Coakley makes with her description of this range of sensitivity is critical to our discussion. In the modern period, she notes, we have mostly lost this multileveled perspective of spiritual senses; during the Reformation it was replaced with Calvin's generalized sense of God. We have a whittling down of Augustine's memory, will, and understanding to Descartes's undivided doubting self.[14] The Pietist movement and its Romantic heirs recognized this loss and sought to recover something of this rich inner world.

Calvin's rich sense of living life in the presence of God is probably not fairly represented by Coakley's observation, but it is surely the case that the Reformers reacted against the medieval picture of the Christian life as a journey to God.[15] We do not climb a stairway to God, Luther famously remarked; rather, he has come to us in the manger of the Christ-child. We noted earlier that Calvin believed in the spiritual sensitivity of the human heart, but he had become suspicious of what the medieval mystics had made of this. But were these practices as mistaken as he imagined? What was really happening in Calvin's view of the spiritual senses? And how does this relate to the worship practices

---

13. Coakley, *Powers and Submissions*, p. 139, emphasis hers.
14. Coakley, *Powers and Submissions*, p. 77.
15. It is certainly inaccurate to claim, as Coakley does, that "for Calvin, this necessarily elitist and progressivist model is replaced by a theory of double predestination" (*Powers and Submissions*, p. 139). Calvin has a great deal to say about the progressive growth of Christian piety. Interestingly, though Calvin quotes from time to time from Bonaventure's *Commentary on the Sentences*, he never cites *The Journey of the Mind to God*.

that he proposed? To answer these questions, we need a deeper sense of his context and what he set out to do.

Calvin and the Locked Church

One can argue that Calvin was in fact deeply concerned to recover, and not to diminish, the personal experience of faith. One example may be taken to illustrate this concern. In his instructions on church order, John Calvin included a significant detail. He insisted that outside of regular worship hours, the church building should be locked. This instruction is illuminating on several fronts — quite apart from explaining why Protestant churches are usually locked during the week. In fact, we might take it as a kind of metaphor for what I want to argue in this chapter. Calvin gave these instructions so that "no one outside the hours [of the service of worship] may enter for superstitious reasons." He went on, "If anyone be found making any particular devotion inside or nearby, he is to be admonished; if it appears to be a superstition which he will not amend, he is to be chastised."[16]

What lies behind Calvin's concern? Two aspects of Calvin's theological program lie behind these instructions. On the one hand, Calvin was convinced that too many things that went on inside the church — the novenas, the penances, the pomp and processions — were not founded on genuine faith, and so were not conducive to true spirituality. He wanted to clear away this thicket of superstitious practice so that nothing would distract worshipers from the preaching of God's word — he wanted, almost literally, to empty the worship space, so that it could be filled with God's word. As he said, "We shall not establish an order in those trifling pomps which have nothing but fleeting splendor."[17] He wanted to clear away what he called "vain pleasure" so that nothing would distract worshipers from the preaching of the word; he wanted to supplant all of this by the light of God's word, so that all observances would "display manifest usefulness" (4.10.32). No doubt his concerns were justified, and he was right in withdrawing an emphasis on these

---

16. John Calvin, *Theological Treatises*, ed. J. K. S. Reid (London: SCM Press, 1954), p. 79.

17. John Calvin, *Institutes of the Christian Religion*, Library of Christian Classics, vols. 20-21, ed. John T. McNeill, trans. Ford Lewis Battles (Philadelphia: Fortress Press, 1960), 4.10.29.

external practices *during his time*. It seems clear, however, that Calvin was not against ceremonies in themselves, but rather what they had become. In fact, he implied that his injunctions were not intended to be permanent. "This present age," he wrote just after his complaints listed above, "offers proof of the fact that it may be a fitting thing to lay aside, as may be opportune in the circumstances, certain rites that in other circumstances are not impious or indecorous" (4.10.32). In the interim there can be no question that Calvin sought to make what went on inside the church a matter of serious spiritual formation. Still, though *he* might have felt that the ban on ceremonies was only temporary, for many it is still firmly in place five hundred years later!

On the other hand, he was equally concerned about what went on *outside* the church; he believed that all that goes under the name of worship need not be confined to church buildings — for example, the believer can pray at home, at work, or while lying in bed. Indeed, for Calvin the focus of Christian worship and discipleship was not on the space of the church but on life in the world, what he frequently called a theatre for the glory of God. During Calvin's tenure, Geneva was emerging as an important city with a rapidly growing population, much of which was desperately poor. Calvin and his colleagues were concerned to make the larger society into a more just and godly community. Indeed, much of their polemic against images and ceremonies had a strong social-justice motive. In 1530, Martin Bucer, Calvin's close colleague in Strasbourg, wrote a tract defending the removal of images. "The goodness of God," Bucer wrote, "shineth in all his creatures." But the true image of God, Bucer claimed, is to be found in your neighbor. All the goodness we see around us urges us to "be to others as God is to us." Images necessarily impede this work: "For suche expenses which ought to have been made upo [sic] poore nedy folke (whom as beynge the very lyve image of God it was convenyent to have socoured and made our frendes with our lyberalyte) we have wastefully bestowed upon styckes and stones."[18] Devotion directed at images and ceremonies is not only misdirected; it is wasteful of resources that are better spent in serving one's needy neighbor.

18. Martin Bucer, *A Treatise Declaring and Showing... That Pictures and Other Images Are Not to Be Suffered in the Temples and Churches of Christian Men* (London: W. Marshall, 1535), STC 24238. W. Marshall translated J. Bedrohte's Latin translation of Bucer's German original, *Das einigerlei Bild* (1530). The quotations in the text are from the English edition, which is not paginated.

This emphasis on life outside of worship is consistent with the nature of the Protestant aesthetics that we explored in the last chapter. It must not be thought that Calvin opposed any role for sight or the visual in his theology. In creation and in our neighbor, God has placed before us much that should stimulate our praise and encourage our discipleship; it is there that the drama and beauty are to be sought.[19]

Protestant spirituality has been indelibly marked by both of these concerns. For Protestants, the movement of the liturgy, while embodying ends in themselves, finds its telos as God's people live out and seek to realize God's shalom in the world. Nicholas Wolterstorff describes the traditional Protestant view in this way: "The Church is most fully realized as the body of Christ in the world . . . at those points where the poor hear good news, where the captives are sprung free . . . where the oppressed are liberated."[20] In this Reformed Protestant view, Christian worship, and thus the spirituality that we need to encourage, ought to motivate a worldly discipleship. It follows that the practices of devotion, and even the symbolic embodiment of these in religious art, more properly belong in the world and not in the church. Devotional practices are instruments of the Christian's struggle in the world; they seek to anticipate the shalom that God will one day bring about.

In many ways I am sympathetic with Calvin's emphases. No doubt locking the church during the week did something to discourage the debilitating practice of indulgences. And surely the fact that half the population of Geneva was desperately poor justified Calvin's call to embody faith in works of righteousness in the world. Still, it is just as clear that in the recovery of the outward movement of faith into the world, something was lost when the church was locked (and the monasteries were closed). In a later chapter I will be arguing that the physical arrangements of worship space, and what takes place therein, are not incidental to heartfelt worship. In his architectural re-organization, Calvin inadvertently closed the door on spiritual practices that might prove useful in developing the inner life. He unintentionally shut out, I sug-

---

19. Cornelis Van der Kooi, *As in a Mirror: John Calvin and Karl Barth on Knowing God: A Diptych*, trans. Donald Mader (Leiden: Brill, 2005), pp. 80-81. According to Van der Kooi, Calvin believed that God has shown us ample visual evidence of his glory; the problem arises when the human agent gets involved in the design of such things!

20. Nicholas Wolterstorff, "Trumpets, Ashes, and Tears," *The Reformed Journal* 36, no. 2 (February 1986): 17-22. In fairness, this does not represent Wolterstorff's own views; he prefers to say the norms of both inform each other.

gest, the rich and variegated levels of contemplation that the medieval humanists and mystics had developed.[21]

What happened to contemplation during the Reformation? Here is what I think: In recovering at least the possibility for personal spirituality and opening up the inner life for development, Calvin appeared at times to open this inner door of worship by closing an outer one — unnecessarily privileging the ear over the eye in worship. Listen to one example of his emphasis:

> In the preaching of the word, the external minister holds forth the vocal word and it is received by the ears. The internal minister, the Holy Spirit, truly communicates the thing proclaimed through the word that is Christ to the souls of all who will, so that *it is not necessary that Christ or for that matter his word be received through the organs of the body*, but the Holy Spirit effects this union by his secret virtue, by creating faith in us by which he makes us living members of Christ.[22]

Now there is much that is good in this — the Spirit enlivening the preached word, the need for personal appropriation, all seen in a corporate context — but there is an implication that ought not to be overlooked. If any external mediation is unnecessary and the Spirit only works within, there is a threat to traditional understandings for what the church had known as sacraments (or sacramentals). To put it another way, the sacraments now can only *picture* this inward work. Although in his understanding of signs Calvin sought to counter the minimalism of Zwingli, in the end nothing external can be essential to this process. We are not encouraged, as with Bonaventure, to move from meditation on the beauty of creation to the reflection of that beauty within and above us. (Incidentally, as near as I can tell, it was around this time that people began to close their eyes during corporate prayer to better focus their minds.) As a result, though Calvin probably did not intend this, over time it became the case that people, especially in the Pietist stream of this tradition, had no way of finding any sub-

---

21. In fact, in many of Calvin's instructions it seemed clear that he was influenced by the medieval tradition and seeking to preserve its best elements. See *Biblical Interpretation in the Era of the Reformation: Essays Presented to David C. Steinmetz*, ed. Richard R. Muller and John L. Thompson (Grand Rapids: Wm. B. Eerdmans, 1996), especially Chapter One, which focuses on the continuity with the medieval period.

22. Calvin, *Theological Treatises*, p. 173, emphasis added.

stantial theological meaning in any external object or act. There was no longer anything for their eyes or their feelings to hold and indwell.

Descartes was key here. I believe that one can argue that he was working in the shadow of this Calvinist heritage when he said in 1642, "I am certain that I cannot have any knowledge of what is outside of me, except by what is in me."[23] The view that we should have more confidence in what is in our minds than what is before our eyes led to what Charles Taylor calls a "mediational epistemology" (the notion that knowledge is mediated through ideas in our mind), and to the split between public and private religion, seen perhaps in its earliest form in Descartes. This distrust of the unity of sense and spiritual knowledge was surely one of the conditions, if not the cause, of his splitting inner and outer knowledge. Such a view tends to privilege the ear over the eye, and, as a result, language over other symbolic forms.[24]

Two Practices of Reading

Nowhere is this clearer than in the practices of reading that developed after the Reformation, which we introduced in the last chapter. In medieval times, reading, closely allied with practices of remembering, was integral to the soul's journey. This is best seen in the medieval practice of *lectio divina*, or sacred reading, which sought to focus the mind in contemplative attention on God's Word. It involved first a primary reading *(lectio)* in which a part of Scripture was taken in as food for the soul. Next came meditation *(meditatio)*, in which the mind "chewed over" the passage and memory processed its meaning. This led to various forms of prayer *(oratio)*, spontaneous responses of the soul to God. Finally, in contemplation *(contemplatio)* one lost a sense of self and was united with God.[25]

---

23. Letter to Gibieuf, 19 January 1642, in René Descartes, *Philosophical Letters*, trans. and ed. Anthony Kenny (New York: Oxford University Press, 1970), p. 123, quoted in Charles Taylor, *Sources of the Self: The Making of Modern Identity* (Cambridge: Harvard University Press, 1989), p. 144. Here is the quoted line in French: "Je me suis assuré que je ne puis avoir aucune connaissance de ce qui est hors de moi, que j'ai eu en moi."

24. One positive result of this was the way that Calvin emphasized linguistic imagery. See the comprehensive survey of Calvin's images in Randall Zachman, *Image and Word in the Theology of John Calvin* (Notre Dame: University of Notre Dame Press, 2007).

25. See Mary Carruthers, *The Craft of Thought: Meditation, Rhetoric, and the Making of Images, 400-1200* (Cambridge: Cambridge University Press, 1998).

Note that this reading was an aesthetic as well as a spiritual process and that the role of memory insured that it was visual as well as oral. One moved through the various *topoi* (or places) of memory through meditation on external objects and texts through the stages that lead to inward reflection. As James Fodor says, for the medieval mystic "reading was a type of 'seeing,' and seeing was a type of 'reading.'"[26] Since it was an embodied journey, it had its landmarks and its stepping stones. To read a text created memorial paths that corresponded to the larger liturgical movements that employed objects and ritual to stimulate and facilitate the inward journey to God. All the medieval practices of processions and pilgrimages found their meaning in this practice of reading as seeing.

In Chapter Three I described the Protestant practice of reading which emerged in the sixteenth century. At its best, I argued, this practice was a recovery of the ancient *lectio divina*. But too often the Protestant reader tended to see Scripture's truth as an agent of liberation rather than as a stimulus to prayer and meditation — something that is clearly illustrated in *The Pilgrim's Progress*. Behind this lay a particular form of logic developed by the French dialectician Peter Ramus (d. 1572).[27] Ramus believed that all truth could best be captured through a process of discrimination by dichotomies, in which the matter under consideration was laid out in a detailed schema. Following Agricola, he called the points of his schema *topoi*, or places. The significance of "places," however, changed from medieval views of memory. They were no longer actual spaces or rooms of the memory which could be pictured, as they were in the Middle Ages, but abstract places which were visually organized in what today we call an outline. Memory was replaced by reason, concrete places by abstractions. Only in this way, Ramus believed, do we come to know things as they *truly are*. What is significant for the present discussion is the way in which Protestant reading reversed the direction in which the movement of reading proceeds. For the medieval believer, the soul's journey moved from external sacraments and practices inward to the soul and then upward to God; the Protestant reader moved outward from within. For the Protes-

---

26. Fodor, "The Beauty of the Word Re-membered," p. 179. I am dependent on his excellent discussion of the *lectio divina*.

27. For a further elaboration of this development in logic and its implication for aesthetics, see William Dyrness, *Reformed Theology and Visual Culture: The Protestant Imagination from Calvin to Edwards* (Cambridge: Cambridge University Press, 2004), pp. 127-33.

tant, as we noted earlier, seeing became a form of reading, as reading itself became a function of understanding.

If one can have no knowledge of anything external except by what is inside oneself, any possibility of symbolism or "contemplation" in the positive sense I am using it is weakened — indeed, the symbolic function of visual art and architectural arrangements more generally is undercut. And any symbolic acts and objects in the church beyond the sacraments are mostly eliminated. This is surely part of the reason that this tradition has sponsored music but little in the visual arts; it has stimulated a worship strong in piety but lacking in rich symbolic acts and objects. Although this may not be what Calvin intended, as his view of the sacraments shows, it is what happened to the tradition of thought he founded.[28]

Contemplation in Faith and Art

In the light of these comments, let me see if I can make some progress toward defining, and then defending, the role of "contemplation" in art and worship, and connecting this with the affective practices of everyday life that are the underlying theme of this book. Assuming for the moment that Calvin was right in what he affirmed but partly mistaken in what he excluded, I want to make a modest suggestion in the direction of a more ecumenical liturgical sensitivity. Since I have argued that art has replaced religion for many people, let me begin by comparing and contrasting contemplation in the sense that I am using it with the perceptual contemplation that modern art encourages. Much of modern art — too much, I would say — does nothing to encourage real contemplation — that is, the active indwelling of forms and colors that spark our affection, even our love. High modernism certainly sought a kind of contemplation when Clement Greenberg's artists hung their work in the reverent, carpeted New York galleries of the 1950s and 1960s. Surely some artists are more successful in this than others. But lately we have seen much art that serves other functions than contem-

---

28. It is the tendency of the tradition that I want to emphasize. There is growing evidence that the levels of medieval reading continued in other forms during the Reformation but were subsequently lost with, among other things, the rise of critical approaches to Scripture. See attempts to recover these pre-critical reading practices in *Biblical Interpretation in the Era of the Reformation*, ed. Muller and Thompson.

plation: art meant to shock us, to make us uneasy about our bodies or the world we live in, or to toy with our perceptions. Of course, these are not necessarily perverse functions, but, at its best, art has used functions of this kind for a higher purpose: to move the viewer toward a deeper contemplation of life, toward delight or dismay. Where this is lacking, the viewer is left to examine the surface of things. The best art has always encouraged deep reflection, and people continue to respond to art that probes these depths. Indeed, I believe that many secular people find art important precisely because it appeals to the contemplative side of their lives — something that our harried existence too often suppresses. It may also be that art is critical for many people just because it does offer them a surrogate eternity — and their rapt attention suggests a hunger for the real one. And maybe this attraction is also a symptom of what too often characterizes Christian worship — too many words, not enough quiet and rest.

Let me put it another way. Despite the best efforts of cell phones, iPods, BlackBerries, and 24-hour broadband Internet access to stamp out all possibility of the contemplative, people still long to stand transfixed before an image of power and beauty, to walk on the beach at sunset, or to sit quietly in prayer. I believe that behind these contemporary hungers lie deep reasons why Protestants ought to allow contemplative practices back into their spiritual lives — to unlock their churches to their affective lives. I want to describe three of these reasons — two contextual reasons that I will explore more briefly, and a third substantial (and theological) reason that I will explore at greater length.

In the sense that I am using contemplation, I define it, after John Navone, as "a vision kindled by the act of turning toward something in love and affirmation."[29] I believe that this gets at the heart of what the liturgy and spiritual practices are meant to do. Indeed, Navone believes that all true love and friendship require the practice of contemplation. He writes, "There can be no true love without approving contemplation."[30] Spiritual contemplative practices take us further to stimulate what might be called an active awareness of the presence of God, what Sarah Coakley calls "a regular and willed practice of ceding to the divine ... [a] willed engagement in the pattern of cross and resurrection, one's

---

29. John J. Navone, *Toward a Theology of Beauty* (Collegeville, Minn.: Liturgical Press, 1996), p. 6.

30. Navone, *Toward a Theology of Beauty*, p. 25.

deeper rooting and grafting into the body of Christ."[31] As she describes this process of active waiting on God, she notes that this is ritually inscribed and symbolized in baptism and the Eucharist, the central places and practices where spiritual growth is nurtured.

Contemporary Pointers to Contemplation

So why is it important to have spaces of contemplation in our lives? I have described some of the reasons for this in the first chapters of this book, and I will briefly review some of them here. The reason that contemplation is especially important for modern persons lies in their post-Romantic sensitivities. To begin with, contemplation has become indispensable for what we might call psychological reasons. I can remember not long ago when it was a sign of a lack of faith to need psychological counseling. Counseling was treated much like my atheist friends treat faith: as a crutch that strong people (in this case, Christians) should not need. Now, by contrast, it is hard to find Christians who have not had therapy, let alone any who think it is unspiritual. What I have been arguing is that the change in our attitudes is an indication of the growing importance of the inward life for the modern person.

Charles Taylor described this process in his discussion of the development of the modern self.[32] That "we are creatures of inner depths" (111) may *seem* a universal fact, Taylor argues, but it is not. Tracing this back to Augustine as interpreted by Descartes, Taylor argues that the way to God for the modern person lies within. He says, "By going inward, I am drawn upward" (134). There are problems with what we have done with this inner way — in seeing it as our choice rather than something given by grace, and understanding this as individualist and disembodied rather than communal — but the demand for an inner journey defined by personal commitment is inescapable (185). And therefore the hunger for personal resonance and depth in what we believe is unrelenting.

I am struck by the centrality of sight — of vision — to these developments. Whether this is recognized or not, behind this lies Augustine's notion that the self is defined not by what it knows but by what it sees

---

31. Coakley, *Powers and Submissions*, pp. 34, 35.
32. Taylor, *Sources of the Self*. Subsequent pages cited in the text refer to this work.

and loves. Although ignorant of its source, and confessedly non-creedal, postmodern people are radically committed to this Augustinian creed. They are living examples of the medieval adage: You become what you behold. Just look at a typical football fan on Saturday afternoon, or a groupie during a rock concert. The modern person's life is defined, often unconsciously, by what they contemplate — the vision of what they indwell in affirmation and affection.

A central argument of this book is that whatever we make of the distortions, we must reckon with this internal landscape, what Frederick Buechner calls "these hungering depths." The genie of inwardness is out of the bottle, in a way that Augustine (to say nothing of Calvin) could not have anticipated. The hunger for contemplation is deeply human and is nothing new, but it has grown in our lives into an inescapable and universal longing, whether fed by the quest for self-discovery, for the ultimate patterns of reality, or for an encounter with God. But what is an opportunity for false quests and imagined eternities is also a chance to pursue genuine spiritual growth, to find spiritual direction and discover living communities in which to pursue personal experiences of the sacred. What people long for in this rediscovery of the sacramental is the experience of contemplation and, through this, to know and feel the love of God.

The second factor is a sociological one: Contemplation is more important to the contemporary person because of the simple fact that in general she has vastly more leisure time, education, and financial resources than her grandparents had to pursue a good (i.e., beautiful) life. And the available evidence points to the fact that this time and these resources are frequently used for what might broadly be called spiritual and aesthetic purposes. Contrary to what was expected by secularization theorists, religion does not appear to be disappearing. Its continued vitality appears to be inseparable from aesthetic elements. Earlier I referred to Robert Wuthnow's study of aesthetic and spiritual practices, and his argument is particularly relevant here. The picture he draws goes something like this.[33]

According to the dominant secularization thesis, during the last two centuries more and more functions previously filled by religion

---

33. Robert Wuthnow, *All in Sync: How Music and Art Are Revitalizing American Religion* (Berkeley and Los Angeles: University of California Press, 2003). Subsequent pages cited in the text refer to this work.

have been taken over by other specialized institutions. First politics, then social services, then education, and, more recently, counseling — all activities that once fell within the purview of the church — have been taken over by professional groups that operate quite independently of church authority and even its influence. Gradually, then, the influence of the church has retreated into the domestic sphere, and religion has become privatized. In this restricted space its presence has become almost invisible and its influence weakened. The theory goes on to predict that gradually religion will lose its hold even in this private space and eventually disappear altogether.

Seldom has a hypothesis of social science proven more mistaken. Not only has religion not disappeared — in the past generation it has experienced a period of renewal. And it turns out that the private sphere of the home and personal life, expanding as it has because of the benefits of industrialization, has provided a space for religion and spirituality to flourish. As Wuthnow puts it, "The private sphere was not so much a last frontier for religion as a new or expanding frontier" (14).

Of course, people's increased leisure time and resources provide opportunities to pursue mischief as well as spirituality. But we are claiming that the appeal of a better life, of travel to new destinations, even of volunteering at a soup kitchen represent a desire for satisfaction that in the broadest sense is spiritual. But beyond this there is evidence that people are using this time for more traditionally spiritual activities. And in this renewal of spirituality the aesthetic dimension is critical. Wuthnow's research has demonstrated that the growing interest in religion is correlated with increasing involvement in the arts. For the arts open up affective spaces in which meditation and prayer can come naturally to expression. Rather than seeking intellectual arguments for their faith, many people today find their faith validated "aesthetically through repetition and familiarity" (54). Often, Wuthnow has found, the attraction to the arts is correlated not with an eclectic, vague spirituality, as is often assumed, but with commitment to a tradition of faith and to deep spiritual growth (23-43). And aesthetic factors are increasingly important in people's choice of church.

So in the light of the growing personal inclination toward contemplation and the social space available for it, it is not surprising that cultural producers seek to fill this space with false gods and alternative experiences. There is clearly a strategic opportunity for Christians here, but I will not pursue that in this book, because the motivation to allow a space for contemplation is not merely strategic — it is theological. The more important reason for making contemplation central to Christian worship and spirituality is that it is central to biblical spirituality and the Christian tradition — or at least it *was* central until it became challenged since the Reformation. This constitutes the most substantial reason for us to unlock the door of the church.

To illustrate this, let me point to some biblical examples and then an example from the Christian tradition. The Protestant tradition famously argues for the centrality of Scripture, and this has been among its strengths. But too often the Protestant reader has limited the uses of Scripture to the narrowly catechetical and cognitive, in contrast to the ancient practice of *lectio divina,* which sought a deep encounter with Scripture. My recent reflection on Scripture has led me to see how often biblical narrative, especially that which contains instructions (torah), is embedded in a striking vision of God or the divine majesty that calls for meditation and reflection. Moses comes down from his encounter with God on the mountain to give the law; David frequently grounds his testimony in his contemplation of God in the temple; Peter's sermon at Pentecost follows the experience of wind and fire; and so on.

A good example is Isaiah's vision of God (Isaiah 6) in the year of King Uzziah's death (a vision probably sparked by the regal symbolism associated with this earthly king):

> I saw the Lord sitting on a throne, high and lofty; and the hem of his robe filled the temple. Seraphs were in attendance above him; each had six wings: with two they covered their faces, and with two they covered their feet, and with two they flew. And one called to another and said: "Holy, holy, holy is the LORD of hosts: the whole earth is full of his glory." The pivots on the thresholds shook at the voices of those who called, and the house filled with smoke. (Isa. 6:1-4)

Reformed theologian John De Gruchy points out that this experience changed the direction of Isaiah's life. The vision of God's glory did not turn him away from the world but turned him toward it, and "sent him to proclaim God's demand for social justice." De Gruchy concludes that "true contemplation and social action are complementary."[34]

---

34. John W. De Gruchy, *Christianity, Art, and Transformation: Theological Aesthetics in the Struggle for Justice* (Cambridge: Cambridge University Press, 2001), p. 222.

Contemplation and action are complementary — that is the best Reformed reading of this passage, and there is much truth in it. But is this what Isaiah intends? My sense is that Isaiah would want to go beyond this complementary view. Perhaps he would want us to see the telos of his life and ministry in this vision of God — which was visually anticipated in temple worship and was the likely stimulus of Isaiah's vision. As Walter Brueggemann comments, "The liturgical experience in the temple has a powerful aesthetic dimension, for the God of Israel is known to be present in an environment of physical, visible loveliness."[35]

It is not as though Isaiah had this experience and then *left it behind* to do ministry — this is, if I may say so, the Protestant reading of this text. Rather, Isaiah *indwelt* this experience as he did his ministry. It was the controlling vision to which he returned — which may be why it is placed here and not in the first chapter of the book. This vision is what enabled him to see the earth and its future as potential carriers of God's glory, to see that "the mountain of the LORD's house shall be established as the highest of the mountains . . . [and] all the nations shall stream to it" (2:2). I have heard many sermons on Isaiah 6, but in my memory they all focus on verse 8, and Isaiah's reply: "Here am I; send me!" I was often reminded that it is the holiness of God that should motivate my response, but as far as I can remember, I was never encouraged to spend any time on the *vision* itself. But Isaiah clearly intends us to do so — the details of wings and coals and smoke were clearly meant to engage our imagination. And not simply as a "means" to the end of our ministry, as it is often made out to be, but as embodying the end to which our ministry is to lead, and the substance that our ministry is to express.

Interestingly, Calvin in his commentary on this verse can appreciate the emotional impact of the vision. He allows that "there was no feeling in [Isaiah] which was not overpowered by the presence of God, so that, like one who had lost his senses, he willingly plunged himself in darkness, or rather, like one who despaired of life, he of his own accord chose to die." Further, this appearance of the invisible God in visual form reflects God's ability to accommodate to people according to their ability to receive, "to cause some kind of mirror to reflect the rays of his

---

35. Walter Brueggemann, *Theology of the Old Testament* (Philadelphia: Fortress Press, 2005), p. 427, quoted in De Gruchy, *Christianity, Art, and Transformation*, p. 223.

glory."[36] But the intent of the vision, as the frequent references to this passage in the *Institutes* make clear, is to convince people of their sinfulness and their separation from the majesty of God.

By contrast, the medieval reader spent a great deal of time reflecting on the vision itself, allowing this to move the will and the emotions in a positive way. It was meditation on this passage, with the winged seraph in the form of the Crucified, that led St. Francis to his identification with Christ, marked on his body in the form of the stigmata — wherein he received the marks of Christ's suffering. St. Bonaventure, when he withdrew to the same place on Mount Alverno, had a vision of the seraph which he said pointed out the way "that state of contemplation may be reached." Thus he proposes, "The six wings of the seraph can be rightly understood as signifying the six progressive illuminations by which the soul is disposed, as by certain grades or steps, to pass over to peace through the ecstatic transports of Christian wisdom."[37] The levels of interpretation common to medieval writers are evident here. There is the literal level of Isaiah's vision in the temple the year that King Uzziah died. Then there is the ethical level, in which we are reminded of the holiness of God and our own impurity. But beyond this there is an allegorical level in which the image of the seraph becomes a symbol of the stages the soul must go through to see God. Finally, the anagogical level reminds us that the goal of our lives, anticipated in Isaiah's vision, is the vision of God in heaven. To absorb these levels of meaning involved a long process of reflection and meditation, which constituted a central aspect of the medieval process of spiritual growth.

John's vision in the first chapter of Revelation parallels Isaiah's vision in many ways. While in exile on Patmos, John has a vision on the Lord's Day. Listen to his description: "I saw one like the Son of Man, clothed with a long robe and with a golden sash across his chest. His head and his hair were white as white wool, white as snow; his eyes were like a flame of fire, his feet were like burnished bronze, refined as in a furnace, and his voice was like the sound of many waters" (Rev. 1:13-15). Commentators typically spend their time deciphering the symbolism — "The Ancient of Days" is from Daniel 7; the imagery is from the tem-

---

36. John Calvin, *Commentary on the Book of the Prophet Isaiah*, trans. William Pringle (Edinburgh: Calvin Translation Society, 1850), pp. 198, 200. See pp. 200-202 for the following discussion.

37. St. Bonaventure, *The Journey of the Mind to God*, Prologues 2 and 3.

ple; and so on. But of the two dozen biblical scholars I consulted, only George Caird refers to its aesthetic intent. He notes that John's allusions are used not only for instruction but also for their "evocative and emotive power" to "set echoes of memory and association ringing."[38]

This vision is meant to arrest us, as it did John. When he confronted this splendor — not unlike that described in Isaiah — John fell as though dead. The brilliance, whose only parallel John could think of is the noontime sun, was overwhelming. (Consider how frequently biblical visions end with witnesses struck down as though dead — surely a potent image of what an experience with God is meant to do.) This vision recalls — and may actually stand behind — John's words in his Gospel: "And we have seen his glory, the glory as of a father's only son, full of grace and truth" (1:14). Clearly, the instructions to the churches which follow in Revelation are meant to be controlled by this vision — "write what you see" (v. 11), the Lord tells John. Indeed, we can say with some confidence that the vision is the reason for which the instructions are given. The One who was dead and is alive for evermore, who has the keys of death and hell, stands over our life and work. This Lord is to be seen, loved, and contemplated — this is a vision to which we are to return again and again, as John did in his book. That the vision is meant to kindle affection as well as awe is evident from the fact that language parallels that of the description of the bridegroom in the Song of Solomon 5:10-16 — radiant, gold, altogether desirable.

And why is it that we return to such a vision? Because we are the image of God, and this experience represents the end for which we are made. It addresses us on many levels, as medieval believers knew: we relive John's vision; we feel the impact of the symbolic elements; we anticipate the joy of the beatific vision in heaven. We are meant to indwell these images. This is evident in the centrality of the Sabbath in Scripture as an eschatological image — arguably a central metaphor for an understanding of worship (perhaps even more important than shalom). The basic meaning of the Hebrew word *Shabbat* is "to stop." In the original instructions to Israel, God says, "Six days shall work be done, but the seventh day is a sabbath of solemn rest, holy to the LORD;

---

38. See George Caird, *A Commentary on the Revelation of St. John the Divine,* Harper's New Testament Commentaries (New York: Harper & Row, 1966), p. 25. Interestingly, Calvin makes no reference at all to this passage in his *Institutes* (and he did not write a commentary on Revelation).

whoever does any work on the sabbath day shall be put to death" (Exod. 31:15). Clearly, the telos of work is the Sabbath, not the reverse — for after his work of creation, God also rested. And the homily of Hebrews describes the future hope of God's people in this way: "A sabbath rest still remains for the people of God; for those who enter God's rest also cease from their labors as God did from his" (Heb. 4:9-10).

There is no question in these passages of placing meditation on the vision over against the obedient response of the person, as though the vision was a distraction from the business of obedience — both are valid levels of response. The biblical visions are meant to *enable and encourage* active obedience. By indwelling the vision, Christians are transformed into people who see through the events that surround them to what is actually present in them — that is, the work of God bringing about what these visions show.

Earlier I described the medieval theologians' understanding of our life as a road to God, and I want to return to this notion of a mystical journey as a further piece of evidence for the importance of contemplation. According to St. Bonaventure, "By ... praying we are given light to discern the steps of the soul's ascent to God. For we are so created that the material universe itself is a ladder by which we may ascend to God."[39] We journey toward the day when we will see as we are seen (1 Cor. 13:12; 1 John 3:2). In many ways, Bonaventure's journey is the subtext of Dante's journey to God in *The Divine Comedy*. In Dante's classic description of the soul's journey to God, there is an interesting parallel between the first and last canticles, the *Inferno* and the *Paradiso*. In both, the movement is rapid at the beginning and grows slower and slower throughout the canticle until it comes to rest — in the vision of Satan in hell in the *Inferno* and in the vision of God in heaven in the *Paradiso*. In the *Inferno*, it is the Neutrals who in Canto III run eternally to and fro, "hateful to God and to his enemies" (III, 63),[40] recalling the vision of those who in the last days will go to and fro, like traffic on a Los Angeles freeway. In Canto V the carnal sinners are blown about forever by stormy winds: "The hellish hurricane, which never rests,/drives on the spirits with its violence: wheeling and pounding, it harasses them" (V, 31-33); in Canto XIV the violent against God "must move about incessantly" (XIV, 24). Later, thieves are

---

39. St. Bonaventure, *The Journey of the Mind to God*, p. 5. Cf. p. 21.

40. Dante, *The Divine Comedy*, trans. Allen Mandelbaum (New York: Knopf, 1995). Subsequent citations in the text refer to this work.

set upon by serpents, and in Canto 32 two traitors are frozen in one hole, where one gnaws on the other until the travelers see Lucifer with three heads half-frozen in the ice — all movement has stopped.

In the beginning of the *Paradiso*, Dante and Beatrice are transported rapidly through the spheres. Gradually, movement is eclipsed by a deepening vision; action is replaced by sight. By Canto X, the reader is invited to join Dante in looking on the beauty of the order — or, better, in experiencing the fullness of that order: Dante sees "that one who contemplates/That harmony cannot but taste of Him" (X, 5-6). In Canto XIII, the twenty-four theologians dance and sing around Dante as he is directed toward — by sight, not movement — the "bright source," that Living Radiance. In Canto XXI, mystics ascend the ladder of contemplation. Gradually Dante's eyes are purified by drinking in the light so that he can contemplate the Virgin and then God: "And turn our vision to the Primal Love,/that, gazing at Him, you may penetrate/as far as that can be — His radiance" (XXXII, 142-44). Finally, Dante's purged sight enters deeper into the beam of sublime light "which in Itself is true./From that point on, what I could see was greater/than speech can show: at such a sight it fails — /And memory fails when faced with such excess" (XXXIII, 54-57). Notice that as Dante nears the goal, his sight is progressively purified and deepened; it is not eclipsed. In fact, it is speech that "fails." Interestingly, in the final canto Dante refers to this final vision as a book bound by love, a book that gathers together all that lies scattered in the universe (line 85). This vision stops the reader, as it does the traveler, in his tracks, and opens up a depth that can only be contemplated.

These instances, to which many others could be added, indicate that vision and the contemplation it invites not only direct our journey but animate it as well. But here is the more important implication of this: At its best, the liturgy and our spiritual practices are meant to be a stimulus for this kind of vision. I ended with Dante because I believe that his poetry, shaped as it is by the medieval liturgical tradition, reenacts a kind of cosmic liturgical drama into which the reader is drawn. His journey is clearly laid out in terms of liturgical events — from the penitence and baptism of the *Purgatorio* to the catechetical questions and ecstatic vision in the *Paradiso*. This is no private, free-floating journey of the individual soul.[41] The medieval contemplative

---

41. Recent scholarship has emphasized the way in which Pseudo-Dionysius and St. Bonaventure were rooted in the medieval monastic and liturgical traditions. See Denys

journey was corporate and embodied — it focused on the communal worship life of the people in the same way that the visions of Isaiah and John do. My argument, then, is that when Calvin locked the church against the "superstition" of his day, he unwittingly excluded this rich liturgical tradition of contemplative worship, and for too many churches it has not been let back in. As a result, part of the richness of Protestantism's own biblical and liturgical heritage was lost to the Protestant imagination.

Conclusion: *Ora et Labora*

There are still readers who no doubt feel that this reading of things diminishes the stark biblical call to active discipleship. Doesn't the focus on contemplation necessitate an evasion of our human responsibility in the world? After all, Calvin's locked church had a positive intent: to *extend* Christians' worship to everyday life; to seek the glory of God in all of life. As we saw earlier, Nicholas Wolterstorff believes that this danger is reflected in twentieth-century developments in the art world. Art has become captive to what he calls the purposes of aesthetic contemplation — a situation reflected in the atmosphere and structure of contemporary museums.[42] Art seems to occupy its own, often rarefied world, and it demands our full and undivided attention. But, he wonders, doesn't such an exclusive gaze ignore the larger aesthetic dimension of the whole of human life? If life is a distraction to one who contemplates, one might also say that contemplation also risks distracting from the business of Christian obedience.

Martha Nussbaum has articulated a similar critique of what might be called an aesthetics of transcendence with great force. In particular, she sees Christianity's insistence on a transcendent meaning and goal for life as a cop-out from the diligent and necessary work of finding and constructing meaning in the present order of things, and of shaping deeply felt and supremely *human* works of art. She has defined this Christian aspiration in terms of the Greek notion of hubris. Over

---

Turner, "How to Read the Pseudo-Denys Today?" *International Journal of Systematic Theology* 7, no. 4 (October 2005): 428-40.

42. Nicholas Wolterstorff, *Art in Action: Toward a Christian Aesthetic* (Grand Rapids: Wm. B. Eerdmans, 1980), Chapter 1.

against this wish to transcend the fragility of this life, she suggests a more appropriate response:

> There is a kind of striving that is appropriate to a human life; and there is a kind of striving that consists in trying to depart from that life to another life. This is what *hubris* is — the failure to comprehend what sort of life one has actually got, the failure to live within its limits . . . the failure, being mortal, to think mortal thoughts. . . . Correctly understood, the injunction to avoid hubris is not a penance or denial — it is an instruction as to where the valuable things *for us* are to be found.[43]

And the valuable things for us are to be found in this life, with all of its beauty and its heartache, however much we may strive against its limits. And the essence of the Greek aesthetic that Nussbaum treasures is to struggle as a human being against all the enemies of human flourishing. But what she emphatically rejects as incoherent "is the aspiration to leave behind altogether the constitutive conditions of our humanity and to seek for a life that is really the life of another sort of being — as if it were a higher and better life for *us*."[44] For this rejection clearly makes impossible the this-worldly dramatic aesthetic she admires.

Nussbaum's argument is important — in many ways it resonates with Protestant arguments against contemplation. The Reformers resolutely set themselves against pursuing any mystical journey of escape from the world. They sought to reckon with the sort of life that God had given in creation and that Christ had died to recover. And, as we have seen, art and drama migrated with them out of the sanctuary and into the world. The problem is that in losing its long-standing connection to worship — indeed, to anything religious — art has become a completely secular pursuit. We are left, Nussbaum believes, to work out as best we can the dramatic life that is offered in this immanent order. Any appeal to transcendence — whether religious or aesthetic — is escapist.

Let me respond to Nussbaum in a way that connects with the overall argument of the book and that prepares us for the next two chapters.

---

43. See Martha Nussbaum, *Love's Knowledge: Essays on Philosophy and Literature* (Oxford: Oxford University Press, 1990), p. 381, her emphasis. Nussbaum is responding here to Charles Taylor, who had written a lengthy critique of her earlier work titled *The Fragility of Goodness* (Cambridge: Cambridge University Press, 1986).

44. Nussbaum, *Love's Knowledge*, p. 379, her emphasis.

Calvin, the Locked Church, and the Recovery of Contemplation

The starting point of this book is the recognition that contemporary post-Romantic people are *already engaged* in practices that spark affection and move them toward a vision of a good life. They may not see these activities as referencing any transcendent realm, and they usually do not think of them as religious, but they are nevertheless practices that offer meaning and delight, and around which they order their lives. Humans are naturally devotional animals.

In response to this starting point, we have surveyed Catholic and Protestant responses as possible ways to interpret this natural devotion. Catholicism, especially in its medieval form, seeks more directly to affirm these movements of the soul; Protestantism is more wary of these practices as too often inclining toward various kinds of idolatry. The former seeks to make a more direct appeal to the imagination, an approach we have called (after Justin Klassen) "rhetorical"; the latter seeks indirectly to move the will to a life of faith in the world, an approach we have called "dialectical." In this chapter we are proposing that the Reformation tradition made some gains in classically defining this way of indirection, but nevertheless lost an important part of its biblical and historical heritage that needs to be recovered. Some of the richness and depth of medieval spirituality, especially what we are calling contemplation, was mislaid.

Although he uses different terms, C. S. Lewis has described these two ways in his *Preface to "Paradise Lost."* There he argues that whereas Milton's *Paradise Lost* is meant to be a poem depicting the objective pattern of things, Dante's *Divine Comedy* is the poetical expression of religious experience. For the Protestant Milton, "the cosmic story — the ultimate *plot* in which all other stories are episodes — is set before us. We are invited, for the time being, to look at it from the outside. And that is not, in itself," Lewis notes, "a religious exercise."[45] In Milton we are invited to consider the whole pattern in which the spiritual life arises; in Dante we *experience* that spiritual journey. Lewis sees in these great writers two kinds of imaginations at work. One, illustrated by Milton, he defines in terms he calls "rhetorical," but which we are calling "dialectical." In this way of putting things, imagination is for the sake of passion and thus of action — that is, the appeal is made *indirectly* to the imagination. But there is another kind of imagination that is illus-

---

45. C. S. Lewis, *A Preface to "Paradise Lost"* (Oxford: Oxford University Press, 1942), p. 128.

trated by Dante. This Lewis describes in terms of poetry (what we have called the "rhetorical"). In poetry, passion is for the sake of imagination and therefore for the sake of wisdom and spiritual health — it teaches by delighting. This art leads indirectly to action, but its primary purpose lies elsewhere — in "the rightness and richness of a man's total response to the world."[46]

It is this teaching by delighting that aesthetic contemplation encourages. Good art will always have this "poetic" dimension, and so will healthy worship. When things are put in this way (and to anticipate the argument of the next chapter), we might ask, Do we see worship as poetry or as rhetoric? Worship, of course, can be both a call to responsible action and a call to imaginative richness. But in Calvin's reading of things — in closing the church — this integration is precluded. The great contribution of the Reformation, and of Calvin in particular, is reopening both the human heart and the Christian's life in the world to the movements of grace. By his emphasis on careful preaching and his view that the sacraments join the promise with the sign, he restored important media by which the Spirit could work in the congregation. But he, like Milton, tended to present the objective pattern within which the spiritual life arises rather than a stimulus to enjoy that life — to instruct rather than to delight. The locked church stands for the absence of objects and actions inviting contemplation, leaving it merely a place of instruction and insight. The movements of the Spirit were to lead *outside,* to the external work of shalom-making; the dancing was to take place, if at all, outside the sanctuary.

But closing the church, arguably necessary for his time, was not essential to Calvin's positive project. The great intellectual pattern which Calvin understood so well and which forms the structure of his preaching and his *Institutes* can only be enhanced by its embodiment in liturgical images and actions of power that move the affections, where we may again be "struck dead" by biblical images and poetic interventions. Why must these appeals be escapist, as Nussbaum argues? There is no reason why richly embodied liturgies, dancing, and drama could not so inspire worshipers that their everyday lives would be transformed. Because, remember, this life is meant to be lived in anticipation of a better life that will be fulfilled only when the new earth is a temple. Worship, then, as our Orthodox friends say, is to resonate with a heavenly liturgy

---

46. Lewis, *A Preface to "Paradise Lost,"* p. 54.

Calvin, the Locked Church, and the Recovery of Contemplation

— it is a celebration of life, not its denial. Prayer, praise, and celebration of the Eucharist move worshipers toward their true end. As Samuel Taylor Coleridge once told his nephew, "Prayer is the very highest energy of which the human heart is capable: prayer, that is, with the total concentration of all the faculties."[47] This goal Calvin himself often endorsed, even if he denied some of the possible means to reach it.

We need not lose sight of what was gained during the Reformation — what we might call a religious re-ordering of life in the world — in order to recover the importance of contemplation and the spiritual practices that promote this. The vision of God is meant — throughout Scripture and Christian history — to animate our life in the world, to draw us out into the work of God leading to shalom. But, with the church door closed, too often the focus was placed on the will as opposed to the affections, and thus the rich potential of Christian spirituality was diminished. As a result, the Christian life, the richly embodied life of faith in the world, which is the crowning achievement of the dialectical imagination, was seen too often as a victory of the will over the various assaults of the affections, rather than as a progressive transformation of these through the practices of reading and prayer. In *The Pilgrim's Progress,* the will ordered the affections. But, I want to ask, why cannot the affections be embraced to nurture the will? After all, it is within the deeply lived texture of everyday life that the affections are exercised and nurtured. John Navone has shown how impossible it is to separate the contemplation of God from our life in the world. This is how he expresses the relationship: "The way in which we envision God is always determined from the start by the way we love and treasure the things/persons presented to us within the context of our life's story. Human experience is both cognitive and affective."[48] In this way, spiritual practices and the rituals of everyday life are complementary; they are both part of a life lived in the presence of a loving God. I suspect that even Calvin would agree with the nineteenth-century Russian bishop Theophan the Recluse when he described life's integration in these terms: "The principal thing is to stand before God with the intellect in the heart, and to go on standing before him day and night until the end of life."

---

47. Coleridge, quoted in Alexander Whyte, *Lord, Teach Us to Pray: Sermons on Prayer* (London: Hodder & Stoughton, 1923), pp. 49-50.
48. Navone, *Toward a Theology of Beauty,* p. 71.

This brings us to the subjects of the next two chapters. If the role of contemplation, or what we are calling poetic theology, is recovered — if the church doors are opened to the creative movement of the Spirit — what will that mean for the Christian community and its worship? And then, with this re-orientation in place, what will this mean for the work of justice-making in the world?

The Trajectory of Poetic Theology:
Where Can We Go?

CHAPTER 8

The Aesthetics of Church

Introduction

If there is truth in what we argued in the last chapter — that the Protestant tradition needs to recover aspects of spirituality and form practices and objects that spark contemplation — then it may be that we need to rethink the nature of the church as the primary site for these activities. Like Isaiah, we need a fresh vision of God apart from and before we work for justice. So I want to propose we reverse the usual order of Protestant aesthetics, where beauty is to be sought primarily outside the sanctuary where God's people work for shalom. Perhaps, I want to argue, we must first see it *within* the sanctuary, so that we will have eyes sharpened to recognize it elsewhere. And to do this, we must recognize that the church is the primary location for articulating and constructing the commitments we make as Christians.

This has been a longtime concern of mine. As newly arrived missionaries in the Philippines years ago, our family attended a church that our mission was planting. In the beginning it met each week in a Boy Scout hall. The walls were covered with faded pictures of present and former scout troops, lists of awards, and schedules. As I recall, one of the missionaries brought a vase of flowers each week to put in front of the small podium that served as the pulpit. Otherwise, the room was unadorned. Of course, this was not supposed to matter — this was a temporary space, and besides, what mattered was the singing, praying, and preaching that happened there, and the response of the people who gathered. It was not *supposed to* matter, but of course it *did* matter — to me, and I suspect for others. I found the place dreary and depressing. I thought at the time that this must have affected our worship, but I wasn't sure how.

I also did not realize at the time how this reflected a long tradition of worship practice, one we described in the last chapter with the metaphor of Calvin's locked church. When Calvin locked the church building, he did not intend this to be an innovation in church architecture, though in fact it was. Nor did he intend it to be a hugely influential symbolic move, though it was this as well. Although he gave relatively little attention to the physical arrangements of space in worship, Calvin did make two significant changes in the physical space of St. Peter's in Geneva. First, he moved the altar out into the middle of the worship space, where it was reconceived as the table around which the congregation gathered for a common meal. Second, he moved the pulpit toward the front of the church so that everyone could better see and hear the preacher. These were both significant symbolic gestures that contributed to a focus on the congregation as active participants in hearing the Word, and signaled their unity in the communion.[1] This was consistent with Calvin's intention to place the emphasis on the people and their discipleship in the world and not on the space of worship in the church — but his rearrangement of the worship space had unwitting consequences.

This influence is evident, in part, in the inclination of his followers to frequently stress that the church is not a building; it is a fellowship of people living their lives to the glory of God. So what people do outside the church is clearly more important than what goes on inside it. As with other innovations made during the Reformation (as we saw in the previous chapter), this move involved gains and losses. While it is certainly true that "church" is not a building, an overemphasis on the scattered nature of the church tended to undercut the value of the gathered nature of the church's life — as a people gathered in celebration and praise. In the previous chapter, I described the implications of this tension for spirituality; here I want to focus more on the implications for the visible form this takes and the ritual practices it encourages (or prevents).

There are striking signs today that this space of the church — the gathering rather than the scattering — needs fresh attention. Let me

---

1. For a description of these changes, see André Biéler, *Architecture in Worship: The Christian Place of Worship* (Philadelphia: Westminster Press, 1965), pp. 47-61.

The Aesthetics of Church

mention a few of these briefly. On the one hand, we live in a period of worldwide spiritual renewal and experimentation with new ways of being church. And as we have frequently been reminded of late, this growth and vitality are not limited to North American churches but are occurring throughout the world. As the African theologian John Pobee commented recently in Kenya, churches in Africa are experiencing a spiritual "bubbling up" as well as a loosening of old forms and a lively search for the new.[2] Beyond this, we are confronted with many forms of churchless Christianity emerging in various places — believers in Christ who identify themselves as Hindu in India or as Moslem in Bangladesh. Closer to home, consider the implications of the "emergent churches" in North America and Britain, congregations led by twenty-somethings who make creative use of art and media but remain deeply conflicted about their place in Christian tradition. And what do we make of the controversy accompanying the struggle to find relevant forms of worship? Or the widespread experimentation with classical forms? In one way or another, many of these streams of renewal (and others we could mention) have ties to the evangelical movement, and all of them raise questions that relate directly to ecclesiology and to the place where Christians gather in particular.[3]

Yet, on the other hand, all this "bubbling up," while wonderfully invigorating to watch (with some notable exceptions), is accompanied by little theological reflection on the *form* this bubbling up should take. Put another way, while these groups are earnestly engaged in the search for some stability of form, for some place to stand and display themselves to the world, their theological beliefs do not seem to help them much in this pursuit. This need for visible (and attractive) form will be the focus of this chapter. Here I am picking up on Hannah Arendt's comment that what the institution adds to belief is the public space of its appearance.[4]

---

2. John Pobee, in a personal interview with the author at St. Paul's Theological College, Limuru, Kenya, 24 October 2003.

3. See Eddie Gibbs, *ChurchNext: Quantum Changes in How We Do Ministry* (Downers Grove, Ill.: InterVarsity Press, 2001), and Eddie Gibbs and Ryan Bolger, *The Emerging Church: Creating Christian Community in Postmodern Churches* (Grand Rapids: Baker Book House, 2005). See also Web sites like theooze.com, emergentvillage.com, and so on.

4. Hannah Arendt, quoted in Paul Ricoeur, *Figuring the Sacred: Religion, Narrative, and Imagination,* ed. Mark I. Davis, trans. David Pellauer (Minneapolis: Fortress Press, 1995), p. 88.

This visible representation has always been difficult for Protestants — especially the varieties of evangelicals[5] — but today the challenge is especially acute. And this need is complicated by the widespread disillusionment, especially among younger generations, with institutions of any kind. In recent years the church itself has become the target of a good deal of criticism and, for many, has simply been dismissed as a meaningful player in contemporary culture. And yet, all the while, as we have seen, there is an increasingly urgent desire for images that capture something of the depth and beauty of life, for practices that can structure one's life and spark affection. Religion has always been the custodian of such symbols, and they were the center of the church's life from the beginning. Yet the sad fact is that few people turn to the church for such symbols today. What has gone wrong?

George Hunsberger thinks he knows one reason at least. In a recent book about the church and its mission, he argues that the Reformers left us with an unintended consequence which influences how we understand the church today. That consequence is the understanding of the church as the "place where certain things happen" — preaching, sacraments, discipline, and so on.[6] Hunsberger obviously sees this focus on place — what he calls the church's spatial disease — as a negative inheritance, the hangover of Christendom. Moreover, this focus impedes the church's sense of mission. Only a recovery of the centrality of mission, he thinks, can restore the church's proper role in the world.

One would not want to argue against the need to recover the centrality of the church's missionary calling — especially within the so-called mainline churches. But I would argue that most evangelical churches have very nearly the opposite problem. The evangelical focus on mission and spirituality has all but extinguished any reflection on the *place* the church occupies in its community and its culture and the ritual practices this should engender. Another way of putting this is to point out that, while much consideration is given to incarnating Christianity in our homes and communities, relatively little thought is

---

5. The special focus on evangelicals in this chapter reflects the fact that the substance of the argument (in a much earlier form) was first given as a part of the theology conference at Wheaton College in April 2004 on evangelical ecclesiology. See *The Community of the Word: Toward an Evangelical Ecclesiology*, ed. Mark Husbands and Daniel J. Treier (Downers Grove, Ill.: InterVarsity Press, 2005).

6. George Hunsberger, in *The Missional Church: A Vision for the Sending of the Church in North America*, ed. Darrell L. Guder (Grand Rapids: Wm. B. Eerdmans, 1998), pp. 79-80.

given to the incarnation of the *church* in such settings. In reviewing evangelical books on "the church," I am struck by how frequently the exposition is really not about church at all, but about "mission," "evangelism," or even "spirituality": the church is a missional community, a purpose-driven community, a world-oriented community, and so on. The "church" part of this constitutes whatever shape or trajectory this mission or activity happens to take at a given time — bursts of Christian energy responding, often creatively, to a rapidly changing environment.

Artur Grabowski sees an even more serious side to this absence of reflection on place and representation. He refers to the contemporary focus on desire which I have described in the earlier chapters, and notes that it implies widespread and deep-seated hopes. But, he asks, "can we hope for anything we cannot imagine?"[7] And can we imagine anything without representation? Today, he believes, we have corporately lost our ability to commune with images. Grabowski thinks that despite the plethora of images in our environment, we have all become iconoclasts. "We've been deprived of our ability to trustingly gaze, and it's been replaced by a distanced looking around at pictures from which we expect nothing more than a glittering surface."[8]

Activity has supplanted receptive contemplation, just as exegesis has replaced *lectio divina*. Clearly, the priority of mission, even the bias for action, represents historically the strength of the Protestant movement, and more recently that of the evangelical movement. For Protestant churches generally, "what happens" at church (and then, as a result, outside of church) is the key to understanding the nature of that church. As Gerhard Nebel has argued, during the Reformation the church became more of an event than a place. In fact, in his book on Protestant aesthetics — which he calls, interestingly, *The Event of the Beautiful* — Nebel goes so far as to argue that "event" plays the same role in Reformational ontology that "substance" plays in Thomistic-Aristotelian metaphysics.[9] For both Luther and Calvin, it was the event of the preaching of the Word that constituted the church and called it

---

7. Artur Grabowski, "Unapologetic Visibility," *Image* 59 (Fall 2008): 70.
8. Grabowski, "Unapologetic Visibility," p. 71.
9. Gerhard Nebel, *Das Ereignis des Schönen* (Klett, 1953), p. 17, quoted in Hans Urs von Balthasar, *The Glory of the Lord: A Theological Aesthetics*, trans. Erasmo Leiva-Merikakis (Edinburgh: T&T Clark, 1982), p. 56. So Nebel proposes a Protestant "analogy of event" to replace the more static (and Catholic) "analogy of being."

back to its biblical roots. In much of the best Reformational writing, this event, and the performance of worship that surrounded it, was described in strong and even majestic terms. This experience was meant literally to be life-changing and world-changing. Indeed, according to Calvin, the whole course of nature would be subverted if the church did not fulfill its role of offering praise to God: "The creation of the world would serve no good purpose, if there were no people to call upon God."[10]

For Calvin, the performance of the preaching of the Word and its reception were theologically central to his understanding of the church — this fact literally defined the space and the symbolism of the sanctuary. He saw the act of preaching as a performative utterance that was the locus of God's presence.[11] In the congregational singing, in the public prayers, in the words of institution, and above all in praise — all that is allied to the preaching of the Word — the Body of Christ is constituted. Indeed, Belden Lane has put this even more strongly, arguing that for Calvin these performances actually *effect* what they celebrate and honor. He writes, "The exaltation of God's glory is a performative act, extending and enhancing what it sanctifies. . . . The character of praise, then, is not simply celebrative, or even restorative, but also *constitutive* of the world maintaining its life and well-being."[12]

While the focus on the event of worship gave worship a dynamic and living character, it could also give it a vaguely disembodied feel — a weakness that will serve as the subtext of what I want to say in this chapter. As Calvin made clear, no physical mediation is necessary for God to work (though in fact the ear is clearly the privileged organ); union with Christ is accomplished inwardly by the Holy Spirit. His reaction against the medieval practices of worship made him highly suspicious of any external or spatial symbolism. The elements of the communion, for example, had meaning only in the *performance* of the Eucharist; they carried no symbolic weight outside of this context. Tellingly, even though it was enjoined in Scripture, the Reformers could not even bring themselves to pour oil on a sick person for fear that the meaning would at-

---

10. John Calvin, commentary on Psalm 115:17, in *Commentary on the Book of Psalms*, vol. 4 (Edinburgh: Calvin Translation Society, 1847), p. 358.

11. See Belden Lane, "Spirituality as the Performance of Desire: Calvin on the World as a Theatre of God's Glory," *Spiritus: A Journal of Christian Spirituality* 1, no. 1 (Spring 2001): 1-30, esp. pp. 18-19.

12. Lane, "Spirituality as the Performance of Desire," pp. 18-19, his emphasis.

tach itself to the oil rather than the offered prayer.[13] The pulpit and the table were all that remained in Calvin's St. Peter's Church, and the table was set only during communion.

What, then, of the place in which this took place? It was the stage on which the performance of worship was played out, and when that was finished, the place had no further role to play. In the metaphor of Protestant attitudes toward worship space that we explored in Chapter Seven, Calvin insisted that outside of regular worship hours — outside of the event of this performance — the building was to be locked. One could not even enter for prayer, because Calvin believed that prayer is unconnected to any particular space; the ministry of the Christian is to permeate the whole of life. Worship was everywhere, but it was nowhere in particular. The space of worship was in practice abolished.

This direct knowledge of God was the treasured fruit of the Reformation, and, as mediated by the Pietist movement and the evangelical revivals, it came to characterize the evangelical movement. This experiential Christianity was given eloquent expression by the Puritans who came to settle New England, and it powered the Wesleyan renewal and the Pentecostal awakenings of the twentieth century. One comes to church to feel the touch of God — that is what church is for. As a Pentecostal preacher put it recently in Nairobi, the house of God is the house of healing. The church is here to bring people into contact with the God of power. People need this power because they are sick. So the worship — indeed, the congregation itself — is constituted by the activities — the prayer, preaching, lively singing, even dancing — that make possible the powerful touch of the healing God.

None of this is wrong, of course; it is biblically and theologically important. But, although it is important, I want to argue that it is not sufficient for a developed ecclesiology. As I have argued previously, Calvin was right in what he affirmed, but sometimes wrong in what he denied. And what he gave up was, in part at least, a theological conception of the representation, the space the church occupies. He had a great deal to say about the necessity of the church as the mother of believers; the outward means as the ordinary way God uses to form believers; and the

---

13. See Brian Gerrish, *Grace and Gratitude: The Eucharistic Theology of John Calvin* (Minneapolis: Augsburg/Fortress Press, 1993), p. 162. And see Carlos Eire, *War against the Idols: The Reformation of Worship from Erasmus to Calvin* (Cambridge: Cambridge University Press, 1986), p. 223n.130.

details of the order of worship and government. But his polemic against the abuses of the Catholic Church of his day inclined him to discount the role of symbolic places and practices. Calvin knew well enough that the church is not simply the gathering of believers into the body of Christ by the power of the Spirit to the glory of God in some spiritual sense alone. The church is defined by certain ritual practices that constitute its worship: prayer, preaching, praise, confession, ministry, and the sacraments.[14] But, in a way that Calvin seemed not to appreciate, these should be seen as historically and culturally situated places that present some shape to the world — some specific testimony to God. In this chapter, I want to argue that these spheres of practice and representation are related in ways that are theologically significant. In ignoring the representation, the church risks becoming "docetic," a place that is only *apparently* real.

Evangelicals have claimed since the Reformation that they are simply following Scripture in their understanding of the church. But they have not always seen that hidden in this claim is a particular way of reading these authoritative texts. The way the church lives out its corporate life in the world and the form that life takes constitute a hermeneutical activity — the people of God interpret Scripture by the way they shape their life together. In this sense, there is no timeless or universal essence the church must express; rather, under God it constitutes itself afresh in each generation — it must become, theologically, a real presence.

The church is what it does — that is, at its heart are certain ritual practices that connect it to God. But what is the public appearance of these practices? What space do they occupy? And what does this look like? In this chapter I will use "space" as a trope for the way the church comes to cultural and social expression — the forms it takes. I want to ask, What are the spaces of these forms? And what theological or symbolic meanings do they have? I want to consider this aspect of space in three ways — socially, historically, and symbolically — as dimensions of place which can counter the docetic tendency of the Protestant church. I want to argue that these dimensions are integrally related; a weakness in one necessarily affects the others.

---

14. I have discussed these in more detail in William Dyrness, *A Primer on Christian Worship: Where We've Been, Where We Are, Where We Can Go* (Grand Rapids: Wm. B. Eerdmans, 2008).

The Aesthetics of Church

The Social Space of the Church

Whether it is recognized or not, the church constitutes a particular social space. Although the church, theologically, is the eschatological community which is the sign and instance of God's new creation in Christ, formed by the Holy Spirit, it is at the same time people from a particular region who come together at particular times and, using one language or another, do things together — indeed, they are to be a people who in their very corporate (embodied) existence point to the world to come. As the recent Amsterdam Declaration puts it, "Here in the world, the Church becomes visible in all local congregations that meet to do together the things that according to the Scripture the Church does."[15] Moreover, this visible aspect of the church has theological significance: how these people shape their lives together directly reflects the presence of Christ by his Spirit.

The personal presence of Christ is typically celebrated in evangelical churches. Indeed, the emphasis on the church as the gathered people of God (as opposed to people living within certain geographical boundaries) may be the major contribution of Protestants in general and of evangelicals in particular to the church universal. Protestants, Wolfhart Pannenberg argues, are custodians of a unique heritage in this respect. Protestants have championed the idea that "a church office did not exist for its own sake. Its purpose was to serve the gospel and thus the faith of those entrusted to its care, in order to help them come to their own relationship with God, and not leave them in a state of immaturity."[16]

But while the spiritual presence of Christ is celebrated, Christ's corporate and visible presence is frequently ignored. The awareness of their spiritual unity typifies evangelicals around the world — witness the meaning of "hermano/a" among Latin Americans and the deep awareness of the "Christian family" among African Christians. But evangelicals often do not value the earthen vessel in which this treasure is found. They do not appreciate that the focus on the people of God and their corporate relationship to God implies a social space that takes on a particular cultural and political shape. More significantly,

---

15. "Amsterdam Declaration," *First Things,* January 2001, pp. 65-66.
16. Wolfhart Pannenberg, *The Church,* trans. Keith Crim (Philadelphia: Westminster Press, 1983), p. 91.

what they overlook is the important correlation between the social space and the spiritual reality represented. How is this so?

In the first place, the social space of the church consists in *the interpersonal unity of all the people of God*. In his important study of the church, Miroslav Volf seeks to discover the nature of "ecclesiality" — what makes the church the called people of God. His search leads him to the question I am raising — the one about the church's external conditions. "If one is to speak meaningfully about ecclesiality, one must know not only what the church is, but also how a concrete church can be identified externally as a church; one must also be able to say *where* a church is."[17] Although he goes on to say that features of the church cannot be purely external, he argues that "questions about the identity and identification of the church are inseparable" (130).

Pointing to sixteenth-century separatist John Smyth, Volf argues that this early expression of free-church ecclesiality rests on the theological importance of the visible organization of the church. Smyth's "entire ecclesiology is based on the fundamental *theological* conviction that *Christ's dominion is realized through the entire congregation*" (p. 132, his emphasis). Smyth wrote, "We say the Church or two or three faithful people Separated from the world & joyned together in a true covenant have both Christ, the covenant, & promises, & the ministerial powre of Christ given to them . . . [such a] true visib[l]e church is Christs kingdome."[18]

This church, then, may be identified by its external representation: the corporate lives of church members are characterized by obedience to the Scripture and, therefore, the freedom from all known sin; they assemble at a specific place and time; and they corporately confess their faith in Jesus Christ before and with others. This pluriform, intersubjective confession of faith, Volf argues, is the basis of free-church ecclesiality. He argues,

> That which the church *is*, namely, believing and confessing human beings, is precisely that which (as a rule) also *constitutes* it. It is not that each person constitutes himself or herself into a member of the

---

17. Miroslav Volf, *After Our Likeness: The Church as the Image of the Trinity* (Grand Rapids: Wm. B. Eerdmans, 1998), p. 129, emphasis his. Subsequent pages will be cited in the text.

18. John Smyth, *The Works of John Smyth*, ed. W. T. Whitley (Cambridge: Cambridge University Press, 1915), pp. 403 and 267, quoted in Volf, *After Our Likeness*, p. 132 (emphasis in Volf).

The Aesthetics of Church

church; rather, through their common pluriform confessing all the members together are constituted into the church by the Holy Spirit. (151-52, his emphasis)

Volf later defines this pluriformity in terms of the church's "polycentric" character, which is expressed both in a Christian call to faith and in the charismata — that is, the gifts of the Spirit (224-25). More significantly, he notes, this conviction is grounded in a particular understanding of the Trinity as characterized by symmetrical relations. "This yields the ecclesial principle that the more a church is characterized by symmetrical and decentralized distribution of power and freely affirmed interaction, the more will it correspond to the trinitarian communion" (236). So the unity that is envisioned, as Colin Gunton has argued, is not "an organic, so much as . . . an interpersonal unity: the personal unity of distinct but freely related persons."[19]

While Volf seeks to place Smyth's ecclesiology into a more consistent theological framework, he wants at the same time to underline the significance of this communal life together that is open to other churches and to all human beings. Theologically central to church is a particular way of being people together. This view of sociality not only makes visible the dominion of Christ in the whole congregation, but also serves as the basis for a theology of the whole church — the whole people of God. Historically, this impulse had a major impact on the Wesleyan conception of small-group accountability and the evangelical revivals — which, in promoting these values, became arguably the most important social space in frontier America. This focus on the church as "the Pilgrim People of God" appears prominently in the documents of Vatican II, indicating perhaps the broader influence of these currents.[20]

A second dimension of the social space of the church is the *particular practices that make this people what it is.* The importance of this has emerged frequently in our explorations in this book: People constitute themselves and express their identity through regular ritual practices.

---

19. Colin Gunton, "The Church on Earth: The Roots of Community," in *On Being the Church: Essays in Christian Community,* ed. Colin E. Gunton and Daniel W. Hardy (Edinburgh: T&T Clark, 1989), p. 75.

20. The broader influence of this in the worldwide church has been pointed out recently by Mark Noll, who argues that this polycentric sense of the church is dominant in non-Western settings. See *The New Shape of World Christianity: How American Experience Reflects Global Faith* (Downers Grove, Ill.: InterVarsity Press, 2009), pp. 41-60.

Moreover, for Christians, these practices come to clearest expression in the space of the church. A powerful contribution to this aspect of the church's visible representation came recently from Stanley Hauerwas. He argues that the church as a "contrast society" has a particular political profile. Like John Howard Yoder before him, Hauerwas believes that the cross of Christ is not simply an abstract transaction between God and the world, but implies a particular set of political arrangements that reveals the nature of the broken world. "In fact," Hauerwas argues, "the God we worship and the world God created cannot be truthfully known without the cross, which is why the knowledge of God and ecclesiology — or the politics called the church — are interdependent."[21] This politics implies a specific ethic that is consistent with the narratives of our lives as God's children and followers of Jesus Christ.[22] Hauerwas believes that this politics, which defines the church, not only derives from the Gospel but is actually *constitutive* of it (145) — indeed, it is constitutive not only of the church's own redemption but of the redemption of the world (194).

Hauerwas insists that the church's witness is correlated to the way things are in the world (203, 223); its witness is appropriate and necessary because the world itself lives off the values of the Gospel (223). Hauerwas's contribution here is to focus on the concrete life of Christians — their politics — as central to the theological meaning of the church, since it grows out of and reflects the narrative of the cross. His insistence here is on the life and practice of Christians together, rather than on their work and witness in the larger community. This emphasis gives concreteness to the church in much the same way as John Smyth's focus on the local congregation. Clearly, this focus on the particular shape of the local congregation, what Yoder called the "hermeneutics of peoplehood," represents a compelling description of the nature of the church. One appreciates the shift of focus away from the church universal and invisible and toward the visible community that gathers in God's name. Even if Hauerwas runs the danger of investing the political character with too much theological authority — making it, as he

---

21. Stanley Hauerwas, *With the Grain of the Universe: The Church's Witness and Natural Theology* (Grand Rapids: Brazos Press, 2001), p. 17. Subsequent pages will be cited in the text.

22. Hauerwas spelled out the content of this narrative ethic in his earlier work: *A Community of Character: Toward a Constructive Social Ethics* (Notre Dame: University of Notre Dame Press, 1981).

puts it, constitutive of redemption — his underlining the theological significance of the church's politics is welcome.

For Hauerwas, particular political practices are authoritative, for they constitute a particular construal of biblical truth, one that by the Spirit should embody the external form of the Gospel. Growing up in an evangelical environment, I frequently heard that "being in a church does not make one a Christian any more than living in a garage makes one a car." The impulse behind this, of course, was to insist that the commitment to Christianity must be personal and not simply nominal. But I have come to believe that this overly spiritual emphasis undercuts the social space of the church. It does not recognize that in an important sense the disciplines and practices of the people of God *do* form a person into the likeness of Christ, just as they constitute the most visible witness to the Gospel. It may not matter where we park our car, but it does matter where, week by week, Christians put *themselves*. Calvin expresses it this way: "We see that God, who might perfect his people in a moment, chooses not to bring them into manhood in any other way than by the education of the Church.... To make us aware, then, that an inestimable treasure is given us in earthen vessels [2 Cor. 4:7], God himself appears in our midst, and, as Author of this order, would have men recognize him in his institution."[23] Perhaps the problem is that evangelicals conceive of their relationship to the church in the same way a car is related to the garage: as a place where they are "parked" rather than a spiritually dynamic social space.

Third, a conception of the social space of the church makes it easier to understand *the relation of this space to all other spaces*. If the church occupies a real social location and exhibits a particular polity as the eschatological community which anticipates God's eternal purposes, it implicates all spaces. Gerhard Lohfink has argued that the church as a spiritual community within human hearts, dating from Augustine's *City of God*, has undermined the biblical conception of church as a "visible, tangible community."[24] Lohfink argues that Jesus came to recon-

---

23. John Calvin, *Institutes of the Christian Religion*, Library of Christian Classics, vols. 20-21, ed. John T. McNeill, trans. Ford Lewis Battles (Philadelphia: Fortress Press, 1960), 4.1.5. This is why Calvin can refer to the church as mother. These references indicate that our argument here develops rather than conflicts with the insights of the Reformation.

24. Gerhard Lohfink, *Jesus and Community: The Social Dimension of Christian Faith*, trans. John P. Galvin (New York and Philadelphia: Paulist Press and Fortress Press, 1984), p. 5. Subsequent pages will be cited in the text.

stitute Israel as a new family, a visible contrast society "precisely in order to make this people a visible sign of salvation" (28). This community is constituted by the gift of the Spirit and is characterized by its togetherness, its elimination of social barriers, and its renunciation of violence — all the practices that flow from the narrative of the Gospel. But this community is characterized most of all by its orientation toward the world. Precisely in its role as a contrast society, Lohfink argues, it transforms the world (66). As he says,

> The rule of God comes not only in word, but also in deed. It grasps the whole of our existence; we never exist as individuals. The society which surrounds us is part of us. For this reason, Jesus' healing miracles cannot be seen solely as actions on behalf of individuals. They are always concerned with the people of God. Many diseases are curable only if the environment of the sick person is also healed. . . . When the reign of God becomes present, its healing power must not only reach deeply into human corporeality but also extend deeply into the social dimension of human existence. (82-83)

Thus, by extension, the social space of the church refers to all spaces — an idea that I will develop in the next chapter. By the Spirit the church is made to visibly embody something of the righteousness and justice that God intends for all creation.

A focus on the particular social shape of the church, therefore, is important in allowing specific Christian practices to be given theological "voice" and a specific social presence. I would argue that theological conversation about the multiform social shapes of the church best enables us to welcome the gifts and graces of the many cultures of the world into the body of Christ (see Rev. 21:24, 26). However, these theological and biblical warrants raise the question of whether in fact one sees signs of this reality in churches today. Referring here to my own context, I ask, Does the evangelical church intentionally consider its social space to be a form of its ministry in the world? Or, put differently, in the light of the social and political challenges it is facing, what impact is the church, as a social space, having on its community? What authority does this space exert?

The importance of this question is underlined by the fact that in many of the neediest places in the world, the church exists as the only functioning institution. Edgar McKnight argues this in the case of our inner cities in America.[25] In Africa, where civil strife, AIDS, and bad government have created widespread poverty and underdevelopment, the churches often stand as the only remaining institution with credibility. Even if, all too often, these congregations do not have a vision that incorporates the whole community, they still represent an essential resource for the development of these places. Whether they recognize it or not, they carry in themselves the meaning of all places, and this meaning calls for visible expression.

The question arises: What is necessary to make this social space effective and visible? In order for this to happen, the church needs something else: it must also intentionally occupy a historical space.

The Historical Space of the Church

In addition to its social space, every church necessarily occupies a particular historical space. For evangelicals, the focus on the church as event and on experiential Christianity has not served to highlight historical continuity. But, as Pannenberg argues, "the public exposition and transmission of Christianity, which nourishes the faith of individual Christians, have no other form than that of the denominations."[26] Denominations, or the historical form that churches have taken, embody the historical traditions that, for better or worse, have shaped Christianity into its present form. Too often, however, evangelical expressions of the church (especially in America, but increasingly in other parts of the world as well) do not believe that they are the product of anything except the Bible, refusing sometimes even to call their groupings of churches "denominations."[27] It is as though the autonomous individual has found a sociological counterpart in the autonomous local church! The event orientation of Protestant worship reveals itself here in its most worrisome aspect, as though the body of Christ was reinventing itself from scratch week by week. In spite of the view of evangelicals toward denominations, it is a fact that one cannot be a Chris-

---

25. See Edgar McKnight, *The Careless Society: Community and Its Counterfeits* (New York: Basic Books, 1995).

26. Pannenberg, *The Church*, p. 14.

27. Recently those claiming to be "non-denominational" for the first time passed Presbyterians as the largest group of students at the seminary where I teach (Fuller Theological Seminary).

tian without being the product of one or another of the traditions of the Christian church.

At the same time, ironically, Christians of this generation are experiencing a revival of historical consciousness — or at least an awareness of the importance of history. On the popular level, so-called emergent churches are busy exploring history for relevant worship resources. Their Web sites reveal a fascination with aspects of the tradition that evangelicals have rarely valued: Celtic worship, medieval spirituality, the Iona community, Taizé worship, and so on. This exploration shows promise, even if the attraction is not based on much thought and reflection. Lutheran pastor and researcher Karen Ward reported in conversation the experience she had as a speaker at a conference of the emergent churches. The worship leader at one point put the Nicene Creed on an overhead for the people to recite together. Karen noticed that many were writing down the creed, and she overheard one of them say, "This is wonderful. Where did this come from?"

There are, of course, thoughtful resources that these groups make use of. Most prominent among them are writings of the late Robert Webber, whose *Ancient-Future Faith* provides a kind of outline for those searching for historical resources, even historical roots. Webber insists that the authority of Christianity and of Scripture in particular will be recovered in the postmodern era only by returning the Bible "to its rightful place in the development of the entire spectrum of Christian thought in the first six centuries of the church."[28]

Outside North America and Europe, Christian churches are experiencing a similar interest in their past. Previously their history has been limited to their own colonial and missionary history. Now, however, the wholesale disparagement of their traditional histories, which occurred during the colonial period, is being widely questioned, and a reevaluation is in process. Outside the West, a post-colonial reading of history is in progress. In his book *Theology and Identity,* for example, Ghanaian Kwame Bediako argues that the missionary importation of Western Christianity was a modern application of the New Testament party of the circumcision (that is, those who insist on circumcision for

---

28. See Robert Webber, *Ancient-Future Faith: Rethinking Evangelicalism for a Postmodern World* (Grand Rapids: Baker Books, 1999), p. 31. See also Brian McLaren, *Everything Must Change: Jesus, Global Crisis, and a Revolution of Hope* (Nashville: Thomas Nelson, 2007).

all males baptized in the name of Christ), in which Christianity was assumed to take a particular cultural form.[29]

Perhaps the most important of the movements of historical retrieval, which I introduced in Chapter One, is Radical Orthodoxy, which deserves close examination and reflection. According to its self-description, Radical Orthodoxy "combines a sophisticated understanding of contemporary thought, modern and postmodern, with a theological perspective that looks back to the origins of the church."[30] It is a *radical* orthodoxy in the sense that it wants to return to the roots of Christian theology, especially its patristic sources, to recover a more coherent vision of Christianity. On its reading of history, this coherence was lost both in the biblicism of the Protestant Reformation and in the authoritarian legalism of Catholicism coming from the Council of Trent.[31] This project involves a careful rereading of the earlier tradition in order to discover resources with which to address the dilemma caused by the collapse of modernity.

Graham Ward has made perhaps the most explicit application of this historical method to ecclesiology in his book *Cities of God*.[32] In this book, Ward combines a careful analysis of the contemporary city, which is ruled by what he calls the disordered erotics of desire, with a recovery of the wisdom of the ancient church, especially that of Augustine and Gregory of Nyssa. From Augustine, Ward recovers the Christian notion of desire. He argues that "desire is fundamental to our nature as human beings, as God created us" and that "theology will have to show how Christian desire operates in a way that does not accord with the operation of desire in secular culture, the culture of seduction" (76). From Gregory of Nyssa, Ward develops an ontology that matches this theology of desire. Gregory helps us avoid the commodification of reality as self-grounded, which, he argues, is a form of over-realized es-

---

29. Kwame Bediako, *Theology and Identity: The Impact of Culture upon Christian Thought in the Second Century and in Modern Africa* (Grand Rapids: Wm. B. Eerdmans, 1993). See also *Christianity in Africa: A Renewal of a Non-Western Religion* (Edinburgh and Grand Rapids: Edinburgh University Press and Wm. B. Eerdmans, 1995).

30. This is on the book jacket of volumes in the "Radical Orthodoxy" series, edited by John Milbank, Catherine Pickstock, and Graham Ward.

31. See *Radical Orthodoxy: A New Theology*, ed. John Milbank and Catherine Pickstock. See the introduction by the editors, especially pp. 2-3.

32. Graham Ward, *Cities of God* (New York and London: Routledge, 2000). Subsequent pages cited in the text refer to this work.

chatology. Rather, as Gregory believed, materiality is an expression of divine energy, a mode of Trinitarian "dunamis" (89). Corporeality, then, is to be read spiritually, for nature exists through the prioritization of the spiritual; this animating principle "enables nature to prosper" (88). Since everything subsists only in God, Ward argues, the "world is a Eucharistic offering" (91). Christ in his risen and ascended reality has been displaced from his historical (and gendered) rootedness and now exists "transcorporeally" in the *corpus mysticum,* which indicates not the Eucharist as it has traditionally been understood, but the displaced and extended body of Christ. The church, then, is the social body of Christ that signifies this sacramental body to the world (92, quoting Michel de Certeau).

Institutional churches are necessary places for the display of this *corpus mysticum,* Ward thinks, but they are not ends in themselves. "They are constantly transgressed by a community of desire, an erotic community, a spiritual activity.... The body of Christ desiring its consummation opens itself to what is outside the institutional church" (180). This view of the mystical body, Ward believes, best answers to the contemporary erotics of desire, and it best shows "what it is to be called by God as an embodied soul to participate in Christ's body" (77).

Both the retrieval of historical sources and the attention to contemporary erotics are admirable and instructive in many ways. We have seen previously how Gregory of Nyssa can help us recover a kind of spiritual reading that forms readers, something we have incorporated into a Protestant hermeneutic. Still, Gregory was successful in contextualizing the faith into his Neoplatonic context. But this is not our context. Further, one must also examine the ways in which this tradition developed in the medieval period and led — fatally, in the minds of the Reformers at least — to a confusion of divine and human activity. These Reformation developments may constitute not a fall into positivism and rationalism, as Ward believes (see his discussion, 60-66), but an alternative reading of the way that God relates to the world — one they believed to be more biblical — and of the way the church is conceived.

Christoph Schwöbel has argued that the primary intention of the Reformers focused precisely on this attempt to define the relationship between the work of God and that of humans. While distinguishing God and creation, both Luther and Calvin believed that "the action of God, Father, Son, and Spirit makes human action possible and enables human beings to act in accordance with the will of the creator."³³ God's action in calling the church into existence, like all God's works, establishes and makes possible both real relationship with God by the Spirit and a genuine human response — an idea that resonates with views of artistic creation, which is our focus. It is true that this construal of the relationship between God and the world could lead to Descartes and the radical dichotomy that Ward deplores, but it does not *have to* do so. It could also lead to the Pietist renewal and the spirituality of a Jonathan Edwards or a John Wesley.

The issue here is the nature of participation that we explored earlier. Granted, the person and thus cultural processes are dependent on God as creator and sustainer. But the question is this: *How* does the creature participate in God? In short, Radical Orthodoxy has proposed that before the Reformation, believers understood that everything participated in God, and so there was no secular/sacred split. During the Reformation, this was denied; the world came to be understood apart from God, and secularism (and even nihilism) inevitably resulted. On this reading, we must recover our sense of being creatures rooted in God. But must we construe this rootedness in terms of participation as defined by medieval theologians? Surely all Christians agree that we live and move and find our being in God. But, as we have noted, the issue hinges on the nature of this "participation." Calvin, in fact, had a strong sense of our need to be joined to God; he saw this not as a substantial union but as a participation in God that was effected by the Spirit. Julie Canlis has argued that for Calvin, communion involved a very real sense of "participation." But it is a "non-substantial participation in the person of Christ, made possible by . . . the Holy Spirit, who is a safeguard against substantial participation."³⁴ The model for this, as we have stressed, is not the methexis of Plato, by which the particulars are said to "participate" in the forms, but New Testament *koinonia,* a sharing of the divine nature in Christ and through the Spirit. Because of our view of the Trinitarian basis of creation, Alan Torrance argues, we have "a real and given event of *communion* between the divine and hu-

---

33. Christoph Schwöbel, "The Creature of the Word: Recovering the Ecclesiology of the Reformers," in *On Being the Church,* ed. Gunton and Hardy, p. 119.

34. Julie Canlis, "Calvin, Osiander, and Participation in God," *International Journal of Systematic Thelogy* 6, no. 2 (April 2004): 184. Canlis cautions against seeing Calvin as opposed to all forms of participation. "There is more than 'room' in Calvin's thought for real communion; rather, 'participation in God' is how we make sense of his view of the Christian life" (p. 184).

man orders. To the extent that created reality requires to be interpreted in the light of this communion ... we may speak of ... real participation of created and contingent humanity in the triune life of God."[35]

The point is not that this Reformed reading of developments is privileged, but that theological conversation has a historical and cultural context that must be taken into account. This leads to a second problem with Ward's project. One of the most admirable aspects of his book is the attempt to address Christianity in terms that relate to contemporary worldviews. But at the same time, it is precisely this project which raises an additional question. His dependence on a fourth-century bishop and his dismissal of the last five centuries of Christian thought lead him to make a radical disjunction between the contemporary culture of desire and Christian desire embodied in the mystical body of Christ. Because Ward cannot see any possible use for Reformation developments, he has to be overly critical of contemporary products of that worldview and the rationalities it fostered — virtual reality, for example. Surely seeing theology as a developing conversation, one that responds to actual cultural situations, would better enable him to address realities that, in one way or another, resonate with that conversation.[36] A living theological tradition, while it always risks being compromised by its context, also offers the best prospect of challenging that context.

But this exchange only serves to underline my argument in this chapter. Churches, like theological conversations, are in fact situated in some historical trajectory. Consciously or not, every church displays its convictions about the way history works. Although evangelicals have sometimes been resistant to the idea of tradition, this has not kept them from embodying a tradition that is quite easy to specify — from the Reformation through the various Pietist movements and evangelical revivals. For them, then, history is constituted by a series of renewals or, in some circles, "repristinations," and that is reflected in the need, week by week, to construct — often from scratch — a worship experi-

---

35. Alan Torrance, *Persons in Communion: An Essay on Trinitarian Description and Human Participation, with Special Reference to Volume One of Karl Barth's "Church Dogmatics"* (Edinburgh: T&T Clark, 1996), p. 347; the quotation is from p. 356. See also p. 310, where he proposes on the basis of this a doxological model of the theological enterprise, something that resonates with the argument of this book.

36. This is something that Graham Ward does accomplish in a later book — *Cultural Transformation and Religious Practice* (Cambridge: Cambridge University Press, 2005).

ence that is spiritually renewing. This is true of evangelical churches and students everywhere. Recently, while I was lecturing on the value of theological traditions in Kenya, one student expressed the view of most of the class by saying, "I think we would say that we want to examine all traditions and take what is good from them, but that we do not have a tradition ourselves" — which is not a bad summary of the evangelical use of history in general. I tried (unsuccessfully) to get him to see that he was giving very articulate expression to a particular — that is, evangelical — tradition of hermeneutics.

The danger, then, in the contemporary use of history is that an eclectic ecclesiology would result that has no sense of the historical sources (and implications) of the practices being adopted — resulting in a kind of liturgical potpourri: "This month, let's do icons!" History is meant to define and nourish our ecclesiastical identity. It is not a collective attic through which we rummage for some interesting and exotic practices with which to embellish our worship experience. Nor is the solution to modern secularization or postmodern pluralism found in a leap back to a previous era. Rather, we must find ourselves by recognizing that we do stand in a living tradition — Reformed, Anabaptist, Wesleyan, Roman Catholic — which represents gifts that can be brought to the work of our corporate maturity in Christ. Having a place to stand historically is not a limitation; it is a grace, making possible a situated reading of Scripture that can mediate the special gifts of our cultural particularity. The church occupies a particular historical place, but it also needs to take a particular visible shape so that it can be made into an object of desire — and that need has yet to be addressed.

The Symbolic Space of the Church

These considerations of spaces lead naturally to a third notion of space, what I will call the church's symbolic space. The church not only comprises a social space; it not only occupies a historical space; it also embodies and displays a symbolic space. Consistent with the thesis of this book, I will argue that if this is not the most important theological aspect of the visible church for postmodern people, it is the most salient. And for Protestants in general and evangelicals in particular, it is clearly the most challenging, for it can bring to expression the underlying longings of our culture that we have reviewed — or it may ignore them.

I am arguing that with the eclipse of Enlightenment rationality, for most educated people in the West, the quest for truth and knowledge has been replaced by a search for pleasure and beauty. As Graham Ward notes, in the modern city the pleasure principle has replaced the reality principle. "For enjoyment now belongs to the symbolic order, the symbolic exchange in which we invest all our hopes for the fulfillment of our desires. A euphoria follows from the new lightness of being. Aesthetics, rather than ethics or even physics, provides the sole criterion for judgment."[37] Although Ward wants to recapture a Christian notion of desire, he has trouble seeing anything but problems with many of the products of this contemporary situation. Ironically, evangelicals usually have the reverse problem: while they have eagerly made use of the products of modern technology, they have resisted the broader implications of the aesthetic turn. But here recall the poetic practices I described in the first chapter. Contemporary people like Adam and Lisa have found meaning in a wide variety of affective and aesthetic practices. For them, these activities have taken on a religious character. The language of the symbol is the language that we must learn to frame the Gospel for these friends, and the church, I am arguing, is the place where this must be centered.

A Return to the Symbol

But Adam and Lisa do not look at the church as a source of practices that spark affection. Why is this so? For evangelicals, I believe the problem is not simply the tradition of suspicion toward culture, though this certainly plays a role. More critical is what might be called the symbolic incapacity of the evangelical tradition. To get at this, we must recall the transformation of the imagination represented by the Reformation. In our previous discussion, we have noticed that the Reformers were suspicious of two kinds of symbolic entities: images that refer to particular persons and events, and ceremonies that enact meaning. These, of course, were central to medieval worship. Even the surrounding spaces of medieval churches were designed to accommodate and focus on certain images and facilitate particular actions. All of this was swept away during the Reformation. Edward Muir has described this revolution by

---

37. Ward, *Cities of God*, p. 60. Ward refers here to the work of Jean Baudrillard.

arguing that, after the Reformation, practices of the upper body replaced those of the lower body — the emphasis shifted from ritual practices involving the whole body to those focusing on the head alone.[38] During the Middle Ages, he notes, "believers approached sacred objects in a highly sensual way that cannot easily be distinguished from an aesthetic response" (165). For these, however, the rich aesthetic response eclipsed any intellectual grasp — believers were not encouraged to trouble themselves with theological niceties. "They were to adore," Muir says, "not think" (172). With their frequent sermons and regular catechism, Reformers insisted that understanding should replace sensual bodily experience of objects and practices. Muir comments, "In a very literal sense, . . . the word of Scripture and an understanding of it replaced the material object of the host at the core of religious practice in Geneva" (184). Believers in Geneva, one might say, were to close their eyes and listen: they were to think and not adore.

This transformation, I want to argue, had important consequences not only for religious practice, but for the understanding of "symbolism" in this tradition. Creation, to be sure, carried meaning for Calvin in that it pointed to and extolled its creator; it was "symbolic" in this sense. And some in this tradition have even gone so far as to say that creation is "sacramental" — though clearly this use of the term would differ from its use in Bonaventure or, for that matter, among present-day Catholics.[39] In the nineteenth century, for example, George MacDonald, who was heavily influenced by the Calvinist tradition, insisted that creation carried its own symbolic meaning. He believed that the work of the human imagination is to grasp the forms inherent in nature and "unveil" them in language. But the primary meaning of any imaginative word is dependent on and extracted from the outer world.[40] So, MacDonald castigated George Herbert for seeking to construct symbols beyond what is given in nature. MacDonald believed that the seventeenth-century poet had grown too enamored with artificial symbols. For it is "the things made by the hands of God and not the things made by the hands of men," he said, "that afford the truest sym-

---

38. Edward Muir, *Ritual in Early Modern Europe* (Cambridge: Cambridge University Press, 2005). Subsequent pages cited in the text refer to this work.

39. Nicholas Wolterstorff argues for a Protestant sacramentalism in *Until Justice and Peace Embrace* (Grand Rapids: Wm. B. Eerdmans, 1983), p. 160.

40. George MacDonald, "The Imagination: Its Function and Its Culture," in *A Dish of Oats* (Whitethorn, Calif.: Johannesen, 1996 [1893]), pp. 7-8.

bols of truth."[41] As Calvin had taught, art and aesthetics should focus centrally on the objects that God has created — which is the reason why art influenced by the Reformation tended to feature landscapes and portraits, things God had made and declared good.

But beyond these, the richly elaborated man-made symbols, so important to the Christian tradition, and the practices of contemplation they solicited, were lost during the Reformation. In one sense, these artifacts were replaced by (also human) formulations of truth; it is not accidental that the word *symbol* (in Latin, *symbolus, symbolum*) came to be used for the creeds. As a result, Protestants, especially those on the evangelical side of the spectrum, usually do not appreciate and thus cannot understand symbolic objects and practices. Since they are often hostile to these things, they do not understand how objects, specially inscribed spaces, and ritual acts can teach, form, and nurture believers. What is worse, since symbolic sensitivities have been effectively leached out of their tradition, evangelicals view this situation as normal. This weakness obviously has important implications for their understanding of the visible church.[42]

Humans are *homo symbolicus* — they respond to the world symbolically whether they are aware of it or not. I once attended a prominent Presbyterian church in southern California in which the distinguished pastor liked to come down in front of the communion table to preach without notes. He would bring his Bible with him, read the text, and then turn to put the Bible behind him on the communion table while he preached. I'm sure he had not given the practice much thought, but its symbolic impact was still powerful: It said, "Now I have finished with this text." I was sure that this is what the act communicated to his listeners, whether he intended it to or not. Similarly, a chapel in a seminary in Africa where I go to teach has a giant wooden door behind the pulpit — it is the only thing visible in the space besides a Bible verse. Every time I go into the chapel, I am reminded of Psalm 24:7: "Lift up your heads, O gates! And be lifted up, O ancient doors!" But when I inquired, I discovered that there was no such

---

41. George MacDonald, *England's Antiphon* (Whitethorn, Calif.: Johannesen, 1996 [1868]), p. 187. This is consistent with Calvin's view that God can institute symbols, but humans cannot. See Cornelis Van der Kooi, *As in a Mirror: John Calvin and Karl Barth on Knowing God: A Diptych*, trans. Donald Mader (Leiden: Brill, 2005), pp. 80-81.

42. I have explored this weakness through a series of ethnographic interviews. See William Dyrness, *Senses of the Soul: Art and the Visual in Christian Worship* (Eugene, Ore.: Cascade Books, 2008).

intent; my meaning was accidental and unintended — even though the placement of the door seemed to say otherwise. Or consider the practices of standing to sing hymns and sitting to listen to Scripture in many evangelical services. These practices seem meaningful — but in fact they have no intrinsic meaning. My point is that we look for meaning, even if the service and space are designed to frustrate this search. And, although our buildings and spaces do express an unconscious aesthetic, they do not express a discerning symbolic sensitivity — certainly not one that is grounded in Scripture or the traditions of the church.

Calvin's locked church became a metaphor for a space that was symbolically vacant. In the worship spaces that resulted, there was no particular place or object or ceremony that, either by itself or in concert with other things, would inform one about God, salvation, or the Christian life. The centrality of the pulpit, of course, had a kind of symbolic significance as the place where the word of God was preached. But the pulpit itself had none of the symbolic or iconic significance that medieval images had, nor did preaching have the same intrinsic meaning that the liturgy had had earlier. Preaching "happened" in relation to particular times, not particular spaces — indeed, some of the most famous preaching in this tradition took place outdoors. The sacraments, of course, continued to have theological and symbolic meaning, but they had no relationship, symbolic or otherwise, to the spaces in which they took place. Their meaning was related to their performance, and this was controlled by the preached word.

This does not mean that this tradition could not sponsor noteworthy developments in church architecture (or in the allied arts like church music). After a fire destroyed eighty-four of the churches in central London, Sir Christopher Wren (1632-1723) was chosen as the architect for about fifty of the new churches, including remodeling the most famous, St. Paul's Cathedral — the largest space for Protestant worship in the world. In their restrained beauty, many of these structures are admirable, but their central purpose was not to provide spaces symbolic of heaven or throne rooms for Christ the king; they were designed simply as meetinghouses for the congregation. Wren's primary concern was that "all who are present can both hear and see." He even calculated how close people had to be to hear distinctly. In fact, his auditory plan became the norm for Protestant architecture for two centuries.[43] One can certainly

---

43. See Frank C. Senn, *Christian Liturgy: Catholic and Evangelical* (Minneapolis: Fortress Press, 1997), pp. 30-31.

even speak of a "grounded aesthetic" of simplicity, silence, and order that characterizes these spaces.[44] But this aesthetic is largely innocent of specially constructed symbolic objects or actions.

Objects and actions inevitably did come to fill Protestant spaces. Pews, pulpits, and tables — all these could become beautiful objects, but they had no intrinsic religious significance. And the space they occupied had a strictly utilitarian function. Separatist pastor Francis Johnson in seventeenth-century Holland captured nicely the common attitude toward such space when he made this observation:

> Now there is not any one place holy, and peculiarly consecrate [sic] to the ministrations of the Lord's Supper, as there was of old for sacrifice only at Jerusalem. So as now therefore a place being a generall circumstance that perteyneth to all actions, commodious and necessairie for people to meet in together, and to be kept from injurie and unseasonableness of the weather.[45]

There was frequently symbolic significance in the *location* of the worship structure, at least in New England. It was to be placed in the center of town, as nearly equidistant as possible from the location of people's houses. It was in one sense the "center" of life, but the space of that center was — theologically and symbolically — "empty."

This emptiness is the reverse side of the positive impetus to see one's Christian vocation, and the glory of God, diffused throughout all of life, as Calvin liked to say. As one hears frequently in this tradition, the church is people, not a building — which is the kind of aphorism that too often passes for theological reflection. So, looking around today, one is not surprised to see churches in storefronts, in banquet halls of large hotels, in nightclubs — even, as in my experience, a Boy Scout hall! Some time ago, a black megachurch in Los Angeles, Faithful Central Baptist Church, purchased the Great Western Forum, the former home of the Los Angeles Lakers basketball team. In a front-page article in the *Christian Science Monitor,* Bishop Kenneth Ulmer defended the church's new location this way: "Church is how you behave

---

44. Paul Willis defines a "grounded aesthetic" as an aesthetic value that grows naturally out of the life and commitments of a community. See *Common Culture: Symbolic Work at Play in the Everyday Cultures of the Young* (Boulder, Colo.: Westview Press, 1991).

45. Johnson, quoted in Marian C. Donnelly, *The New England Meeting Houses of the Seventeenth Century* (Middlebury, Conn.: Wesleyan University Press, 1968), p. 100.

in society after the sermon, how you live your life after the benediction. . . . The building is not important, except as a vehicle through which we dispatch and deploy others."[46] The emptiness, then, is the other side of a positive impulse to extend the impact of the Gospel into the world, but I want to argue that it is by no means a necessary component of that impulse.

Indeed, there is growing evidence that our symbolic poverty may actually *impede* the imaginative work that is necessary to creative ministry. Both Scripture and contemporary psychology agree that embodiment is essential to our humanity. Earlier I pointed out ways in which our emotional life is dependent on our being embodied. Therefore, visual objects, ritual acts, and one's emotions are inextricably related.[47] Thus Calvin, insofar as he insisted on the uniqueness of the Word in mediating God's presence, was unrealistically isolating the experience of hearing from the larger context of objects and actions in which this takes place. People move about in space, see and touch their environment, in ways that are not only practical but also affective.

Here, then, I want to propose that since the church occupies a particular social space and represents a historical trajectory, its visible shape should symbolize this space and this trajectory. Further, if these factors have theological significance — that is, if God's Trinitarian purposes *necessarily* involve a social shape and a historical engagement — then the visual shape should represent a charged image of these purposes, one where God is present in power. The church should be in the business of reflecting, visibly and concretely, "the desire of all nations," not just because that answers to contemporary longings, but because that best represents this Triune God.

Performance and Symbolism

Two notions are key to the charged space of the church: performance and symbolism. We noted that Calvin's notion of preaching was close to what today we call "performative" utterance. That is, preaching was

---

46. Daniel B. Woods, "Black Churches as Big Players in City Renewal," *Christian Science Monitor,* 25 January 2001, p. 4.
47. See Antonio R. Damasio, *The Feeling of What Happens: Body and Emotion in the Making of Consciousness* (New York: Harcourt, Brace, 1999).

meant to embody the truth that it announced, and, since it was tied to the activity of the Holy Spirit in worship, it was meant to effect in worshipers what it embodied. But why should this performance be limited to preaching (or, as often happens today, to singing)? Why not insist that the whole of the place of worship be re-oriented around the notion of the performance of faith, around practices and objects that embody something of the glory that belongs to God? Philip Stoltzfus has argued that theology can be best understood in the language of performance, as in the performance of a piece of music. Our experience with God should be likened, he thinks, to the "acquisition of a certain practice through the performance environment of hearing, playing, and living with a piece [of music] over time."[48] The spaces of worship, then, may be better understood as places of performance, where we experience, by the form and rhythm of our language, actions, and gestures, the commitments that we make.

But for this to happen, we must recover a robust sense of symbols. Symbols, I argued in an earlier chapter, are objects or practices that recognize, construct, and celebrate the relationships in which we have been created — our connections with each other, with creation, and ultimately with God. They not only forge connections; they celebrate them — they create a charged field in which we are drawn together with each other and God. For the church, the proclamation of the Word and the celebration of the Eucharist are the central symbols of God's presence and work in Christ, and so they are foundational to our understanding of symbolism. They are both a model and a performance of what human symbolism and imaginative projection should be. Although Christians differ over the precise meaning of sacraments, they agree about their centrality to the life of faith. These "symbols" and their ritual performance connect us with each other, especially with the poor and marginalized, with the created order, and with God. They are symbols that represent reconciliation, hospitality, and nourishment — both physical and spiritual — which are to influence all of life.[49] William Cavanaugh has argued movingly that the Eucharist represents an alternative narrative to that of torture and violence (which he docu-

---

48. Philip Stoltzfus, *Theology as Performance: Music, Aesthetics, and God in Western Thought* (New York: T&T Clark, 2006), p. 225.

49. I have elaborated this function of worship in Chapter Five of *A Primer on Christian Worship*.

ments in Chile during the 1970s and 1980s). To participate in it — that is, to eat and drink the body and blood of Christ — is, Cavanaugh says, "to live inside God's imagination."[50] Similarly, Graham Ward calls the Eucharist a dynamic symbol, or, as he prefers, "the dynamism and semiosis of allegory."[51] Symbols of this kind are active agents in human life, performing what they represent. So as we read (and re-enact) this narrative in the liturgy, we "participate in divine disclosure,"[52] and we readers (and hearers) are trained in the reading to read the world theologically — that is, to interpret it in the light of these symbols. Cavanaugh in particular reminds us how these practices, especially the Eucharist, are often subversive of the dominant cultural ideologies and the resulting oppressive practices. But I want to emphasize the way in which they also *fulfill* contemporary longings and the devotional practices and ritual that embody these. They express not simply an alternative world but a better world.

The focus on the Eucharist reflects the Catholic and Anglo-Catholic perspective of Cavanaugh and Ward, but the symbolic import of the Eucharist can be endorsed by Christians of all traditions. A Reformed perspective would focus more attention on the vibrant practice of the proclamation of the Word. While preaching is not symbolic in the same sense as the sacraments are, it clearly qualifies as an active and symbolic practice. The Reformers insisted that theologically the Word and the Spirit were correlated. Where the Word is truly preached, Calvin insisted, there the Spirit is present in power. Moreover, Calvin insisted that the Word interprets the sign of the Eucharist and so must always supplement it. Thus preaching, which elaborates the narrative of the Gospel, is also a dynamic symbol that connects the hearer with the larger world and with God. These are performances which, when successful, engage the imagination and stir the affections, but beyond this, they connect us with the grace and power of God.[53]

But why not insist that other practices — singing, confession,

---

50. William Cavanaugh, *Torture and Eucharist: Theology, Politics, and the Body of Christ* (Oxford: Blackwell, 1998), p. 279.

51. Graham Ward, *Christ and Culture* (Oxford: Blackwell, 2005), p. 220. He thinks that allegory best expresses a rhetoric of temporality, which suits the narrative of the Gospel.

52. Ward, *Christ and Culture*, p. 224.

53. See the important book by Clayton J. Schmit, *Too Deep for Words: A Theology of Liturgical Expression* (Louisville: Westminster John Knox Press, 2002), where the aesthetic dimension of preaching is developed.

prayer, and sharing the peace — are also potentially transformative performances in which Christians engage? Surely these are also theological practices, since both God and the believer are active in them. Their nature suggests that the worship space can become a "performance environment" (Stoltzfus) that sparks the affections and stimulates the imagination by the work of the Spirit.

It is critical that we understand the significance of this for what I am calling the aesthetics of church. My argument in this book began with the assumption that contemporary people pursue a beautiful life; they seek a life in which their imaginations, and not just their wills, are engaged. Moreover, they seek and construct, and are drawn to, images and practices which fire their imaginations and affections. For many of these people, the church no longer provides the experiences they seek, and so they have sought them elsewhere. But now we are proposing that the central practices of the church — preaching and the sacraments — are dynamic symbols that are privileged sites of God's presence which can not only engage the imagination but also, by the dynamic presence of the Spirit, transform both imagination and will.

But if this is so, participation in these dynamic practices should enable the believer not only to live a morally transformed life in the Spirit, but also to live a life that fulfills and satisfies the longing for beauty. It should enable the worshiper not only to *do* good but to *see* it as well. Living inside God's imagination means construing the world according to the figural splendor that creation embodies, and appreciating the beauty toward which the Spirit moves it. Surely Christians are not the only ones to recognize the splendor of the sunset or the wonder of great art, but if the church does not stimulate an appreciation of these things, it is not the church of Christ the creator.

The Eucharist is a unique symbol, of course, designated and fenced off by what we call "sacrament," and the Reformers insisted that while Jesus could make an object into a sacrament, we cannot.[54] But surely, while we cannot make objects into sacraments in the biblical sense, we do make them into symbols that can reflect the world formed by this sacrament. Indeed, I would argue that sacraments fall short of their full impact if they do not move us to shape other objects and actions into meaning-filled symbols. The ability to imbue objects with depth and

---

54. However, as Edward Muir points out, even the Reformers stumbled when it came to explaining what the sacrament did. See *Ritual in Early Modern Europe*, p. 179.

richness of meaning is what gives art its special power. And a fully developed theology of Christian art would surely argue that art finds its full meaning in a larger "sacramental" context that ultimately refers to Christ's own incarnation and the affirmation this provides of God's good creation. All good art, I argue, even against its will, echoes this reality. The critic George Steiner has argued that this symbolizing potential is indebted to Judeo-Christian theology: "Our endeavors to pass from letter to spirit are the immediate heirs to the textualities of western Judeo-Christian theology.... It is from there that we have borrowed our theories of symbol, our use of the iconic, our idiom of poetic creation and aura."[55]

Sacraments cannot stand alone as symbolic in our life; they call for a wider pattern of symbolization that extends — and reiterates — the meaning of the sacraments throughout our lives. James White argues that one of the unfortunate tendencies in the history of worship is the way the church progressively reduced the number of sacraments — from a large number to seven in the Middle Ages, and then to two during the Reformation. Why would anyone want to *diminish* opportunities for wonder, he asks: Why not seek to extend this sacramental vision more widely?[56] Why not indeed? In fact, this question provides the starting point of my argument in the following chapter on justice-making and aesthetics.

Excursus: Why Is the Ear Privileged over the Eye?

The tradition of Calvin, in its privileging of the ear over the eye, has been deeply suspicious of symbolism. Perhaps this is the place to explore further the theological reasons for this. Michael Horton has recently given articulate expression to this suspicion in his excellent book *Covenant and Eschatology*.[57] While it is not central to his argument, underlying his plea for making the covenant and our eschatological hope central to our understanding of theology is a consistent critique against vision and the

---

55. George Steiner, *Real Presences,* The Leslie Stephen Memorial Lecture, Cambridge University, 1 November 1985 (Cambridge: Cambridge University Press, 1986), p. 22. This lecture was eventually enlarged and published as *Real Presences: Is There Anything in What We Say?* (London: Faber, 1989).

56. James White, *The Sacraments in Protestant Practice and Faith* (Nashville: Abingdon Press, 1999).

57. Michael S. Horton, *Covenant and Eschatology: The Divine Drama* (Louisville: Westminster John Knox Press, 2002). Subsequent pages cited in the text refer to this work.

visual. He contrasts his model of praxis with that of vision. The former reflects the Reformational concern for the doing of truth. The paradigm of vision, he thinks, is ultimately Platonic, in which the realm of appearance is the mirror image of eternal ideas. Its central defect lies in encouraging contemplation rather than active involvement in the world (252, 253). Further, he follows Coleridge in suggesting that the despotism of the eye suggests that what cannot be seen cannot exist (187). But the deeper reason for this negative view of sight is theological: a focus on vision suggests an over-realized eschatology, a direct sight of the One rather than a faithful hearing of God's instructions (35). Horton sums up the contrast between hearing and sight in this way:

> A theology of vision corresponds to a *theologia gloriae*, while a theology of promise corresponds to the *theologia crucis*. The former craves an unmediated encounter with the sacred in a realized eschatology, while the latter patiently and joyfully receives the mediated encounter with a personal God in the "already" and "not yet" tension that belongs to faith rather than sight. (145; his emphasis)

Much of this resonates with the dialectical vision that we have developed in this book. Horton's description of theology based on God's personal covenant promise is a rich and compelling account which leads to chapters that describe God's call as a cosmic drama that invigorates the imagination. But why should all this be based only on the word and not on the image? Why should theology be always a telling and not also a showing — indeed, it is hard to imagine a drama that does not do both. Interestingly, Horton bases his claim, in part, on 1 Corinthians 13. Here he thinks Paul is saying that faith and hope are pilgrims who are on the journey, and that this is suited to hearing the preached Word (35). But why should that be the case? In fact, in this passage (in 1 Cor. 13:12, which Horton quotes), Paul pointedly does not oppose faith and sight, but contrasts sight in a mirror (or literally, in Greek, "in enigma") with face-to-face sight — that is, he contrasts sight which is incomplete with that which is perfect. In other words, we do have glimpses of a vision that will one day be filled out, an imperfect view of what will one day be perfected. To deny this is to deny that Christ has *already* inaugurated a redemptive process that is not yet complete.[58]

---

58. The prejudice against the visual seems to reflect, in part, an incomprehension of

The Aesthetics of Church

Our discussion of biblical imagery in the last chapter emphasized the imaginative power of the biblical drama. Indeed, one might ask, how can there be a dramatic presentation of God's covenant promise, which Horton describes so well, *without* symbolic and metaphorical carriers? He can even praise a divine *poesis* in the biblical drama while insisting that this is something only God can do, not his human creation (182, 245). The worry connected with this emphasis recalls Kierkegaard, who did not want the aesthetic to trump the ethical — a fear to which we will return in the next chapter on justice. Those in this tradition do not want the splendor of some false glory to distract believers from actually hearing the Word and putting it into practice — as in Bunyan's story, beauty is reserved for the heavenly city. The impulse behind this is sound. Part of the insistence of Reformed spirituality, as with Kierkegaard, is on what might be called the critical absence of the divine. That is, we do not yet "see" God; we are waiting earnestly for God's appearance (i.e., the "parousia"). This waiting opens up space for us to be obedient, to be about our Father's business. We do not sit on the mountain waiting for Christ's return, as Paul reminded the Thessalonians; we work with our hands so that we can serve our neighbor and thus honor God.

But if we do not yet see God, we do see God's work in creation, and especially in our neighbor. And while we are about our Father's business, it matters a great deal what exactly our hands are making and what we do with what we make, especially in our spaces of worship. We can be making things that we will store away in our barns (i.e., investment accounts) so that, as the retirement commercials remind us, we can sleep easily at night, or we can take what we make and pour it lavishly on Jesus' feet like the nameless woman in Matthew. Significantly, Jesus called this promiscuous, wasteful giving a "beautiful work" (*ha ergon kalon,* Matt. 26:10b). But the Protestant habit of privileging the inner over the outer discourages such beautiful work. There is an irony here. Calvin sought to purify the heart precisely by removing distracting images. But in doing so, he inadvertently discouraged the shaping of objects that stimulate the imagination and fire the heart, thus di-

---

how images actually work. In one place, Horton argues for the use of analogies by contrasting them to pictures "which capture an image, and because of their identical representation are inflexible to interpretation" (p. 18). But this ignores the fact that both hearing and seeing require discerning interpretation.

minishing the scope of the very inner life he meant to celebrate. In terms that we developed earlier, if we are discouraged from shaping outward expressions of inward grace or sculpting objects to contemplate, how can we be stimulated to make a beautiful life for ourselves and our family?

It is important to remind ourselves how often postmodern people, including many of our children, are put off by the symbolic poverty of our worship and find a home in other traditions, or form alternative church structures with symbolic and aesthetic richness. Or they leave the church altogether in search of imaginative stimulus. They intuitively understand that ritual and ceremony are necessary for lives that are fully human.

Conclusion

We have come a long way from the medieval cathedral in which every act and object has intrinsic and deeply theological meaning. The splendor of many sacramentals was reduced by some Reformers to the seven sacraments, by others to two, and in many respects even these, for modern people, have lost their sacramental depth. I am reminded here of the important intervention by Cardinal Godfried Danneels of Belgium at the May 2001 Consistory of Cardinals in Rome. The modern person, he noted, tends to be "in love with rites and ritualization, but is allergic to the Christian sacraments." The sacraments, he commented, are no longer the center of gravity for Catholic pastoral life. He might have said that this center has become empty — though it is still "filled" with words and preparation for *diakonia*. He went on to say, "The church seems to be nothing more than a place where one speaks and where one places oneself at the service of the world. The sacramental life is shifting from the center of the church to its periphery. Is it, perhaps, a matter of a slow and unconscious Protestantization of the church from within?"[59]

Visits to a variety of our contemporary evangelical worship spaces lead me to wonder if our worship spaces, filled as they are with words — preaching, announcements, even our singing — can fix and hold our faith for us? Can words ultimately, by themselves, fix our minds and

---

59. Godfried Danneels, "Intervention," *America,* July 30–August 6, 2001, pp. 6-7.

hearts in a way that shapes us theologically? Like the ever-changing images on the omnipresent screen, lacking any fixed spatial reference point, do words too slip and slide around?

These questions — indeed, all the challenges of the visible representation of the church that I have addressed — raise the issue of "authority" in the church. I have said that the life of the visible church is an ever renewed (and embodied) interpretation of Scripture. I would argue that these three spaces — social, historical, and symbolic — are necessary for such an embodied interpretation and a Spirit-filled authority. These spaces give us fixed points by which we orient ourselves and from which we give our situated witness. Together they give us a communal, historical, and concrete identity. We interpret Scripture by our corporate life together, the social space that is formed by the Holy Spirit; we construe the text in ways that reflect the historical place which we find ourselves in (or that we have chosen) and which we will do our part to enlarge and elaborate; but above all we make our interpreted witness by the shapes and objects of our worship. The authority of Scripture must always take some historical shape to become visible. These spaces provide churches with the opportunity to exhibit the reality of their evangelical commitments. As Artur Grabowski says, "Without the arts the religion of the revealed Word will not have a representative in the world of phenomena; it will not present itself and will live dimly. No other method of revealing it can substitute for metaphors and images. In them we come to know and confess the Creator."[60]

In the end, this symbolic space may be more important than the social and historical space for us Protestants because this make possible the representation of these other spaces. For corporate ritual acts and symbolic objects cement our social lives; they give us visible and public points — concrete metaphors — around which we can orient our lives. These also give important expression to the historical place that we stand in — recalling with gratitude ancient practices and images that Christians have lived with for centuries. Indeed, the symbolic spaces and objects give form to the social and historical spaces; they become places where these spaces coalesce, places which, by the Holy Spirit, can be used to shape us together into the body of Christ. They can become — indeed, by God's grace, they are meant to become — divine objects of desire.

---

60. Grabowski, "Unapologetic Visibility," p. 75.

However, I believe that the most important role these sharpened sensitivities can play is not only theological but also pastoral. Understanding the sacramental — or perhaps I should say the incarnational — dimension of worship may force us to give new attention to the forms and reminders of our baptism and the Lord's Supper. More importantly, it may force us to think with many of our Christian mothers and fathers, mystics and saints, about the implications of the fact that God became part of the human creation in Jesus Christ. We might learn to say with John of Damascus, "I salute all remaining matter with reverence, because God has filled it with his grace and power."[61] In short, evangelicals may come to see that the church is not at all like a garage; it is more like a richly furnished home into which we may gladly invite our friends and neighbors.

---

61. St. John of Damascus, "First Apology," 16, in *On the Divine Images,* trans. David Anderson (New York: St. Vladimir's Seminary Press, 2002), p. 23.

CHAPTER 9

Aesthetics and Social Transformation

"Beauty will save the world."

Fyodor Dostoyevsky

Beauty and the Poor

If the church is the site of a fresh vision of the world, how does this extend itself out into the world? If, as Protestants have insisted, worship has its final reference in our work for shalom in the world, how might this relate to the project of poetic theology? It is to these questions that we turn in this chapter.

In the introduction to his book *Christianity, Art, and Transformation*,[1] John De Gruchy tells of a colleague who asked him why, during the period of apartheid, South Africa produced such ugly architecture. De Gruchy admits that he had not noticed it, but that it was certainly true. He goes on to say that as far as he knows, this connection has never been explored — something that he sets out to do in his book. De Gruchy's comments are important because they immediately connect what is usually unrelated — justice and aesthetics, or, in this case, injustice and ugliness. This is a set of concerns I want to address here. With De Gruchy I want to argue for a connection between the spheres of aesthetics and human transformation.

---

1. John W. De Gruchy, *Christianity, Art, and Transformation: Theological Aesthetics in the Struggle for Justice* (Cambridge: Cambridge University Press, 2001).

THE TRAJECTORY OF POETIC THEOLOGY

Let me specify what kind of connection I am proposing. Relating beauty and human flourishing is not to suggest that poor people simply need to be introduced to aesthetics as part of their (social and economic) advancement. I am not proposing an aesthetic development program. Indeed, as the history of popular music (and popular arts more generally) makes clear, creative innovations are as likely to travel *from* poor and marginalized communities to the broader culture than the reverse. My claim is more basic: the aesthetic sense is fundamental to humanity. People seek to create beauty, to make something of their lives, not because they are educated or economically privileged, but because they are created to reflect God. Since symbolic practices are fundamental to human flourishing, any project of human betterment will seek to appreciate and celebrate the aesthetic impulse that is already present in the community.

For much of her life, my mother-in-law, Grace Strachan Roberts, was active in poor areas of San Jose, Costa Rica, organizing the women there in ways that nurtured their many gifts. One of the things that constantly amazed her, and that she frequently pointed out to us, was the way these women always managed to adorn their houses and yards to make them attractive — a wall painted in festive blue and white; flowers set out in discarded tin cans. Whatever else she needed to do, she did not have to introduce to them the notion of aesthetic delight!

Given that aesthetic impulses characterize people everywhere, I want to ask how this relates to larger issues of human flourishing. How do we think about community development and aesthetics together? I have been arguing that the Reformed Protestant tradition has expressed consistent concern for social transformation. Reformed sensitivities were often sharpened by the Bible's persistent concern for the poor. Calvin's emphasis on creation as the sphere in which the glory of God can be realized encouraged believers to be busy with human need. Especially in the last generation, Protestants in this tradition have called for integration of Christian witness and justice.[2]

And, as I argued, there are resources here for understanding our work in the world in aesthetic categories. While John Calvin, for exam-

---

2. In addition to De Gruchy's book, see, among others, Bryant Myers, *Walking with the Poor: Principles and Practices of Transformational Development* (Maryknoll, N.Y.: Orbis Books, 1999), and Nicholas Wolterstorff, *Until Justice and Peace Embrace* (Grand Rapids: Wm. B. Eerdmans, 1983).

ple, did forbid bringing images into the worship experience, he also conceived of worship and human life more generally in terms of a great drama. If creation is a theatre for God's glory, one of the chief places this glory is visible is in the human image. If we are to reflect and display this glory, we can do no better than to cultivate and care for this image. In an earlier chapter I referred to Reformer Martin Bucer's argument that making images was the chief obstacle to the proper cultivation of God's beauty. Rather than shaping material objects to honor God, Bucer says, let us remember that the whole of creation is meant to reflect God's glory. Thus we should labor to have the whole frame of the world as "a monument . . . to put us in remembrance of God." On this great canvas, the glory of God is to be seen.[3]

Biblical discussions as well often link outward splendor with proper social order and justice; I described some of these connections in an earlier chapter. So there are ample biblical and historical precedents for linking beauty and justice, even if these have too often been separated in the tradition. In the previous chapter I argued that one of the characteristics of Christian — and congregational — maturity is aesthetic and symbolic depth. Similarly, it would seem likely that one of the criteria for successful projects in human development would be aesthetic. So here I will ask how this might be so. But before doing this, I must spend some time addressing theological priorities which have sometimes discouraged the integration I want to encourage.

Aesthetics and Eschatology

In the last chapter we inquired into the form the church takes: How does it represent itself to the world? Here I might start by asking a similar question: What form does justice take? What does the work of justice-making look like? What might be the formal shape of such work in communities? In an earlier chapter I argued that the Protestant focus on the narrative of the Christian life led to a uniquely storied aesthetic. Indeed, a central focus of this book has been the delight that humans can take from the encounter with God in this earthly life. The

---

3. Martin Bucer, *A Treatise Declaring and Showing . . . That Pictures and Other Images Are Not to Be Suffered in the Temples and Churches of Christian Men* (London: W. Marshall, 1535), n.p.

dramatic narrative of salvation grows out of and articulates, as it were, the created context in which God has set this story. That is to say, while Christians wait eagerly for the final revelation of glory, they find a spiritual depth and even joy in their embodied life. Moreover, many people today are initially drawn toward God through the desire sparked by their experience of the goodness and beauty of creation.

But if God will one day transform the world, once and for all, into his splendid kingdom, it is not hard to see why many Protestants, when it comes to aesthetics, want to focus on what is still to come, when Christ returns in glory. The Reformers' reaction against medieval mystical (and artistic) practices was in part an attack on an over-realized eschatology, and on the tendency, especially of the monastic orders, to retire from involvement in the world — to anticipate, so to speak, the rest of heaven. So, many Protestants argued, contemplation (what was called in the medieval period the *vita contemplativa*, the contemplative life), and thus art and beauty, would be characteristic of our heavenly life; meanwhile, we are called to pursue the active life (what was called the *vita activa*). For these, then, art and aesthetics really belong to the "not-yet" rather than the "already" side of the eschatological equation. This is why Bunyan reserved his most specifically aesthetic language in *The Pilgrim's Progress* for the precincts of heaven and the Delectable Mountains. Glory, on this view, is not easy to see during this dispensation. Indeed, there are those such as Michael Horton, whom we met in the last chapter, who discourage us from even looking for it here. Karl Barth seems to agree. "Art must be considered in an eschatological context," he writes in his *Ethics,* because in this form of human action, our duties "cannot be made intelligible to us except as play."[4] Meanwhile, we wait, he says, but we also play. Play now reminds us not to take this life with final seriousness "because the perfect has still to come beyond all that we do now. . . . We cannot be more grimly in earnest about life than when we resign ourselves to the fact that we can only play" (504-5). So, he thinks, the artist's work is "homeless" in the deepest possible sense — it belongs to a world that is yet to come. But in the meantime, "art plays with reality" (507).

4. Karl Barth, *Ethics,* ed. Dietrich Braun, trans. Geoffrey Bromiley (New York: Seabury Press, 1981), pp. 506-7, quoted in Roger Lundin, "The Beauty of Belief," in *The Beauty of God: Theology and the Arts,* ed. D. J. Treier, Mark Husbands, and Roger Lundin (Downers Grove, Ill.: InterVarsity Press, 2007), p. 207. Other quotations are also from this page; page numbers from Barth's original volume are cited in the text.

Aesthetics and Social Transformation

Barth's words suggest a significant connection between the present experience of aesthetics and play, something that we will want to pursue later in the chapter. This fits with the thinking of other Protestants who want to hold out for a serious playfulness characterizing the human drama. Abraham Kuyper, we noted earlier, thought that the opening up of the whole of life to the artist's vision, which took place at the Reformation, was a good thing. This enabled artists to find enthralling drama and lively harmonies in the most humble circumstances — even to suggest a connection between these and the glory that is to come. Marilynne Robinson celebrated this aesthetics of everyday life in her recent novel *Gilead*. She describes the old Presbyterian minister John Ames as finding exquisite beauty in his simple life. Ames knows that the amazing things he sees with his childlike eyes are "all mere apparition compared to what awaits us." Still, he continues,

> But it is only lovelier for that. There is a human beauty in it. And I can't believe that, when we have all been changed and put on incorruptibility, we will forget our fantastic condition of mortality and impermanence, the great bright dream of procreating and perishing that meant the whole world to us. In eternity this world will be Troy, I believe, and all that has passed here will be the epic of the universe, the ballad they sing in the streets.[5]

This homey narrative, Ames thinks, is too dense, too substantial, for any other reality to put it in the shade. No eschatology, however pious, asks this of us. And this hint of glory suggests ways that aesthetics will surely connect with projects which promote human flourishing.

We have seen that a Protestant aesthetic would be one in which aesthetic values are dispersed rather than concentrated; they relate, broadly, to all of life and creation, not only to a separate sphere that might be called "aesthetic." And since, according to this view, it is God's purpose to ultimately transform the whole cosmos — until the glory of the Lord covers the earth "as the waters cover the sea" (Hab. 2:14) — present injustice has to be experienced as a major obstacle. And, since this is so, injustice is, in part, aesthetic — an ugly blot that must be challenged and eventually effaced. It follows that any project of addressing this condition must also be poetic.

---

5. Marilynne Robinson, *Gilead: A Novel* (New York: Farrar, Straus & Giroux, 2004), p. 57.

Aesthetics versus Ethics: Levinas and Kierkegaard

But the objection to a present focus on aesthetics is not only eschatological; it is also, more seriously, ethical. Here we might recall the warning embodied in the Second Commandment: "You shall not make for yourself an idol, whether in the form of anything that is in heaven above, or that is on the earth beneath, or that is in the water under the earth" (Exod. 20:4). The Jewish and Christian tradition has often interpreted this restriction to imply that image-making involves an evasion not only of spiritual responsibility but of moral responsibility (which was a major theme of Bucer's argument). This is certainly the reading given this commandment by the Jewish philosopher Emmanuel Levinas, who believes that "the proscription of images is truly the supreme command of monotheism."[6] Levinas seems to find three problems with art-making, at least in the form of making images. First, he thinks it neutralizes our active engagement with objects (132). He thinks that we have a real and ethically significant relationship with the world around us and, most importantly, with other people through our active response to these. Art, however, moves us in a totally different direction, away from responsibility. We understand by and through action, Levinas believes; art obscures understanding by an invasion of the shadow — that is, the image.

This is because — and here is the second problem with art-making — in art the real is replaced by the not real, truth by non-truth (i.e., the image). Levinas believes that "a represented object, by the simple fact of becoming an image, is converted into a non-object" (134). Reality, he thinks, is disincarnated by art. This means — and here is the third problem — that by making or enjoying the art object, we evade the responsibility that the real object invariably places upon us — the moral situation of the created order to which we have frequently referred. The image, morally speaking, "lets us off the hook." Levinas says, "Art brings into the world the obscurity of fate, but it especially brings the irresponsibility that charms as a lightness and grace. It frees. . . . Do not speak, do not reflect, admire in silence and in peace — such are the counsels of wisdom satisfied before the beautiful" (141). Images register their hold over us — they choose us — and thus confirm us in our passivity rather

---

6. Emmanuel Levinas, "Reality and Its Shadow," in *The Levinas Reader*, ed. Sean Hand (Oxford: Blackwell, 1989), p. 141. Subsequent pages will be cited in the text.

than encouraging our initiative toward the other. In the face of the image, Levinas asks, how can we love our neighbor as ourselves?

There is much in this complaint that our previous reflections have made familiar, and that many Protestants would applaud. Art, at least in the modern period, in claiming our exclusive attention, *distracts* us — from worship, from moral responsibility. In this way it veers toward idolatry. But something else is familiar in Levinas's worry: the refusal of symbolism. These perceived elements, he insists, "do not serve as symbols, and in the absence of the object they do not force its presence, but by their presence insist on its absence" (136). It is not completely clear whether his lament is for art more generally or for what has become of art in the modern period. "Perhaps," he suggests near the end of his essay,

> the doubts that ... since the Renaissance, the alleged death of God has put in souls, have compromised for the artist the reality of the henceforth inconsistent models, have imposed on him the onus of finding his models anew in the heart of production itself, and made him believe he had a mission to be creator and revealer. (143)

But in refusing symbolism, one wonders, how are we to put a face on the world that will inspire love and joy? How are we to shape in our imaginations the winsome *connections* among things? The image is not necessarily empty; it is often full of (previously) unheard melodies, of unseen harmonies, that can send us back to the world with new eyes and fresh spirits. The imagery of Hopkins' kestrel expands all possibilities for birds in flight; the mulberry tree of Van Gogh makes us wonder if we have ever really looked at a tree. Levinas notes that listening to music is not the same thing as dancing. But how will we dance without music?

Søren Kierkegaard has also been enlisted in the chorus of those promoting the ethical over the aesthetic. He famously argued that the poet is one who *avoids* suffering. "Who is a poet?" he asks at the beginning of *Either/Or*. He answers, "An unhappy man who hides deep anguish in his heart, but whose lips are so formed that when the sigh and cry pass through them, it sounds like lovely music."[7] A generation after Schiller and Goethe, *Either/Or* seems on the surface to be a response to

---

7. Søren Kierkegaard, *Either/Or: A Fragment of a Life,* ed. Victor Eremita, trans. Alastair Hannay (New York: Penguin Books, 1992 [1842]), p. 43. Subsequent pages will be cited in the text.

the aestheticism of the Romantic poets. Indeed, Kierkegaard wrote substantial portions of this work during one of his few trips out of Denmark, to Berlin, where he listened to lectures by Schelling. In this 1843 work, Kierkegaard portrays the aesthete, whom he calls *A,* carrying on an epistolary conversation with Judge Vilhelm, who defends the ethical life. In his "Seducer's Diary," *A* seems to anticipate Nietzsche's fear that morals extinguish the aesthetic life. *A* has fallen in love with Cordelia. All seems to be going well with their relationship, *A* believes, when moral obligation ruins everything: "Beneath the sky of the aesthetic everything is light, pleasant, and fleeting; when ethics comes along, everything becomes hard, angular, and unending ennui" (305). Because, *A* thinks, "the glory and divinity of aesthetics is just this, that it only enters into relation with the beautiful; all it has to do with, essentially, is fiction and the fair sex" (361).

The judge responds that although *A* thinks he has chosen this aesthetic life, it is not a choice at all. Beauty, the judge insists (anticipating Levinas), is not a choice that he makes, but something that chooses him in the moment. And it does not produce evil so much as indifference. Aesthetics, the Judge says, is observing life with your hands in your pockets. But to live truly, Kierkegaard says, one must choose. By choosing, we become who we are. So appears the absolute choice, the either/or: "The personality, through choosing itself, chooses itself ethically and excludes the aesthetic absolutely" (491).

On these grounds, Kierkegaard has been placed among those promoting ethics over aesthetics. But when one follows the argument further, it turns out that what Kierkegaard excludes absolutely is not aesthetics or beauty, but the sense that one can by desire *escape* an ethical choice — that one can, by aesthetics, escape choosing what is right. What he excludes is Kant's notion of disinterested beauty. But when one chooses the ethical and the religious, Kierkegaard claims, beauty is given back in another, higher form. *A* has persuaded himself that romantic love is aesthetic, while marriage is its denial. The Judge (and, one supposes, Kierkegaard) disagree. How can marriage be aesthetic? the Judge asks. Only by adding the resources provided by the ethical and the religious. The beautiful marriage in fact is actually incommensurate with poetic representation. It can be represented only by being lived — it is, he says, like music, which only lives in performance. The highest aesthetic can only be realized in the actual living of life. "This is how aesthetics transcends itself and reconciles itself with life": by be-

Aesthetics and Social Transformation

ing lived (461). Notice the way that Kierkegaard adds the aesthetics of drama to the life of obedience. The realization of the highest in the aesthetic, Kierkegaard believes, is the life of

> [one who has the] sense of being a character in the play written by God . . . a play where the playwright and prompter are not different people, where the individual, like the trained actor who has made himself one with his part and his lines, is not put off by the prompter but feels that what is whispered to him is what he himself would say, so that he begins almost to doubt whether it is the prompter that is putting the words into his mouth or he putting them into the prompter's; he who in the deepest sense feels himself at once composer and composition. (462)

It turns out, then, that Kierkegaard is not against aesthetics in itself but only against a constricted sense of desire that is divorced from the larger moral situation in which we find ourselves. It is this larger moral situation that catches David Lurie in J. M. Coetzee's novel *Disgrace*, which we discussed in the first chapter. While he sought to follow what was good in the desire he felt for his student, he was not able to see this in the larger moral order, and so his desire became destructive rather than life-giving. Thus, Kierkegaard is giving us resources for finding in the narrative of human life, especially one lived in the conscious presence of God, an aesthetic quality which can attract by desire.

Kierkegaard's reflections, when put together with John Ames's words, imply something even more far-reaching for the claims that we want to make in this chapter. The way to the higher meaning is not made by a mystical leap or a peak experience, but through the transformation of ordinary desires — by living them out within a larger moral and spiritual framework. Sexual love is not abandoned in marriage, but it is transfigured into something better — even, the Scriptures say, into an image of God's own relation with his people. Desire is not suppressed by the larger social and cultural context, but enlarged and expanded.

The Split between Aesthetics and Human Transformation

But even if Kierkegaard is not to be blamed, we are still saddled with this insistent and pernicious divide between the good and the beautiful. As Nietzsche saw, religious people in particular have trouble seeing the connection, but they are not alone. How did this separation between the beauty and the good come about?

For a variety of reasons, during the Renaissance, art began to be considered separately from the rest of life, as an activity that had its own values and ends. This did not happen all at once, nor was it noticeable at the start, but the process began there. This separation received its definitive impulse in the Romantic movement in the nineteenth century, when sensitive (what we today call artistic) people began to be appalled at the horrors of industrialization (the ancestors of those who are appalled at the similar horrors of urbanization and globalization today). As Raymond Williams has argued, these poets and critics began to define their work in terms of values that have come to be synonymous with "culture." This world of culture was placed in contrast to "society," with its industrial blight and crowded urban slums. Aesthetics and art were the province of those who pursued "culture"; "society," meanwhile, was left in the hands of the social engineers. (I recently met a scholar who argued that there was a parallel phenomenon in nineteenth-century economics — that it progressively grew away from larger moral and religious values and concentrated on narrow mathematical calculations.) These words of D. H. Lawrence echoed those of many of his nineteenth-century predecessors:

> The Pisgah-top of spiritual oneness looks down upon the hopeless squalor of industrialism, the huge cemetery of human hopes. This is our Promised Land.... The aeroplane descends and lays her eggshells of empty tin cans on the top of Everest, in the Ultima Thule, and all over the North Pole; not to speak of tractors waddling across the inviolate Sahara and over the jags of Arabia Patraea, laying the same addled eggs of our civilization, tin cans, in every camp-nest.[8]

Artists sought refuge in an aesthetic of being rather than one of doing; in contemplation, not action; on Mount Pisgah rather than the plains of industrialism. As a result, art in the twentieth century struggled, usually unsuccessfully, to find a public voice, succeeding occasionally — Pi-

---

8. D. H. Lawrence, "Climbing Down Pisgah," quoted in Raymond Williams, *Culture and Society, 1780-1950* (New York: Penguin Books, 1963), pp. 199-200.

casso's *Guernica* is one example — but mostly recording private states of consciousness. For purposes of our discussion, it is important to note that for most twentieth-century artists, the very notion of beauty became problematic.

At the beginning of a new century, we find ourselves heirs of this serious split. On the one hand, there is a growing world of sophisticated non-governmental organizations anxious to correct the ills and excesses of industrialization — to pick up, as it were, the tin cans scattered about. Meanwhile, on the other hand, the other universe called the art world, with its phalanx of critics, galleries, museums, and publications, generously supported by philanthropists and large foundations, has developed a life of its own — but one that rarely intersects with the world of human need.

In the twenty-first century, we ask, What does the rarefied world of culture, the worldwide gallery and auction system, have to do with the developmental goals of the United Nations? Nor is this only a problem for religious believers; non-believers face a similar gulf. Elaine Scarry (whom we have met previously) wrestles, from her secular perspective, with the private nature of beauty and the apparently public call of justice. She attempts to undertake a phenomenology of beauty that might allow for concerns with justice. Her struggles are instructive. She begins by noting the holistic character of beauty:

> At the moment one comes into the presence of something beautiful, it greets you. It lifts away from the neutral background as though coming forward to welcome you — as though the object were designed to "fit" your perception. In its etymology, "welcome" means that one comes with the well-wishes or consent of the person or thing already standing on that ground. It is as though the welcoming thing has entered into, and consented to, your being in its midst. Your arrival seems contractual, not just something you want, but something the world you are now joining wants.[9]

Notice that she speaks of objects of beauty, not beauty itself. For the idea of beauty — even discussions about it, she admits — have become decidedly out of favor. Scarry revisits the typical political argument

---

9. Elaine Scarry, *On Beauty and Being Just* (Princeton: Princeton University Press, 1999), pp. 25-26. Subsequent pages will be cited in the text.

made against beauty, by both believers and unbelievers, in this way: "Beauty, by preoccupying our attention, distracts attention from wrong social arrangements. It makes us inattentive" (58). Here, voiced by an unbelieving Protestant, reappears that very Protestant fear of beauty as a *distraction*. But there is something wrong with this way of putting things, she thinks. Recalling her earlier description of beauty as implying a kind of contract between viewer and viewed, she underlines the connection between these. The experience of beauty not only confers on the perceiver the gift of life, she thinks, but "also confers on the object the gift of life. The pacific quality of beauty comes in part from the reciprocal, life-granting pact" (69).

Two things follow from this life-giving pact. First, when we experience something beautiful, we find ourselves with "an urge to protect it, or act on its behalf" (80). Second, as a result, we find ourselves wanting to extend this attention to other objects around. Scarry says, "It is as though beautiful things have been placed here and there throughout the world to serve as small wake-up calls to perception, spurring lapsed alertness back to its most acute level" (81). Perceptual interest in beauty "enlists us" in regard for others. Beautiful things, then, "give rise to the notion of distribution, to a life-saving reciprocity" (95).

Beauty and the viewer each welcome the other in a reciprocity that seeks extension, Scarry claims. This claim she elaborates in two ways. First, this reciprocity is grounded in a substantial notion of equality that implies both pleasure and goodness. For this reason, equality has to be that to which all things aspire. Here, significantly, she quotes the following from Augustine's *De Musica:*

> The higher things are those in which equality resides, supreme, unshaken, unchangeable, eternal.... This rhythm is immutable and eternal, with no inequality possible. Therefore it must come from God.... Beautiful things please by proportion ... equality is found not only in sounds for the ear and in bodily movements, but also in visible forms. (98)

Does anyone emerge from this "cascade of paragraphs," she wonders, without having their commitment to this equality (and its broader extension) deepened (99)? More important, can there be any doubt that the moral pull and the aesthetic surface of this are deeply connected? This, of course, moved Augustine — but not Scarry — to say "Therefore it must

Aesthetics and Social Transformation

come from God."[10] Similarly, George Steiner has argued that what lies behind the weight of an aesthetic object is a presence that he calls a logos. He writes, "Without some axiomatic leap towards a postulate of *meaningfulness*, there can be no striving towards intelligibility or value judgment.... Where it elides the 'radical' — the etymological and conceptual root — of the *Logos*, logic is indeed vacant."[11]

But even if our attention is drawn by the weight of the call to equality, even if the form of beauty pulls us, what moves us to take up *action* in that direction? What might shake us from being transfixed by our regard? This leads Scarry to the suggestion, secondly, that the experience of beauty is radically de-centering (111). Here Scarry is forced to call in another Christian witness, Simone Weil. Beauty, according to Weil, calls us "to give up our imaginary position as the center.... A transformation then takes place at the very roots of our sensibility, in our immediate reception of sense impressions" (111). The experience of beauty, then, calls us out of ourselves. Rather than veering in the direction of idolatry, here it pushes us in the direction of giving up ourselves for another. One is even reminded of Paul's words: "I have been crucified with Christ; and it is no longer I who live, but it is Christ who lives in me" (Gal. 2:19-20). Beauty, of course, can only suggest this; only God can make it happen. Weil — though again, not Scarry — knows this well enough.[12]

---

10. Scarry has earlier considered, then dismissed, the possibility that the loss of this "metaphysical depth" makes discussion of beauty impossible: "But if the metaphysical realm has vanished, one may feel bereft not only because of the giant deficit left by that vacant realm but because the girl, the bird, the vase, the book now seem unable in their solitude to justify or account for the weight of their own beauty." But in a move that reflects her Romantic influence, she thinks that Matisse (among others) helps us see that beauty can carry greetings "from within," if not from above (p. 47).

11. George Steiner, *Real Presences,* The Leslie Stephen Memorial Lecture, Cambridge University, 1 November 1985 (Cambridge: Cambridge University Press, 1986), pp. 17-18, his emphasis. In the lecture, Steiner goes on to acknowledge the debt this expresses to theology (which was omitted in the later publication): "It is loans of terminology and reference from the reserves of theology which provide the master readers in our time ... with their license to practice. We have borrowed, traded upon, made small change of the reserves of transcendent authority. Very few of us have made any return deposit" (p. 20).

12. In fact, just before the section that Scarry uses, Weil says, "By loving the order of the world, we imitate the divine love which created this universe of which we are a part." She goes on to say that this creation involved giving the creature an imaginary likeness of God's power so that the human creature could imagine "himself" at the center, so that "he also, although a creature, may empty himself of his divinity." See Simone Weil, *Waiting for God,* trans. Emma Craufurd (New York: Harper & Row, 1951), p. 158.

Still, Scarry's conclusion from these reflections is sound: Can anyone emerge from this experience without wanting this beauty for others? Do we want future generations to look back on us and say, Why did you leave the world in such a way that a beautiful life is no longer possible? Or, to put this question another way: Do we, so zealous for human flourishing, wish to deny the poor, in the name of our zeal for development, experiences of life-giving beauty?

It would be naïve, however, to suggest that communities simply need to have their own sense of beauty and goodness awakened in order to advance, especially in the light of the suffering and despair that characterize certain areas of the world today — Darfur and Zimbabwe are the names that come to mind, but there are others. For many in situations of extreme need, the struggle is not to make a life that is attractive but simply to survive through another dark night. Jacques Maritain takes these situations as a different kind of wake-up call than the aesthetic experiences Scarry describes. In fact, he argues that Christians especially are all too prone to ignorance about these dark places. In his classic book *Integral Humanism,* he writes,

> Human weakness is always trying to go to sleep; if it is not the doubt of the old humanist stoic, it is the eternal truths it will take for its pillow. If he is not kept awake by a sorrowing communion with all the suffering and outcasts of mortal life, the Christian is apt to take for his pillow the very love which he has received.[13]

Maritain believes that the human creature can be rehabilitated only as she recognizes her rootedness in God (72), and that basic temporal development is essential to provide material conditions for one to pursue higher spiritual goals (176). On this ground, one might argue that attention to the aesthetic needs of a community must be postponed until more basic needs are met. But aren't affective attractions critical even at this basic level? One only has to reflect on the motivation, itself grounded in affection and commitment, provided by the hope for a better life for one's children to see the importance of this emotional

---

13. Jacques Maritain, *Integral Humanism: Temporal and Spiritual Problems of a New Christendom,* trans. Joseph Evans (Notre Dame: University of Notre Dame Press, 1968, 1973 [1936]), p. 55. Subsequent pages will be cited in the text.

and aesthetic dimension. All people at all times want to make a life for themselves and their children that is attractive.

Beauty, then, is something we want; but it is also something the world wants. It is a basic human value. Here is where the connection between beauty and community health and transformation emerges. Our neighbor wants moral goodness, of course, but as Hans Urs von Balthasar points out, it is beauty that makes such goodness attractive. Justice remains distant and vacuous unless it is embodied in relationships and connections that take concrete form — forms that move one not simply to understanding but to action. So what people desire, what we all want, is life that is full and beautiful. Advertisers know this, of course, and they make their promised world sparkle with color and brightness. But though theirs is a reflected light, it still speaks of the presence of One who lights everyone (and everything) coming into the world (John 1:9). It is no insult to the creature when the Christian asks, Why enjoy only moonlight, when Christ the light has dawned? But even if the practices of making beauty and doing good are related, what shape might this relationship actually take? It is to this question that I now turn.

Cultivating Aesthetic Practices

Let me suggest, briefly, some practices that might become indices of community health — practices that speak of the aesthetics of community in a similar way to what we have called the aesthetics of church. We set the discussion in the context of what is called "community development," though it could just as well be framed differently. In a general sense, community development involves activities that seek to promote human flourishing. But workers in this field know that statistical indices of per-capita income and infant mortality are not sufficient indicators of community health. As a result, recent literature has begun to address issues like core livelihood values, or sustainable, long-term solutions to injustice and poverty. It is understood that the processes of development must be comprehensive, community-based, and people-centered.[14] Current strategies often make use of what is called appreciative inquiry, promoting practices that seek to discover what the felt

---

14. The best introduction to these issues is Bryant Myers, *Walking with the Poor*.

gifts of the community are as well as its felt *needs*. Building on these recent approaches, I would like to propose what might be called aesthetic criteria for the health of communities.

Before I do this, I want to return to the split referred to earlier between culture and society, the one side including all that concerns art and aesthetics, the other comprising those activities concerned more directly with human welfare. In the developing nations today, one will find nongovernmental organizations representing both sides of the culture/society split, but rarely does one find these integrated. In other words, it appears that we have simply exported the split between the sciences and the humanities that has become entrenched in our Western university system. For guidance in addressing this split, I turn again to someone who brings resources to bear from outside these Western dichotomies: the Hispanic theologian Roberto Goizueta.[15] The problem, Goizueta reminds us, is to suppose that aesthetic values are somehow outside the community and must be introduced so that the community can become healthy. Just as development workers now understand that the resources to move the community toward wholeness are to be found, in the first instance, within the community and not introduced from outside, so the aesthetic values and realities that the community needs to flourish *already exist within that community*. This is because, Goizueta says, for the Hispanic community (as for many non-Western cultures), the cosmos "is an intrinsically relational reality where, as in an organism, each member is necessarily related to every other member" (50). Moreover, these relationships are not primarily defined by their societal roles — that is, functionally; rather, they are constituted by what Goizueta calls "emotional warmth" (63). This, Goizueta thinks, provides the basis for a deeper and more inclusive understanding of aesthetics. In the West, he says, people have come to privilege an "objective" knowledge. But the knowledge that truly motivates, he notes, is not objective but subjective, involving "empathetic fusion."

But what does this have to do with aesthetics? Building on the work of Mexican philosopher José Vasconcelos, whom we introduced earlier, Goizueta notes that when we listen to a beautiful piece of music or look

---

15. Roberto Goizueta, *Caminemos con Jesus: Toward a Hispanic/Latino Theology of Accompaniment* (Maryknoll, N.Y.: Orbis Books, 1995). Subsequent pages cited in the text refer to this work.

at a beautiful object, we do not hold ourselves separate from the object but become "fused" with it (91). So it is with actions that realize and promote our relationships with others in the community. Interpersonal action, he thinks, is fundamentally aesthetic action. "Only through an aesthetic, empathetic fusion with another can I truly relate to the other as a person" (92). He goes on to say that practices of play and dance are essentially aesthetic precisely because we become one with the action — we do not hold ourselves at a distance. So the practices that best promote human community and health, what Goizueta calls "aesthetic praxes," are those activities which promote and extend the loving relationships that are fundamental to that community — especially as these are seen in the family and the church. So those activities that express and encourage these relationships — what we have called symbolic practices — reflect, to a greater or lesser extent, the natural aesthetics that constitute healthy communities.[16]

While Goizueta writes from his perspective as a Hispanic Catholic, much that he says resonates with the everyday-life aesthetic that I have sought to develop in this book. The gifts that allow people to come together and make a beautiful life for themselves are reflective of their creation in the image of God. While sin and self-regard have done much to distort these gifts, they still have the potential of reflecting something higher and finer. Building on Goizueta's work, let me propose the following axiom: Activities that encourage and facilitate the empathetic connections within the community will do more in the long run to promote the health of that community than work done for the alleviation of poverty alone. One of Goizueta's most important contributions is his suggestion that the pursuit of liberation, which was the goal of a generation of liberation theologians in Latin America, was insufficiently comprehensive. He suggests that the goal of "praxis" which motivated the liberation theologians needs to be expanded to include the aesthetic dimension of life and relationships as ends in themselves rather than means to other ends — to the building of homes rather than simply houses (83). While others may claim that liberation is central and aesthetics is secondary, Goizueta reverses this: the aesthetic reality, the empathetic fusion within the community is primary; liberation is a byproduct. If this is so, we might judge success in development projects

---

16. Goizueta thinks that the rituals of popular Catholicism provide the best examples of such forms. See *Caminemos con Jesus*, pp. 101-11.

by different standards than we have previously used — or by standards more capacious of the values resident in the community, of persons and things already loved.

These ideas are supported by research done by Paul Willis among working-class youth in Britain. His investigations led him to propose the presence of what he terms "symbolic creativity" in the lives of these young people. This creativity was expressed in the everyday activities and relationships of these communities by which they expressed their value commitments and, finally, in terms of which they developed their identity. This is expressed in the symbolic creativity of their work. (Willis builds here on Eric Gill's notion that work is holy.)[17] While typical arrangements for work today often suppress this informal symbolic creativity, young people in their appropriation of media and fashion find ways to express this. In these activities, Willis claims, young people express a "grounded aesthetic." He describes this as "the creative element in a process whereby meanings are attributed to symbols and practices and where symbols and practices are selected, reselected, highlighted, and recomposed to resonate further appropriated and particularized meanings" (21). While for the most part official art (in museums and galleries) is unavailable to the youth from this subculture, elements of common culture — its media, its rituals, and its fashions — are always available. They are ready to be appropriated in the expression of popular desires, providing symbolic charges that they will further mediate in the creation of their own style. Elements of popular culture, Willis thinks, provide agreeable materials for making something of oneself (25, 26).

Since the impulse and the materials for a grounded aesthetic are already present in cultures, whether of the rich or the poor, it follows that the work of encouraging human community must also include aesthetic reconstruction. J. N. K. Mugambi of the University of Nairobi defines this as follows:

> Aesthetic reconstruction entails an appreciation of the values upon which a society is founded, and a commitment to build on this foun-

---

17. Eric Gill was a Roman Catholic who, like Maritain, saw in the medieval workshop a model for art and work today. See Paul Willis, *Common Culture: Symbolic Work at Play in the Everyday Cultures of the Young* (Boulder, Colo.: Westview Press, 1991), p. 9. Subsequent pages will be cited in the text.

dation a mode of life that is constructively responsive to the challenges of the present and the future.[18]

Only in this way, Mugambi says, will communities freely express their own hopes and dreams and avoid living the stories of another. The criteria will include the ability to express the symbolic activity of this grounded aesthetic. Here, then, is a developmental axiom: *Those activities which enable communities to express in symbolic activities their grounded aesthetics are an essential part of social reconstruction.*

What, then, might be the criteria by which such activities are judged? I have heard development workers speak of the fact that the health of refugee camps can be evaluated by children's games. They note that in the worst situations, children no longer play but walk or lie listlessly about. In healthier places, children laugh and run about. Children's play becomes the canary in the coal mine — that is, the marker able to depict the presence or absence of justice. I believe this common observation deserves further study. Here I would like to focus on the way that activities of this kind display the inner health of a community and suggest an important connection between aesthetics and justice. These obviously have implications for work among the poor, but the implications of their importance extend well beyond this.

Theologians have rarely addressed these issues. But one who has consistently had his eye on such questions is Jürgen Moltmann. He has recently made a case for the importance of beauty in human community, which he describes as all that resonates with and furthers the life of people.[19] He develops this into a range of activities and processes that contribute to what he calls the integrity of life. Among other things, these will integrate the individual into the community, encourage the reverence for life, heal relationships, and give hope. All such activities, Moltmann believes, further God's own covenant with life, and thus are intrinsically theological. What furthers life, he thinks, makes Christ present and recognizes the energies of God that are always working for life.

These are helpful benchmarks that reference God's presence, but the question is, How can these be made visible? What form might such

---

18. J. N. K. Mugambi, *Christian Theology and Social Reconstruction* (Nairobi: Acton, 2005), p. 49.

19. Jürgen Moltmann, *Experiences in Theology: Ways and Forms of Christian Theology* (Minneapolis: Fortress Press, 2000), pp. 149-51.

values take? These deep human values remain abstract until they are embodied in specific practices and objects. And we have argued that these practices, at their best, become symbolic of the deep values and commitments of a people, and (potentially) expressive both of God's presence, as Moltmann says, and of their own human dignity. Because of the created situation in which people find themselves, and because of God's active presence, through the Spirit, calling creation to its completion in Christ, people are inclined to make something of themselves. And, at their best moments, what they want to make is a life that is attractive. So we ask: In places where community development is in progress, what sorts of practices might best reflect this impulse?

Community Life and Play

Let me briefly describe three such practices that might be taken as markers of the health of a community (or indeed of a family). The first is the category of *playfulness*. One of the gifts of childhood is to remind us of the fundamental joy of life in God's good creation.[20] This means a central part of God's call to obedience is not only to care for creation but to celebrate it by playing in and with it. Adam clearly enjoyed the Garden before (and while) he took care of it. Jesus' parables often feature play and celebration. So, I argue, fundamental to the promotion of human flourishing is the provision of spaces which are conducive to play. In the West, we sometimes have reversed God's order and made work the center of our lives rather than play (what is sometimes called the Puritan work ethic). But according to biblical values, it is the rest and playfulness of the Sabbath that is to be central in our lives. We work from rest, not toward it, and, the Epistle to the Hebrews tells us, at the end we will finally enter completely into this rest (Heb. 4:4-11). Moreover, what the Bible calls justice and righteousness, especially those justice-making acts of God — the Cross, the Resurrection, and Pentecost — provide the basis of the rest that God's people are invited to share, just as the Sabbath itself was a sign and memorial of the deliverance that the Exodus provided. By contrast, I believe that one could also show that injustice is always in some way or other implicated in the inability to play.

20. For a development of this theme, especially in relation to creation, see Robert K. Johnston, *The Christian at Play* (Grand Rapids: Wm. B. Eerdmans, 1983).

So a community is healthy to the degree that spaces appear in which people are invited to play, or dance, or sing. This is not necessarily a result of programs, though creative programs can encourage it; it is an expression of the gifts of God and the freedom of God's children to express those gifts. So the evaluation of any development program might ask, Does this community find places where the elders are free to tell their stories? Where the musicians are encouraged to sing and play? Where old and young are encouraged to enjoy the zarzuela or the tango? If such spaces are increasing, the community is growing more healthy. If not, there are reasons for concern: injustice is likely the cause.

Community Life and Celebration

A second criterion related to this is the promotion of what might be called practices of *celebration*. This is related to play, of course, but there are not only games; there are also parties. The impulse to celebrate events and achievements with food, ritual, and dance is universal. Many cultures of the world seem to live to gather and celebrate — any significant event provides reason to have a party: a birthday, a marriage, a first communion. This speaks of the larger need that people have to celebrate their values and achievements, and ultimately their God. Of course one cannot celebrate freely if one is suffering or hungry or displaced from home. In other words, all that reflects the brokenness of the world and its injustices is also that which impedes human celebration. How can we sing the Lord's song in a foreign land? the psalmist asks (Ps. 137:4). How can I celebrate when I have lost my home to a typhoon or fraud? Here too, one cannot program celebrations; they flow naturally from spirits liberated from care or pain. So we must address these symptoms, but we cannot feel that we have done our work until someone calls for a party!

Celebrations, of course, are a part of all human cultures. And sometimes the cost of traditional ritual celebrations becomes a drag on the economic development of communities. Robert Chambers has observed that frequently in India or Africa the celebration of marriages and funerals results in an increase in the poverty of people and communities. He notes, "The cost of ceremonies and social transactions did often drive people deep into debt."[21] But such cases testify to the deep-

---

21. Robert Chambers, *Rural Development: Putting the Last First* (London: Darton,

seated need to celebrate life and community. And surely the flourishing of communities as they address poverty and injustice will, sooner or later, include joyful celebration.

There is a moving scene at the end of the movie version of the book *Bridge over the River Kwai*, released in 2001 as *To End All Wars*, which illustrates this point. The American prisoners in the Japanese POW camp decide to celebrate the graduation of the inmates who have completed their camp "university." They all come together to celebrate the accomplishments of the students — some bearing the scars of their imprisonment, all thin from malnourishment — to hear music played on makeshift instruments and to enjoy food carefully preserved from their rations and made available for this special occasion. There in the midst of injustice they celebrate the existence of another world of hope, wisdom, and joy. And at the same time, they celebrate the developing health of their community.

So one important index of a successful community development program is the existence of celebratory practices — the opportunities for people to come together around achievements and gifts, to rejoice, and often to praise their God. Where these exist, and to the extent they exist, the community is a healthy community; where they do not, one can presume that injustice is the cause.

Community Life and Ritual Practice

Although I am sure there are many other criteria one might mention, one final category I want to highlight is *ritual practice*. For our purposes I will define this as a prescribed form of words and actions which embody the meaning of a community. Often this is used, in Protestant circles at least, in a negative sense to refer to something that is "merely ceremonial" without deeper meaning. But I believe this understanding is a mistake, because it fails to recognize the importance of acted ceremony for human flourishing. Rituals are important, I want to argue, precisely because they embody the aesthetic side of our life together. I use "ritual" here in the sense of regular, prescribed, and elaborated activities which

---

Longman & Todd, 1983), p. 115. I owe this reference to Bryant Myers. See also Sheldon Annis, *God in a Guatemalan Town* (Austin: University of Texas, 1987). He argues that evangelical conversion promoted economic growth by eliminating costly religious ceremonies.

hold life (and the community) together and represent (visually) its meaning. And I believe that ritual is a critical notion because it holds together the idea of "order," or what we call in America "due process," with the satisfying and even beautiful actions that a community develops over time.

Order or security, as any development worker knows, is critical to the functioning of any community. But order in a healthy community cannot simply be imposed from without. Proper order implies justice because it does not work unless it involves the whole community and allows the free expression of that community's values and gifts. When certain segments of the community are excluded from the decision-making process or from resource distribution, order will surely break down. Also, this order must be embodied in a set of actions that present this — the president is sworn in; the graduates receive their diplomas; the communicant goes forward to take communion. And the more significant the event, the more elaborate is the ceremony of the ritual. But most important — and this is the point of my argument — the most highly elaborated rituals, those reflective of a more highly developed and highly functioning community, will display the highest level of aesthetic awareness and even beauty. In medieval Italy, every city set aside a day to honor its patron saint. All the members of the various guilds and fraternities would turn out in the gowns of their profession and carry banners through the city. At the end of the procession, they would hold a special ceremony of dedication and gratitude to their patron saint and to God in the cathedral on the city square. So important to the civic life of the town were these events that they were frequently celebrated in special paintings that display all the splendor and pride of the community.

Long-standing suspicion toward ceremonies (and not just by Protestants!) should not be forgotten entirely. For we all know of ceremonies that serve only the interest of the powerful or by their very beauty trample on the rights of the poor. Amos has some harsh things to say about religious ceremonies of this kind (Amos 5:21-24). But clearly one sign of a healthy community is ritual that meaningfully involves a wide range of interests and elaborates these in ways that show the community's pride and gifts. These are rituals in which the community takes justifiable pride. So the presence of ritual is a criterion of successful community development: Has the community been able to develop healthy practices of ritual which embody and even elaborate aesthetically its values and intentions?

There are no rules for the promotion of these practices. Indeed, the argument of this book is that the impulse to celebrate and forge delightful objects is built into human nature. It is a reflection of the image of God — people are made to play and dance and love. No just arrangements can assure this, nor can injustice efface it entirely. But injustice may be said to be relevant in at least one important respect. Nicholas Wolterstorff has recently argued that human justice is constituted by enjoying rights — normative social relationships that accrue to people because they are created and loved by God. Their rights reflect their intrinsic dignity as humans.[22] In an application of this to questions of aesthetics, Wolterstorff argues that justice demands that urgent issues of food, clothing, and housing be given priority. But human dignity demands much more than this, he thinks — education, freedom, and respect are among these additional elements. And there is one thing more. Poverty reflects injustice, Wolterstorff says. But "it is just as true that when social arrangements force some of our fellow human beings to live in aesthetic squalor, they are wronged, treated unjustly. Living in aesthetic decency is not an optional luxury but a moral right. Justice requires it."[23]

Conclusion

It might seem that I have avoided what was to be a main theme of the chapter: how to help the poor develop their communities, as we so inelegantly put it. Well, that must be done, surely. But, I want to insist, that is not the end of the matter. Asserting that aesthetics is essential to human flourishing is simply affirming that one does not live by bread alone. Nor should these suggestions be taken to mean that aesthetic practices should be encouraged when food, clean water, clothing, or shelter is unavailable. But what they do suggest is that a house is meant to be made into a home; food is provided for the sake of mounting a feast. Of course a community needs the basic provisions of life. But these must contribute to something richer and higher; they must give

---

22. See Nicholas Wolterstorff, *Justice: Rights and Wrongs* (Princeton: Princeton University Press, 2008).

23. Nicholas Wolterstorff, "Beauty and Justice," *The Cresset* 73, no. 4 (Easter 2009): 15. This view of justice and rights leads Wolterstorff to take issue with Scarry's definition of justice as equal regard.

hope, suggest games, even call people to dance. Remember that it was when the Lord was tempted to provide for his own physical needs that he told Satan that one does not live by bread alone, but by "every word that comes from the mouth of God" (Matt. 4:4). Interestingly, Jesus is quoting Moses' words in Deuteronomy 8:3, where that prophet reminded Israel that God had let them hunger before feeding them with manna (which neither they nor anyone else had ever seen before) so that they would understand that "one does not live by bread alone, but by every word that comes from the mouth of the LORD" (8:3c). That is to say, in the very manner in which they were provided with physical nourishment, they were reminded that food is symbolic of deeper relationships — with one another, with the earth, and, most importantly, with God. They had seen for themselves that one expression of God's word involved new forms of nourishment.

People must see that they belong to God. Here we get to the heart of the matter in community development. For bread to really provide hope (and laughter and joy), it must finally become Eucharist — the basic meaning of which is "thanksgiving." It is not accidental that the three practices that I have described all resonate with the practices of Christian worship. Writers on liturgy frequently compare worship to a kind of holy playfulness, or, as Marva Dawn puts it, "a royal 'waste' of time."[24] At the center of worship is what we refer to as the celebration of the sacraments. And of course ritual itself, for the Christian, finds its highest meaning in the words and actions of the liturgy. This is to say that one sign of a healthy community involves the practices of play, celebration, and ritual — and these will always resonate with the deeper practices of religious ritual. This, then, is the most comprehensive framework for development. Human life in community tends to develop and elaborate patterns, games, and parties because this is how people were made to live together. Moreover, I believe that these practices are all — sometimes unwittingly — tributes to the Good News which Christ brought into the world. For the transformation that he made possible not only liberates us to play and celebrate together, but it invites us in these very activities to anticipate the final celebration of joy and ritual associated with the marriage supper of the Lamb — pictured as a grand celebration of cosmic proportions. It is this celebra-

---

24. See Marva J. Dawn, *A Royal "Waste" of Time: The Splendor of Worshiping God and Being Church for the World* (Grand Rapids: Wm. B. Eerdmans, 1999).

tion that we anticipate in our regular celebration of communion — until he comes to make it happen. Liturgy schools us in justice, but it also anticipates shalom and the rest and joy of the Sabbath.

It is the practices of worship that, among other things, sharpen our eyes to see beauty where we might otherwise miss it. At the end of the movie *American Beauty,* the murdered Lester Burnham is made to speak: "It's hard to stay mad when there's so much beauty in the world — it flows through me like rain, and I can't feel anything but gratitude for every single moment of my stupid little life. You have no idea what I'm talking about, I'm sure . . . but don't worry, you will someday." Many critics have taken this to be a mystical evasion of the horror that his murder represents. But what if it reflects something deeper? What if this observation recognized that beauty resides at the deepest level of reality because God is there — a presence no human effort can efface!

This quote is at least evidence of the fact that in this period of history especially — and, I would add, in advanced Western countries in general — we overlook aesthetics at great peril. In *Waiting for God,* Simone Weil argues (not many pages after the section that impressed Elaine Scarry) that there are three means that God uses to bring us to himself: religious practices, suffering, and beauty. In the West at least, she says, religious practices and suffering no longer function in this way. Their meanings have been debased. "On the other hand," she notes, "a sense of beauty, although mutilated, distorted, and soiled, remains rooted in the heart of [people] as a powerful incentive. It is present in all the preoccupations of secular life. If it were made true and pure, it would sweep all secular life in a body to the feet of God."[25]

A reflection by Kathleen Norris captures this aesthetic dimension of truth and morality as well as anything I have seen. She writes, "Once while delivering a meal to an elderly woman in a cruel winter, I was startled by the presence of beauty in a place where I did not expect it. Summoning the ghost of John Keats, I wrote: 'Valentine roses have lost their bloom; wrinkled, they droop on their stems, as if weighted by beauty.'" Where did Norris see beauty? In the widow's icy front walk? In her gnarled fingers on the lap robe? In the musty living room? Well, yes, even there, and especially in the Bible open on her lap to Isaiah 35, where it says,

---

25. Weil, *Waiting for God,* p. 162.

> The wilderness and the dry land shall be glad,
> the desert shall rejoice and blossom;
> like the crocus. It shall blossom
> and rejoice with joy and singing.
> The glory of Lebanon shall be given to it,
> the majesty of Carmel and Sharon.
> They shall see the glory of the LORD,
> the majesty of our God.

Beauty and hope are everywhere if we look with eyes nourished by the liturgy, the bread of life. Even in the wrinkly smile of this widow, Norris says, "as I knock and enter. Beauty, yes. All of it. And truth."[26]

---

26. http://www.forbes.com/asap/2000/1002/252_print.html as posted 30 May 2002.

Conclusion

CHAPTER 10

Living and Reflecting Poetically: Systematic Implications

I bear my mortal body across your world. So may your deepest longing soon be appeased and you be lodged within the heaven that's most full of love.

Dante Alighieri, *Purgatorio*, XXVI, 60-63

What, then, is poetic theology? In this chapter I will try to summarize where we are, and seek to show the role of poetic theology in imagining and moving us toward a better life. Then we will move to consider, briefly, what poetic theology might contribute to traditional questions of theology. Does it supplant or supplement these? Here I will suggest ways that theological reflection might proceed differently and, perhaps, as a result, appear more attractive. The reader is bound to be dissatisfied with this summary, for the implications of a poetic theology are still largely to be worked out. This is merely a preliminary drawing — notes for a poem.

Poetic Theology, Poetic Life

Dante is our frequent guide with respect to poetic theology, In his journey through the Inferno, he often encounters people he knows from Florence, right alongside those he has read about in classical poetry. In climbing down to the seventh circle in Canto XII, for example, he finds centaurs firing arrows at those who seek to escape their punishment.

One of them, the mythical Nessus, who carried Deianira across a river with evil intention and was shot by Heracles' poisoned arrow, points out (the historical) Guy de Montfort, who avenged the death of his father, Simon, by murdering Henry, son of the Earl of Cornwall in church. Although Dante notes that the centaurs, typically, were running around "as, in the world above, they used to hunt" (*Inferno,* XII, 57), he knows as well as anybody that they never did run around in the world above. Guy's murderous deed, however, was, as we say, historical, and earned him his place in hell. Yet, with a touch of irony, Dante has the centaur point out Guy to the travelers — the fictional specifies the historical.

What is going on here? How can myth occupy the same space as history, let alone illumine the historical? The background of this endorsement of fiction over history is Aristotle's famous treatment of poetry. There the Philosopher differentiates between the poet and the historian in this way:

> The one [historian] relates what has happened, the other [poet] what may happen. Poetry, therefore, is more philosophical and a higher thing than history: for poetry tends to express the universal, history the particular.

The poet describes what is universal, "what such or such a kind of man will probably or necessarily say or do," while the historian merely describes what happened to have been.[1] When put in these terms, it is not hard to see that the universal, the work of poetry, is clearly superior to the historical.

Contemporary readers of Dante (and of Aristotle) are regularly puzzled by this apparent confusion over truth and history. It as if, during our journey through hell, Scarlett O'Hara appeared and pointed out Lee Harvey Oswald to us! For in many respects this order has been exactly reversed for modern readers — the poetic has been supplanted by the historical. It is not possible here to trace the path that has led to this way of thinking — though the Reformation and its focus on the Gospel narrative, and on everyday life, had something to do with it. Nor do I wish to simply suggest that this reversal is entirely mistaken. But what we must recognize is what has been lost in this development.

---

1. Aristotle, *Poetics,* trans. S. H. Butcher (Mineola, N.Y.: Dover, 1997), Ch. 9, 5, 1451, p. 17.

Living and Reflecting Poetically

Dante and his contemporaries understood intuitively that a universal story — that is, a narrative that encompasses the whole of humanity and its history — should guide our reading of a particular story. And for them there was no question that the story of God's historical actions in Christ and the Spirit, especially as these were mediated through the liturgical life of the church, was the ultimate universal story. But they were also convinced that other great world-shaping stories could also embody universal truths, that they could help us fill in the details of God's universal saga. Dante believed that the incorporation of ancient mythology could contribute to his spiritual aim, which was "to remove those living in this life from a state of misery, and to bring them to a state of happiness."[2] Along with the frequent citations of Scripture, this cultural wisdom, for Dante, could play a role in the pilgrim's growth "to maturity, to the measure of the full stature of Christ" (Eph. 4:13).

It would be foolish indeed to suppose that because we moderns know better, there is no truth to Aristotle's (and Dante's) assumptions. Moreover, what truth there is to this proposition was certainly not limited to medieval art and literature. This book has sought to explore what this meaning might be for the twenty-first century. Poetic theology, as we are using the term, suggests that the Christian faith, and consonant human flourishing, are to be shaped in part by embracing the play of light and love that is to be found in the wisdom of the surrounding culture — what sparks affection in its objects, patterns, and tales. It means allowing contemporary struggles and joys, especially as they are made into striking cultural artifacts, to move us as we seek to reach full submission to the authority of Christ. The significance of this, however, reaches beyond the circle of faith. For many people, aesthetic and emotional experiences — what we have called symbolic practices — arrive with a kind of universal intent. As Henri Nouwen writes to his atheist friend, "Aren't you, like me, hoping that some person, thing, or event will come along to give you that final feeling or inner well-being that you desire?"[3] Nouwen implies that any conversation about God should start with those desires: Don't you imagine that there is finally some trip, some relationship, some experience that will fulfill your deepest desire? Poetic theology

---

2. Letter to Con Grande, in *Dantis Alagherii Epistolae: The Letters of Dante,* trans. and ed. Paget Toynbee (Oxford: Clarendon Press, 1920), X, p. 202.

3. Henri Nouwen, *Life in the Beloved: Spiritual Living in a Secular World* (New York: Crossroad, 1992), p. 35.

seeks to do a religious reading of these deep-seated cultural longings. For these longings, insofar as they reflect the goodness of the created order and God's loving presence there, constitute a partial vision of God — indeed, for many people they are the only grounds for hope they know.

Surely, someone will say, Scripture in the hands of the Spirit is quite capable of accomplishing this maturing and shaping work; it does not need any help from a culture shaped by sinful people. We have discussed this objection earlier, but let me recall two points. First, as I argued in the first chapter, we never approach and interpret Scripture outside of some cultural context — it comes to us in the terms provided by Hebrew and Greek culture. And we read it through the glasses provided by our own cultural situation. So the question is not whether we will employ culture in our obedient reading of Scripture, but whether we will use the best that cultural wisdom has to offer, or use some poorly considered bits and pieces. In other words, the question is whether we will, as Paul says, reflect on what is good, or simply be taken in by what is most popular (Phil. 4:8).

Second, we need to remind ourselves that culture itself is made up of materials provided by the good creation which God has made. In spite of the disobedience of the human caretaker, creation still proclaims the glory of God (Ps. 19:1). Poetic theology takes its starting point from the assertion that creation is still the dramatic stage for God's glory. Further, then, culture, in the perspective of this book, is what humans make of this good creation. Because of human rebellion and self-seeking, we may misuse this gift, and we often do. But we may also make something good and beautiful of it as well. This means not only that we may enjoy the blessings of the gathering light of sunrise, or the newborn's first smile, but that these may be taken up into the imagination of artists and refracted through their own divine image. Particular parents and grandparents may understand the joy of birth of their child; everyone can feel the exquisite delight that William Blake has voiced:

> Sweet Babe, in thy face
> Soft desires I can trace,
> Secret joys and secret smiles,
> Little pretty infant wiles.[4]

4. Wiliam Blake, "A Cradle Song," in *The Complete Poetry and Selected Prose of John Donne and The Complete Poetry of William Blake* (New York: Modern Library, 1941), p. 568.

Let me be clear: In the framework I am proposing, Scripture is the final interpreter of my experience, but it is not the *only* authority. Just as medieval practitioners of the *theologia poetica* read classical sources in the light of Scripture, so we must allow this to shed light on all lesser guides. It was Scripture that gave direction and meaning to many of the stories that they employed in shaping their *theologia poetica* — they looked *through* the stories of Rome, whether mythical or historical, to the Story of the Rome that is above. Beyond this, the authority of Scripture is "final" in a more comprehensive sense. The impact of Scripture is to be felt not only on our minds but on the whole of our lives. We are to love God with heart, mind, and soul — even, if we are painters or pianists, with our fingertips. What God desires in our submission to Scripture is never simply an awareness of its stories, or even an understanding of its God. Rather, what is demanded is a total transformation of our minds, wills, and imaginations, what Paul calls growing up in Christ in all things (Eph. 4:15-16). For this to happen effectively, our minds, wills, and imaginations have to be enriched and expanded, not only by the tutelage of Scripture but also by the exercise and richness that cultural wisdom provides. This all becomes material for our growing to maturity. But the fact that this takes place in the light of Scripture means that the actual authority of Scripture — that is, its formative power — will *increase* through the use of these other sources. Reading a great story, as Dante knew, increases our capacity to be a follower of Christ. While we assume the authority of Scripture in doing theology, what we are after, and what poetic theology seeks to promote, is the progressive realization of this authority in the habits, thoughts, and practices of our lives together.

The Kingdom: From Above or Below?

There is another objection that might be raised to this method: Doesn't this focus on culture get in the way of the supernatural character of the new creation which Christ brings from God? Does this not risk making the kingdom a kind of human achievement? Surely the kingdom comes from God, but it does not follow from this that it comes from outside of culture. Further, it is not altogether clear that Christ did not solicit our participation in making this kingdom visible. Consider the first parable in all the Synoptics: the parable of the sower (Matt. 13:3-9; Mark 4:3-9;

Luke 8:4-8). All three Synoptic writers record this wisdom parable as the beginning of Jesus' teaching — suggesting that special attention is to be paid to it. In this simple story, Jesus starts with one of the most common images of his agricultural society: a farmer sowing his seed. Every listener would have been familiar with the various effects of soil, rocks, and weeds on the harvest. The story comes to life out of their corporate experience. But, as he frequently does, Jesus springs the trap at the conclusion of the parable: "Other seeds fell on good soil and brought forth grain, some a hundredfold, some sixty, some thirty. Let anyone with ears listen!" (Matt. 13:8-9). Jesus has slipped in a surprise ending, and he asks, Did you catch it? Scholars think that thirtyfold, even sixtyfold could have been imagined. But a hundredfold? That would have shocked listeners — as it should shock us.

The significance of this story, then, is twofold: it is significant because of what Jesus employs from his listeners' experience, and it is significant because of the way he proposes something which transcends that experience. First, the wisdom story implies that creation has an ordered and regular way of working that wise people learn and exploit. As often as possible, the farmer seeks to put seeds in good soil and keep them away from the rocks and thistles. Jesus does nothing to suggest that this order is wrong or unimportant. On the contrary, his teaching affirms this: just as he urges his listeners to consider the lilies of the field, or the birds of the air, so here he asks them to consider the way seeds grow. But he does suggest that the words that he is sowing — his life and teaching — will bear a fruit that transcends this order of things. This teaching is introducing his followers to a new order of living that he calls the way of the kingdom, and that Paul will call a new creation. But notice: this new way of life does nothing to overturn and everything to affirm the order from which it emerges. In other words, the stories that Jesus is telling about loving one's neighbor, caring for the poor — even raising the dead — grow up out of their stories. Indeed, his stories incorporate them into the more expansive imaginary he is bringing about. Surely, just as the encounter with Jesus did nothing to make the farmer think his work with seeds and soil no longer mattered, so too no farmer that heard this parable would think about planting and growing in the same way after his encounter with Jesus!

We do not stand outside of culture, and it turns out that this is no handicap for God. An important subtext of this book is that since the

Romantic movement, religious motives and influences have been culturally mediated and subjectively appropriated. Most people today, even religious believers, live their lives within a radically immanent frame. Since most educated people intuitively reject any transcendent reality, perhaps we should take this as our starting point. Rather than seeking to overturn these assumptions, I want to argue that, initially at least, we work with them. I propose that we begin not with a conversation that they cannot comprehend, but with the conversation that God has *already begun* with them in the way they seek a beautiful life.

The kingdom is from God, the new creation is God's work, but these do not emerge out of the blue. They emerge, as it were, from within culture — specifically, in the case of the parable stories, from God's incarnate presence within first-century Palestinian culture. This is just as true for our own twenty-first-century situation. God is working from within the multiple cultural realities of this century — from within all our little stories. Now it is true that, although God works in culture in Christ and by the Spirit, God is not bound by culture. God stands outside of culture as well and will one day appear to judge and restore the creation and human culture. But *we* do not stand outside of culture. We are, through and through, cultured beings who, with God's help, strain and stretch toward the transcendent goal which God holds out for us. As Paul puts it, we "press on toward the goal for the prize of the heavenly call of God in Christ Jesus" (Phil. 3:14).

Meanwhile, for the time being, we seek to describe the human journey to God with the materials that our human wisdom provides, in the light of Scripture and by the Spirit's empowerment. We seek to approve what is good in this wisdom. As Paul says, Meanwhile, as we seek to reflect on all that is worthy of praise (4:8), "let us hold fast to what we have attained" (3:16). W. H. Auden captures this sense of filling up the time after (the first) Advent, as best we can, in his poem "For the Time Being":

> Once again
> As in previous years we have seen the actual Vision and failed
> To do more than entertain it as an agreeable
> Possibility, once again we have sent Him away . . .
> . . . In the meantime
> There are bills to be paid, machines to keep in repair,
> Irregular verbs to learn, the Time Being to redeem

> From insignificance. The happy morning is over,
> The night of agony still to come; the time is noon . . .⁵

But while we're at it, we might as well hold fast to what is worth looking at, thinking about, and taking into account as praiseworthy (Phil. 4:8-9). We are not simply insisting that there are many worthy ecological, pacifist, conciliatory, and creative projects in which we might be engaged. We are proposing that, *for us,* the kingdom will largely emerge out of and in terms of these projects. And in this book I have tried to call particular attention to those aesthetic objects and practices that probe the depths and roots of our human experience, and that stretch our imaginations in the direction that God is leading us. Because whether or not the artist recognizes this, he or she is working with gifts that image something (and Someone) beyond his or her imagining. These gifts are not a specific word from God, but they can provide real guidance and insight which enrich our reading of Scripture and, in turn, are qualified and directed by that reading.

So our little stories and our big projects constitute the necessary arena of our Christian stewardship. As Trevor Hart reminded us in an earlier chapter, the calling of artists is to take the materials of creation — the episodes of life — and make of these a narrative that can be offered up to God in gratitude. Artists put things together in ways that expand our vision. In our treatment of interpretation in Chapter Three, we saw, following Paul Ricoeur, that our putting together of things we see or read in stories and images is itself a poesis, a making. But Ricoeur goes beyond this to insist that this imaginative work is metaphoric. That is, we do not simply put the pieces of life together like a puzzle, but we are able to see *through* the pieces that we have shaped to something new and higher. Objects which artists have made, and which we in turn incorporate into our imaginaries, are "semanticized," as Charles Taylor put it. They innovate.⁶

This movement toward fresh vision is critical because most of the time the deepest meaning of things cannot be reached by scientific explanation — not even, dare I say, by abstract theological formulation

---

5. W. H. Auden, "For the Time Being," in *Collected Longer Poems* (New York: Random House, 1969), pp. 195-96.

6. Here I have learned from the fine discussion of these things in Graham Ward, *Cultural Transformation and Religious Practice* (Cambridge: Cambridge University Press, 2005), pp. 125-33.

alone. Most meaning which grasps us can only be suggested; its character, as Calvin Seerveld says, remains allusive. People and life are mostly ungraspable in literal terms; they are shot through with mystery. But this is precisely the strength of poets and the poetic imagination, and these offer the language best suited to gesturing toward the transcendent. Handling, ever so carefully, the fire of this language may allow us, for the moment at least, to reverse the hermeneutical flow — to hear in it a word from God. Who knows? It may turn out that Scarlett O'Hara — or, better, Raskolnikov — might be able to shed some light on Lee Harvey Oswald after all!

Is There a Poetic Reading of Theology?

From our review of theological reflection on aesthetics over the last few centuries, and our discussion of Dante and Bunyan earlier, we discerned two distinctly different ways of embodying God's work aesthetically. On the one hand, those in the Catholic tradition tended to locate and appreciate this divine splendor in particular objects, to look for God in the *form* of the progressive revelation of divine glory in Christ and the church (as in von Balthasar). On the other hand, Protestants have tended to focus on the narrative and drama of God's redemptive acts. It is the Gospel story, Protestants argue, and one's own internalization of that story which contribute to making life attractive.

Here, then, are two quite different ways of understanding the possible role of aesthetics for human life. The one tradition stresses the splendor of *form* of the progressive revelation of the divine glory; the other stresses the *act* — one might say the drama — of a created order called to praise God. Another way of framing this is to say that one side earnestly contends for the visibility of God's revelation in history; the other just as jealously guards the transcendence and thus the invisibility (or hiddenness) of God, especially in Jesus Christ. But, even if one inclines in one direction or the other, must one ultimately choose one side or the other? Surely one of the principal functions of art and the artist — at least as we have come to understand this in the modern period — is rendering another world in terms of this one — that is, seeing this world metaphorically. But isn't it equally true that we are called not simply to see but to work toward this world?

Poetic theology, as we have developed it, suggests a way that these frameworks may be reconciled. Traditionally, theology has been understood as the systematic explication of Scripture as this has been understood in the various traditions of the church. Culture and our experience, then, are to be read in the light of this exposition. Poetic theology intends to reverse this order of things: it insists that we start with the cultural artifacts, especially those symbolic practices and experiences around which contemporary persons orient their lives. Scripture and tradition are thus constantly reread in the light of the human drive to create a beautiful life. It is crucial that this be understood as an active and imaginative process. We have defined this in terms of two key notions: emplotment and performance.

Following Ricoeur, we have described the way that people naturally seek to construe the events of their lives — especially those focal and symbolic events — in terms of a narrative. But we have found that people seek not simply to perceive a structure but to actively create one. Emplotment is an activity, not simply a structure — it reflects the persistent human drive to make something of life. And it is in terms of this struggle to make a life that, inevitably, one reads Scripture. Graham Ward describes the role that Scripture and especially the Gospels play in this process. The unique character of the Gospel writings, Ward thinks, comes from their participation in the dynamic of the story they recount — their unique genre reflects their special intention. In the Gospels (literally the Good News), Ward says, "the telling itself participates in [the disclosure of God] and produces a divine pedagogy."[7] For our part, then, following this story produces a kind of phronesis, or practical wisdom, in which we are gradually shaped by the story that we follow. Notice that this process is active but that it is also fundamentally aesthetic — that is, we are creatively arranging the bits and pieces of our lives in the light of this story. And as we make a life, we are engaged in a process that is driven by affections as much as by convictions. As we learn the practical wisdom of this narrative, we create new "Gospels" of our own which are shaped Spiritually — i.e., by the Spirit — by our reading and following of the original accounts. Moreover, this wisdom draws out the deep meaning of the pivotal events of our

---

7. Graham Ward, "Spiritual Exercises: A Christian Pedagogy," in *Christ and Culture* (Oxford: Blackwell, 2005), pp. 224-25. This is why Jean-Luc Marion says of the Gospels that they are "destined for prayer." See *God without Being: hors-texte,* trans. Thomas A. Carlson (Chicago: University of Chicago Press, 1991), p. 155.

Living and Reflecting Poetically

lives, even as it is eventually embodied in new (symbolic) expressions of such events.

The second critical notion for this poetic theology is performance. Aesthetic and symbolic practices are important because they become the sites where we express and live out the commitments that we have made. But, Philip Stoltzfus has argued, the idea of performance contains a further implication: in the lived rhythm of our language, feelings, and actions, we not only enact our deepest beliefs — we form and deepen them. Stoltzfus uses the idea of "performance practice" to underline the idea that when an artist performs music, she does not simply express some timeless truth or her own deep feeling, but progressively and more deeply rediscovers (and re-creates) the music. Thought of in this way, our experiences — those games, hobbies, and artistic practices with which we began the book — can be the means of the "acquisition of a certain practice through the performance environment of hearing, playing, and living with a piece over time."[8] Obviously, the creative potential of these popular practices is limited, but it is not insignificant. What if these symbolic projects resonate with a larger set of practices that engage the presence and activity of God? Indeed, what if already, in these small stories, God is already at work?

Stoltzfus thinks that theology is like music: while embodying various traditional formulations, it "resists satisfactory expression in propositional form."[9] This is because, as in drama or music, theology is more naturally embodied in various performances. The metaphor of performance has sometimes been criticized as suggesting a static following of a script or score and not being sufficiently open to contingency and the future.[10] But if performances are also at the same time practices which allow new and deeper resonances to emerge, this criticism is avoided. Like the performance of the liturgy, our active engagement in this poesis orients "itself in a forward-thinking way toward the possibilities of the next yet-to-be-enacted series of public performances."[11]

---

8. Philip Stoltzfus, *Theology as Performance: Music, Aesthetics, and God in Western Thought* (New York: T&T Clark, 2006), p. 225; see also pp. 196, 259. His purpose is to see music not as a thing but as an act (p. 254).

9. Stoltzfus, *Theology as Performance*, p. 196.

10. This is the criticism that Jeremy Begbie endorses in "Resonances and Challenges," in *Faithful Performances: Enacting Christian Tradition*, ed. Trevor Hart and Stephen Guthrie (Aldershot: Ashgate, 2007), p. 277.

11. Stoltzfus, *Theology as Performance*, p. 256.

CONCLUSION

Poetic theology understood as active emplotment by means of performance shows promise of overcoming the dichotomy of form and action. The aesthetic figure and its attraction are essential to the charged field of human motivations. But they are not inert objects — symbols are dynamic agents in life. Human life is put into play by these aesthetic elements — they represent those things for which we live and die. People are literally set in motion by the moral and affective practices because they represent, so I have argued, the soul's movement toward God. But this is true only because God is present and active in these practices, making them potential instruments of the Spirit, who moves creation toward its fulfillment. For, as Paul says, "creation itself will be set free from its bondage to decay and will obtain the freedom of the glory of the children of God" (Rom. 8:21).

Theology and Aesthetics: Seeing the Way Forward

If theological construction, in personal terms, involves constructing and performing a life, then we might ask how traditional theological categories contribute to this task. How might these be reframed? If, moreover, we wish to insist that theology needs to organize itself around various symbolic practices in which God is present, we might ask how we might describe and discern such practices. I cannot develop this in any detail — this project is lifelong and ongoing — but I want to make some initial suggestions.

First, I suggest that theological proposals should spark affection in a way that moves the believer in the direction of human flourishing — what the New Testament calls maturity in Christ.[12] If the human person finds meaning, as I have argued, in a charged moral (and ultimately) spiritual field, the final construal of God's presence ought to come alive in particular ways that spark our love. Calvin Seerveld has proposed that "truth is the way God does things."[13] Perhaps we could expand on Seerveld's striking aphorism by saying that, if truth is the way God does things, beauty is what

---

12. In thinking about theology pastorally in this way, I have been much helped by Ellen Charry's work. See *By the Renewing of Your Minds: The Pastoral Function of Christian Doctrine* (New York: Oxford University Press, 1997).

13. Calvin Seerveld, "The Relation of the Arts to the Presentation of the Truth," in *Truth and Reality: Philosophical Perspectives on Reality Dedicated to Professor Dr. H. G. Stoker*, ed. Vincent Brummer et al. (Braamfontein, S.A.: De Jong's Bookshop, 1971), p. 162.

this looks (and feels) like. Since God's acts express love, they will attract as well as convince. If we may accept that this is so, it would seem likely that we would find much in Scripture that would reflect the beauty of God's activity and that would move the reader. During the Reformation, the major Reformers insisted that the word of Scripture, whether preached or read, is accompanied by the life-giving presence of the Spirit. In other words, Scripture is a privileged site of spiritual reading. While critical exegesis has sometimes discouraged such contemplative reading, I have argued that this must be recovered. A generation ago, Erich Auerbach underlined the importance of the aesthetic character of the Christian story. In the Christian story, he noted, the figural meaning predominates over the sensory (or the purely historical). "The story speaks to everybody and everybody is urged and indeed required to take up sides for or against it."[14] The story, in other words, constitutes a charged arena in which readers are challenged and eventually formed.

Second, this means that the theological themes drawn from this material will themselves resonate with this figural account. That is, theological insight should captivate the imagination and draw the believer in certain directions, making possible certain ways of living and discouraging others. Philip Stoltzfus has argued that this means that we think about doctrine not as a barrier to *thinking* certain ways, but rather as a path to making certain ways of *living* possible that otherwise would not be. Doctrine should be considered not as a "break from the outside, but as an activity of freeing up the 'interplay' of forces such that one can live completely differently."[15]

But finally we recognize that the material under consideration in theology is meant, as Auerbach says, to challenge and motivate. Biblical truth — the way God does things — draws readers into the drama so that they are formed by the story they read. This is why contemplative reading, which is analogous to the religious reading of culture that we are proposing, is essential. Reading Scripture in this way gives it a kind of discursive power, which, as Graham Ward points out, is much like prayer and confession — indeed, it is a spiritual practice like these: "Reading as contemplation is a form of ethical praxis, integral with the pursuit of virtuous life."[16]

---

14. Erich Auerbach, *Mimesis: The Representation of Reality in Western Literature* (Princeton: Princeton University Press, 1953), pp. 48-49.

15. Stoltzfus, *Theology as Performance*, pp. 210-11.

16. Ward, "Spiritual Exercises: A Christian Pedagogy," p. 241.

CONCLUSION

With this framework in mind, then, let me turn to some biblical material in terms of some traditional theological themes. These materials, I will argue, give us an aesthetic in which both the *event* of encounter and the *form* of God's appearance and work play a role — the one providing the dramatic movement, the other the splendor of the contour of revelation. And these together can form readers communally into a new fellowship of love. Let's call such beauty and symbolic practice *the splendor of a God-graced order*. So, if you want to see beauty, you have to watch what God does, and — to anticipate — if you want to be beautiful, you must pray for grace to love the kind of things that God loves. If this is true, then the mistake in not connecting, say, beauty and justice is fundamentally a theological mistake — it is separating event from form, or emplotment from performance. Let me briefly develop the theological grounds for making this claim by referring to a series of theological elements that grow out of the biblical material: creation; Christ, suffering, and the Christian life; and heaven or the new creation.

Creation

In this book we have frequently made use of John Calvin's compelling metaphor of creation as a theatre for the glory of God. This metaphor combines two very important notions. First, it implies that there is a drama that is going on around us whose central actor (and director) is God; God has something in view for this booming, budding confusion; it is not, as Shakespeare said, "a tale told by an idiot, full of sound and fury, signifying nothing." But, second, it is in this world that one must look to contemplate the divine "beauty." It is here before our eyes. But since this is theatre, beauty is not only to be *seen* here; in an important sense, it is meant to be *performed* here. We too are actors in this theatre.

Seeing creation as divine theatre means that, however broken this order is at present, it is toward creation itself that one looks to see "vestiges" of the divine splendor. The creation bears traces of its creator. In Genesis, one God saw the progressive creation as "good" — *tov,* a Hebrew word that includes both moral and aesthetic dimensions — and brought the work to its climax by creating an actual "image" of divinity. And when everything was said and done, God definitively pronounced it all "very good." So, the psalmist can say, the heavens "are telling the glory of God" (Ps. 19:1); and the human creation is "crowned . . . with glory and honor" (Ps. 8:5) — two of the important words used for *beauty* in the Old Testament.

When studying the various words for beauty and splendor in the Old Testament, one is struck with the cavalier way that descriptions of ordinary life are mixed in with references to temple worship, even to God and the future — often biblical words for beauty refer simply to what is "fitting" or "appropriate."[17] For example, the Hebrew word *yapa* — meaning "to be fair or beautiful" — which is used sixty-three times in all its forms, can refer to the beloved in the Song of Solomon (4:10) or simply to an "olive tree, fair with goodly fruit" (Ezek. 16:12-14; Jer. 11:16). But it can also be used to refer to God's presence in Zion: "Out of Zion, the perfection of beauty, God shines forth" (Ps. 50:2, cf. 48:2). And, significantly, it is used to describe God's people in the last days (Zech. 9:17). Note that this usage implies that the loveliness of creation should be seen in the context of the beauty of temple worship and even of the final work of God in the new creation — as though even the beauty of olive trees could not be fully understood outside this larger context. While Protestants are inclined to focus only on the beauty of creation and Catholics are inclined to focus only on liturgical beauty, the biblical materials imply that these kinds of beauty must be seen and appreciated together — that the latter is a kind of distillation of the former.

This integration of the liturgical and the diurnal is theologically significant, because it means that God wants us to see in the world evidence, even sparks of his own glory and greatness — in both what God does and what we do with this. Looking at the world invariably involves enjoying what is there, which in turn becomes a kind of performance practice for "seeing" God in the beauty of holiness. John Calvin expresses it this way: "For in this world God blesses us in such a way as to give us a mere foretaste of his kindness, and by that taste to entice us to desire heavenly blessings with which we may be satisfied."[18] It is significant that Calvin uses language here that recalls Paul's references to the Holy Spirit in the New Testament, for it is the Spirit who enlivens the created order and works redemption within it, even as He gives us a

---

17. I am using material from a more complete description of biblical beauty in William Dyrness, "Aesthetics in the Old Testament: Beauty in Context," *Journal of the Evangelical Theological Society* 28, no. 4 (December 1986).

18. Calvin, commentary on 1 Timothy 4:8, quoted in Belden Lane, "Spirituality as the Performance of Desire: Calvin on the World as a Theatre of God's Glory," *Spiritus: A Journal of Christian Spirituality* 1, no. 1 (Spring 2001): 9.

foretaste of heavenly glory. As Paul says, "we ourselves, who have the first fruits of the Spirit, groan inwardly while we wait for adoption, the redemption of our bodies" (Rom. 8:23). If this is right, part of the failure of the human response to God is a lack of delight in what God has made. Hildegard of Bingen referred to Adam and Eve's sin as a failure to take delight in all the trees of the garden, focusing perversely on only one.[19]

The word associated with this visible splendor is "glory" (*kabod* in Hebrew; *doxa* in Greek). It combines the idea of weight with that of outward and visible display. When this word appears in Scripture, the reader is alerted to pay special attention: its centrality implies that the process of transfiguration is central to creation, wherein God takes what is ordinary and makes it extraordinary. The "Glory of the Lord" is what Christopher Cocksworth calls "the sensory impact of the invisible God."[20] It is seen in a cloud in the wilderness (Exod. 16:7, 10) and in the temple: "Lift up your heads, O gates! And be lifted up, O ancient doors! that the King of glory may come in" (Ps. 24:7; see also 1 Kings 8:11). And it is seen especially at the end of the story, when Ezekiel sees the rebuilt temple: "And there, the glory of the God of Israel was coming from the east; the sound was like the sound of mighty waters; and the earth shone with his glory" (43:2). Ezekiel might have said, "I have seen a place not yet discovered, where we will once again worship freely, *and yet,* it is this earth." Those who saw the glory of God in the face of Jesus Christ could say with Paul that the glory of God dwells corporeally in Jesus Christ, but he was also one of us. Born of Mary, subject to hunger, fatigue, and suffering, yet transfigured before the disciples' eyes. Notice that the beauty of this was a dramatic event, but it was also a manifestation of the splendor of God in human (earthly) form. It makes a great story — indeed, in many ways it lies behind all the stories of Western literature — but it was also embodied in forms which we may contemplate and before which, like John the Apostle in Revelation 1, we fall as though dead.

Much of this can be found in contemporary theological treatments of creation. But two implications of this deserve more attention than they have been given. First, God's continuing presence, just as virtually all divine activity, is too often defined in terms of power; it is seldom de-

---

19. Noted in Lane, "Spirituality as the Performance of Desire," p. 9.
20. Christopher Cocksworth, *Holy, Holy, Holy: Worshiping the Trinitarian God* (London: Darton, Longman & Todd, 1997), p. 127.

scribed in terms of glory. As a result, creation is seen as a play of political forces rather than a field of desire. And so we miss its symbolic richness. Why do people, of all ethnicities and religious persuasions, consistently rhapsodize over the delights of creation? Surely it is because they have experienced it as an order that sparks their affections and solicits their praise — where they can be and feel at home. Creation cannot be understood apart from its divine excess, which, Jean-Luc Marion notes, expresses its gift character. Only agape, Marion says, can put such things on earth.[21] It is this gift character that moves us to respond with such joy. After all, we are sensing the loving presence of the giving God — indeed, we are being invited to indwell that presence. Much current ecological discussion would be enhanced if human beings were understood to be a part of the created order, made to respond to it as lovers and not just as stewards. Octavio Paz has lamented the decline of love in our dealings with nature — those affective connections and figures that poets have so often celebrated. He writes, "Today love can be, as it was in the past, a way of reconciliation with nature. We cannot change ourselves into springs or oak trees, birds or bulls, but we can *recognize ourselves* in them."[22]

But if we are to recognize ourselves in the material order, there is a further theme that needs celebration: the centrality of the body in our dealings with God. Sometimes theological conversation, even about creation, proceeds as though human and divine encounter takes place mentally — in our hearts, as Protestants like to say. But in truth we know and love God in the same way that we know and love each other — by means of bodies. Just as we touch, see, and listen to each other through bodily senses, so we celebrate God's presence through touch and movement — by dancing and kneeling. A poetic theology cannot proceed without a body, because poetry, like life, relies on senses as well as thought — indeed, it calls for thought out of and through the senses. So there is no other way to God than through and by means of the body and the senses. Christianity has always insisted on this; that is part of its uniqueness. As Paz points out, "In this respect Platonism is the opposition of the Christian vision: the Platonic eros seeks disincarnation, whereas Christian mysticism is, above all, a love of in-

---

21. Marion, *God without Being,* p. 106.
22. Octavio Paz, *The Double Flame: Love and Eroticism,* trans. Helen Lane (New York: Harcourt, Brace, 1995), p. 270, his emphasis.

carnation, following the example of Christ, who became flesh in order to save us."[23]

The final meaning of the embodied creation is to call forth the praise of the creature. This meaning is performed in the first instance by the worship of God's people, which reiterates the affirmation of creation that God himself pronounces. There is a very interesting verse in the great psalm of nature — Psalm 104: "May the glory of the LORD endure forever; may the LORD rejoice in his works" (v. 31). In his commentary on this verse, Calvin argues that God here appears almost to sustain or hold up creation by the very act of taking delight in it. Calvin says, "Unless the Spirit of the Lord attracts everything, it all lapses back into nothingness."[24] This yearning of God for creation is met, Belden Lane notes, "by the thunderous applause (and yearning) of creation itself," an applause that we are invited to join. So the central meaning is liturgical — or, one might say, human life finds its highest end in celebration.

Christ, Suffering, and the Christian Life

The paradox of Christ embodies the paradox of the Christian life: Christ, who comes from God, is born, lives, and dies within the confines of first-century Palestinian culture. His life and ministry emerge from within a very specific culture, and yet that proves no barrier to the more-than-human reality that he introduced. Jesus' ministry grew from within the patterns of hospitality, friendship, and family life of his culture — indeed, it only made sense in that context. The Gospels put these little stories together into a narrative that performs what it describes. Amazingly, these stories show that Jesus, working within this limited context, put together a new way of living that attracted the devotion of the crowds as well as the hostility of religious leaders.

Thus, the first response to Jesus' ministry ought properly to be amazement. How can such a person, without the benefits of family and class, make much of himself? Can any good thing come from Galilee? The fact that he made so much of his life and experiences led Karl Barth to say that *wonder* is one of the words that best describes the life of

---

23. Paz, *The Double Flame*, p. 256.
24. Calvin, commentary on Psalm 104:31, quoted in Lane, "Spirituality as the Performance of Desire," p. 5. Lane's quote which follows is from this page.

Christ and, by extension, the task of theology itself. "Wonders," Barth wrote, "are the occurrence, presence, and activity of what is basically and definitively incompatible and unassimilable to the norm of common experience."[25] Barth especially applies the term to the special events of the life of Christ: "As fundamentally *astonishing* stories, they function first of all in a formal way as a sort of *alarm signal,* which is the reason the New Testament likes to term them 'signs'" (p. 65, his emphasis). All of this indicates that these miraculous events are also at the same time symbolic events that are meant to ground and orient the performance of this new thing that Christ came to embody, what he calls the kingdom of God. When Jesus says, "Your faith has made you whole," "Lazarus, come out!" or "Peace! Be still," he is indicating a "change in the ordinary course of the world and nature which threatened and oppressed men" (p. 66).

The most common response to such activity, as to Jesus' teaching, was amazement. But this was meant to attract the hearer to the ultimate response that Jesus sought — an intimacy based on love. At the center of the upper-room discourse in John, Jesus returns to wisdom imagery — wherein God is a vinegrower, and the relationship that Jesus seeks with his disciples is that of a vine and branches. As he says, "Abide in me as I abide in you" (John 15:4). The significance of this metaphor can hardly be overemphasized. Jesus was not satisfied with the accepted relationship between the rabbi and his students. Based on his own intimacy with the Father, he sought a depth of relationship that was to transform these disciples and, indeed, to shape the Christian tradition. As he said, "As the Father has loved me, so I have loved you; abide in my love" (15:9).

So in Jesus' life we see a development from an external relationship of attraction and wonder to a deeply personal relationship of love. He intended the symbolic acts to spark interest, even affection, but ultimately he sought a communion that would eventually transform the notion of the person. The human person had always been formed by family and community, and Christ does not change this cultural fact. But now a relationship of love creates space for the development of per-

---

25. Karl Barth, *Evangelical Theology: An Introduction,* trans. Grover Foley (London: Collins, 1965 [1963]), p. 63. Barth says, "If anyone should *not* find himself astonished and filled with wonder when he becomes involved in one way or another with theology, he would be well advised to consider once more . . . what is involved in this undertaking" (p. 61, his emphasis). Subsequent pages will be cited in the text.

sonal identity and depth through mutual reciprocity. Paul, as the primary interpreter of this reality, describes this in Galatians: Now I no longer live by the law, Paul writes, but "I have been crucified with Christ; and it is no longer I who live, but it is Christ who lives in me. And the life I now live in the flesh I live by faith in the Son of God, who loved me and gave himself for me" (Gal. 2:19-20).

But this deeply personal transformation had its ground in an aesthetic transformation of humanity represented by the Incarnation, which itself can be understood only within a Trinitarian context. From the Gospels and Paul, it is clear that Christ already on earth was transformed into the splendor of what Paul will call the "Lord of glory" (1 Cor. 2:8). The disciples saw a demonstration of this when Christ was transformed before their very eyes, by the work of the Spirit, into the Glory that came from the Father, a transfiguration that was made publicly manifest in the Resurrection and the Ascension (which is why, after the transfiguration, Christ strictly charged his disciples not to tell anyone what they had seen). Jürgen Moltmann says of this event, "As the exalted, transfigured man of God he works on downtrodden, barely human and mortal man not only through his liberating power and new demands, but through his perfection and his beauty as well."[26]

This beauty and the joy it elicits are both a present experience and, according to the New Testament, a down payment on the future transformation. Notice how Paul stresses this: "And all of us, with unveiled faces, seeing the glory of the Lord as though reflected in a mirror, are being transformed into the same image from one degree of glory to another; for this comes from the Lord, the Spirit" (2 Cor. 3:18). Our transformation is a real (figural!) anticipation of the future revelation of God's glory. The figure presents (and represents) the inner spiritual reality that shines through it. Moltmann notes that without this aesthetic dimension, our imitation of Christ too often becomes legalistic and joyless. With this aesthetic dimension, as Athanasius says, "The risen Christ makes of human life a continual festival."[27]

This combination of aesthetic attraction and personal, loving presence makes possible Augustine's treatment of the world as a field of

---

26. Jürgen Moltmann, *The Church in the Power of the Spirit: A Contribution to Messianic Ecclesiology* (Minneapolis: Fortress Press, 1993), p. 109.

27. Athanasius, cited in Moltmann, *The Church in the Power of the Spirit*, p. 109.

aesthetic signs, which, used rightly, leads one to love the One who alone is worthy of love. It led mystics in the twelfth century to define the goal of their lives as union with God.[28] It led Bernard of Clairvaux to propose that love was the only human power that allows one to deal reciprocally with God — of which the best image was marital love. When we love God, Bernard said, "then God is indeed experienced, although not as he truly is, a thing impossible for any creature, but rather in relation to your power to enjoy. Then you will experience your own true self."[29] This mystical spirituality played an important role in the Reformation, influenced the rise of Pietism in the seventeenth century, and later left its mark on Romanticism. In the modern period, Jacques Maritain believes this personal revelation of God in Christ makes possible a theological understanding of the value of the self that resonates with the modern artist's self-understanding. Maritain writes that Western art moved from a sense of the human self grasped as object to, "in the sacred examplar of Christ's divine Self, . . . a sense of the human Self finally grasped as subject, or in the creative subjectivity of man himself, man the artist or the poet."[30] Christ's own revelation of personal love, understood within the Trinitarian relationships, illumines the rise of the self in Western spirituality and even illumines the triumph of subjectivity in contemporary art.[31]

For Christians, performance in the drama of Christ's life is linked to baptism and the subsequent relationship with Christ. Like the Old Testament, the New Testament doesn't hesitate to mix together the joys and delights of this world with its brokenness as part of the splendor of the drama, with present struggles tending toward — even strangely anticipating — a dazzling future. Evelyn Underhill claims that there is a parallel development between Christ's earthly life and that of the Christian with respect to suffering. The first phase of the Christian life reflects that of Christ, "with its confident movement within the natural

---

28. Bernard McGinn believes that the idea of union does not appear before the twelfth century, when it became widespread. See "Love, Knowledge, and Mystical Union in Western Christianity: 12-16th Century," *Church History* 56, no. 1 (1987): 8-9.

29. Bernard of Clairvaux, *Sermons on the Song of Solomon*, vol. 3, trans. Killian Walsh and Irene Edmonds (Kalamazoo, Mich.: Cistercian Publications, 1979), pp. 35-36.

30. Jacques Maritain, *Creative Intuition in Art and Poetry* (Cleveland and New York: Meridian Books, 1954), p. 20.

31. On the religious roots of modern developments, see Daniel Siedell, *God in the Gallery: A Christian Embrace of Modern Art* (Grand Rapids: Baker Book House, 2008).

world; mending what is wrong with it, using what is right in it, and sharing the social life of men."[32] But after the transfiguration, everything changes: the conflict with the world deepens, and one begins to realize that what is wrong can be mended only by suffering. Reading these Gospel accounts, following Christ's via dolorosa, forms the reader into a person who will have to perform what is read, especially responding to Christ's call to "Take up your cross and follow me." But it is only in reading along with these writers, and living along with the Spirit, that these differences are discovered, that the believer proves in practice what God desires. In this way, through an embodied, cultured obedience, the believer discovers the wisdom that is from above — through a progressive conversion of the affections.

The Apostle Peter, who stresses the trials (and injustices) associated with this present life, actually calls on believers, oddly, to rejoice in these difficulties — so that, he writes, "your faith . . . may be found to result in praise and glory and honor when Jesus Christ is revealed. Although you have not seen him, you love him; and even though you do not see him now, you believe in him and rejoice with an indescribable and glorious joy" (1 Peter 1:7-8). Paul places a similar emphasis on suffering and goes so far as to say, "I consider that the sufferings of this present time are not worth comparing with the glory about to be revealed to us" (Rom. 8:18).

It may seem strange to say, but I believe that both Peter and Paul have picked up on a side of the Christian life that should be called aesthetic. They recognize that human life is motivated by a deep longing for communion with God, and for the joy and glory that are part of God's life. But at the same time, strangely enough, they link this precisely with earthly struggles over pain and injustice — the hopes and fears over these things are connected. To miss this connection is to make a serious theological error. Jürgen Moltmann has argued that there is at present a theological overemphasis on the political and moral lordship of Christ, and that this has suppressed the aesthetic side of his resurrection. This has resulted, he thinks, in a Christianity that is stern and unattractive.[33] The desire for joy and glory must be cultivated and seen to be centered in God.

---

32. Evelyn Underhill, *Lent with Evelyn Underhill: Selections from Her Writings*, ed. G. P. Mellick Belshaw (London: Mowbray's, 1964), pp. 102-3.

33. Moltmann, *The Church in the Power of the Spirit*, p. 109.

But Christians cannot be united with Christ and celebrate the joy of his resurrection without being thrust back into the struggle of the cross. We cannot celebrate the light of Easter without passing through the darkness of Good Friday. Here is where our aesthetic theology seems to meet its greatest challenge, but perhaps also where it may realize its greatest potential. How can one look into this darkness and speak of beauty? For in the haunting and prophetic words of Isaiah, "He had no form or majesty that we should look at him, nothing in his appearance that we should desire him. He was despised and rejected by others; a man of suffering. . . " (53:2-3). The Lord of glory was also the obedient servant of the cross. According to Kierkegaard, this is the paradox against which reason beats its head until the blood comes.

But, John De Gruchy asks, what if "in some mysterious way this corrupt world is redeemed by the beauty concealed in the crucified Christ"?[34] If beauty is what God's work looks like, then there *must* be beauty hidden, as it were, in the cross, in "the manner in which God's goodness gives itself and is expressed by God and understood by man as the truth."[35] It is beautiful precisely because through this humiliation the world is transformed — precisely in this darkest moment, Christ is glorified. This is the clear teaching of John, where Christ insists that his death is the hour of his glorification (John 17:5). In saying this, Claus Westermann argues, John "captures . . . the whole of the being of Jesus for this world: 'he revealed his glory.'"[36] And in Philippians 2:5-10, Paul similarly argues that Christ's exaltation is based on his humbling himself unto death, even the death of the cross.

For Calvin, this event is at the very center of the splendid drama of creation, and so it also reflects something of that splendor. This is what he says in his commentary on John 13:31:

> For in the cross of Christ, as in a splendid theatre, the incomparable goodness of God is set before the whole world. The glory of God shines indeed, in all creatures on high and below, but never more brightly than in the cross, in which there was a wonderful change of things — the condemnation of all men was manifested, sin blotted

---

34. John W. De Gruchy, *Christianity, Art, and Transformation: Theological Aesthetics in the Struggle for Justice* (Cambridge: Cambridge University Press, 2001), p. 101.

35. De Gruchy, *Christianity, Art, and Transformation*, p. 104.

36. Claus Westermann, "Biblische Asthetik," *Die Zeichen der Zeit* (1950), p. 286.

out, salvation restored to men; in short, the whole world was renewed and all things restored to order.[37]

Dietrich Bonhoeffer refers to the love of God as the *cantus firmus* (the fixed melody) of the Christian life. In *Letters and Papers from Prison,* he writes,

> God wants us to love him eternally with our whole hearts — not in such a way as to injure or weaken our earthly love, but to provide a kind of cantus of the *cantus firmus* to which other melodies of life provide the counterpoint. . . . Only a polyphony of this kind can give life a wholeness and at the same time assures us that nothing calamitous can happen as long as the *cantus firmus* is kept going.[38]

In late medieval polyphonic music, the composition was formed by adding contrapuntal voices to the fixed melody. De Gruchy applies this image to the cross in particular, as that place where the love of God is seen in its clearest form.[39] This is a striking image for a number of reasons. Fundamentally, it reminds us that the cross as the central expression of God's love is *the* fixed melody of the Christian life — not an optional melody that adds flavor to our otherwise happy lives. As Christ went the way of the cross, so we too are called to take up our own cross and follow him. The injustices of this fallen order necessitated Christ's via dolorosa, and if we follow him, they will also lead us there as well. But the additional element of the image of polyphony is that it is only against this fixed melody, this plain chant, that the other melody lines find their meaning and make their unique harmony.

A major element in these contrapuntal melodies is the celebrative motif of the transfiguration. As we have seen, the aesthetics of the cross are bound up theologically with the glory of transfiguration and of the Resurrection and the Ascension. The moments of joy and hope that we are given then find their particular splendor when set against the dark background of the cross. Christ was not defeated by the powers of darkness but was triumphant over them, and through the Holy Spirit contin-

---

37. Calvin, commentary on John 13:31, quoted in Lane, "Spirituality as the Performance of Desire," p. 11.

38. Dietrich Bonhoeffer, *Letters and Papers from Prison,* ed. Eberhard Bethge (New York: Macmillan, 1967), pp. 150-51.

39. De Gruchy, *Christianity, Art, and Transformation,* p. 242.

ues to work the transforming power of the cross. The secret of this relational subjectivity is Trinitarian. In the patristic period, this mutuality and exchange that are characteristic of the Triune life of God were called perichoresis — which described the process by which the three persons mutually interpenetrate one another. It turns out that this Greek word comes from the joining of *peri* and *choresis* (from *choreuo,* meaning "to dance in chorus" — a meaning which is preserved in our word *choreography,* the composition of dance movement). In other words, the inner life of God, which is bound up inextricably with the redemptive, justice-making activity of God in the world, is characterized at its core by a dance or chorus, a dance that is the ground and end of all beauty. Notice that at this deepest level of God's being, an aesthetic image takes precedence over abstract terminology. For, as it turns out, this comes closest to expressing the mystery that is the life of God.

But a poetic theology is not content simply to state these propositions, even to point out their aesthetic character. For the nature of Christian doctrine that we propose is one in which these propositions, in part because of their aesthetic and symbolic character, make possible certain ways of understanding and living with suffering that would not otherwise be available to us. The texts that describe these earth-shattering events are to be read devotionally, which means they are to be practiced rather than simply understood — or, better, *they will be understood only when practiced.* We are to read them as an adjunct to our vocation of making a life that is attractive and sparks affection. James Fodor has proposed that this reading can be seen as a kind of liturgical journey, a pilgrimage — making and following several routes of memory that are rational and emotional. He writes, "These memorial pathways are comparable to the routes of liturgical processions and pilgrimages, stations of the cross — external, bodily movements which are themselves forms of prayer grounded in arts of remembrance."[40]

This reminder of the liturgical structure of the life of faith is important for reasons that we have noted at various points in this study. This understanding by means of devotion reminds us that our life with God is mediated — through our reading of Scripture, our faith, and our life of prayer and worship. The distance to God, Jean-Luc Marion says, can

---

40. James Fodor, "The Beauty of the Word Re-membered," in *The Beauty of God: Theology and the Arts,* ed. D. J. Treier, Mark Husbands, and Roger Lundin (Downers Grove, Ill.: InterVarsity Press, 2007), p. 179.

be traversed only in praise — that is, liturgically.[41] Scriptural texts disclose "the nature of the world," Graham Ward reminds us, but only indirectly.[42] Because of our sin and our cultural constraints, we cannot see this world directly; we can see it only by means of metaphor — that is, aesthetically — and we can appropriate it only liturgically — that is, through prayer and praise. But here the movement of aesthetic encounter, or what Ward calls allegory, is a distinct asset rather than a liability. Because of our encounter with this dynamic field of symbols that we call Scripture, we are allowed to imagine the world beyond the limits of our own life and culture. Moreover, by the Spirit, we are given permission and impetus to live into this world. We have access to this world only by faith and by the obedient life that a faith-based imagination makes possible. This is why the imaginative vision is essential to such a life.

Heaven or the New Creation

When one examines the many words for beauty, splendor, glory, and goodness in Scripture, as I have pointed out, it is striking how many of them refer to the future of creation (and how many include the presence of justice) — what is called the New Jerusalem or heaven. Surely there are reasons why many Christians want to locate aesthetic theology in eschatology. Isaiah says, "In that day the LORD of hosts will be a garland of glory, and a diadem of beauty, to the remnant of his people; and a spirit of justice to the one who sits in judgment" (Isa. 28:5-6); and in that day God says through the prophet, "I will put salvation in Zion, for Israel my glory [beauty]" (Isa. 46:13c). At the final settlement, God will "shake all the nations, so that the treasure of all nations shall come, and I will fill this house with splendor, says the LORD of hosts" (Hag. 2:7; see also the allusion to this verse in Rev. 21:24). In the New Testament, Jesus urges believers to lay up their treasures (in Greek, *thesauros*) in heaven where they cannot be destroyed (Matt. 6:19-21). And Paul, as we have noted, frequently speaks about the glory and the joy that await the believer in heaven. He thinks that present sufferings "are not

---

41. Marion, *God without Being*, pp. 65-77. This leads him to say that theology has to do not with God, but with faith in the crucified Christ.

42. Ward, "Spiritual Exercises: A Christian Pedagogy," p. 236.

worth comparing with the glory" that is to come (Rom. 8:18), because "no eye has seen, nor ear heard, nor the human heart conceived, what God has prepared for those who love him" (1 Cor. 2:9). Although invariably contrasted with present sufferings and injustices, they imply that the promised future, whatever else it is, is clearly an aesthetic event of monumental proportions. The Revelation of John shows that it will comprise visual, dramatic, musical, and kinesthetic elements in a grand cosmic opera.

These references to the beauty of God's people in the last days, and the insistence on visibility and on incarnation, signal a typical and central progression in the biblical materials. As Hans Urs von Balthasar likes to say, God's work represents a progressive "figuration" that tends to the "splendid," seen supremely though provisionally in Christ, but anticipated all the way through the Old Testament.[43] The various ways in which God is indicated in the Old Testament materials, within the field of desire, prepare readers to recognize the particular splendor that Christ will embody, and, beyond that, solicit and prepare them for the final chorus and banquet which the book of Revelation anticipates.

The seventeenth-century Puritans made great use of these images to encourage believers and even to persuade unbelievers. Richard Baxter wrote his famous treatise *The Saints' Everlasting Rest* to urge believers to use their affections to imagine the glories of heaven so that their earthly lives would be transformed thereby. Thinking about heaven, or hearing sermons on heaven, does not make one heavenly, he notes. "To get these truths from thy head to thy heart, and that all the sermons which thou hast heard of heaven . . . be turned into the blood and spirits of affections, thou must feel them revive thee, and warm thee at thy heart."[44] In John Bunyan's famous *Pilgrim's Progress*, which he wrote a generation later (1678), the final range of mountains reached by the travelers is called the Delectable Mountains. From here they could catch sight of the beauties of the heavenly city.[45] Notice that these images are meant not to distract the travelers from

---

43. Hans Urs von Balthasar, *The Glory of the Lord: A Theological Aesthetics*, vol. 1: *Seeing the Form*, trans. Erasmo Leiva-Merikakis (Edinburgh: T&T Clark, 1982), passim.

44. Richard Baxter, *The Saints' Everlasting Rest*, 4th ed. (London, 1653), p. 122; originally published in 1649/50.

45. See discussions of this in James McClendon, "Toward an Ethic of Delight," in *Ethics, Religion, and the Good Society: New Directions in a Pluralistic World*, ed. Joseph Runzo (Louisville: Westminster John Knox Press, 1992), pp. 53ff.

their journey but to animate them — indeed, to allow them to see the beauties of the journey (as well as its trials) as pointing beyond themselves to a final celebration. They suggest that ethics and aesthetics are intrinsically related.

But this also suggests that what we call eschatology cannot be approached apart from the use of the believer's imagination. The passages I cited are loaded with expressive connotations that strike deep emotional chords. They make possible a different way of thinking about life and the future, but this potential cannot be realized apart from envisioning a new way of living. Using the imagination, as Richard Bauckham notes, is not the same thing as surrendering to fantasy or wishful thinking. For the promise of God is literally beyond our wildest dreams — how then can it be a wish fulfillment, as Feuerbach proposed? And the only way in which these promises can be apprehended is imaginatively. As Bauckham says, "The revelatory promise of God appeals to the human imagination . . . seizes, transforms, and expands it, and makes it the locus and vehicle of human reception of God's promise."[46] Only in this way, he says, can God's promise actually empower Christian living.

Consider the images Scripture uses to portray the future: resurrection, the marriage supper of the Lamb, Sabbath rest, the river of the water of life, and many others. These images are fundamentally aesthetic in character — whatever their historical reference, they are metaphors. And this fact allows them to open up windows of possibilities that expand our perception in dramatic ways. They push back the barriers that our culture has raised for us, insisting that something is possible beyond what we currently know. As Augustine insisted, real freedom must have its end as life in God. That is, living into God, which is our present experience with Christ through the Spirit, has a future telos as a life in God, and the future cannot be separated from the present. Through our devotional celebration of this life — our prayers, our praise, and our sharing the Eucharist until Christ returns — our affections are reoriented and directed toward a new future.

---

46. Richard Bauckham, "Eschatology," in *Oxford Handbook of Systematic Theology*, ed. John Webster, Kathryn Tanner, and Iain Torrance (Oxford: Oxford University Press, 2007), p. 317. See also Richard Bauckham and Trevor Hart, *Hope against Hope: Christian Eschatology in Contemporary Context* (London: Darton, Longman & Todd, 1999).

Conclusion

Believers are invited, then, to participate in this narrative, first by means of contemplation, by what I have called a liturgical reading — what in the medieval period was called *lectio divina,* which brings about a transformation of the affections. Then participation is invited by the call to embody the story in the particular setting of our lives. As Kierkegaard was fond of reminding his readers, we are not spectators sitting in the gallery (as Hegel and Kant imagined themselves to be); we are on the stage — we are part of the cast. And a critical dimension of the performance is aesthetic — we are called to perform it. We are called to indwell the narrative imaginatively so that we can follow it obediently. Moreover, as we learned from von Balthasar, we are to look for visual forms of that figural reality — in other words, we are meant to see the form of its inner splendor as we follow and enact the event of the drama. To see and live in this world in terms of God's promised future is the secret to being in but not of the world.

In my experience, artists intuitively understand this connection of worlds — even when they would deny the existence of a transcendent world. Indeed, the best example I know of is found in an incident from one of David Malouf's novels, *Harland's Half Acre.*[47] The leading character, Frank Harland, grows up in the home of a poor farmer in Australia; his mother had died before he knew her. Inspired by his father's incredible ability to create real worlds in the stories he tells, Frank becomes an artist, drawing everything he sees and things he dreams about.

As Frank learns the elements of drawing from a local artist who takes him under his wing, Malouf offers this description of Frank's development:

> [Frank] was freed into discipline, then freed again into his old happy state of dreamlike self-discovery, but with a sureness of touch in which the adventuring mind moved out into uncharted spaces, over horizons that were merely notional . . . with nothing to guide you at last but a firm hand, and the assured, all-risking, ever watchful and untiring spirit. (39)

---

47. David Malouf, *Harland's Half Acre* (New York: Vintage International, 1997 [1984]). Subsequent pages cited in the text refer to this work.

CONCLUSION

Later, when his work is becoming known, Frank comes to live with a musician named Knack. Knack likes Frank's work and stands in front of it for long periods of time with his hands behind his back, as though looking out a window. One day, while Knack is looking at a scene Frank had painted, he and Frank have an interesting conversation:

> "I like this country you have painted, Frank. This *bit* of it. It is splendid. A place, I think, for whole men and women, or so I see it — for the full man, even if there are no inhabitants as yet. Perhaps it is there I should have migrated."
>
> He gave a dark chuckle. It was one of his jests.
>
> "But it is *this* country," Frank said . . .
>
> Knack looked.
>
> "No, Frank, I don't think it is. Not yet anyway. It has not been discovered, this place. The people for it have not yet come into existence, I think, or seen they could go there — that there is space and light enough — in *themselves*. And darkness. Only you have been there. You are the first." (116)

Creation itself, Paul says, yearns for the revelation of this new country for which we all long — which, as Knack says, is "a place for whole men and women." But Scripture also insists, like Frank, that it is *this* country. And this, after all, is the final secret of poetic theology: To have eyes to see through this country to the place where there is space and light enough, where we will live in God.

Bibliography

Abrams, M. H. *The Mirror and the Lamp: Romantic Theory and the Critical Tradition*. New York: Oxford University Press, 1971.

Aquinas, Thomas. *Summa Theologica*. In *Basic Writings of Saint Thomas Aquinas*. Edited by Anton C. Pegis. New York: Random House, 1945.

Archer, Margaret. *Being Human: The Problem of Agency*. Cambridge: Cambridge University Press, 2000.

Aristotle. *Poetics*. Translated by S. H. Butcher. Mineola, N.Y.: Dover, 1997.

Auden, W. H. "For the Time Being." In *Collected Longer Poems* by W. H. Auden. New York: Random House, 1969.

Auerbach, Eric. *Mimesis: The Representation of Reality in Western Literature*. Princeton: Princeton University Press, 1953.

Augustine. *City of God*. Translated by Philip Levine. Cambridge: Harvard University Press/Loeb, 1966.

———. *Confessions*. Edition 1. Translated by Henry Chadwick. Oxford: Oxford University Press, 1992.

———. *On Christian Doctrine*. Translated by D. W. Robertson. Indianapolis: Library of the Liberal Arts/Bobbs-Merrill, 1958.

———. *On Christian Teaching*. Translated by R. P. H. Green. Oxford: Oxford University Press, 1997.

———. *Ten Homilies on the First Epistle of John*. In vol. 7 of *The Nicene and Post-Nicene Fathers*, Series 1. Edited by Phillip Schaff. 1886-1889. 14 vols. Reprint: Peabody, Mass.: Hendrickson, 1995.

Auksi, Peter. "Simplicity and Silence: The Influence of Scripture on the Aesthetic Thought of the Major Reformers." *The Journal of Religious History* 10, no. 4 (1979).

Bakhtin, M. M. *The Dialogic Imagination: Four Essays*. Edited by Michael Holquist. Translated by Caryl Emerson and Michael Holquist. Austin: University of Texas Press, 1981.

Balthasar, Hans Urs von. *The Glory of the Lord: A Theological Aesthetics*. Translated by Erasmo Leiva-Merikakis. Edinburgh: T&T Clark, 1982.

———. *Theo-Drama: Theological Dramatic Theory,* vol. 4: *The Action.* Translated by Graham Harrison. San Francisco: Ignatius Press, 1994 (1980).
Barfield, Owen. *Owen Barfield on C. S. Lewis.* Edited by G. B. Tennyson. Middletown, Conn.: Wesleyan University Press, 1989.
Barnard, F. M. *Herder's Social and Political Thought: From Enlightenment to Nationalism.* Oxford: Clarendon Press, 1965.
Barth, Karl. "The Architectural Problem of Protestant Places of Worship." In André Biéler, *Architecture in Worship: The Christian Place of Worship.* Translated by Odette and Donald Elliot. Philadelphia: Westminster Press, 1965.
———. *Church Dogmatics: The Doctrine of God,* vol. 2. Edited and translated by G. W. Bromiley and T. F. Torrance. Edinburgh: T&T Clark, 1957.
———. *Evangelical Theology: An Introduction.* Translated by Grover Foley. London: Collins, 1965 (1963).
Barzun, Jacques. *From Dawn to Decadence: Five Hundred Years of Western Cultural Life.* New York: HarperCollins, 2000.
Batson, Beatrice. *John Bunyan's "Grace Abounding" and "Pilgrim's Progress": An Overview of Literary Studies, 1960-1987.* New York: Garland, 1988.
Bauckham, Richard. "Eschatology." In *The Oxford Handbook of Systematic Theology.* Edited by John Webster, Kathryn Tanner, and Iain Torrance. Oxford: Oxford University Press, 2007.
Bauckham, Richard, and Trevor Hart. *Hope against Hope: Christian Eschatology in Contemporary Context.* London: Darton, Longman & Todd, 1999.
Baxter, Richard. *The Saints' Everlasting Rest,* 4th ed. London: n.p., 1653.
Bediako, Kwame. *Christianity in Africa: A Renewal of a Non-Western Religion.* Edinburgh and Grand Rapids: Edinburgh University Press and Wm. B. Eerdmans, 1995.
———. *Theology and Identity: The Impact of Culture upon Christian Thought in the Second Century and in Modern Africa.* Grand Rapids: Wm. B. Eerdmans, 1993.
Begbie, Jeremy S. "Created Beauty: The Witness of J. S. Bach." In *The Beauty of God: Theology and the Arts.* Edited by D. J. Treier, Mark Husbands, and Roger Lundin. Downers Grove, Ill.: InterVarsity Press, 2007.
———. *Theology, Music, and Time.* Cambridge: Cambridge University Press, 2000.
———. *Voicing Creation's Praise: Towards a Theology of the Arts.* Edinburgh: T&T Clark, 1991.
Berlin, Isaiah. *The Roots of Romanticism.* Edited by H. Hardy. Princeton: Princeton University Press, 1999.
Bernard, Saint. *Sermons on the Song of Solomon.* 4 vols. Kalamazoo, Mich.: Cistercian Publications, 1971-1980.
Biéler, André. *Architecture in Worship: The Christian Place of Worship.* Philadelphia: Westminster Press, 1965.
Birtwistle, Graham. "H. R. Rookmaaker: The Shaping of His Thought." In *The Complete Works of Hans Rookmaaker,* vol. 1. Carlisle, U.K.: Piquant, 2002.
Blake, William. "A Cradle Song." In *The Complete and Selected Prose of John*

Bibliography

Donne and The Complete Poetry of William Blake. New York: Modern Library, 1941.

Boccaccio, Giovanni. *The Decameron of Giovanni Boccaccio.* Translated and edited by Mark Muse and Peter E. Bondanella. New York: W. W. Norton, 1977.

———. *The Earliest Lives of Dante.* Translated by James Robinson Smith. New York: Henry Holt, 1901.

Boersma, Hans. "Accommodation to What? Univocity of Being, Pure Nature, and the Anthropology of St. Irenaeus." *International Journal of Systematic Theology* 8, no. 3 (July 2006).

Bonaventure, Saint. *The Journey of the Mind to God.* Translated by Philotheus Boehner. Indianapolis: Hackett Publishing Company, 1990 (1956).

Bonhoeffer, Dietrich. *Letters and Papers from Prison.* Edited by Eberhard Bethge. New York: Macmillan, 1967.

Bouwsma, William J. *John Calvin: A Sixteenth-Century Portrait.* New York: Oxford University Press, 1988.

———. "The Two Faces of Humanism: Stoicism and Augustinianism in Renaissance Thought." In *A Usable Past: Essays in European Cultural History.* Berkeley and Los Angeles: University of California Press, 1990.

Brown, Frank Burch. *Religious Aesthetics: A Theological Study of Making and Meaning.* Princeton: Princeton University Press, 1989.

Brown, Peter. *Augustine of Hippo.* Berkeley and Los Angeles: University of California Press, 1967.

Brunner, Emil. *Man in Revolt: A Christian Anthropology.* Translated by Olive Wyon. Philadelphia: Westminster Press, 1947.

Bucer, Martin. *A Treatise Declaring and Showing . . . That Pictures and Other Images Are Not to Be Suffered in the Temples and Churches of Christian Men.* STC 24238. W. Marshall translated J. Bedrohte's Latin translation of Bucer's German original, *Das einigerlei Bild,* 1530.

Buckley, Michael. *At the Origins of Modern Atheism.* New Haven: Yale University Press, 1987.

Bunyan, John. *The Pilgrim's Progress from This World to That Which Is to Come, Delivered under the Similitude of a Dream.* Chicago: Moody Press, n.d. (1678/84).

Caird, George. *A Commentary on the Revelation of St. John the Divine.* Harper's New Testament Commentaries. New York: Harper, 1966.

Calvin, John. *Commentary on the Book of Psalms.* Vol. 4. Translated by James Anderson. Edinburgh: Calvin Translation Society, 1847.

———. *Commentary on the Book of the Prophet Isaiah.* Translated by William Pringle. Edinburgh: Calvin Translation Society, 1850.

———. *Institutes of the Christian Religion.* Library of Christian Classics, vols. 20-21. Edited by John T. McNeill. Translated by Ford Lewis Battles. Philadelphia: Fortress Press, 1960.

———. *Theological Treatises.* Edited by J. K. S. Reid. London: SCM Press, 1954.

Canlis, Julie. "Calvin, Osiander, and Participation in God." *International Journal of Systematic Theology* 6, no. 2 (April 2004).

Carnell, Corbin Scott. *Bright Shadow of Reality: C. S. Lewis and the Feeling Intellect*. Grand Rapids: Wm. B. Eerdmans, 1974.

Carruthers, Mary. *The Craft of Thought: Meditation, Rhetoric, and the Making of Images, 400-1200*. Cambridge: Cambridge University Press, 1998.

Cavanaugh, William T. *Torture and Eucharist: Theology, Politics, and the Body of Christ*. Oxford: Blackwell, 1998.

Chambers, Robert. *Rural Development: Putting Last Things First*. London: Darton, Longman & Todd, 1983.

Charry, Ellen T. *By the Renewing of Your Minds: The Pastoral Function of Christian Doctrine*. New York: Oxford University Press, 1997.

Chesterton, G. K. *The Common Man*. New York: Sheed & Ward, 1950.

Coakley, Sarah. *Powers and Submissions: Spirituality, Philosophy, and Gender*. Oxford: Blackwell, 2002.

Cocksworth, Christopher. *Holy, Holy, Holy: Worshiping the Trinitarian God*. London: Darton, Longman & Todd, 1997.

Coetzee, J. M. *Disgrace*. New York: Penguin Books, 1999.

Cook, Nicholas. *Music: A Very Short Introduction*. Oxford: Oxford University Press, 1998.

Damasio, Antonio R. *The Feeling of What Happens: Body and Emotion in the Making of Consciousness*. New York: Harcourt Brace, 1999.

Dante Alighieri. *Dantis Alagherii Epistolae: The Letters of Dante*. Translated and edited by Paget Toynbee. Oxford: Clarendon Press, 1920.

———. *The Divine Comedy*. Translated by Allen Mandelbaum. New York: Knopf, 1995.

———. *The Divine Comedy: Hell*. Translated by Dorothy Sayers. London: Penguin Books, 1949.

Danto, Arthur. *The Philosophical Disenchantment of Art*. New York: Columbia University Press, 1986.

Dawn, Marva J. *A Royal "Waste" of Time: The Splendor of Worshiping God and Being Church for the World*. Grand Rapids: Wm. B. Eerdmans, 1999.

De Duve, Thierry. *Look: One Hundred Years of Contemporary Art*. Translated by Simon Pleasance and Fronza Woods. Brussels: Ludion, 2000.

De Gruchy, John W. *Christianity, Art, and Transformation: Theological Aesthetics in the Struggle for Justice*. Cambridge: Cambridge University Press, 2001.

Descartes, René. *Philosophical Letters*. Translated and edited by Anthony Kenny. New York: Oxford University Press, 1970.

Dickson, Gwen Griffith. *J. G. Hamann's Relational Metacriticism*. Berlin: Walter de Gruyter, 1995.

Donnelly, Marian C. *The New England Meeting Houses of the Seventeenth Century*. Middletown, Conn.: Wesleyan University Press, 1968.

Dooyeweerd, Herman. *A New Critique of Theoretical Thought*. Vol. 2. Philadelphia: Presbyterian and Reformed Publishing Company, 1969.

Dyrness, William A. "Aesthetics in the Old Testament: Beauty in Context." *Journal of the Evangelical Theological Society* 28, no. 4 (December 1986).

———. "Caspar David Friedrich: The Aesthetic Expression of Schleiermacher's Romantic Faith." *Christian Scholar's Review* 14, no. 4 (1985).

———. *The Earth Is God's: A Theology of American Culture*. Maryknoll, N.Y.: Orbis Books, 1997.

———. *A Primer on Christian Worship: Where We've Been, Where We Are, Where We Can Go*. Grand Rapids: Wm. B. Eerdmans, 2008.

———. *Reformed Theology and Visual Culture: The Protestant Imagination from Calvin to Edwards*. Cambridge: Cambridge University Press, 2004.

———. *Senses of the Soul: Art and the Visual in Christian Worship*. Eugene, Ore.: Cascade Books, 2008.

Eco, Umberto. *Art and Beauty in the Middle Ages*. Translated by Hugh Bredin. New Haven: Yale University Press, 1986.

Edwards, Jonathan. *The Great Awakening: A Faithful Narrative*. Vol. 4 of *The Works of Jonathan Edwards*, edited by C. C. Goen. New Haven: Yale University Press, 1972.

———. "The Mind." In Jonathan Edwards, *Scientific and Philosophical Writings*, vol. 6 of *The Works of Jonathan Edwards*, edited by Wallace E. Anderson. New Haven: Yale University Press, 1980.

Eire, Carlos. *War Against the Idols: The Reformation of Worship from Erasmus to Calvin*. Cambridge: Cambridge University Press, 1986.

Elkins, James. *On the Strange Place of Religion in Contemporary Art*. New York: Routledge, 2004.

Erickson, Kathleen Powers. *At Eternity's Gate: The Spiritual Vision of Vincent Van Gogh*. Grand Rapids: Wm. B. Eerdmans, 1998.

Farrow, Douglas. "Beyond Nature: Shy of Grace." *International Journal of Systematic Theology* 5, no. 3 (2003).

Fodor, James. "The Beauty of the Word Re-membered." In *The Beauty of God: Theology and the Arts*, edited by D. J. Treier, Mark Husbands, and Roger Lundin. Downers Grove, Ill.: InterVarsity Press, 2007.

Ford, David, and Daniel W. Hardy. *Living in Praise: Knowing and Worshiping God*. London: Darton, Longman & Todd, 2005.

Freedberg, David. *The Power of Images: Studies in the History and Theory of Response*. Chicago: University of Chicago Press, 1989.

Fryberger, Betsy G., et al. "Painting as Performance: The Case of Picasso." In *Picasso: Graphic Magician: Prints from the Norton Simon Museum*. Palo Alto, Calif.: Iris and B. Gerald Cantor Center, Stanford University, 1998.

Fuller, Robert C. *Wonder: From Emotion to Spirituality*. Chapel Hill: University of North Carolina Press, 2006.

Furlong, Monica. *Puritan's Progress*. New York: Coward, McCann, & Geoghegan, 1975.

Gadamer, Hans-Georg. *Truth and Method*. New York: Seabury Press, 1975.

Gerrish, Brian. *Grace and Gratitude: The Eucharistic Theology of John Calvin*. Minneapolis: Augsburg/Fortress Press, 1993.

Gibbs, Eddie. *ChurchNext: Quantum Changes in How We Do Ministry*. Downers Grove, Ill.: InterVarsity Press, 2001.

Gibbs, Eddie, and Ryan Bolger. *The Emerging Church: Creating Christian Community in Postmodern Churches*. Grand Rapids: Baker Book House, 2005.

Goizueta, Roberto S. *Caminemos con Jesus: Toward a Hispanic/Latino Theology of Accompaniment*. Maryknoll, N.Y.: Orbis Books, 1995.

Gonzalez-Andrieu, Cecilia. "Lorca as Theologian: The Method and Practice of Interlacing the Arts and Theology." Ph.D. dissertation. Graduate Theological Union at Berkeley, 2007.

Grabowski, Artur. "Unapologetic Visibility." *Image* 59 (Fall 2008).

Guder, Darrell L. *The Missional Church: A Vision for the Sending of the Church in North America*. Grand Rapids: Wm. B. Eerdmans, 1998.

Gunton, Colin E. "The Church on Earth: The Roots of Community." In *On Being the Church: Essays in Christian Community*, edited by Colin E. Gunton and Daniel W. Hardy. Edinburgh: T&T Clark, 1989.

———. "Creation and Re-creation: An Exploration of Some Themes in Aesthetics and Theology." *Modern Theology* 2, no. 1 (1985).

———. *The One, the Three, and the Many: God, Creation, and the Culture of Modernity*. Cambridge: Cambridge University Press, 1993.

———. *The Triune Creator: A Historical and Systematic Study*. Grand Rapids: Wm. B. Eerdmans, 1998.

———. *Yesterday and Today: A Study of Continuities in Christology*. London: SPCK, 1997 (1985).

Hamann, Johann Georg. "Aesthetica in Nuce." Translated in *Johann Georg Hamann's Relational Metacriticism* by Gwen Griffith Dickson. Berlin: Walter de Gruyter, 1995.

Hart, Archibald D. *Thrilled to Death: How the Endless Pursuit of Pleasure Is Leaving Us Numb*. Nashville: Thomas Nelson, 2007.

Hart, David Bentley. *The Beauty of the Infinite: The Aesthetics of Christian Truth*. Grand Rapids: Wm. B. Eerdmans, 2003.

Hart, Trevor. "Hearing, Seeing, and Touching the Truth." In *Beholding the Glory: Incarnation through the Arts*, edited by Jeremy Begbie. Grand Rapids: Baker Book House, 2000.

Hart, Trevor, and Stephen Guthrie, eds. *Faithful Performances: Enacting Christian Tradition*. Aldershot: Ashgate, 2007.

Hauerwas, Stanley. *A Community of Character: Toward a Constructive Social Ethics*. Notre Dame: University of Notre Dame Press, 1981.

———. *With the Grain of the Universe: The Church's Witness and Natural Theology: Being Gifford Lectures Delivered at the University of St. Andrews in 2001*. Grand Rapids: Brazos Press, 2001.

Hauerwas, Stanley, and William Willimon. *Resident Aliens: Life in the Christian Colony*. Nashville: Abingdon Press, 1989.

Hawkins, Peter. *Dante's Testaments: Essays in Scriptural Imagination*. Stanford, Calif.: Stanford University Press, 1999.

Heaney, Seamus. "The Fire i' the Flint." In *Preoccupations: Selected Prose, 1968-1978*. London: Faber & Faber, 1980.

Heidegger, Martin. "The Origin of a Work of Art." In *Philosophies of Art and*

Beauty, translated and edited by Albert Hofstadter and Richard Kuhns. New York: Oxford University Press, 1964.
Horton, Michael S. *Covenant and Eschatology: The Divine Drama.* Louisville: Westminster John Knox Press, 2002.
Husbands, Mark, and Daniel J. Treier, eds. *The Community of the Word: Toward an Evangelical Ecclesiology.* Downers Grove, Ill.: InterVarsity Press, 2005.
James, William. *Writings: 1902-1910.* Edited by Bruce Kuklick. New York: Library of America, 1987.
John of Damascus. *On the Divine Images.* Translated by David Anderson. Crestwood, N.Y.: St. Vladimir's Seminary Press, 2002.
Johnson, Barbara A. *Reading "Piers Plowman" and "The Pilgrim's Progress": Reception and the Protestant Reader.* Carbondale, Ill.: Southern Illinois University Press, 1992.
Johnson, Mark. *The Body in the Mind: The Bodily Basis of Meaning, Imagination, and Reason.* Chicago: University of Chicago Press, 1987.
Johnson, Steven. *Everything Bad Is Good for You: How Today's Popular Culture Is Actually Making Us Smarter.* New York: Riverhead Books, 2005.
Johnston, Robert K. *The Christian at Play.* Grand Rapids: Wm. B. Eerdmans, 1983.
———. *Reel Spirituality: Theology and Film in Dialogue.* Grand Rapids: Baker Book House, 2000; 2d ed., 2006.
Jüngel, Eberhard. "Even the Beautiful Must Die! Beauty in the Light of Truth: Theological Observations on the Aesthetic Relation." In *Theological Essays,* vol. 2, translated by J. Webster and A. Neufeldt-Fast. Edinburgh: T&T Clark, 1995.
Kaufmann, U. Milo. *"The Pilgrim's Progress" and Traditions in Puritan Meditation.* New Haven: Yale University Press, 1966.
Kierkegaard, Søren. *Either/Or: A Fragment of a Life.* Edited by Victor Eremita. Translated by Alastair Hannay. New York: Penguin Books, 1992 (1842).
———. *Purity of Heart Is to Will One Thing.* Translated by Douglas W. Steere. New York: Harper & Row, 1956.
King, John N. *English Reformation Literature: The Tudor Origins of the Protestant Tradition.* Princeton: Princeton University Press, 1982.
Klassen, Justin D. "Truth as 'Living Bond': A Dialectical Response to Recent Rhetorical Theology." *International Journal of Systematic Theology* 10, no. 4 (October 2008).
Kreitzer, Larry. *Gospel Images in Fiction and Film: On Reversing the Hermeneutical Flow.* Sheffield: Sheffield Academic Press, 2002.
Kuhn, Daniel. "The Joy of the Absolute." In *Imagination and the Spirit: Essays in Literature and the Christian Faith Presented to Clyde S. Kilby,* edited by Charles Huttar. Grand Rapids: Wm. B. Eerdmans, 1971.
Kuyper, Abraham. *Lectures on Calvinism: The Stone Foundation Lectures.* Grand Rapids: Wm. B. Eerdmans, 1931.
Lane, Belden. "Spirituality as the Performance of Desire: Calvin on the World as a Theatre of God's Glory." *Spiritus: A Journal of Christian Spirituality* 1, no. 1 (Spring 2001).

Lee, Sang Hyun. *The Philosophical Theology of Jonathan Edwards.* Princeton: Princeton University Press, 1988.

Levinas, Emmanuel. "Reality and Its Shadow." In *The Levinas Reader,* edited by Sean Hand. Oxford: Blackwell, 1989.

Lewalski, Barbara K. *Protestant Poetics and the Seventeenth-Century Religious Lyric.* Princeton: Princeton University Press, 1979.

Lewis, C. S. *Christian Reflections.* Edited by Walter Hooper. Grand Rapids: Wm. B. Eerdmans, 1967.

———. *The Discarded Image: An Introduction to Medieval and Renaissance Literature.* Cambridge: Cambridge University Press, 1964.

———. "On Stories." In *Of This and Other Worlds,* edited by Walter Hooper. London: Collins, 1982.

———. *A Preface to "Paradise Lost."* Oxford: Oxford University Press, 1942.

———. *Surprised by Joy: The Shape of My Early Life.* London: Fontana, 1955.

———. "Transposition." In C. S. Lewis, *"Screwtape Proposes a Toast" and Other Pieces.* London: Fontana, 1965.

Lohfink, Gerhard. *Jesus and Community: The Social Dimension of Christian Faith.* Translated by John P. Galvin. New York and Philadelphia: Paulist Press and Fortress Press, 1984.

Lundin, Roger. "The Beauty of Belief." In *The Beauty of God: Theology and the Arts,* edited by D. J. Treier, Mark Husbands, and Roger Lundin. Downers Grove, Ill.: InterVarsity Press, 2007.

Luxon, Thomas H. "Calvin and Bunyan on Word and Image: Is There a Text in Interpreter's House?" *English Literary Renaissance* 18, no. 3 (1988).

Lynch, Gordon. "Film and the Subjective Turn." In *Reframing Theology and Film: New Focus for an Emerging Discipline,* edited by Robert K. Johnston. Grand Rapids: Baker Book House, 2007.

Lyotard, Jean-François. *The Postmodern Condition: A Report on Knowledge.* Translated by G. Bennington and B. Massumi. Minneapolis: University of Minnesota Press, 1979.

MacDonald, George. *England's Antiphon.* Whitethorn, Calif.: Johannesen, 1996 (1868).

———. "The Imagination: Its Function and Its Culture." In *A Dish of Oats.* Whitethorn, Calif.: Johannesen, 1996 (1893).

MacIntyre, Alasdair. *Three Rival Versions of Moral Inquiry.* Notre Dame: Notre Dame University Press, 1990.

———. *Whose Justice? Which Rationality?* Notre Dame: Notre Dame University Press, 1988.

Malouf, David. *Harland's Half Acre.* New York: Vintage International, 1997.

Manning, Russell R. "Towards a Critical Reconstruction and Defense of Paul Tillich's Theology of Art." *Arts: The Arts in Religious and Theological Studies* 16, no. 2 (2004).

Marion, Jean-Luc. *God without Being: hors-texte.* Translated by Thomas A. Carlson. Chicago: University of Chicago Press, 1991.

Bibliography

Maritain, Jacques. *"Art and Scholasticism" and "The Frontiers of Poetry."* Translated by Joseph W. Evans. New York: Scribner's, 1962.

———. *Creative Intuition in Art and Poetry.* Cleveland and New York: Meridian Books, 1954.

———. *Distinguish to Unite; or, The Degrees of Knowledge.* Translated by Gerald B. Phelan. New York: Scribner's, 1959.

———. *Integral Humanism: Temporal and Spiritual Problems of a New Christendom.* Translated by Joseph W. Evans. Notre Dame: University of Notre Dame Press, 1968, 1973 (1936).

Marsh, Clive. "On Dealing with What Films Actually Do to People." In *Reframing Theology and Film: New Focus for an Emerging Discipline,* edited by Robert K. Johnston. Grand Rapids: Baker Book House, 2007.

Maslow, Abraham H. *Toward a Psychology of Being.* 2d ed. Princeton, N.J.: D. Van Nostrand, 1968.

McClendon, James. "Toward an Ethic of Delight." In *Ethics, Religion, and the Good Society: New Directions in a Pluralistic World,* edited by Joseph Runzo. Louisville: Westminster John Knox Press, 1992.

McFague, Sallie. *Speaking in Parables: A Study in Metaphor and Theology.* Philadelphia: Fortress Press, 1975.

McGinn, Bernard. "Love, Knowledge, and Mystical Union in Western Christianity: 12-16th Century." *Church History* 56, no. 1 (1987).

McInerny, Ralph. *Art and Prudence: Studies in the Thought of Jacques Maritain.* Notre Dame: University of Notre Dame Press, 1989.

McKnight, Edgar. *The Careless Society: Community and Its Counterfeits.* New York: Basic Books, 1995.

McLaren, Brian. *Everything Must Change: Jesus, Global Crisis, and a Revolution of Hope.* Nashville: Thomas Nelson, 2007.

Meltzoff, Stanley. *Botticelli, Signorelli, and Savonarola: Theologia Poetica and Painting from Boccaccio to Poliziano.* Florence: L. S. Olshki Editore, 1987.

Milbank, John. "Beauty and the Soul." In John Milbank, Graham Ward, and Edith Wyschogrod, *Theological Perspectives on God and Beauty.* Harrisburg: Trinity Press, 2003.

———. "Knowledge: The Theological Critique of Philosophy in Hamann and Jacobi." In *Radical Orthodoxy: A New Theology,* edited by John Milbank and Catherine Pickstock. London: Routledge, 1999.

———. *Theology and Social Theory: Beyond Secular Reason.* Oxford: Blackwell, 1990.

Milbank, John, Graham Ward, and Catherine Pickstock, eds. *Radical Orthodoxy: A New Theology.* London: Routledge, 1999.

Mitchell, Louis J. *Jonathan Edwards on the Experience of Beauty.* Studies in Reformed Theology and History, no. 9. Princeton: Princeton Theological Seminary, 2003.

Mitchell, W. J. T. *What Do Pictures Want? The Lives and Loves of Images.* Chicago: University of Chicago Press, 2005.

Moltmann, Jürgen. *The Church in the Power of the Spirit: A Contribution to Messianic Ecclesiology.* Minneapolis: Fortress Press, 1993.

———. *Experiences in Theology: Ways and Forms of Christian Theology.* Minneapolis: Fortress Press, 2000.

Morris, Colin. *The Discovery of the Individual, 1050-1200.* London: SPCK, 1972.

Mugambi, J. N. Kanyua. *Christian Theology and Social Reconstruction.* Nairobi: Acton, 2003.

Muir, Edward. *Ritual in Early Modern Europe.* Cambridge: Cambridge University Press, 2005.

Muller, Richard R., and John L. Thompson, eds. *Biblical Interpretation in the Era of the Reformation: Essays Presented to David C. Steinmetz.* Grand Rapids: Wm. B. Eerdmans, 1996.

Myers, Bryant. *Walking with the Poor: Principles and Practices of Transformational Development.* Maryknoll, N.Y.: Orbis Books, 1999.

Navone, John J. *Toward a Theology of Beauty.* Collegeville, Minn.: Liturgical Press, 1996.

Nee, Watchman. *Love Not the World.* Wheaton, Ill.: Tyndale House, 1978.

———. *The Normal Christian Life.* Ft. Washington, Pa.: Christian Literature Crusade, 1963 (1957).

Neuhaus, Richard John, ed. *Augustine Today.* Grand Rapids: Wm. B. Eerdmans, 1993.

Nietzsche, Friedrich Wilhelm. "The Anti-Christ." In *The Portable Nietzsche,* edited by Walter Kaufmann. New York: Viking Press, 1954.

———. *The Birth of Tragedy.* Translated by Francis Golffing. Garden City, N.Y.: Doubleday, 1956.

Noll, Mark. *The New Shape of World Christianity: How American Experience Reflects Global Faith.* Downers Grove, Ill.: InterVarsity Press, 2009.

Nouwen, Henri. *Life in the Beloved: Spiritual Living in a Secular World.* New York: Crossroad, 1992.

Nussbaum, Martha. *The Fragility of Goodness: Luck and Ethics in Greek Tragedy and Philosophy.* Cambridge: Cambridge University Press, 1986.

———. *Love's Knowledge: Essays on Philosophy and Literature.* Oxford: Oxford University Press, 1990.

O'Doherty, Bryan. *Inside the White Cube: The Ideology of the Gallery Space.* Santa Monica, Calif.: Lapis Press, 1976; 2d ed., 1999.

Ong, Walter J. *Orality and Literacy: The Technologizing of the Word.* London: Methuen, 1982.

———. *Ramus, Method, and the Decay of Dialogue: From the Art of Discourse to the Art of Reason.* Cambridge: Harvard University Press, 1958.

Pannenberg, Wolfhart. *The Church.* Translated by Keith Crim. Philadelphia: Westminster Press, 1983.

Paz, Octavio. *The Double Flame: Love and Eroticism.* Translated by Helen Lane. New York: Harcourt Brace, 1995 (1993).

Perkins, William. *The Art of Prophesying.* In *Works of That Famous and Worthy Minister William Perkins,* vol. 2. London: John Legatt, 1631.

Bibliography

Pico della Mirandola, Giovanni Francesco. *On the Imagination*. Translated and edited by Harry Caplan. New Haven: Yale University Press, 1930.
Polanyi, Michael. *The Tacit Dimension*. New York: Routledge & Kegan Paul, 1967.
Postman, Neil. *Amusing Ourselves to Death: Public Discourse in the Age of Show Business*. New York: Penguin Books, 1985.
Postrel, Virginia. *The Substance of Style: How the Rise of Aesthetic Value Is Remaking Commerce, Culture, and Consciousness*. New York: HarperCollins, 2003.
Redeker, Marin. *Schleiermacher: Life and Thought*. Translated by John Wallhausser. Philadelphia: Fortress Press, 1973.
Ricoeur, Paul. *Figuring the Sacred: Religion, Narrative, and Imagination*. Edited by Mark I. Wallace. Translated by David Pellauer. Minneapolis: Fortress Press, 1995.
———. *Time and Narrative*. Vol. 1. Translated by Kathleen McLaughlin and David Pellauer. Chicago: University of Chicago Press, 1984; 1990.
Robinson, Marilynne. *Gilead: A Novel*. New York: Farrar, Straus & Giroux, 2004.
Romanowski, William, and Jennifer L. VanderHeide. "Easier Said Than Done: On Reversing the Hermeneutical Flow in Theology and Film." *Journal of Communication and Religion* 30 (March 2007).
Rookmaaker, Hans R. *Modern Art and the Death of a Culture*. Downers Grove, Ill.: InterVarsity Press, 1970; reprint: Crossway Books, 1994.
Rothko, Mark. *The Artist's Reality*. Edited by Christopher Rothko. New Haven: Yale University Press, 2004.
Rowland, Tracey. *Culture and the Thomist Tradition: After Vatican II*. London: Routledge, 2003.
Ruskin, John. *Modern Painters*. In Raymond Williams, *Culture and Society: 1780-1950*. Middlesex, England: Penguin Books, 1958/1963.
Sayers, Dorothy L. *Introductory Papers on Dante*. London: Methuen & Co., 1954.
Scarry, Elaine. *On Beauty and Being Just*. Princeton: Princeton University Press, 1999.
Schaeffer, Francis. *Escape from Reason*. London: InterVarsity Fellowship, 1968.
Schiller, Friedrich. *On the Aesthetic Education of Man in a Series of Letters*. Translated by Reginald Snell. New Haven: Yale University Press, 1954.
Schleiermacher, Friedrich. *Dialektik*. Edited by Ludwig Jonas. Berlin: G. Reimer, 1839.
———. *On Religion: Speeches to Its Cultured Despisers*. Translated by John Owen. New York: Harper & Row, 1958 (1799).
Schmit, Clayton J. *Too Deep for Words: A Theology of Liturgical Expression*. Louisville: Westminster John Knox Press, 2002.
Schwöbel, Christoph. "The Creature of the Word: Recovering the Ecclesiology of the Reformers." In *On Being the Church: Essays in Christian Community*, edited by Colin E. Gunton and Daniel W. Hardy. Edinburgh: T&T Clark, 1989.
Seerveld, Calvin. *A Christian Critique of Art and Literature*. Toronto: Association for Reformed Studies, 1968.

———. *Rainbows for the Fallen World: Aesthetic Life and Artistic Task*. Toronto: Tuppence Press, 1980.

———. "The Relation of the Arts to the Presentation of the Truth." In *Truth and Reality: Philosophical Perspectives on Reality Dedicated to Professor Dr. H. G. Stoker*. Braamfontein, S.A.: De Jong's Bookshop, 1971.

Senn, Frank C. *Christian Liturgy: Catholic and Evangelical*. Minneapolis: Fortress Press, 1997.

Sherry, Patrick. *Spirit and Beauty: An Introduction to Theological Aesthetics*. Oxford: Oxford University Press, 1992.

Sidney, Philip. "A Defense of Poetry." In *Miscellaneous Prose of Philip Sidney*, edited by K. Duncan-Jones and Jan van Dorsten. Oxford: Clarendon Press, 1973.

Siedell, Daniel. *God in the Gallery: A Christian Embrace of Modern Art*. Grand Rapids: Baker Book House, 2008.

Smith, James K. A. *The Fall of Interpretation: Philosophical Foundations for a Creational Hermeneutics*. Downers Grove, Ill.: InterVarsity Press, 2000.

Steiner, George. *Real Presences*. The Leslie Stephen Memorial Lecture, Cambridge University, 1 November 1985. Cambridge: Cambridge University Press, 1986.

Stewart, Susan A. *Poetry and the Fate of the Senses*. Chicago: University of Chicago Press, 2002.

Stoltzfus, Philip. *Theology as Performance: Music, Aesthetics, and God in Western Thought*. New York: T&T Clark, 2006.

Summers, David. *Real Spaces: World Art History and the Rise of Western Modernism*. New York: Phaidon, 2003.

Swain, Kathleen M. *Pilgrim's Progress: Discourses and Contexts*. Urbana: University of Illinois Press, 1993.

Tanner, Kathryn. *Theories of Culture: A New Agenda for Theology*. Minneapolis: Fortress Press, 1997.

Taylor, Barry. *Entertainment Theology: New-Edge Spirituality in a Digital Democracy*. Grand Rapids: Baker Book House, 2008.

Taylor, Charles. *A Secular Age*. Cambridge: Belknap/Harvard University Press, 2007.

———. *Sources of the Self: The Making of Modern Identity*. Cambridge: Harvard University Press, 1989.

Tillich, Paul. *On Art and Architecture*. Edited by John and Jane Dillenberger. New York: Crossroad, 1987.

———. "On the Idea of a Theology of Culture." In *Visionary Science: A Translation of Tillich's "On the Idea of a Theology of Culture" with an Interpretive Essay*, edited by Victor Nuovo. Detroit: Wayne State University Press, 1987.

———. *Systematic Theology*. Vol. 1. Chicago: University of Chicago Press, 1951.

Tolkien, J. R. R. "On Fairy-Stories." In *Essays Presented to Charles Williams*, edited by C. S. Lewis. New York: Oxford University Press, 1947.

Torrance, Alan. *Persons in Communion: An Essay on Trinitarian Description and*

Bibliography

Human Participation, with Special Reference to Volume One of Karl Barth's "Church Dogmatics." Edinburgh: T&T Clark, 1996.

Tracy, David. *The Analogical Imagination: Christian Theology and the Culture of Pluralism.* New York: Crossroad, 1981.

Trinkaus, Charles Edward. *"In Our Image and Likeness": Humanity and Divinity in Italian Humanist Thought.* London: Constable, 1970.

Turner, Denys. "How to Read the Pseudo-Denys Today?" *International Journal of Systematic Theology* 7, no. 4 (October 2005).

Underhill, Evelyn. *Lent with Evelyn Underhill: Selections from Her Writings.* Edited by G. P. Mellick Belshaw. London: Mowbray's, 1964.

Van der Kooi, Cornelis. *As in a Mirror: John Calvin and Karl Barth on Knowing God: A Diptych.* Translated by Donald Mader. Leiden: Brill, 2005.

Vanhoozer, Kevin J. *The Drama of Doctrine: A Canonical-Linguistic Approach to Christian Theology.* Louisville: Westminster John Knox Press, 2005.

Vanhoozer, Kevin J., Charles A. Anderson, and Michael J. Sleasman, eds. *Everyday Theology: How to Read Cultural Texts and Interpret Trends.* Grand Rapids: Baker Book House, 2007.

Viladesau, Richard. *Theological Aesthetics: God in Imagination, Beauty, and Art.* New York: Oxford University Press, 1999.

Volf, Miroslav. *After Our Likeness: The Church as the Image of the Trinity.* Grand Rapids: Wm. B. Eerdmans, 1998.

———. *Exclusion and Embrace: A Theological Exploration of Identity, Otherness, and Reconciliation.* Nashville: Abingdon Press, 1996.

———. "When Gospel and Culture Intersect: Notes on the Nature of Christian Difference." In *Pentecostalism in Context: Essays in Honor of William W. Menzies,* edited by Wonsuk Ma and Robert P. Menzies. Sheffield: Sheffield Academic Press, 1997.

Wakefield, Gordon. "To Be a Pilgrim: Bunyan and the Christian Life." In *John Bunyan — Conventicle and Parnassus: Tercentenary Essays,* edited by N. H. Keeble. Oxford: Clarendon Press, 1988.

Walford, E. John. *Jacob von Ruysdael and the Perception of Landscape.* New Haven: Yale University Press, 1991.

Ward, Graham. *Christ and Culture.* Oxford: Blackwell, 2005.

———. *Cities of God.* New York and London: Routledge, 2000.

———. *Cultural Transformation and Religious Practice.* Cambridge: Cambridge University Press, 2005.

———. *True Religion.* Oxford: Blackwell, 2003.

Ward, W. R. "Pietism." In *Global Dictionary of Theology,* edited by William A. Dyrness and Veli-Matti Kärkkäinen. Downers Grove, Ill.: InterVarsity Press, 2008.

Webber, Robert. *Ancient-Future Faith: Rethinking Evangelicalism for a Postmodern World.* Grand Rapids: Baker Book House, 1999.

Weil, Simone. *Waiting for God.* Translated by Emma Craufurd. New York: Harper & Row, 1951.

Westermann, Claus. "Biblische Asthetik." *Die Zeichen der Zeit* (1950).

White, James F. *The Sacraments in Protestant Practice and Faith*. Nashville: Abingdon Press, 1999.
Whyte, Alexander. *Lord, Teach Us to Pray: Sermons on Prayer*. London: Hodder & Stoughton, 1923.
Williams, Charles. *The Figure of Beatrice: A Study in Dante*. London: Faber & Faber, 1963.
Williams, Raymond. *Culture and Society, 1780-1950*. New York: Penguin Books, 1963.
Williams, Rowan. *Grace and Necessity: Reflections on Art and Love*. London: Continuum, 2005.
Willis, Paul E. *Common Culture: Symbolic Work at Play in the Everyday Cultures of the Young*. Boulder, Colo.: Westview Press, 1991.
Wills, Garry. *Saint Augustine*. New York: Viking Press, 1999.
Wolff, Hans Walter. *The Anthropology of the Old Testament*. Minneapolis: Fortress Press, 1974.
Wolterstorff, Nicholas. *Art in Action: Toward a Christian Aesthetic*. Grand Rapids: Wm. B. Eerdmans, 1980.
———. "Beauty and Justice." *The Cresset* 73, no. 4 (Easter 2009).
———. *Justice: Rights and Wrongs*. Princeton: Princeton University Press, 2008.
———. "Trumpets, Ashes, and Tears." *The Reformed Journal* 36, no. 2 (February 1986).
———. *Until Justice and Peace Embrace*. Grand Rapids: Wm. B. Eerdmans, 1983.
Wuthnow, Robert. *All in Sync: How Music and Art Are Revitalizing American Religion*. Berkeley and Los Angeles: University of California Press, 2003.
Zachman, Randall. *Image and Word in the Theology of John Calvin*. Notre Dame: University of Notre Dame Press, 2007.
Zizioulas, John. *Being as Communion: Studies in Personhood and the Church*. Crestwood, N.Y.: St. Vladimir's Seminary Press, 1985.
Zuckerman, Phil. *Society without God: What the Least Religious Nations Can Tell Us about Contentment*. New York: New York University Press, 2008.

Index

Abrams, M. H., 104
"Aesthetica in Nuce" (Hamann), 22, 102
Aesthetics, defining, 11, 154, 162
Aesthetic turn in post-Romantic culture, 3-36, 211; challenges from Radical Orthodoxy, 14-18, 22-23, 233-36; creation and culture, 21-24; creativity/creative imagination and, 12-13, 19-20, 25-26; dangers of, 28-31; defining aesthetics, 11, 154, 162; defining poetics, 11-12, 38; desire and, 26-27, 32-34, 50-53, 57-61; hunger for contemplation, 200-209; modern rationalist theology and, 7-9; post-Romantic sensitivities, 13-36; and Romanticism's inward turn, 25-26, 28, 79; secular rituals and practices, 3-6, 52-57, 69-70, 187-88, 200-209, 211; symbols and symbolic potential in cultural forms, 20-21, 52-57, 63-70; theological objections, 13-18, 22-23. *See also* Contemporary *theologia poetica;* Twentieth-century aesthetics
American Beauty (film), 278
Amsterdam Declaration, 225
Ancient-Future Faith (Webber), 232
Apologetic theology, 6-7, 10
Aquinas, Thomas, 15, 126-27

Archer, Margaret, 53, 111
Arendt, Hannah, 219
Aristotle, 11, 39-40, 47, 50, 85, 284
Arndt, Johann, 101
Art and Scholasticism (Maritain), 127
Art-making: Begbie, 149-51; eschatological implications, 148; Gunton, 146-49, 150; Levinas and problem with (aesthetics versus ethics), 258-59; participation and, 147-48; Trinitarian aesthetics and theological practice of, 146-51
The Art of Prophesying (Perkins), 175-76
"Art world," twentieth-century, 115-16, 187, 209, 262-63
Auden, W. H., 289-90
Auerbach, Erich, 88n, 295
Augustine: on beauty, 264-65; Calvin and, 100; humanism and notions of the self, 43-44, 47-49, 51, 188, 200-201; idea of the will, 42, 100, 188; and intertextual dimensions of Scripture, 92; journey of the affections, 64, 100, 111, 155, 188, 310; and medieval *theologia poetica,* 39, 40-44, 188; understanding of time and narrative (and the intention of the soul), 84-85; view of symbols/signs, 42-43, 58, 64, 100,

INDEX

155; views of love and desire, 25, 33, 35, 41-42, 58, 59, 188, 233
Auksi, Peter, 173-74

Bakhtin, M. M., 91-92
Balthasar, Hans Urs von, 93, 131-35, 267, 291, 309, 311
Barfield, Owen, 118n
Barney, Matthew, 65-66, 67
Barth, Karl, 9, 132-33, 256-57, 300-301
Bauckham, Richard, 310
Baxter, Richard, 163, 309
Beauty: Augustine on, 264-65; Balthasar on, 93, 267; Barth and, 132-33; creation and, 21, 286, 296-300; Hart on desire and, 121-22, 123-24; justice and, 263-65; and the poor, 253-55; as radically de-centering, 265-66; Scarry on, 263-66; as transcendental form of God's presence, 93
Bediako, Kwame, 232-33
Begbie, Jeremy, 21, 149-51, 172
Berlin, Isaiah, 104, 106, 136
Bernard of Clairvaux, St., 189, 303
Bildung, 17, 18
The Birth of Tragedy (Nietzsche), 183-84
Blake, William, 27, 59, 286
Boccaccio, Giovanni, 45-46
Boersma, Hans, 52n
Bonaventure, St., 32, 155, 189-90, 195, 205, 207
Bonhoeffer, Dietrich, 306
Boonyakiat, Satanun, 156n
Bourdieu, Pierre, 111n
Bouwsma, William, 43n, 47n, 49
Brain studies and aesthetics/consciousness, 8
Brown, Frank Burch, 11, 154, 162, 166
Brown, Peter, 41
Brueggemann, Walter, 204
Brunner, Emil, 90
Bucer, Martin, 193, 255
Buechner, Frederick, 201

Bultmann, Rudolf, 86
Bunyan, John, 100. See also *Pilgrim's Progress* (Bunyan)

Caird, George, 206
Calvin, John: aesthetics and creation, 21, 100, 239-40, 296-98, 300; Augustine and, 100; commentary on Isaiah 6 text, 204-5; and contemplation during the Reformation, 195; the cross/suffering of Christ and, 185, 305-6; and devotional practices in Reformed Protestantism, 193-94; drama and, 185, 254-55; emphasis on worship and discipleship outside the church, 193-94, 218, 223-24; humanism and, 47-49; and the locked church, 191-96, 209, 212, 218, 223-24, 241; and medieval picture of Christian life as journey to God, 191-92; and medieval *theologia poetica*, 39, 47-49; and "participation" in God, 171, 235; preaching emphasis, 139, 167, 212, 221-22, 243-44, 245; and Reformation suspicion of symbolism, 222-24; Romanticism and, 100-101; and sight/the visual, 194; and social space of church, 229; and split between sense knowledge/spiritual knowledge, 167-68, 170-71, 196
Canlis, Julie, 235
Carnell, Corbin Scott, 119
Catholic Church: Aquinas and neo-Thomist tradition, 126-27; Balthasar and visual forms of figural reality, 131-35, 291, 311; Bunyan/Dante and differences between Catholic and Protestant aesthetics, 162-66, 177; Maritain and, 127-31, 134, 146, 148; Second Vatican Council, 16-18, 37-38, 127, 130; twentieth-century theologies of aesthetics, 126-35, 138
Cavanaugh, William, 244-45
Celebration/celebratory practices and community life, 273-74

328

Index

Cézanne, Paul, 113
Chambers, Robert, 273
Chesterton, G. K., 32-33
Christianity, Art, and Transformation (De Gruchy), 253
Christmas Eve Dialogue (Schleiermacher), 110
Church aesthetics, 217-52; Calvin and, 218, 222-24, 229, 241; Calvin's locked church and the congregation, 218, 223-24, 241; historical space of church, 231-37, 251; issue of "authority" in the church, 251; the particular practices expressed in church, 227-29; preaching and, 221-22, 243-44, 245; and Reformation prejudice against vision/the visual, 247-49; and Reformation suspicion of symbols, 222-24, 238-40; the relation of the church space to all other spaces, 229-31; ritual performance and symbolism, 243-47; sacraments and, 224, 241, 244-47, 250; searches for stability of form, 219-20; signs that contemporary Protestant ecclesiology needs attention, 217-24; the social space of church, 225-31, 251; symbolic incapacity of the evangelical tradition, 238-43; the symbolic space of church, 237-43, 251; Volf on free-church ecclesiality and polycentric character, 226-27
Church Dogmatics II/I (Barth), 132
Cities of God (Ward), 233-34
City of God (Augustine), 42, 44, 229
Coakley, Sarah, 68, 188, 191, 199-200
Cocksworth, Christopher, 298
Coetzee, J. M., 27, 64, 261
Coleridge, Samuel Taylor, 213, 248
Community development and aesthetics, 267-76; aesthetic criteria for the health of communities, 271-76; "aesthetic praxes," 269-70; celebration/celebratory practices, 273-74; play/playfulness, 256-57, 272-73; ritual practice, 274-76;

"symbolic creativity" in everyday activities, 270. *See also* Social transformation and aesthetics
Confessions (Augustine), 35, 40-41, 42, 84-85
Contemplation, 61-63, 78-79, 187-214; Calvin and the locked church, 191-96, 209, 212, 218, 223-24; in contemporary faith and art, 198-200, 209; contemporary importance of, 200-209; evangelical movement and, 221; and post-Reformation practices of reading, 196-98; post-Romantic hunger for, 200-209; Reformation Protestant spirituality and, 187-214; sight/vision and, 200-201; social action and, 203-4; spiritual contemplative practices, 199-200; as way of knowledge, 61-63. *See also* Reading of Scripture (Protestant poetics)
Contemporary *theologia poetica,* 50-70; and activity of artistic contemplation, 61-63; and biblical notions of the symbolic, 57-61; connections between seeing and desiring, 57-59; desire and, 26-27, 32-34, 50-53, 57-61; historical parallels to contemporary struggles with culture, 50-52; ideological approaches to culture, 73-78; Maritain and connection between God and contemporary aesthetic situation, 61-63; moral and spiritual situation of contemporary Christians, 71-78; symbolism/symbolic practices, 52-57, 63-70. *See also* Aesthetic turn in post-Romantic culture; Medieval *theologia poetica;* Twentieth-century aesthetics
Covenant and Eschatology (Horton), 247-49
Creation, 296-300; beauty/order of, 21, 286, 296-300; Calvin and, 21, 100, 239-40, 296-98, 300; centrality of the body/embodied creation, 299-300; culture and, 21-24; the

economic Trinity and, 24, 60-61; glory and, 298-99; and "participation" in God, 24-25; Reformation and, 21-23, 24, 239; symbolic meaning, 239-40
Creative Intuition in Art and Poetry (Maritain), 62
Creativity: and aesthetic turn in post-Romantic culture, 12-13, 19-20, 25-26; Neo-Romantic and Neo-Medieval views of, 117-22, 123-24; Romanticism and, 25-26, 105-7; Willis and "symbolic creativity" in everyday activities, 270
Critique of Judgment (Kant), 104
Cross of Christ: Calvin, 185, 305-6; the paradox of Christ, 303-7; and Protestant emphasis on brokenness of the world, 169, 171
Cubism, 114
Culture/society split, 115-16, 262, 268-69

Dada, 67, 69, 143-44
Damasio, Antonio, 8, 53n, 90, 111n
Danneels, Godfried, 250
Dante Alighieri, 33-34, 283; Boccaccio and, 46; medieval *theologia poetica* and, 39, 40, 44-45, 46, 154. See also *Divine Comedy* (Dante)
Danto, Arthur, 184-85
Darwin, Charles, 14
Dawn, Marva, 277
De Certeau, Michel, 72, 234
De Duve, Thierry, 65
De Gruchy, John, 203, 253, 305, 306
Descartes, René, 191, 196, 200, 235
Desire: Augustine's views of love and, 58, 59, 233; constructive engagement with (as movement outside oneself), 32-34, 52-53; contemporary *theologia poetica*, 26-27, 32-34, 50-53, 57-61; creation and, 58, 60-61; Hart on beauty and, 121-22, 123-24; James and, 58-59; Lewis on experiences of longing and, 117-21; and Neo-Romantic and Neo-Medieval views of art and creativity, 117-22, 123-24; sight/vision and, 57-59
Dialectical theology/discourse, 93-94, 153, 166, 181-82, 211
Dialektik (Schleiermacher), 109
Disgrace (Coetzee), 27-28, 34, 261
Divine Comedy (Dante), 33-34, 44-45, 154-58, 162-66, 207-9, 211, 283-84; and Augustine's world of signs, 155; and Bunyan's *Pilgrim's Progress*, 158-59, 162-66; and differences between Catholic and Protestant aesthetics, 158-59, 162-66; *Inferno*, 34, 44, 156, 207, 283-84; intended readers, 163; *Paradiso*, 157, 164, 207-9; *Purgatorio*, 156-57, 164, 208; purpose/aims in writing, 163; role of sight/vision, 164-65, 208; and the soul's journey to God, 44-45, 154-58, 165-66, 207-9; symbolism, 162-63
Dooyeweerd, Herman, 143, 144
Dostoyevsky, Fyodor, 172-73, 253
Duchamp, Marcel, 69, 144

Eco, Umberto, 127
Edwards, Jonathan, 139-41
Either/Or (Kierkegaard), 259-60
Eliot, T. S., 119
Emerson, Ralph Waldo, 125
Emplotment, process of, 83-90, 292; prefiguration, 86-87; configuration, 87-89; refiguration, 89-90; and a shared "theological standpoint," 89-90
The Entombment of Christ (Holbein), 172-73
Erickson, Kathleen, 174-75
Eschatology: aesthetic theology and, 308-10; Gunton's Trinitarian ontology and implications of art-making, 148; and Reformation prejudice against vision/the visual, 248; Reformers' reaction against, 248, 256; social transformation and aesthetics, 255-57
Ethics versus aesthetics, 258-61

Index

Eudaimonism, 31, 33
Evangelical Christians and Church aesthetics, 219-24; emergent churches, 219, 232; focus on mission and spirituality but absence of reflection of place/form, 220-21; and historical space of the church, 231-32, 236-37; and social space of church, 225-26; spiritual "bubbling up" and churchless Christianity, 219; symbolic incapacity/lack of symbolic sensitivity, 238-43. *See also* Church aesthetics
Expressionism, 113-14, 143-44

Faith, progressive nature of, 94-95
Faithful Central Baptist Church (Los Angeles), 242-43
Feuerbach, Ludwig, 104, 310
Fodor, James, 197, 307
Ford, David, 45, 51, 78
Forms of figural reality, 131-35, 291, 311
Foster, John, 177, 178
Foucault, Michel, 123
Francis, St., 190, 205
Freedberg, David, 56
Freud, Sigmund, 14
Friedrich, Caspar David, 103
Fuller, Robert, 29
Furlong, Monica, 173

Gadamer, Hans-Georg, 82-83, 86, 89
Gaudium et Spes, 17, 37
Gilead (Robinson), 257
Gill, Eric, 128, 270
Glaubenslehre (The Christian Faith) (Schleiermacher), 109-10
Goizueta, Roberto, 54-56, 137-38, 268-70
Grabowski, Artur, 221, 251
Gregory of Nyssa, 181, 233-34
"Grounded aesthetics," 242, 270-71
Guernica (Picasso), 87, 263
Gunton, Colin, 146-49, 150, 227

Hamann, J. G., 22, 23, 101-3, 104, 108, 135
Hardy, Daniel, 45, 51, 78
Harland's Half Acre (Malouf), 311-12
Hart, Archibald D., 30n
Hart, David Bentley, 121-24, 126; Balthasar's influence on, 132; on beauty and desire, 121-22, 123-24; on symbolism, 122-23; and Trinitarian revival, 124
Hart, Trevor, 149-50, 290
Hauerwas, Stanley, 15, 228-29
Hawkins, Peter, 166n
Heaney, Seamus, 25-26
Hedonism, 30-31
Heidegger, Martin, 82
Henry, Carl, 9
Herbert, George, 239-40
Herder, J. G., 18, 103, 135-37
Hermeneutics, cultural, 73-78, 80-81; ideological approaches to culture, 73-78; and the "interpretive situation," 74-76; and process of emplotment, 83-90, 292; Ricoeur's hermeneutics and poetic theology, 82-90; Scripture interpretation and, 80-81, 224, 286-87. *See also* Ricoeur, Paul
Hildegard of Bingen, 298
Historical space of church, 231-37, 251; evangelicals and, 231-32, 236-37; post-colonial/post-missionary churches, 232-33; Radical Orthodoxy, 233-36; revivals of historical consciousness, 232-36
Holbein, Hans, 172-73
Hopkins, Gerard Manley, 20, 25-26, 45
Horton, Michael, 115, 247-49, 256
Humanism: Augustinian humanism and medieval *theologia poetica*, 43-44, 47-49, 51, 188, 200-201; Calvin and, 47-49; commitment to rhetoric, 49; sense of accommodation, 48-49; Stoicism and, 43-44
Human transformation, split between aesthetics and, 262-67

INDEX

Humboldt, Karl Wilhelm von, 17, 135
Hunsberger, George, 220

"The Idea of a Theology of Culture" (Tillich), 112
Imagination: and the arts in contemporary Protestant Christianity, 182-86; Pico della Mirandola and medieval *theologia poetica*, 46-47; and the prophetic, 177-80
Industrial Revolution of late-nineteenth century and emergence of "art world," 115-16, 262
Inferno (Dante), 34, 44, 283-84
Institutes of the Christian Religion (Calvin), 47-48, 205, 212
Integral Humanism (Maritain), 266
Isaiah's vision of God in the year of King Uzziah's death (Isaiah 6), 203-5

James, William, 28-29
John of Damascus, 252
John Paul II, Pope, 17
Johnson, Barbara, 163-64
Johnson, Francis, 242
Journey of the Mind to God (St. Bonaventure), 189
Jüngel, Eberhard, 182
Justice: Goizueta and aesthetics in relation to, 54-56; Scarry on beauty and, 263-65; Wolterstorff on human dignity/rights and, 276

Kandinsky, Wassily, 18, 25, 150
Kant, Immanuel, 14, 16, 103-5, 123; Hart and, 122, 123; Pietism and, 103-4; Schleiermacher and, 109
Kaufmann, U. Milo, 163n
Kierkegaard, Søren, 94, 104, 111, 186, 249, 259-61, 311
King, John N., 153
Kingdom of God, 287-91
Klassen, Justin, 93-95, 166, 211
Knowledge: contemplation as way of, 61-63; Reformed Protestant aesthetics and split between sense knowledge and spiritual knowledge, 166-73, 196; Schleiermacher's aesthetics and, 109-11
Koinonia, 24, 150, 169, 235-36
Kreitzer, Larry, 80n
Kuhn, Daniel, 118n
Kuyper, Abraham, 141-43, 144, 257

Lane, Belden, 185
Lawrence, D. H., 262
Lectio divina (sacred liturgical reading), 182, 196-98, 203, 311
Lectures on Calvinism (Kuyper), 141-42
Lee, Sang Hyun, 139n
Letters and Papers from Prison (Bonhoeffer), 306
Levinas, Emmanuel, 54n, 258-59
Lewalski, Barbara, 153
Lewis, C. S., 14-15, 68, 117-21, 123, 211-12
Liberation theology, 55, 137, 269
Life of Dante (Boccaccio), 46
Lohfink, Gerhard, 229-30
Lorraine, Claude, 168
Luther, Martin, 191, 221-22
Luxon, Thomas, 164-65
Lynch, Gordon, 64
Lyotard, Jean-François, 65

MacDonald, George, 239-40
MacIntyre, Alasdair, 152
Mallarmé, Stéphane, 18
Malouf, David, 311-12
Manning, Russell, 112-13
Marion, Jean-Luc, 23, 185n, 299, 307-8
Maritain, Jacques, 61-63, 114, 266; Christology, 128-29, 148; "connaturality," 62, 129-31; contemporary *theologia poetica*, 61-63; modern Catholic theologies of aesthetics, 127-31, 134, 146, 148, 303
Marsh, Clive, 84
Maslow, Abraham, 29
Mather, Richard, 177, 178

Index

McCarthy, Cormac, 87
McFague, Sallie, 115n
McGinn, Bernard, 303n
McKnight, Edgar, 230-31
Medieval *theologia poetica*, 39-50, 80, 287; Augustine and, 39, 40-44, 188; Augustinian humanism, 43-50, 47-49, 51, 188, 200-201; Calvin, 39, 47-49; Dante, 39, 40, 44-45, 46; Dante's *Divine Comedy* and image of the soul's journey toward God, 44-45, 154-58, 207-9; the imagination, 46-47; Petrarch, 39, 45-46; Pico della Mirandola, 39, 46-47; and practice of *lectio divina* (sacred liturgical reading), 182, 196-98, 203, 311; and the stages of love of God (Christian life as journey to God), 188-92, 207-9
Methexis, 24n, 131, 235
Methods of poetic theology. *See* Aesthetic turn in post-Romantic culture; Contemporary *theologia poetica;* Medieval *theologia poetica;* Poetic stewardship of life
Milbank, John, 15-17, 18, 24, 26, 93
Milton, John, 211-12
Mitchell, W. J. T., 54, 55n, 56
Moltmann, Jürgen, 271-72, 302, 304
Morris, Colin, 190
Mozart, Wolfgang Amadeus, 18
Mugambi, J. N. K., 270-71
Muir, Edward, 238-39, 246n
Murphy, Jeffrey G., 187n
Music, experience of, 146-47, 150-51
Mysticism/mystical experiences, 28-30

Narcissism, 30-31
Navone, John, 199, 213
Nebel, Gerhard, 95n, 180, 221
Nee, Watchman, 7-8
Neo-Reformed tradition and twentieth-century aesthetics, 138-46, 151-52. *See also* Twentieth-century aesthetics
Neo-Thomism, 126-27

Nietzsche, Friedrich, 14, 104, 106, 113; construal of Christianity as the enemy of art/feeling, 99-100, 183-86; divide between the good and the beautiful (ethics and aesthetics), 262
Noll, Mark, 227n
Non-Western aesthetic sensitivities, 54-56, 135-38, 268-70
Norris, Kathleen, 278-79
Nouwen, Henri, 285
Nussbaum, Martha, 29, 209-11, 212

Oak Trees on the Lake with Water Lilies (Van Ruisdael), 168-69, 170
O'Connell, Robert, 58
O'Doherty, Bryan, 80n
On Christian Teaching (Augustine), 41-43, 58, 155
Ong, Walter, 165
"On Stories" (Lewis), 120
On the Aesthetic Education of Man (Schiller), 105-6
On the Imagination (Pico della Mirandola), 46-47

Pannenberg, Wolfgang, 225, 231
Parables of Jesus, 81, 171, 174, 272, 287-89
Paradise Lost (Milton), 211-12
Participation in God: Calvin and, 171, 235; creation and, 24-25; Gunton's Trinitarian ontology and, 147-48; Maritain's analogy of incarnation rather than, 131; and Protestant emphasis on brokenness of the world, 94, 169-71; Radical Orthodoxy and, 16, 22-23, 50-51, 235-36
The Passion of the Christ (film), 171
Paul, Apostle, 15, 58, 94, 248, 287, 289, 294, 302; on creation, 60; eschatology and aesthetic theology, 308-9; references to the Holy Spirit, 297-98; sermon on Mars Hill (Acts 17), 51, 82
Paz, Octavio, 32, 33, 299-300
"Peak experiences," 29-30

INDEX

Pelagianism, 19
Pentecostalism, 223
Performance: poetic theology and metaphor of, 293, 311; preaching as "performative" utterance, 243-44, 245; ritual performance and the symbolic space of church, 243-47
Perichoresis, 123, 307
Perkins, William, 175-76
Petrarch, Francesco, 39, 45-46
Picasso, Pablo, 87, 144, 186, 263
Pico della Mirandola, 39, 46-47
Pietism/Pietist tradition, 22, 101-4, 106, 188
Pilgrim's Progress (Bunyan), 158-66, 173, 176-77, 256, 309; and Dante's *Divine Comedy*, 158-59, 162-66; and differences between Catholic and Protestant aesthetics, 158-59, 162-66; the hermeneutics of suspicion and, 158-61; hidden character of, 163, 173; intended Protestant readers, 163-64; metaphor of reading a text (trope of reading), 164-65, 176; narrative style engaging the reader in interpretation, 179; role of sight/vision, 164-65, 176; symbolism, 162-63
Plato, 59-60, 120, 123
Platonism, 24n, 131, 235, 248, 299-300
Play/playfulness and community life, 256-57, 272-73
Pobee, John, 219
Poesis, 11, 38, 39-40, 107
Poetics, defining, 11-12, 38
Poetic stewardship of life, 71-95; breaking out of practical level of life toward the poetic sphere, 90-95; contemplation, 78-79; hermeneutics and contemporary interpretation of Scripture, 80-81, 224, 286-87; ideological approaches to culture (reflection followed by appropriate response), 73-78; moral agency, 76-77; and moral and spiritual situation of contemporary Christians, 71-78; poetic theology and the active call to live faithfully, 81-82; the process of emplotment (putting our lives in narrative order), 83-90, 292; Ricoeur, 82-90
Poetic theology, systematic implications of, 283-312; the active process of following a narrative (active emplotment), 293, 294; Catholic/Protestant understandings of the possible role of aesthetics for human life, 291; creation, 296-300; eschatology and aesthetic theology, 308-10; the kingdom of God, 287-91; the paradox of Christ, 300-308; performance, 293, 311; reading of Scripture, 286-87; reframing traditional theological categories, 294-96; theological themes that grow out of biblical material, 300-310; universal stories, 284-85
Polanyi, Michael, 75
Pollock, Jackson, 25
positive psychology, 29
Postmodernism, 10, 201, 232, 237, 250
Post-Romantic culture. *See* Aesthetic turn in post-Romantic culture
The Potato Eaters (van Gogh), 174-75
Praxis, 38, 77, 137
Prophetic, the, 177-80
Protestant aesthetics. *See* Church aesthetics; Reading of Scripture (Protestant poetics); Reformed Protestant aesthetics/spirituality; Twentieth-century aesthetics
Puritans, 175-76, 223, 309

Radical Orthodoxy: challenges to aesthetic turn in contemporary culture, 14-18, 22-23, 233-36; and historical retrieval of ecclesiology, 233-36; and "participation" in God, 16, 22-23, 50-51, 235-36
Rahner, Karl, 166-67
Ramus, Peter, 49-50, 100-101, 197

Index

Ratzinger, Joseph (Pope Benedict XVI), 136
Reading of Scripture (Protestant poetics), 177-82, 196-98, 203-7, 292, 295, 307; Bunyan's *Pilgrim's Progress*, 163-66, 176, 179; hermeneutics and cultural interpretations, 80-81, 224, 286-87; medieval practice of *lectio divina*, 182, 196-98, 203, 205, 311; pedagogical reading, 181-82, 292, 295, 308; post-Reformation practices, 196-98; Protestant priority of word and language, 165-66; Protestant readings in contrast to medieval, 197-98, 203-7; reversed direction from within to outward, 197-98, 203-5; Ricoeur and process of emplotment, 83-90, 292; role of sight/vision, 164-65, 176, 197-98, 203-5; "typological" reading, 180, 181
Reformation: attempt to define relationship between God and creation, 234-35; celebration of creation, 21-23, 24; distrust of external symbolism, 222-24, 238-40; distrust of unity between sense knowledge and spiritual knowledge, 167, 196; efforts to disconnect art from its ancient sources, 184-85; and modern developments in the arts, 142, 184-85; preaching and, 221-22; prejudice against vision/the visual, 247-49; Radical Orthodoxy's arguments and, 16, 233-36; reaction against overrealized eschatology, 248, 256
Reformed Protestant aesthetics/spirituality, 153-86; and the arts in contemporary Protestant Christianity, 182-86; Bunyan and, 161-80; Bunyan's *Pilgrim's Progress*, 158-66, 173, 176-77, 179, 256, 309; the cross of Christ and, 169, 171; Dante's *Divine Comedy*, 154-58, 162-66, 207-9; dialectical orientation, 166-80; differences between Catholic and Protestant aesthetics, 158-59, 162-66, 177; dramatic action, 166; hidden character (enigmatic and indirect methods), 173-77; "participation" in God, 169-71; priority of word and language, 165-66; the prophetic, 177-80; recovery of contemplation, 187-214; role of sight/vision, 164-65, 176, 247-49; split between sense knowledge and spiritual knowledge (brokenness of the world), 166-73, 196. *See also* Reading of Scripture (Protestant poetics)
Reformed tradition, 9, 100-101
Rhetorical theology/discourse, 93-94, 166, 211-12
Ricoeur, Paul, 82-90, 168, 179, 290, 292; hermeneutics and poetic theology, 82-90; on process of emplotment, 83-90, 292; and split between sense knowledge and spiritual knowledge, 168
Ritual: church performance and symbolism, 243-47; community life and ritual practice, 274-76; order and, 274-75; preaching (as active symbolic practice/"performative" utterance), 221-22, 243-44, 245; the sacraments, 224, 241, 244-47, 250; symbolic import of the Eucharist, 244-45, 246
The Road (McCarthy), 87
Roberts, Grace Strachan, 254
Robinson, Marilynne, 257
Romanticism, nineteenth-century, 18-26, 99-124; art/aesthetics and theology, 103-7; Calvin and, 100-101; the Christian roots of, 100-103; creation and, 21-23; Hamann, 101-3; Hart, 121-24; and Industrial Revolution's separation of culture/society, 115-16, 262; inward turn of, 25-26, 28, 79; Kant's revolution, 103-5, 123; knowledge and aesthetics, 109-11; Lewis, 117-21, 123;

335

INDEX

modern aesthetic framework and, 18-20; and Neo-Romantic/Neo-Medieval views of art and creativity, 117-24; Pietism and, 22, 101-3, 188; Romantic poets and modern notion of creativity, 25-26, 106-7; Schiller, 105-7; Schleiermacher, 107-11, 152; symbols and symbolism, 20, 63-64, 100, 106, 120; Tillich, 111-17, 152. *See also* Aesthetic turn in post-Romantic culture

Rookmaaker, Hans R., 143-44
Rothko, Mark, 65-70
Rouault, Georges, 128
Rowland, Tracey, 16-18, 52n, 71-72, 82, 136
Ruskin, John, 115-16

Sacraments, 224, 241, 244-47, 250
The Saints' Everlasting Rest (Baxter), 309
Sayers, Dorothy, 162
Scarry, Elaine, 27, 34, 263-66, 278; on beauty and justice, 263-65; on beauty as radically de-centering, 265-66
Schaeffer, Francis, 14
Schelling, Friedrich Wilhelm Joseph von, 109n
Schiller, Friedrich, 17, 18, 105-7
Schleiermacher, Friedrich, 80, 107-11; Kant and, 109; knowledge and aesthetics, 109-11; Pietism and, 103; Tillich and, 111-17, 152
Schoenberg, Arnold, 150
Schwöbel, Christoph, 234-35
Second Vatican Council, 16-18, 37-38, 127, 130
Secular culture and rituals, 3-6, 5, 52-57, 69-70, 187-88, 200-209, 211
Secularization, theories of, 201-2
Seerveld, Calvin, 144-45, 174, 291, 294
Sharrock, Roger, 173
Sherry, Patrick, 150n
Sibbes, Richard, 163

Sidney, Philip, 49-50, 51, 52
Sight/vision: biblical connections between seeing and desiring, 57-59; Bunyan's *Pilgrim's Progress*, 164-66, 176; Calvin and, 194; Dante's *Divine Comedy* and, 164-65, 208; eschatology and, 248; post-Romantic hunger for contemplation and centrality of, 200-201; reading and, 164-66, 176, 197-98, 203-5; Reformation prejudice against, 247-49; visual forms of figural reality, 131-35, 291, 311
Smyth, John, 226
Social space of church, 225-31, 251; Calvin and, 229; evangelicals' neglect of, 225-26; and the particular practices expressed, 227-29; Protestant idea of church as gathered people of God, 225-27; the relation of the space to all other spaces, 229-31; Volf on free-church ecclesiality and the polycentric character of the church, 226-27
Social transformation and aesthetics, 253-79; aesthetic criteria for the health of communities, 271-76; "aesthetic praxes," 269-70; aesthetics and everyday life, 257, 269-70; aesthetics versus ethics, 258-61; beauty and the poor, 253-55; Christian worship practices, 277-78; community development and cultivation of aesthetic practices, 267-76; community life and celebration/celebratory practices, 273-74; community life and play/playfulness, 256-57, 272-73; community life and ritual practice, 274-76; culture/society split and, 262, 268-69; eschatology, 255-57; the fulfilling of basic human needs, 266, 276-77; "grounded aesthetics," 270-71; justice, 54-56, 263-65, 276; the split between aesthetics and human transformation, 262-67
Sociology of religion, 28-29

Song of Solomon, 58, 189
Speeches on Religion (Schleiermacher), 107
Spener, Philip, 101
St. Paul's Cathedral (London), 241-42
Steiner, George, 247, 265
Stewart, Susan, 11
Stoics, 43-44, 51
Stoltzfus, Philip, 108, 109, 110, 244, 293, 295
Suffering of Christ, 303-7
Summers, David, 69, 77, 145n
Swain, Kathleen, 179
Symbols/symbolism: and ambiguity of the human situation, 66; Barney, 65-66, 67; biblical notions of, 57-61; Bunyan's *Pilgrim's Progress*, 162-63; Calvin and, 100; contemporary post-Romantic culture, 20-21, 52-57, 63-70; Dante's *Divine Comedy*, 162-63; defining, 54-56; the Eucharist, 244-45, 246; evangelical tradition and, 238-43; Hart on, 122-23; the human impulse to make symbols, 56-57; Lewis on, 120; Neo-Romantic and Neo-Medieval views of art and creativity, 122-23; preaching as, 221-22, 243-44, 245; Protestant worship spaces and symbolic emptiness, 242-43; Reformation transformation and suspicion of, 222-24, 238-40; ritual performance and, 243-47; Romanticism, 20, 63-64, 100, 106, 120; Rothko and, 65-70; the sacraments, 224, 241, 244-47, 250; style and, 113-14; symbolic space of church, 237-43, 251; Tillich and religious symbols, 114, 116; Tillich's notion of "symbol," 113-15, 116, 122; transcendence and, 66-69

Tavener, John, 151
Taylor, Charles, 67, 83, 142, 290; and development of the modern self, 200; "mediational epistemology," 196; on Romanticism and modern aesthetic framework, 18-20, 25, 63, 105-7, 188; on the "social imaginary," 75-76
Theology, Music, and Time (Begbie), 150
Theology and Identity (Bediako), 232-33
Theophan the Recluse, 213
Tillich, Paul, 111-17, 152; the "art world" and, 115-16; notion of "symbol," 113-15, 116, 122; and Schleiermacher's Romantic view of art in relation to God, 111-17, 152
Time and Narrative (Ricoeur), 83, 84
To End All Wars (film), 274
Tolkien, J. R. R., 185
Torrance, Alan, 24n, 235-36
Toward a Psychology of Being (Maslow), 29
Tracy, David, 93n, 154
"Transposition" (Lewis), 118-19
Trinitarian aesthetics: and art-making as theological practice, 146-51; creation and the economic Trinity, 24, 60-61; Gunton and, 146-49; Hart and, 123-24; perichoresis, 123, 307
Trinkhaus, Charles, 40
True Christianity (Arndt), 101
Twentieth-century aesthetics, 125-52; "aesthetics of the whole of life," 144-46; Aquinas and neo-Thomist tradition, 126-27; Balthasar and the focus on form, 131-35, 291, 311; Barth and God's glory/beauty, 132-33; Begbie, 149-51; Calvinist tradition and, 139, 142-43; Dooyeweerd, 143, 144; Edwards, 139-41; Goizueta, 137-38; Gunton, 146-49, 150; Hart, 121-24; Herder's organic model, 135-37; Kuyper, 141-43, 144; Lewis, 117-21, 123; Maritain, 127-31, 134, 146, 148; modern Catholic theologies of aesthetics, 126-35, 138; music and, 146-47, 150-51; Neo-Reformed tradition, 138-46, 151-52; Neo-Roman-

tic and Neo-Medieval, 117-24; non-Western sensitivities and recognition of cultural/ethnic diversity, 135-38; Rookmaaker, 143-44; Seerveld, 144-45; Trinitarian aesthetics and art-making as theological practice, 146-51; Wolterstorff, 144-46. *See also* Aesthetic turn in post-Romantic culture; Church aesthetics; Social transformation and aesthetics

Ulmer, Kenneth, 242-43
Underhill, Evelyn, 303-4

Van der Kooi, Cornelis, 48-49, 194n
Van Gogh, Vincent, 23, 74, 174-75
Vanhoozer, Kevin, 72-73
Van Ruisdael, Jacob, 168-69, 170, 179-80
The Varieties of Religious Experience (James), 28
Vasconcelos, José, 55, 137, 268-69
Viladesau, Richard, 169
Virgil, 44-45, 155-56
Vita Nuova (Dante), 34
Voicing Creation's Praise (Begbie), 149
Volf, Miroslav, 76, 82, 226-27

Waiting for God (Weil), 278
Wakefield, Gordon, 160n
Walford, John, 168
Ward, Graham, 35n, 38, 64, 238; and Christian notions of reading and spiritual pedagogy, 181-82, 292, 295, 308; Radical Orthodoxy and historical retrieval of ecclesiology, 233-36; and shared "theological standpoint," 89-90; and symbol (allegory), 181, 245, 308
Ward, Karen, 232
Ward, W. R., 101
Webber, Robert, 232
Weil, Simone, 265, 278
Wesley, Charles, 101
Westermann, Claus, 305
White, James, 247
William of Ockham, 16
Williams, Charles, 33-34
Williams, Raymond, 262
Williams, Rowan, 129n
Willis, Paul, 270
Wills, Garry, 42n, 188n
"The Windhover" (Hopkins), 26
Wittgenstein, Ludwig, 7, 147
Wolff, Hans Walter, 26
Wolterstorff, Nicholas, 174, 194, 209; and "aesthetics of the whole of life," 78-79, 144-46; on desire as investment in external events, 32, 33; and eudaimonism, 31, 33; on justice/human dignity and rights, 276
Worship practices, 212-13; aesthetics of church and, 218, 223-24, 241-43; Calvin's locked church and rearranged physical spaces of worship, 218, 223-24; Protestant worship spaces and, 241-42; social transformation and, 277-78
Wren, Sir Christopher, 241
Wuthnow, Robert, 12-13, 79, 201-2

Yesterday and Today (Gunton), 146-47
Yoder John Howard, 228

Zizioulas, John, 62n
Zwingli, Ulrich, 195

www.ingramcontent.com/pod-product-compliance
Lightning Source LLC
Chambersburg PA
CBHW021753230426
43669CB00006B/69